EARLY CINEMA IN ASIA

EARLY CINEMA IN ASIA

Edited by Nick Deocampo

Indiana University Press

This book is a publication of

Indiana University Press
Office of Scholarly Publishing
Herman B Wells Library 350
1320 East 10th Street
Bloomington, Indiana 47405 USA

iupress.indiana.edu

The paper used in this publication meets the minimum
requirements of the American National Standard for Information
Sciences—Permanence of Paper for Printed Library Materials,
ANSI Z39.48-1992.

Manufactured in the United States of America

Cataloging information is available from the Library of Congress.

ISBN 978-0-253-02536-4 (cloth)
ISBN 978-0-253-02554-8 (paperback)
ISBN 978-0-253-02728-3 (ebook)

1 2 3 4 5   22 21 20 19 18 17

For Aruna Vasudev—for her vision and dedication in promoting Asian cinema and making me and a generation of film critics, scholars, filmmakers, and festival programmers appreciate Asian film culture

Contents

Acknowledgments

It has been a long journey to get this book published. For making its publication possible, there are a lot of people and institutions I want to thank. I first express gratitude to the Nippon Foundation, particularly its executive director, Tatsuya Tanami, because of the Asian Public Intellectuals Fellowships grant it awarded me. Through the grant, I was able to organize the Origins of Cinema in Asia Conference in Quezon City, Metro Manila, in 2005. The conference gathered film scholars, critics, festival programmers, and cineastes from Spain, Sweden, the United States, Belgium, Thailand, Australia/Malaysia, and the Philippines. The initial contributions to this book came from among papers presented at the conference. The plenary speaker was Dr. Charles Musser from Yale University, whose paper is included in this book. He became the guiding voice in our discussions on early cinema. As organizer of the event, I thought of the conference as something that would be similar to the annual Pordenone silent film festival in Italy, where early cinema is studied and celebrated. But without a patron, it was hard to continue holding an annual conference or to publish the essays.

A follow-up conference was held in New Delhi, India, two years later. In the Cinefan International Film Festival, organized by Aruna Vasudev, a larger conference was organized, and more countries participated. The papers read at that conference were added to the growing number of essays considered for publication. Again, Dr. Musser lent his support by serving as moderator for the conference panel, which included participants from Asian countries such as India, Malaysia, Indonesia, Philippines, Thailand, Singapore, Iran, South Korea, Japan, Bangladesh, Pakistan, and Sri Lanka. They were joined by participants from Australia, the United States, and the United Kingdom. The idea of holding a conference on early cinema in the region proved appealing, and a third conference, the Conference on Asian Cinema Heritage and Culture, was held in Kuala Lumpur, Malaysia, in 2008. The event had decidedly Asian participation. This was the last of the conferences on early Asian cinema I would organize.

While a sizable number of essays were gathered from the conferences, the book was still far from publication. Dr. Musser made the crucial step of recommending the collection of essays to Indiana University Press. The publication was green-lighted in late 2008. To those who made the cut and who have been patient in writing and rewriting their essays after more than a decade of waiting, I give my heartfelt thanks.

Despite the initial approval, the task of actually getting the book published would still take years and three Indiana University Press editors guiding its arduous journey. For shepherding the project, I thank Raina Polivka, Jenna Lynn Whitaker, and the current editor, who finally got the book printed, Janice Frisch. To them I owe my sincere thanks for their patience and perseverance.

In addition, I offer my sincerest gratitude to all those who helped me in my research work: the library staffs at the Library of Congress (Washington, D.C.), the National Archives (College Park, Maryland), and the National Film Center (Tokyo) and the archivists, librarians, collectors, museum guides, scholars, critics, researchers, cineastes, and private film collectors who diligently took care of the film holdings and records and who personally assisted me at the libraries, film archives, and film museums in Berlin, Frankfurt, Paris, London, New York, Hollywood, Tokyo, Madrid, Barcelona, Belgium, Jakarta, Bangkok, Canberra, Shanghai, Hanoi, Amsterdam, Tampere, Hong Kong, Kuala Lumpur, Singapore, Manila, Cebu, and Iloilo.

Finally, to Charles Musser, for the invaluable help and unwavering support he has given to this project—from recommending the book to Indiana University Press for publication to proofreading individual contributions—my gratitude is boundless.

EARLY CINEMA IN ASIA

Introduction

The Beginnings of Cinema in Asia

Nick Deocampo

Arrival of Film

The history of early cinema in Asia remains largely unwritten, perhaps because the region tends to place a strong emphasis on national cinemas—one that affirms the present-day popularity of motion pictures while forgetting their historical beginnings. When people speak of Asian cinema, they often talk about Japanese, Chinese, Indian, Korean, Thai, Filipino, Malaysian, Indonesian, Hong Kong, Vietnamese, Iranian, Sri Lankan, Taiwanese, and other national cinemas. After more than a century of motion pictures, cinema in Asia has become as diverse as the region's multistate configuration. But what identity did cinema have when it first arrived? Was cinema always identified as "national"?

By examining cinema's historical roots, the authors in this book help establish its diverse identities at the moment of its arrival. (Were the identities colonial, local, or transnational?) Lessons can be learned from studying how cinema first began in Asia. One lesson is that of changing identity: the identity of Asia at the time of film's arrival (during the age of colonization) was far different from the identity the region assumed when film reached its maturity (during the period of nationalism) and will yet assume once globalization has done its share of transforming the region (will this period finally foster a truly Asian cinema?).

When film first appeared, Asia was virtually a continent of colonies (figure I.1).[1] The moving picture device arrived in Asia through Western colonial agents, who left it behind as one of their enduring legacies. The film apparatus was introduced by the French, British, Spaniards, Americans, Dutch, Italians, and Germans, among a few others. Its appearance toward the end of Asia's colonial period makes for an interesting argument that long before countries became independent nation-states and the notion of national cinemas prevailed, there already was cinema. Its identity, however, was far from what we know of the national film industries that exist today.

Film's arrival was tied to the region's modern maritime history. Motion pictures appeared and first flourished in coastal areas along the routes taken by

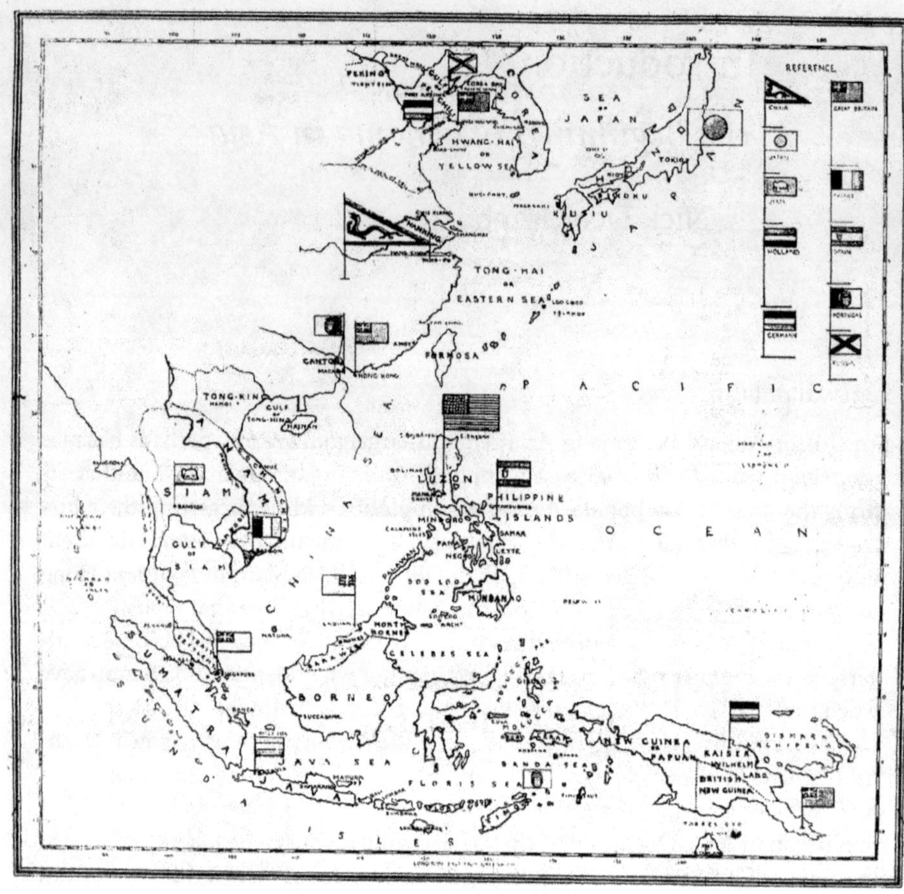

Figure I.1. Asia was once a region dominated by Western colonial powers. The flags shown in this map represent the Western countries that exercised control over their Asian territories. (*Harper's Weekly*, June 11, 1898, p. 570.)

ocean liners. Rightly so, because the end of the nineteenth century was a time when transcontinental navigation created closer relations between West and East: steamships reduced travel time by more than half that of the slow-moving galleons of bygone years. The West's increasingly industrialized economy brought with it new inventions delivered in steel ships, among them the motion picture device. Moving picture shows flourished in seaport cities like Bombay, Manila, Shanghai, Yokohama, Batavia (Jakarta), Hong Kong, Tokyo, Bangkok, Singapura (Singapore), Malacca, Sugbu (Cebu), and Pusan. While it did not take long for motion pictures to move inland, film initially found its home in these seaside cities.

As sites of international commerce, port cities were exposed to cosmopolitan life. International trade was brought in largely by foreign populations as native elites did their best to keep abreast of these entrepreneurial ventures. The increasing cosmopolitanism of these ports created communities where foreign residents replicated the life they were accustomed to living in the West. Besides the basic necessities that foreigners needed to live in their adopted homeland, there came accoutrements that satisfied their needs for comfort and leisure. Familiar with Western ways, the local elite began to crave similar things as well. When the motion picture device emerged as the latest entertainment novelty, Asians were quick to adopt it.

It is little wonder that after film's arrival, both foreign and local elite constituted its first audiences. Were not colonial expatriates—Westerners huddled inside their confined communities—the first to hear about this novelty in the West and want it brought to the East for their own viewing pleasure? Were these not the same people who could well afford to buy admission tickets after reading announcements of film screenings in newspapers? If only a few educated local inhabitants could afford to buy such newspapers, could the rest of the population read them and become informed of film's coming popularity? The story of film's instant acceptance is told in many parts of Asia, where society's elite and royalty were among the first film viewers. They are reported to have become immediately enamored of the experience, unlike in the West, where stories of audiences hiding or running away from the sight of a moving train are among the most striking anecdotes of early film viewing.

There were other reported cases, particularly in places outside urban localities, where local residents were at first too superstitious to watch film shows because they were believed to be handiworks of the Western devil.[2] Some were reluctant to see the moving pictures that were inexplicably thrown on the white screen: they were thought to be ghosts or spirits. Given the strong reservation expressed by some viewers from interior China to the Philippines' northern mountain provinces, one wonders: What process did it take for film to become an object that Asians could call their own? What role did native language play in owning the experience of film watching? As film found its way to islands across the region, how did traditional entertainments, particularly the shadow play, create the uncanny impression that film was only a Western version of the ancient Oriental pastime, where the one marked difference between the two is the technology that could mechanically throw images onto a screen? What influences did indigenous theater—from Japan's Kabuki and Malaya's native opera, *bangsawan*, to India's epic, the *Ramayana*, and the Philippines' Spanish-influenced musical theater, *sarsuwela*—cast on the narrative and performative elements of the motion picture medium? What in the origins of cinema in Asia can we learn about the region itself?

Although Asia's "early cinema" remains elusive in its definition, and its historicity has yet to be fully established, attempts to investigate this phenomenon are slowly being undertaken. Recent conferences held in the region have offered rare opportunities to go beyond the constricting nationalist rhetoric that has conflated film's beginning with cinema's present paradigm, which is defined as being "national."[3] Leaving aside (and at times challenging) the dominant beliefs offered by the all-embracing national cinema concept, conference participants faced the daunting task of finding out what constitutes early cinema and how this reframes Asia's film historiography in the light of colonialism. Current efforts show promise as scholars move beyond the cinemas of Japan, India, and China—three countries that have undoubtedly generated a body of historical knowledge about their early years of cinema. More recent efforts at researching and writing are now providing accounts of cinemas in countries and subregions that were not previously covered—in South Asia (outside India), Southeast Asia, West Asia, Central Asia, even Oceania (or the Pacific Islands in Asia)—although, admittedly the last three still remain seriously understudied.

Early Cinema, Early Cinema in Asia, Early Asian Cinema: Marking Differences

In approaching the beginnings of cinema in Asia, it is helpful to talk in terms of common themes to deal with cinema's polysemous traits emanating from the region's diverse indigenous cultures and varied colonial legacies. For this reason, an effort is made here to develop, for example, one theme—that of "early cinema"—as a generic classification to deal with issues of how motion pictures first evolved in this part of the world, notwithstanding film's many sources, influences, and origins. There is, however, a need to distinguish between concepts such as "early cinema"—with its historical time frame that is mainly Western based, including its practices, personalities, and even the contemporary theories about its nature—and other concepts like "early cinema in Asia" and "early Asian cinema" that would signify how motion pictures found their entry, development, and acceptance in the Asian continent.

Film history began in the West, with the invention of a mechanical motion picture system and the cinematic practices that came out of its first encounters with viewing publics. The study of early cinema engages cinema's formative developments as a system of communication and as an entertainment institution, until film practices evolved into a new and advanced communication system with the establishment of Classical Hollywood cinema, or the vertically integrated studio system.[4] This came about as a new world film order governed its global spread after the end of World War I (around 1918).

The study of early cinema has become institutionalized in Western academic circles, mainly in film studies departments. This has brought to early cinema a

load of Western values and standards that have defined the various ways film's past has been reconstructed. The way early film history has been periodized, for example, charts events that happened in European and North American societies where film was invented, traded, and consumed. Despite the acceptance of early cinema in the West, its time frame is hardly ever fully established and fixed, as there is no consensus among film scholars about its precise time frame and key turning points.[5] Notwithstanding this ambiguity, the notion of early cinema refers to cinema's Euro-American beginnings dated in the late nineteenth century, lasting until around the end of the 1910s. Given the density of meanings early cinema carries as a Western theoretical concept, Asian scholars often find it highly problematic when the term is applied outright to the nascent period when film first appeared in Asia—a period when native cinemas, much less national cinemas, had yet to be established.

In localizing film's first appearance and operation, we may ask: What do we mean by "early cinema in Asia"? How can this Western-based concept be applied to the early years when motion pictures first operated in the East? Objectively speaking, we cannot deny that the arrival of motion pictures in Asia (in Bombay, Saigon, and Manila in 1896) falls near the start of the period that Western scholars have designated as "early cinema."[6] This happened as itinerant cameramen from Europe and the United States traveled across the world, filming people and scenery to enrich their sales catalogues and visual archives back home. They also profited from offering film exhibitions in places where they visited. But should the beginnings of cinema in Asia be conveniently seen as merely an extension, or an appendage, of the Western early cinema period? If yes, what aspects of film's growth in the region may be seen and defined as "early cinema," referring to, and perhaps adhering to, the Western notions and practices carried by the term? Only the aspects of exhibition and viewing consumption? If not, what aspects in the Western concept do not apply to its Eastern experience? Could film production be one? How should we confront the temporal parallax in which early cinema ends in the West as domestic cinemas in many parts of Asia had barely started? We discuss what early cinema means to the region and how its traits were influenced by the global and country-specific realities attendant to film's many appearances and diffusions in Asia.

Furthermore, let us also think about "early Asian cinema"—the last and perhaps the most problematic among the three concepts. Was there ever an early Asian cinema? To what does the term refer? In this phrase, a different object of interest is made implicit in its formulation: the identity of a cinema produced in the region that is described to be both historically early and identifiably Asian. The concern of "early Asian cinema" is to establish the identity of early cinema as Asian, whereas the concern of "early cinema in Asia" is the historical period when a moving picture medium phenomenally occurred in a geographically determined location such as Asia. The first concept presupposes an identity that makes film an intrinsic part of the region—indigenously produced or appropriated through a sense of regional belonging. The second simply denotes that an occurrence like early cinema happened in Asia, and, whichever this term may refer to, it does not bestow the object with an identity that is Asian; for all that anyone cares, the film referred to or the cinematic practice conjured may actually be Western, but it happened or existed in the neighborhood of Asia. We discuss later whether early Asian cinema proves to be a historically tenable concept.

In considering these three early cinema concepts, which is most appropriately used in viewing Asia's early film period? To what and for whom should the notion of early cinema refer and become useful? Whose history does it enunciate? Is it convenient to take up the lens of the Western-inspired early cinema and force its application on the region despite the difference of perspectives between its Western reference and its Eastern application? Doing so will only cut off—and systematically exclude—the time when cinema finally fell into the hands of native filmmakers, simply because the Easterners failed to make their local films before the period ended in America and Europe. As history shows, not until after the end of World War I did many of the homegrown cinemas in Asia begin their first native productions, well outside the time frame designated by the West (late 1890s to mid-1910s). The first films produced by Asians were made in the 1920s, excepting those in India (1897), Japan (1898), Thailand (possibly 1898), and the Philippines (possibly 1918).[7] What should we call this period of initial film production done by Asians after World War I? Is it possible for the notion of early cinema to be reconfigured to provide a basis for the region's own notion of early cinema, freed from the baggage brought about by a Western-determined historical time frame? Will this problem in historical periodization be able to open up new possibilities for cinema in Asia so that it can adopt a definition that fits its own nature and use? Authors in this book provide their own responses to this set of problematic historiographic issues.

Colonial and National Cinemas: Contrasting Notions

Another major distinction to be made while studying early cinema is the difference between "colonial cinema" and what may be considered "national cinema." With the prevailing rhetoric of cinemas in Asia focused on the articulation of a national culture, there is an obvious fallacy when calling a cinema that existed even before the formal nation-state had been created national rather than the more appropriate colonial. As a totalizing paradigmatic discourse, this nationalist rhetoric continues to define much of our understanding of cinema in the region, including, erroneously, its history and identity during the period of colonialism. A nationalist rhetoric has also encouraged historians to mark the beginnings of these national cinemas as the moment when native-born filmmakers founded their own countries' film industries—ignoring that cinema started well before film came into the hands of the local filmmakers. Many of the region's film historians can hardly recount when and how their countries' founders of film obtained the technology used to shoot their first films.

Some of these historians cannot recall how cinema began in the age of colonialism. It is not uncommon to hear them say that the colonial phase of cinema in their countries was not part of their film history. It was dismissed as a history of their colonial rulers. A film archivist who was also a national government functionary living in a francophone country even urged me to go to France if I wished to research the colonial era of that country's cinema because that part of history, this archivist claimed, was not recognized as its cinema's history. It was a "colonial cinema"—uttered with much disdain— defined as a form of cinema that happens when a country is under the domination of a foreign ruler and its film activities, whether reception, production, or distribution, are governed by the administration and fall under the rule of a foreign, colonial power.[8] However, a national cinema happens when a cinema is formed after a country or colony has become an independent nation-state, allowing that country to endow its cinematic products with traits of its newfound political and cultural identity, claiming its films to be national. But it is too simplistic to claim that just because a country or colony has become independent that it has ceased to engage itself culturally with its colonial past. Nor is it correct to think that because a nation has become independent politically, it has established a self-enclosed, autonomous cinematic life that is devoid of any influence or interference from its former colonial master and the rest of the outside world. In truth, many cinemas that are today considered to be national had their roots in their countries' colonial past and continue to engage with or be influenced by their past cinematic experience. The Asian cinemas we know today did not come from nowhere; nor did they indigenously emerge. The dynamics of colonial and national forces determining a cinema's identity and functionality continue to blur and affect each other far beyond the political demarcations set by phenomenal events like granting a country its independence.

As we delve into the study of early cinema, we need to keep in mind how knowledge of early film history allows us to rethink some of the beliefs held dear by a nationcentric film history. This book seeks a more balanced understanding of cinema's past, allowing us to look at cinema's present national realities and its colonial beginnings. This book does not seek a return to the nostalgic past; nor does it wish to make apologies for the Western influences found in the region's present-day cinemas. In studying film's past, we may be able to balance, if not redress, issues that long ago suppressed historical facts to favor one side of a political history while condemning another because of the errors and injustices committed. We may need to seriously reconsider the idea of when to date the start of a country's film history, as well as to whom and to which set of films and filmic practices we attribute cinema's beginnings. Understanding how Asian film cultures developed and to what particular historical precedents they owed their growth can be vital to our understanding of the present-day national cinemas. As recent archival research uncovers new and revealing data, these investigations reveal historical lapses committed in the name of nationalism and offer major challenges to the national cinema paradigm. Historical amnesia has obscured important areas now in need of scholarly investigation. While essays in this book are hardly the first to pursue such tasks, these historiographic investigations un-cover aspects of cinema that were either forgotten or repressed from memory: Western film pioneers and their filmic practices as well as early forms of screen reception that greeted film's initial arrival in the region.

Problematizing the Beginning of Early Cinema in Asia

There are few accounts of early cinema in Asia, and these are primarily limited to film histories of individual countries. Others are sketchy accounts in the opening pages of national film histories. A short list of these works includes Noel Burch's classic *To the Distant Observer: Form and Meaning in the Japanese Cinema* and Jay Leyda's *Dianying: An Account of Films and the Film Audience in China*. More recent publications include Joanne Bernardi's *Writing in Light: The Silent Scenario and the Japanese Pure Film Movement*; Zhang Zen's *An Amorous History of the Silver Screen: Shanghai Cinema, 1896–1937*; and my two books on colonial cinema in the Philippines, *Cine: Spanish Influences on Early Cinema in the Philippines* and its sequel, *Film: American Influences on Philippine Cinema*. There are also lengthy accounts covering early film beginnings, such as Joseph L. Anderson and Donald Richie's *Japanese Film: Art and Industry*; Mihir Bose's *Bollywood*; B. D. Garga's *From Raj to Swaraj*, which discusses nonfiction filmmaking in India; Yves Thoraval's voluminous and photograph-filled *So Many Cinemas: The Motion Picture in India*; *The Cinemas of India 1896–2000*, a film festival catalogue; *19th Hong Kong International Film Festival, 1995*.[9] However, none of these books have defined "early cinema" in a regional sense that would satisfactorily establish this cinema in ways that become inclusive of the collective cinemas of the region, in short, of an Asian early cinema phenomenon.

Faced with the difficult task of periodizing and defining early cinema in the region, we turn to American film historian Charles Musser's study of early film history in the Philippines for help in clarifying problematic issues.[10] He rede-fines early Philippine film history and provides useful insights through both a historical and theoretical perspective. In defining the traits, personalities, and landmark works of early cinema within the American context, Musser discusses how cinema in the Philippines, as a former US colony, manifested traits of early cinema during this period. He also informs us about the intersection of relations between a local cinema and the greater international and regional forces that impinge on its identity and operations.

Musser and other contributors, in studying the region's early cinema, take up issues of *colonial relations* that made possible film's introduction to host societies by colonial agents during the period of late colonialism; *modernity* as a motivating influence driving the region's inhabitants to new innovations regarding film entertainment; *technology* as a revolutionizing agent that redefined local cultures as it made its impact on the collective social space defining the notion of what was public; *identity*, as many educated and affluent classes struggled to attain self-determination for their countries and from whose ranks emerged film's local pioneers; *economic power*, as capitalism offered enticing rewards for profit and economic advancement through film business; and, important to consider among all these, *film reception*, as film appealed to viewers whose sheer volume as consuming audiences made Asia a coveted market for cinema. It is through the mediation of these local audiences that cinema became widely accepted, paving the way for film's entrenchment as a wildly popular public entertainment. This acceptance would one day have strong consequences on ideology formation as film produced new public spheres in the region (as Wimal Dissanayake aptly notes in his chapter), thus becoming an effective instrument for nation building.

As early cinema begins to gain attention in Asia, efforts are complicated by difficulties in assigning a specific time frame for its coverage and duration. This only shows the arduous task ahead for film historians and scholars. Problems start with the various dates for the introduction of film to colonial territories by foreign agents. The year 1896 remains incontestably the date when motion pictures first showed up in the region.[11] This regional appearance puts it well within the commonly held beginning of early cinema in the West, whether Auguste and Louis Lumière's December 1895 film exhibition in Paris or screenings in London or New York during the first months of 1896. But from this first arrival, it is not clear how motion pictures later spread across the vast continent. This book can only attempt to trace film's early circulation.

Looking across Asia, we find it hard to see early cinema applied with the same sense of precision regarding its spread because the arrival of motion pictures in one Asian colony or country does not correspond to another's; nor is its geographic distribution a consequence of a centralized and systematic diffusion process. This is made more difficult by the personalities and racial backgrounds of the colonizing cultures that shaped its early acceptance and development. While this unevenness makes it hard to find strict commonalities in the experience of early cinema regionally, peoples in Asia later developed a sense of a shared film experience (short of becoming a collective one) when their popular acceptance of movie entertainment fueled the phenomenal growth of movie entertainment in the years ahead.

The End of Early Cinema

While noting an absence of regional homogeneity in film's arrival, another significant problematic arises almost as a consequence: When did Asia's early cinema end, and did it end uniformly across the region? Was there a precise time when early cinema stopped? Or like its many beginnings, did early cinema have many endings? Despite the difficulties in finding a common cutoff point for the period when early cinema ended, it may be necessary to establish one if the concept of "early cinema in Asia" is to be of some practical use. Musser suggests pointing to a period after World War I (but without an exact date) as a probable frame of reference to be considered: "Certainly (and not surprisingly), an investigation of cinema in the Philippines, Thailand, China, and elsewhere in Asia reveals factors that confirm and reinforce the legitimacy of seeing the immediate post–World War I moment as an important dividing line." Undoubtedly, the end of World War I brought about new and epochal changes in the world film order, specifically to Asia. The devastating war forced European film brands that dominated the Asian film market to renege on their film quotas and, as a consequence, lose their lead in supplying films.[12] This provided an opportune moment for Hollywood film companies to fill up the void and, with aggressive marketing, shape a new world cinematographic order.

A seismic change happened after World War I. The year 1918 was pivotal for film history, as film industries in individual colonies started changing their market allegiance from Europe to Hollywood. Even more important, although minor in market effect, domestic film productions began to appear. During this new period, film historians find a wide array of activities that have yet to be mined for their historiographic significance. Here the Philippines, with its double colonial domination—first by a European power (Spain) and subsequently by the United States—is a perfect example for revealing the film world's changing balance of power. The Philippines' fledgling colonial cinema became a battleground between the retreating (but unvanquished) European (Spanish, French) film powers and the emergent American (Hollywood) one. In addition to these hegemonic film dislodgements, local (e.g., Tagalog, later to be called Filipino) film productions began to challenge the dominance of Western film control, though only marginally. This three-cornered interaction between foreign and country-specific cultures finding expression in cinema resulted in a "trialectic" of cultural influences shaping what would later emerge as a Filipino cinema.[13] Changes in trade and political relations between Asia and Western countries made the post–World War I period significantly different from the early cinema phase in which only the hegemonic presence of colonial film powers was in place and at work.

Post-1918 Philippines offers clues to developments in the rest of the region: how cinema changed its identity, not hastily, but in time, as a result of a change in film trade relations with film's Western sources. In the pre-1918 situation, London served as the center for much of the global film business, and films could be acquired through auction houses.[14] All this began to change after the war. Hollywood aggressively set up offices in places where agents could engage in direct marketing of American films. As a US colony, the Philippines experienced this shift almost instantly; it was only a matter of time for the rest of Asia. As Musser notes in chapter 2, the Philippines was made part of what he calls "the Hollywood-dominated system of world cinema" after Universal Studios set up a distribution branch in Manila in 1918 and was soon followed by almost all the major American studios. Kristin Thompson provides evidence to this claim as she traces Hollywood's spread in the region.[15] Significantly, too, the first Filipino studio, Malayan Movies, laid the groundwork for Philippine cinema to become "an independent, anticolonial force" after 1918. It happened when the first Philippine-born film director, José Nepomuceno, made his debut feature-length film, *Dalagang Bukid* (Country maiden, 1919), hailed as the country's first native-produced moving picture. In the case of the Philippines, the end of World War I offers a neat demarcation line, leaving behind an early-cinema phase to embrace the beginning of a new film order dominated by Hollywood, while at the same time signaling the start of a domestic film industry.

In China, production did not occur until a year later. As Musser points out in chapter 2, 1920 is seen as a significant dividing line for cinema to become state run after this epochal year. In 1922 the Royal Thai State Railways set up a film production department, Topical Film Service, to produce actualities depicting Thai social life.[16] This department helped produce what some consider to be the first Thai feature in 1923. Also in 1923 the first Hong Kong and Korean features were made.[17] In Taiwan, as Japanese colonization intensified, the first Taiwanese-produced feature film was claimed to have been made in 1925.[18] The Dutch East Indies' (Indonesia) first locally produced film was shown in 1926;[19] in Iran in 1929;[20] Malaya in 1933;[21] as late as 1947 for the Sinhala-language film to be made in Ceylon (Sri Lanka);[22] and not until 1948 for newly independent countries like Pakistan.[23] Significantly, all these dates were after World War I, making it worth investigating how a new world film order affected the internal dynamics of individual film-producing countries. What caused them to finally embark on efforts that put a premium on domestic control over film activities and break away from the domination of foreign film capitalists? What factors allowed this to happen? All across the region, World War I brought an end to the early cinema and sparked the rise of a new era of nationalistic filmmaking.

While 1918 may serve as a convenient dividing line, it is not without historiographic problems, such as the relationship between Hollywood's newfound role as the dominant player in Asian film markets and the almost simultaneous rise of homegrown filmmaking. Are these two phenomena contradictory? Musser, at least, suggests that we should not look at them as a contradiction but as a form of dialectic. How this dialectic played out in each of Asia's film centers may be worth investigating. It is how historians may richly account for Asia's film history.

Another problem with designating 1918 as the end of early cinema is that we may regard (in simplistic duality) the preceding years as a period of colonial cinema and the subsequent period as one of independent, anticolonial (in short, national) cinema. Even though it has been suggested here that a colonial period must be recognized before a nationalist cinema could happen, this otherwise complex situation should not be seen in such a reductivist fashion. Reality was far from this binary, if dialectical, assignation. Colonial powers, being hegemonic forces, continued to exercise their colonial, and dominant, control over their colonized territories long after the first native films were produced (and even after independent nations claimed cinema as their national preserve). Again the Philippines can offer lessons. With the Americans still, if not more, in control of colonial Filipino society after 1918,[24] the period saw a movement toward producing native symbols and practices that fostered the creation of a national identity while under the strict and watchful eyes of the US colonial government. During this time national institutions such as the National Archives, National Library, National Congress, and even the designation of what bird, flower, and hero to adopt as national symbols were determined.[25] Cinema likewise took its infant steps toward becoming national during this time when local filmmaking commenced while Hollywood took firm control of the local film market. Parallel histories may similarly be found in other places in Asia where Hollywood successfully penetrated those local markets.

The Period after Early Cinema: Transition toward National Cinema

In extending the trajectory of cinema's growth from its early to its national episodes, we begin to wonder how to regard the period after 1918. As Hollywood became an integrated film system in the United States after advancing from its early stage in the mid-1910s, was there a similar phenomenon happening in Asia? Did cinemas in Asia become integrated to become an efficient regional film system, or at least within each national territory? Did the period after 1918 result in something like a "classical Asian cinema"? What really happened after the end of Asia's early cinema period? Answering these questions can help us define not only the period that came after early cinema but refine and validate our assumptions concerning early cinema in Asia itself.

The period of peace extending from the end of World War I until the outbreak of World War II (1937–1941), which entirely changed the course of Asia's history and its cinemas, allowed colonial businesses to take root and flourish, including film businesses. Colonial progress brought development to Asia's fledgling cinemas. One can regard the period between 1918 and 1941 as the "post–early cinema" phase—a transitory stage when film was still in the grip of colonial powers, but domestic ownership of film business was in frenzied transition. It was a special period in which, paradoxically, colonial film influences—mostly dominated by Hollywood's overseas studio branches, but for some francophone countries, French and other European film companies lingered—achieved monopolizing supremacy. However, this time also allowed local cinemas to thrive while remaining dependent on Hollywood's raw materials, such as film negatives and technological devices like cameras and projectors. Colonial cinema and the cinema of the colonized coexisted, although not without their difficulties and tension but also not without rewards.

During this period of relative calm (despite the aftermath of war in Europe and the Great Depression of the 1930s in the United States) Hollywood found an opportune moment to expand its market. With the US State Department providing concerted support that forced foreign governments to accept American film products (thus overcoming the growing self-protectionist quota restrictions in the region) and with the economic incentives given by the Department of Commerce to promote films as America's major commodity exports, Hollywood enjoyed the market boost that no other nation's cinema could match.[26] Hollywood films in turn facilitated the entry to overseas markets of other American commodities (from cigarettes to cars and cosmetics), prompting one US official to remark, "Trade follows film."[27] But beyond government and state support, it cannot be denied that Hollywood films truly captivated Asia's viewing millions. This mass popularity may be attributed to the use of simple stories, recognizable genres, and, most important, the stars.

Even as American films began to dominate Asia's screens, a pioneering wave of locally produced films began in the 1920s. Might these productions still be considered part of early cinema? Strictly speaking, and only because we are using the Western standard, these films cannot be considered part of early cinema, even if they were the first and earliest ever to be made in those newly emerging cinemas. Noting that some of Asia's pioneering films were made post-1918 and were already of feature length, they were also produced long after Classical Hollywood cinema had cast its deep influence on the region's local cinemas. Films made during this time contrasted greatly with those made by itinerant cameramen and those shown on the early screens in terms of their film language and the manner in which they were produced and shown. Hollywood films became models of these locally produced films. They provided an obvious template for the cinematic language and aesthetics that many domestic film industries adopted. Hollywood's simple linear narratives appealed to audiences, adding action, sex, and melodrama to stir up popular appeal. With Hollywood films serving as templates, it became an obvious choice for Asia's filmmakers to pattern their stories on the popularity of the Classical Hollywood model, which showed high regard for visual continuity, linear storytelling, and unity of action—contrary to many films made during the early cinema era that were "syncretic, presentational, and nonlinear."[28]

Added to the marked difference of adopting Hollywood's film language, the industrial mode of production became the preferred choice of many domestic studios as they mushroomed across the region. Some of these studios were initiated by foreign residents, while others were built by a growing class of local film entrepreneurs wanting to cash in on the phenomenal motion picture business. A growing material infrastructure was on its way to giving Asia a sustainable and, for a few large companies, an immensely profitable way to produce films commercially, with Hollywood as esteemed model. Considering the crude and simple means once deployed in early cinema—in both its visual language and artisanal production—cinema in the hands of these emerging local filmmakers progressed far beyond film's initial phase.

The emerging Asian film market preferred to show films in the Hollywood classic film style as it also adopted the Hollywood studio system in producing films. These factors greatly influenced the way Asia's first domestic film narratives were aesthetically and materially produced. One could hardly find non-Hollywood styles such as German expressionism or French avant-gardism as significant influences on any of the region's feature-length productions. With the relative calm in the region and the growing prosperity in its film trade with the West, colonial Asia was on its way to developing its own domestic film industries, while at the same time entrenching Hollywood cinematic style and practices—not the least, the Classical Hollywood narrative cinema.

But then World War II shattered the calm. The Pacific War that engulfed Asia was, for cinema, a period as extraordinary as it was brief. Even so, the war interregnum had a deeply profound impact on the changing identity of cinema, although this remains a much-understudied subject. The war provided the region with a game-changing opportunity to eventually own cinema when, after the devastation, formerly colonized countries began to achieve independence. With independence came a shift in paradigm from regarding cinema as a Western entertainment to becoming a national culture. This came about as nation building in each of the former colonies went on in earnest. In this stampede toward creating new beginnings, history needed to be rewritten: early cinema, with its attachment to colonial ties, was to become a better-forgotten episode in a cinema that now had an urgent role to play in fulfilling the nationalist imaginary that would make cinema native.

During the catastrophic war, many incipient movie industries suffered untold destruction as studios were bombed, prints were burned, and artists were persecuted, if not co-opted, to become wartime collaborators. Film ties with the West, both Europe and Hollywood, were drastically severed, allowing strict Japanese military control over film businesses in many of the countries that the Japanese army invaded, such as Singapore, Hong Kong, Indonesia, Malaya, China, and the Philippines. As short as this period may have been, films produced under strict military control offered lessons on how a fellow Asian country (also one of the region's leading film producers) tried to influence emerging national cinemas in ways that reminded Asians that Western film powers once controlled the region's nascent cinemas, although the Japanese militia did so in more controlling ways. Under this scenario, film—used for propaganda and control—became a war instrument.[29]

The Japanese propaganda machinery compelled movie workers in occupied territories to renounce all forms of Western influence as it advocated for the return of Asia to Asians. If the propaganda slogans were to be believed, Asians have their own intrinsic culture that was spoiled with the coming of the Westerners; it was time to drive away the white devils. All these were wrapped in the ideology swaddling Imperial Japan's project to create the Greater East Asia Co-Prosperity Sphere. Acknowledging the role played by cinema in the Japanese war propaganda campaign, one can only wonder how cinema would be presently figured if this Japanese wonderland ever became true. One may speculate about cinema perhaps turning regional, as Japan could have advocated for a motion picture industry that, while centered in Tokyo, may possibly have provided a regional compass for its influence and market. In this (unfulfilled) scenario, Hollywood—like the rest of the Western world except Japan's Axis partners, Germany and Italy—would have been barred from penetrating the region. But this was not to be. The end of World War II brought changes that profoundly affected, again, local cinemas in ways that both the West could not have wished to happen and Japan not have expected to see—as both lost their monopolistic grip over domestic film markets. With Japan's defeat in 1945, national independence movements began to win their struggle to overthrow Western colonial powers. This soon led to a period of frenzied studio filmmaking that would further legitimize every country's claim to a national cinema. This would usher in a world that was to become separated from film's early beginnings. The period after World War II saw Asia then being overcome by nationalist fever, and cinema could only turn national.

Aspiring for One Asia and the Failure of Pan-Asianism

The sweeping movement toward the creation of national cinemas greatly reinforced the region's geographic fragmentation. Further intensified by the trauma caused by the recent war, and made more severe by the incipient Cold War, the region had little chance of developing homogeneous ways to unite the region's enormous population in sharing common aspirations and even a shared cinema. There was, however, toward the end of the nineteenth century, a movement that aimed for a regional solidarity. Pan-Asianism, an intellectual movement that grew among elite intellectuals as a way of conceiving a united Asia in the face of rampant Western colonization, developed at almost the same time as the arrival of motion pictures in the region.[30] If pan-Asianism ever succeeded in its ambition to build a united Asia, could cinema have followed a similar path? However, because of intervening events that tore the region apart, pan-Asianism became sidelined, no longer a viable option for cinema to develop through values of oneness and solidarity. Its aspiration for regional unity was sidetracked by the nationalist fever that resulted in a fragmented region, as each former Western colony established itself as an independent state. Cinema necessarily adapted to the influence of nationalism.

Few actions taken during the early film years pointed to linkages among the region's countries that could be seen as prototypically pan-Asian. In time, however, even these faint signs failed to become a viable regional cinematic system. Several chapters in this book provide examples of these trans-border activities during the period of early cinema. Wimal Dissanayake, Nadi Tofighian, and Hassan Muthalib describe instances when such a condition had marginally prospered through interlinkages among early film markets;[31] and people of various nationalities migrated to work and improved their neighboring countries' local film industries.[32] These efforts ultimately were not sustained and did not result into a pan-Asiatic cinematic institution. The concept has, so far, remained only an unfulfilled aspiration. If it had ever succeeded, Asian cinema could have undergone a vastly different history.

What is the possibility of an "early Asian cinema" ever happening? If the term refers to an identity developing from a sense of film's intrinsic regional belonging, this clearly did not happen, as very few filmmakers embarked—and fewer still succeeded—on a collective effort to initiate film productions and engage in establishing pan-regional activities like building a common film studio or establishing regionwide theater circuits and film-exchange offices (distribution houses) to serve not just one ethnic population but the entire continent.

Historically speaking, there remains no evidence to show that a collective Asian cinema formed during the early film period. While there were seminal efforts at cross-country market penetration and nascent attempts at financial coproductions, the region's division into colonies and the political divides can be seen as major obstacles for a united continental film industry. Other factors are diversity in language, ethnicity, culture, religion, and the region's geographic vastness, which hindered productive interaction between colonies and filmmakers, resulting in a failure to produce common regional film institutions and to achieve a regional identity for cinema during this time of growth. The notion of an early Asian cinema is a sort of imaginary, perhaps an ideal, that one would have wished to fulfill—an imagined collectivity for a region that desperately needed to view itself as a whole despite facing a cracked mirror. While one may have wished for an imagined regional community, one could only despair that it did not happen.

The inability of cinema to take a unifying pan-Asian path only strengthens what later became diverse cinemas. One need not look far to see how the region itself provided the environment for this to happen. Reflecting on Asia's unwieldy nature, we turn to Chinese scholar Wang Hui and his observations about the "idea" of Asia to see how cinema's division into categories (nationality, language, geography, etc.) may best be understood if we were to think of the region as something

> ambiguous and contradictory as it is colonialist and anti-colonialist, conservative and revolutionary, nationalist and internationalist, originating in Europe and shaping Europe's image of itself, closely related to visions of both nation-state and empire, a notion of non-European civilization, and a geographic category established through geopolitical relations.[33]

Wang's observation reinforces that Asia has remained divided as a result of centuries of European (and later North American) colonization, including conditions from within the continent. Cinema could take from the region only what the region could offer. The region's fragmentation (as a result of natural, geographic divisions as well as the political divisions of its colonial past) left behind a cinema that also became fragmented, with varied languages, cultures, practices, and cinematic institutions, determined by their national identities. Hence the fragmented cinemas we now see in Asia are the legacy of the region's fragmented past. Wang notes that the region's history was drawn from epic divisions as well as heroic acts of unification. In all of Asia's complexity, Wang calls for an effort to know Asia by understanding the "specific historical relations" that can help us transcend the "derivativeness, ambiguity and inconsistency" that have characterized the region and by extension—and for our purposes here—its cinemas.[34] Only by studying Asia's historical relations (within and outside itself) can we have a better understanding of its many contradictions and differences. Asia has been conceived both from outside and within its confines as the world's largest and most diverse continent; its cinema, too, contains all the markings of a past filled with varied and shifting identities and realities.

Inspired by Wang's historical study of the evolving ideas about Asia, our collected essays traverse a similar path, looking at historical beginnings and historical relations established between Asia and the West, when motion pictures were first imported and found a new home in Asia. As does Wang, the writers have acknowledged that cinema went through a period of derivativeness during much of its colonial experience. But because of changing political fortunes due to the emergence of nationalism, cinema also followed a path to achieving national identity, which allowed emerging nations (and their cinemas) to forge a way toward self-definition. A major consequence of this momentous change is the shift in perspective of how Asia was now imagined. From pioneer Western filmmakers like François-Constant Girel, James Henry White, Joseph Rosenthal, and E. Burton Holmes; film merchants like Benjamin Brodsky; theater owners like Antonio Ramos; and those with colonial imaginings of peoples and places they encountered in the East, the change of political stewardship of the region brought about new cinematic perspectives that greatly favored natives of the region. Asian pioneers such as Harishchandra Sakharam Bhatvadekar (India), Shiro Asano and Tsunekichi Shibata (Japan), Prince Sanbhassatra (Thailand), Qingtai Ren (China), José Nepomuceno (Philippines), and Mirza Ebrahim Khan Akkas Bashi (Iran); theater magnates such as Jamshedji Framji Madan and Abdulally Esoofally (India); and others who were native born undertook filmmaking themselves and, despite their elitist leanings, turned the alien device to something of their own.

Who is imagining Asia is thus a question of who gets the power to assert their beliefs over the region. As Wang suggests, this can be made apparent by studying the historical relations arising from the region's internal and external political and market ties. Also important are relations between cultures. The essays in this book show how the beginning of motion pictures in Asia favored those who had moving picture technology; it helped them exploit the large markets of the region. Understanding the past that favored their success and the fortunes they gained in nurturing the medium, we can then understand how Asian cinema evolved to become what it is today.

Conceiving Early Cinema in Asia

Considering the preceding discussion, we need to readjust our views of early cinema in Asia. We need to look beyond a precise time frame, which often results in differing views.

We should first appreciate the region's immense size and then realize the complications surrounding film's assimilation into the region: differing colonial administrations with their diverse policies and priorities; the plethora of film devices that were often incompatible with each other; strong native traditions that met the coming of film with resistance, or its reverse, sudden acceptance; and even though films were silent, the babel of languages that hampered pan-Asian film promotion. The growth of cinema was delayed but at times greatly hastened, which causes us to think about the ways historical time can become bent, broken, extended, abbreviated, or transformed after a phenomenon (such as film's introduction) enters into the multilayered social vortex of a region as diverse and vast as Asia.

We need to rethink what should be considered first, early, and beginning in early cinema (including their reverse, end and closure) and how they will have to be adjusted to account for other factors that are not temporal or not specific to film. For example, there may be difficulties in how a film commodity traveled between colonies, passing through local bureaucracies, political administrations, language barriers and cultural impositions, native sensibilities and belief systems, moralities and prejudices—all of which had the capacity to repulse, innovate, or reject even the most well-meaning acts by foreign and local filmmakers or promoters. In situations like these, the notions of being fast or slow, early or delayed, pre- or post- in describing film's regional diffusion may depend on the circumstances in which a film commodity finds itself. What may be early for Westerners (with their rigid time limitations) may not be perceived as the same for Asians, or even between and among Asians. Some may have earlier experiences of motion pictures than others. Thus, the notion of early cinema becomes a contested concept when used to describe the beginnings of cinema in Asia; other determining factors are technological, political, cultural, and social. While there may be objective time frames to observe—such as 1896 for film's arrival year or 1918, as suggested, for marking the probable end to early cinema—all these are considered from the perspective of Western historiography, while in the region reality combined time constraints with cinematic practices that defied strict categorizations and stringent applications. Western historiography can be useful, but it does not tell all that is needed to be said about the phenomenon of early cinema in the region.

In hindsight, to define early cinema in Asia is a struggle. Saying that early cinema started in the region in 1896 and lasted until around 1918 merely assigns a temporal frame. It hardly begins to describe the many differences attending to film's appearance in various locations in the hands of numerous personalities with varying practices under different conditions and experienced by innumerable audiences. However, the exercise in defining early cinema in Asia allows us to find a common prism that offers opportunities to identify important regional commonalities, despite the region's and its cinemas' many historic and cultural variances and the ultimate development of multiple national cinemas. This desire for commonality despite differences provides an antidote to assessing Asia as a mere geographic location fragmented by its overtly and overly determined modern political identity (the emergence of nation-states) and its (almost) fated adoption of national cinemas. Finally, early Asian cinema becomes an aspirational notion, offering us an imagined (though lost) opportunity, when cinema could have galvanized the region into one cinematic institution but did not. Despite all these complexities in understanding the early years of motion pictures in Asia, focusing on early cinema in the region helps us find a common theme in ways of thinking about a continent with many differences, inconsistencies, and ambiguities.

Reflecting on Asia's Early Cinemas

Aware of the challenges in addressing a regional conception of Asia in a situation where cinema was made to embody multiple national identities, this book includes two perspectives on early film history: a regional and a national perspective. As the history of early cinema in the region begins to be addressed, historical data are not readily available for scholars, resulting in uneven historical writing and hampering many of this book's contributors. While we may take pride in being the first to compile a substantial set of articulations on the subject, we accomplish this with difficulty, tentativeness, and perhaps a sense of frustration. It took more than eight years for this project to see fruition, allowing some historical data in this book to be overtaken by new research by other scholars.[35] Many contributors have found it difficult to deeply engage with their subjects. Some articles are available that are rich in historiographic data (not surprisingly, written by Western contributors), but others remain thin in their accounts. Language has something to do with this disparity, particularly for contributors whose English is a second language. Somehow facility of language casts some difficulty in framing the subject of early cinema by a discourse that was first formulated in the West. A diverse set of scholars, film historians, film critics, filmmakers, researchers, film educators, and students provide different perspectives and approaches to the notion of early cinema. Thus, this is a diverse set of historical discourses, some substantially documented while others are more anecdotal in a discursive style.

The regional and national perspectives should not be seen as separate and autonomous; nor should they be regarded as oppositional. Rather, they should be seen as dialectical. A regional perspective can be found in the essays of Wimal Dissanayake, Nadi Tofighian, and Charles Musser. They offer new perspectives in historiographic research beyond the convenient ways offered by the prevailing national approach found in the historical accounts that follow. Their concerns and methodologies involve a comparative approach to the study of filmic phenomenon. They find in film's diffusion an articulation of the region itself. In the second view, cinema as national culture locates cinema's unique cultural identity in specific locations such as individual nations, which again contributes to an understanding of the region's rich cinematic diversity.

Wimal Dissanayake offers an expansive view of Asian cinema that accounts for its beginnings as a colonial legacy until the period when cinema becomes national. Dissanayake's profound knowledge of the subject through his many publications allows him to address a wide range of issues regarding the emergence of cinema in Asia. He chooses to focus on the theme of "public sphere," revealing the role played by early cinema in the efforts at nation building. Cinema provided a cultural space to fulfill a people's sense of nationhood at a time when peoples in Asia were demanding the right to govern themselves and be freed from Western colonial bondage. Recognizing the national identity to which film has come to be popularly known, Dissanayake proceeds to conceive Asian cinema—a central theme in his chapter—by offering traits that help define regional cinema. The author devises a set of conceptual grids meant to understand Asian cinema geographically, nationally, and regionally. The first may seem simple (but it is by no means less problematic), as it refers to films that come out of the geographic location named "Asia." Quoting the author, the second grid refers to "the additive collectivity of diverse national cinemas" such as the way cinemas in the region are currently understood to be Chinese, Japanese, Korean, and so on. The third is the most challenging, as it refers to the "commonalities that bind Asian cinema and how Asian cinema comes to signify more than its national parts." This last concept refers to the yet-to-be-fulfilled (because it is evolving) state of pan-Asian cinema that may produce a form of cinema that will no longer be identified to one country and people but to a diverse group of countries and peoples producing films in the region, thus attaining an identity that circumscribes regionality. These three categorical grids are inscribed with their respective problematics that should allow the readers to view Asian cinema as open-ended and contested, not fixed and unchanging.

Expanding existing notions of the region's cinema, Dissanayake allows his readers to traverse historical time to appreciate the evolution of this cultural form. Inevitably, this brings the author far beyond the domain of early cinema into a period that came after it—the rise of national cinemas. Arriving first as a colonial medium, film soon became nativized through the role it played in the emergence of the public spheres that helped form Asia's national identities and polities. Tracing his conceptual references to the writings of Martin Heidegger and Jürgen Habermas in the sociopolitical field and to the theories developed by Alexander Kluge and Miriam Hansen in cinema studies, Dissanayake widens the conceptual horizon of the public sphere in its application to Asian cinema. Furthering his conceptual framework, the author mentions scholars like Benedict Anderson, Eric Hobsbawm, Partha Chatterjee, Homi Bhabha, and Arjun Appadurai to reflect on how cinema could be implicated as a cultural agency in the formation (and perhaps formulation?) of the national public sphere. Associating public sphere with early cinema, Dissanayake urges us to reflect on the nature and identity of motion pictures during their formative stage.

While Dissanayake links the history of cinema with the identity of the region where it developed, Charles Musser provides another perspective in writing the history of early cinema in the region—that of the emergence of a national cinema. His erudite study of early cinema in the Philippines during the period of America's colonial administration of the islands provides a classic example of how a once-colonial cinema manages to crawl out of its master's shadow and carve its own indigenous film industry. This may be a story not unlike many others in the region except that the Philippine case is made more dramatic by the fact that its master's cinema, Hollywood, became an all-embracing influence, considering the fact that the country has been politically and culturally dominated by American politics and culture. Musser provides valuable historiographic knowledge of an infant Philippine cinema not yet freed from the grip of its American pioneers but already changing hands, technologically, to native filmmakers. Moreover, his case study of early local cinema also shows us how it continues to engage internationally with its foreign market sources and, by virtue of its spread in the region, also in a kind of regional (i.e., Asian) affinity with other seminal film industries on the continent. He shows how Philippine cinema's origin makes it a part of the global and Asian motion picture phenomena.

Three essays in this book illustrate how in one country alone, China, film's initial introduction splintered into three politically diverse geopolitical sites: Shanghai (representing mainland China), Hong Kong, and Taiwan. Ritsu Yamamoto challenges past claims that identify August 11, 1896, as the date when film was said to have been first shown in China.[36] Regarding this date as mere historical theory, Yamamoto offers a later one—May 22, 1897—as the day when film was first shown to a foreign audience at Astor Hall in the Richards Hotel in Shanghai. Two weeks later in Shanghai, on June 4, film may have possibly been shown to a mix of native Chinese and foreigners at Zhang Yuan, an entertainment venue popularly known as Chang Su-Ho's Garden and owned by Shuhe Zhang. Yamamoto's fresh claims offer new arguments regarding film's introduction into China by identifying the date when the first film screening happened and when the "first account of a movie viewing written by a Chinese" happened. These new claims set back film's debut in China by nearly a year. Earlier regarded as next to India in inaugurating a local film exhibition, China is pushed back in time after screenings in Bombay happened on July 7, 1896; film was shot in Saigon on December 1896; and film exhibitions were made in Manila on January 1, 1897, and Osaka on February 15, 1897.

In a contrasting study of another Chinese film culture, Wai-ming Law traces Hong Kong's cinematic beginnings through a look into the island's film exhibition history. Lamenting the lack of documentary materials to establish a precise beginning for Hong Kong's film business, the author makes up for it by finding in a more-established theatrical tradition such as Chinese opera a way of understanding Hong Kong's deep cinematic roots. While he cites anecdotal accounts of film screenings that put 1898 or 1899 as years when films may have possibly been first shown, Law offers February 20, 1900, as the more reliable date for Hong Kong's first film show. The year 1903 proved a watershed when film shows became "a regular part of theater life in the territory."[37]

Daw-Ming Lee analyzes the early years of film in Formosa (now Taiwan) as tied to Japan's political interests. This Chinese territory shares with only a few other Asian countries (such as that in Choson, or Korea) the experience of having film introduced by an Asian rather than Western colonial power. Japanese film interests developed from film screenings into film production with politics as a driving force. A government functionary commissioned a fellow Japanese labor movement activist, Toyojiro Takamatsu, to produce a film in Taiwan to "educate the ignorant Taiwanese." This resulted in a five-hour program of propaganda that made Takamatsu the island's first filmmaker. His success also turned him into a movie mogul who eventually owned eight theaters. A local film culture grew under Japanese tutelage, seeing the growth of film clubs, film journals, and cinephiles who engaged in art movies and amateur filmmaking. Subsequent political events involving Japan, such as the Second Sino-Japanese War, gravely affected film's budding growth in this island colony, forcing its cinema to become a tool for propaganda by the Imperial Japanese army until the end of World War II.

While the arrival of cinema in Japan itself is an often-told tale, little attention has been paid to the ways in which the country's film industry adapted traditional theatrical practices in the age of modernism. Up until the 1920s, filmmakers in Japan not only rarely reshot a scene but typically made only one positive print from a negative. In the age of mechanical reproduction, this appears to be an oddity. Aaron Gerow investigates the reasons why this became a unique feature in early Japanese cinema. Gerow points out that printing only one film copy may conveniently be seen as a marker to differentiate Japanese from Western cinemas, as does the *benshi* (a live commentator on the film), thus pointing out Japan's cultural uniqueness. While this practice may appear as a form of cultural idiosyncrasy, the author explores the relations of industry and culture in a modernizing Japan for a deeper understanding of this practice. He sees it "less as a form of cultural resistance against modernity than as an articulation of cinema as event through an alternative, hybrid form of modernity that problematized the contemporary formation of the nation."

Gerow's essay finds its counterpart in Nadi Tofighian's profile of a major Scandinavian company's film business in Asia: the Danish Nordisk Films Kompagni (commonly known as Nordisk Film). His chapter, which brings back a regional perspective to the book, comes as a welcome addition to a subject that is rarely discussed in early film history: distribution. Tofighian has unearthed documents about the historically obscured trade relations between this Nordic film company and selected Asian countries. He also explores the greater difficulties Nordisk faced in conducting its business than other leading European film companies experienced, such as Pathé and Gaumont. To sell their films in Asia, European producers had to resort to various business strategies such as finding London agents to sell their films or conducting direct sales of their products in countries where they had branches. In most cases, this particular Scandinavian company sold its multiple films outright, making it hard to identify local distribution partners.

To date the history of early cinema in Cambodia, Laos, and Vietnam has been largely invisible. By throwing light on the cinemas of Indochina, Tilman Baumgartel provides this book with one of its most surprising contributions. It is a revelation to discover that, on his way to Japan in late 1896, Lumière's cameraman François-Constant Girel made one of the earliest films ever shot in Asia during his brief stopover in Saigon. With Japan as his destination, Girel did not stay long there. In 1899, he was followed in Japan by another Lumière operator, Gabriel Veyre, who had a more productive experience by also shooting in Indochina. Veyre was commissioned by the governor-general, Paul Doumer, to film five hundred scenes of various activities in those countries, with an aim to show them at the 1900 Paris Exposition Universelle. He was soon followed by a long line of mostly French filmmakers, who shot films in this colonial territory. Among the remarkable works are Leon Busy's films for Albert Kahn's *Archives of the Planet*, Jacques Feyder's *Au pays du roi lepreux* (In the land of the leper king, 1926), as well as the documentaries and educational films that contributed to the Mission cinématographique. Through such efforts, colonial administrators sought to make France known to Indochina and Indochina known to France.

P. K. Nair's chapter on the formation of a national cinema under colonial conditions not only illuminates the struggles of early Indian filmmakers but provides inspiration for Asians still seeking to counter foreign domination of their local motion picture industries. Invoking the long cultural tradition that Indians had in public entertainment, Nair strikes a contrast between Occidental and Indian audiences with regard to the first film viewing experience. He believes that the Indian viewers' familiarity with shadow plays prepared them to watch their first moving pictures and thus not undergo the stress experienced by the Lumières' Parisian audiences. South Asians, Nair contends, had a rich pre-cinematic experience that prepared them to see film's arrival as one merely of technological advancement. Indian cinema is the most diverse in Asia, and Nair takes note of how film developed subregional industries based on various ethno-linguistic traits from languages such as Tamil, Urdu, Bengali, and other languages besides Hindi. There was further expansion overseas when Indian filmmakers started making films in Ceylon, Singapore, and the Malay Peninsula. While Indian films were initially meant for home markets, they soon found overseas audiences, first among diasporic Indian communities and later among the growing global market.

Colonialism is likewise the underlying theme running through my chapter on early cinema in the Philippines. Imported by the Spaniards, the first moving pictures opened wide the gate for European film culture to spread. Led by French products—Lumière, Gaumont, and Pathé—other brands from Italy, Germany, England, and Denmark also shared in the growing domestic market. Film's initial growth was boosted when the Americans took over control of the archipelago from the Spaniards. I recognize the first American film pioneers who made the first motion pictures in and about the country. This generation of itinerant filmmakers was followed by resident Americans who laid the foundations of what would become Tagalog cinema. As cinema progressed away from the early cinema period, its journey toward the Classical Hollywood style augured well with local production, when it was time for homegrown Filipinos to eventually make their own films. Surrounded by all things American, the domestic film industry was molded in the material as well as artistic influence of the American cinema. Seeing how the country's early cinema developed under the influence of colonial forces, it is not hard to see how cinema has become a mirror of the country's own political history.

Hassan Abdul Muthalib deals with the development of film under British colonial rule in the multiethnic Malay Peninsula. Digging into a past that conjures ancient practices such as the shadow play and other forms of public entertainment, Muthalib finds that the Malay people (like many others in nearby parts of Asia) can lay claim to a form of cinema that was indigenous, save for the technology that gives film its modern appearance. Muthalib also recalls the cultural specificities that give films made in what is now Malaysia their localized traits. Forms like the native opera (*bangsawan*) or the language the characters speak (Bahasa Malaysia) are elements that cannot be ignored as cultural attributes that make these films distinctly different from other films made in the region.

Members of royalty were among the first to use motion pictures in some parts of Asia. Shahin Parhami chronicles the development of Iranian cinema since 1900, when Mozaffar al-Din Shah bought a Lumière Cinématographe and assigned his court photographer to make films showing him and life in the royal circle. To contextualize the emergence of motion pictures, Parhami digs even deeper into the visual past of a country that was formerly known as Persia. He situates its relationship to a history of prerevolutionary visual, literary, and performance cultures in modern-day Iran up until the late 1970s. He has described how the kinetic qualities of Iranian pictorial, sculptural, narrative, and dramatic forms are linked to contemporary modes of cinematic representation. As the country began to modernize many years later, films by commoners started to be made, inspired by the foreign films shown in Iran's growing number of movie theaters. Started by a Russian-Armenian immigrant, Ovanes Ohanian, the tradition of filmmaking in the hands of private individuals moved cinema out of the royal court and ushered it through various episodes in Iran's political history. It is gratifying to find how the country's cinema that once started in the hands of the Persian royalty to serve as entertainment among courtly nobles found its way to become one of the world's prominent national cinemas of the last three decades.

Anchalee Chaiworaporn contributes a unique view on the prominent role that Thai royalty played in cinema's acceptance and eventual establishment as public entertainment in the kingdom of Siam (now Thailand). Once King Chulalongkorn was photographed by a Lumière cameraman during his visits to Europe, his fascination with motion pictures spilled over to his royal family. While subsequent film activities were mostly limited to the elite royal society (the king's brother, Prince Sanbhassatra, and later his sons and more of his royal circle became involved in all aspects of film activities), the Siamese upper class also became involved. Nevertheless, even as the royals had their hands full with film activities, Japanese, and most especially, Chinese, entrepreneurs began to shape motion pictures as an industry—something that would be resented later during the height of a nationalist awakening in Thailand. Because both internal political events and external colonial interests were forcing the Thai monarchy to abdicate a monopoly of power over Thai society and government, the change in political governance inevitably caused film to change hands from the monarchy to private ownership.

Stephen Bottomore concludes this book with a triptych of essays that probe the edges of our knowledge of early cinema in Asia. The first, which has a title that evokes Yasujiro Ozu's silent film classic *I Was Born, but . . .* (1932), reflects on film's early history and the many individuals whose achievements have yet to be taken into account. As does Ozu's film, Bottomore reminds those who are still uncomfortable with cinema's colonial, Western origins that we cannot choose our parents, no matter how much we may want to disown them. Bottomore reminds us that "they constitute an undeniable part of the history of cinema on the continent." Remembering the original pioneers—who were Westerners—Bottomore enumerates names that have been obscured by time, such as those who inaugurated motion picture shows in Indochine (or Indochina), Nederlands-Indie (now Indonesia), or Ceylon (now Sri Lanka). Bottomore is the first to make mention of Dr. Harley, who mounted what may have been the "first known appearance of moving pictures in India" (and by extension, probably in the whole of Asia). While he laments that his mention of this fact in an Indian publication did not cause "even a response," we belatedly acknowledge his discovery as an achievement, first of research, then as a triumph of memory. This recollection triggers the unwinding of multiple histories—about the period of colonialism, the early form of market globalism, commodification of fantasy, diffusion of technology in Asia, and the Orientalism that resulted between the interface of the Western camera and the Eastern subject. Bottomore's discovery of the first aspect of film's past in the region, prepares us for the many more facets of film's early history yet to be found.

Bottomore's final two chapters examine two areas in the region that have been ignored, excluded, or obscured in many accounts of film history. He throws light on the exotic, but many times ignored, Oceania and argues for these Pacific islands to be part of geographic Asia. The author starts by considering two cameramen working for Edison Studios, James Henry White and Frederick Blechynden, who shot films in the Hawaiian Islands in 1898 during the Spanish-American War. They were later joined by other American and European filmmakers. Other islands in the Pacific were also brought into the celluloid orbit—Samoa, Fiji, Solomon Islands, and Tahiti. But the apotheosis of film's development in the islands was as location sites for what would one day turn into a worldwide phenomenon of "South Sea cinema," including classics such as Robert Flaherty's *Moana* (1926) and W. S. Van Dyke's *White Shadows in the South Seas* (1928).

Bottomore's last contribution concerns early cinema in Central Asia. The earliest date for the introduction of cinema in this border territory was possibly 1902, the exact date being burdened by the lack of determination of what was actually shown—motion pictures or stereopticon slides. Afghanistan figures as possibly the first among these Central Asian territories to hold the first film exhibition. Not unlike the situation in Thailand and Iran, the amir of Afghanistan (and subsequent amirs) was responsible for introducing the modern invention of motion pictures into his country. In the amirs' interest in photography and their constant travels abroad, they fancied the Cinematograph and used it to film their royal activities. In neighboring Uzbekistan, film may have even been shot earlier than in Afghanistan (although the assumed year of 1900 is still undetermined), when Hudaibergen Divanov made a documentary about his country. Once again royalty introduced film into this region, although commercial hands took over in following years. Film arrived late in Tibet because it is located on a high mountain plateau, not easily accessible to itinerant cameramen. Tibet's first encounter with cinematography did not even happen inside the country, when the spiritual leader, the Dalai Lama, fleeing from Chinese authorities after being deposed, was captured on celluloid while on a procession in northeastern India. Only after this initial encounter between the camera and a prominent Tibetan figure was film finally shot inside Tibet the following year.

Bottomore poses a question that is at the heart of this book: "Does this mean that the Western-oriented history of cinema in this pioneering period (I mean broadly the silent period, up to about 1930) is or should be irrelevant to the history of these countries themselves?" His reflection further validates what has earlier been posed in this introduction. Periodizing the era of early cinema in Asia based on a Western standard poses major problems when applied to cinemas as remote as those found in these territories, where time retards what is deemed the normal progression of film history in Western terms, whether technological or cultural. This is a lag that can be seen only from a Western perspective, one that comes from outside the society and culture being studied.

Like Bottomore, this book asks for a new perspective in looking at origins and notions of development that consider time in relation to the location where film activities happen and from there chart the progress of film's development. This means seeing how a territory owned and created its own history of film considering the time it took for film to grow in that particular place. Echoing Wang's appeal for "specific historical relations," this orientation provides us with a more realistic way of assessing film's early history in many other countries and subregions of Asia. Given the complex challenge this site-specific historical progress demands, there is a necessity for various ways of looking at and defining the concept of early cinema—as early cinema (in its Western connotation), as early cinema in Asia, and as early Asian cinema. While this book affirms that there is a need to establish the Western notion of early cinema and its history of filmic progress, other notions must likewise be considered in studying the phenomenon of film's arrival and early formation in the region.

NICK DEOCAMPO is Associate Professor at the UP Film Institute of the College of Mass Communication, University of the Philippines. He is a filmmaker, author, and scholar who has pioneered several film activities in the Philippines, including the resurgence of interest and study of independent cinema and early cinema. His three books touching on the colonial cycle of Philippine cinema cover the periods of Spanish, American, and Japanese influences. He has served as member of various international film juries and has organized several conferences on film. He is a member of the International Advisory Board of the Network for the Promotion of Asia Pacific Cinema (NETPAC) and the UNESCO Memory of the World Philippine Committee.

Notes

1. The continent was also known by other names to serve various purposes from geographic designation to ideological convenience: Far East, Orient, Pacific, or simply the East. These names came with their own nuances of meaning signifying the layers of colonization the region experienced and the identity the continent assumed in the hands of its colonizers.

Considering Asia's vast size and the way Western colonizers exercised dominion over its parts as the region was partitioned into geographic spheres of influence, Asia may further be divided into the more ancient classifications of Asia Minor and Asia Major; in the more contemporary groupings of Near East, Middle East, and Far East; or subregional groupings like West Asia, East Asia, South Asia, and Southeast Asia. In these designations, countries are designated according to their relation to China and India (e.g., those in Southeast Asia are countries located south of China and east of India).

For a general reference on modern Asia, see Mark Borthwick, *Pacific Century: The Emergence of Modern Pacific Asia* (Boulder, CO: Westview, 2007). A useful source for relating Asia to film development is Annie Tereska Ciecko, ed., *Contemporary Asian Cinema* (Oxford: Berg, 2006).

2. Several articles in US trade journals report that some Asians saw the motion pictures as works of the devil. For an article on Benjamin Brodsky showing films to Chinese audiences, see H. F. H., "A Visitor from the Orient," *Moving Picture World*, May 18, 1912, pp. 620–621; for another account in Hong Kong, see untitled article, *Nickelodeon*, January 21, 1911; and for accounts of Dean C. Worcester screening to mountain tribes in northern Philippines, see "Moving Pictures among Non-Christians of Philippines," *Moving Picture News*, May 18, 1912, p. 29, and "Pictures in the Philippines," *Motography*, July 1911, p. 22.

3. Among the conferences referred to was the Origins of Cinema in Asia, held July 27–29, 2005, in Quezon City, Metro Manila, Philippines, which I organized through a grant from the Asian Public Intellectuals Fellowships of the Nippon Foundation. The conference had representations from Thailand, Philippines, the Association of Southeast Asian Nations (ASEAN; presenting an overview of Southeast Asian cinemas), Australia, United States, Spain, and Sweden, with papers also submitted from Malaysia and India but whose contributors were unable to attend. A second conference, Origins of Cinema in Asia–India, was held July 22–23, 2007, in New Delhi, India, organized by the Network for the Promotion of Asian Cinema (NETPAC) and Osian's Cine Fan Festival of Asian and Arab Cinemas. A third conference, Asian Cinema Heritage and Culture, with topics on Asia's proto-cinema and Malaysian and Indonesian early cinemas, was held November 27–29, 2008, in Kuala Lumpur, Malaysia.

4. See Charles Musser, *The Emergence of Cinema: The American Screen to 1907* (Berkeley: University of California Press, 1990); and David Bordwell and Kristin Thompson, *Film History: An Introduction* (New York: McGraw-Hill, 1994).

5. Several sources have been consulted for definitions of early cinema: Richard Abel, ed., *Encyclopedia of Early Cinema* (London: Routledge, 2005); Anthony Slide, *Early American Cinema* (Metuchen, NJ: Scarecrow, 1994); Simon Popple and Joe Kember, *Early Cinema: From Factory Gate to Dream Factory* (London: Wallflower, 2004); Thomas Elsaesser, *Early Cinema: Space, Frame, Narrative* (London: British Film Institute, 1990); Bordwell and Thompson, *Film Art*; Miriam Hansen, "Early Cinema—Whose Public Sphere?," in Elsaesser, *Early Cinema*, 228–246; Yuri Tsivian, *Early Cinema in Russia and Its Cultural Reception* (Chicago: University of Chicago Press, 1991); Frank Kessler and Nanna Verhoeff, *Networks of Entertainment: Early Film Distribution, 1895–1915* (Eastleigh, UK: John Libbey, 2007); and Richard Abel, Giorgio Bertellini, and Rob King, eds., *Early Cinema and the "National"* (Eastleigh, UK: John Libbey, 2008). Websites that offer information on early cinema include http://www.earlycinema.com, http://www.bfi.org.uk, https://www.acmi.net.au, and http://www.imdb.com.

6. Several sources provide evidence for these claims: for the first screening in Bombay, see Eric Barnouw and S. Krishnaswamy, *Indian Film* (New York: Oxford University Press, 1980); Suresh Chabria, ed., *Light of Asia: Indian Silent Cinema, 1912–1934* (New Delhi: Phoenix Computer Center, 1994); Ashish Rayadhyaksha and Paul Willemen, eds., *Encyclopedia of Indian Cinema* (London: British Film Institute, 1994); Paul Willemen and Behroze Gandhy, eds., *BFI Dossier, No. 5: Indian Cinema* (London: British Film Institute, 1982); Yves Thoraval, *The Cinemas of India* (New Delhi: MacMillan India, 2000); and K. Moti Gokulsing and Wimal

Dissanayake, *Indian Popular Cinema: A Narrative of Cultural Change*, 3rd ed. (London: Trentham Books, 2004); for Saigon, see Michelle Aubert and Jean-Claude Seguin, eds., *La production cinématographique des frères Lumière* [Film production by the Lumière brothers] (Paris: Centre national de la cinématographie, Bibliothèque du Film, 1996); and for Manila, see Nick Deocampo, *Cine: Spanish Influences on Early Cinema in the Philippines* (Manila: National Commission for Culture and the Arts, 2003).

7. These are the years when the first motion pictures were filmed by locals, although these may have been mere experiments.

8. Wimal Dissanayake, ed., *Colonialism and Nationalism in Asian Cinema* (Bloomington: Indiana University Press, 1994).

9. For additional accounts of cinema's early years, see the following anthologies: Aruna Vasudev, Latika Padgaonkar, and Rashmi Doraiswamy, eds., *Being and Becoming: The Cinemas of Asia* (New Delhi: Macmillan India, 2002); David Hanan, ed., *Film in South East Asia, Views from the Region: Essays on Film in Ten South East Asia-Pacific Countries* (Hanoi: SEAPAVAA, Vietnam Film Institute, and National Film and Sound Archive of Australia, 2001); Jose F. Lacaba, ed., *The Films of ASEAN* (Quezon City, Philippines: ASEAN Committee on Culture and Information, 2000); and John A. Lent, *The Asian Film Industry* (Bromley, UK: Christopher Helm, 1990). Single-author books written about various national cinemas also include slim accounts of the subject, but many of their claims are unverified and inadequate.

10. Musser served as keynote speaker at the Origins of Cinema conference held in Manila, Philippines, in 2005.

11. Projected film was first introduced in Bombay on July 7, 1896, although Stephen Bottomore gives the date as December 27, 1895, when the first peepshow presentation using Edison's Kinetophone machine was held in Calcutta.

12. See Kristin Thompson, *Exporting Entertainment: America in the World Film Market, 1907–1934* (London: British Film Institute, 1985); and Kerry Segrave, *American Films Abroad: Hollywood's Domination of the World's Movie Screens from the 1890s to the Present* (Jefferson, NC: McFarland, 1997).

13. The concept of the "trialectic" is inspired by George Wilhelm Friedrich Hegel's "dialectic," but instead of two forces in conflict with each other, the trialectic considers a third element interacting with the two others to arrive at a new thesis. Applied to Philippine cinema, this theory holds that in addition to the Spanish and American influences fighting for dominance in shaping early cinema in the Philippines, the native cinema (referring to the emerging Filipino), although marginalized, also exercised its influence. The struggle and interaction among these three forces resulted in what would become known as the Filipino cinema. See Nick Deocampo, *Film: American Influences on Philippine Cinema* (Mandaluyong: Anvil, 2011).

14. Untitled article, *New York Times*, June 30, 1912.

15. Thompson, *Exporting Entertainment*, 71–76.

16. Anchalee Chaiworaporn, "Endearing Afterglow," in Vasudev, Padgaonkar, and Doraiswamy, *Being and Becoming*, 443.

17. For information on Hong Kong cinema, see Cheuk-to Li, "Zest and Anguish," in Vasudev, Padgaonkar, and Doraiswamy, *Being and Becoming*, 92; on Korea, see Hyae-joon Kim, "The Politics of Memory," in Vasudev, Padgaonkar, and Doraiswamy, *Being and Becoming*, 283.

18. Gene-Fon Liao, "In and Out of Shadows," in Vasudev, Padgaonkar, and Doraiswamy, *Being and Becoming*, 418.

19. Marseth Sumarno and Nan Triveni Achnas, "In Two Worlds," in Vasudev, Padgaonkar, and Doraiswamy, *Being and Becoming*, 153.

20. Houshang Golmakani, "Star within Reach," in Vasudev, Padgaonkar, and Doraiswamy, *Being and Becoming*, 186.

21. Hassan Abdul Muthalib and Wong Tuck Cheong, "Gentle Winds of Change," in Vasudev, Padgaonkar, and Doraiswamy, *Being and Becoming*, 301.

22. Wimal Dissanayake, "Cinema, Nationhood, and Cultural Discourse in Sri Lanka," in Dissanayake, *Colonialism and Nationalism in Asian Cinema*, 190.

23. Aijaz Gul, "A Diffused Light," in Vasudev, Padgaonkar, and Doraiswamy, *Being and Becoming*, 329.

24. The Philippines was granted independence by the United States only in 1946.

25. Resil Mojares, "The Formation of Filipino Nationality under U.S. Colonial Rule, 1900–1940," unpublished paper presented at Sangandaan 2003: An International Conference on Arts and Media in Philippine-American Relations, 1899–2002, Quezon City, Philippines, July 7–11, 2003.

26. See Segrave, *American Films Abroad*, concerning the issue of US government agencies' support of Hollywood in opening up markets in Asia and the rest of the world.

27. "Marion Says Trade Follows Films," *Moving Picture World*, April 5, 1919, p. 54.

28. Musser, *Emergence of Cinema*, 4.

29. See Yukio Fukushima and Markus Nornes, eds., *Media Wars: Then and Now* [Yamagata International Documentary Film Festival Catalogue] (Tokyo: Cinematrix, 1991).

30. For information on pan-Asianism, see Sven Saaler and Christopher W. A. Szpilman, eds., *Pan-Asianism: A Documentary History*, 2 vols. (Lanham, MD: Rowman and Littlefield, 2011).

31. In India, the world's largest film industry, movie theaters flourished. From tents to movie palaces, from cities to interior towns, and from India to across Asia, including Ceylon, Singapore, and the Malay peninsula, Indian film moguls built their fortunes literally from the movie houses they constructed.

32. One instance of cross-border influence occurred between China and Indonesia. As Westerners laid down the foundation for local film production in what was formerly the Dutch East Indies in the mid-1920s, the Chinese were already in control of 85 percent of film theaters. It was only a matter of time until the Chinese ventured into film production. The opportunity came when T. D. Tio Jr., who was born in China, invited the Wong brothers from Shanghai to come to Batavia to produce films. The Wong brothers consolidated much of the Chinese community into supporting their film venture. Obtaining working capital from David Wong, also born in China, they established a film company to produce their films. *Lily Van Java* (Lily of Java, 1928) was the first film made in Batavia rather than Bandung (where earlier films were made by European filmmakers.) The film starred Chinese actors, including Lily Oey, considered the first native-born Chinese actor in film. Chinese-Indonesian actors were able to find work in Shanghai, establishing a link between both film worlds through the strong Chinese film market in the Dutch East Indies.

33. Wang Hui and Matthew Hale, "The Politics of Imagining Asia: A Genealogical Analysis," *Inter-Asia Cultural Studies* 8, no. 1 (2007): 27.

34. Ibid.

35. This long gestation period is also noted by Stephen Bottomore in chapter 15.

36. For those claiming August 11, 1896, as the date of China's first film screening, see Leyda, *Dianying*; and Jihua Cheng, Shaobai Li, and Zuwen Xing, eds., *Zhongguo dianying fazhan shi* [A history of the development of Chinese cinema], 2 vols. (Beijing: ZDC, 1963), on which Leyda may have based his assumption, citing Cheng's source from a newspaper advertisement published in Shanghai's *Shenbao*, August 10 and 14, 1896.

37. Wai-ming Law, "Hong Kong's Cinematic Beginnings, 1896–1908," trans. Stephen Teo, in *Early Images of Hong Kong and China*, ed. Law Kar (Hong Kong: Urban Council, 1995), 20–26.

1 Early Asian Cinema and the Public Sphere

Wimal Dissanayake

COMMENTATORS ON ASIAN cinema usually point out that cinema as a form of mass entertainment is an importation from the West and that cinema was, in the early years, an inferior form of entertainment given over to sentimentality and thoughtless melodrama. These statements are true, as far as they go. However, they need to be immediately qualified for one to attain a deeper and more nuanced understanding of Asian cinema. My objective is to explore the complex and interesting ways in which early Asian cinema was implicated in the public spheres of countries in South Asia and Southeast Asia. The period I cover is from 1910 to 1950. There is nothing magical about the years 1910 and 1950 except that they are a convenient point of demarcation and generally signify the first four decades of indigenous filmmaking in Asia.

Cinema has become one of the most important forms of mass entertainment in Asia. Asia has also become a site in which meanings related to a complex set of issues such as modernity, nationhood, Westernization, feminism, colonialism, urbanization, civil society, and cultural citizenship are negotiated. No cinema emerges from a cultural vacuum. Indeed, all cinemas display the stamp of the culture, society, political structure, and historical moment that produced them. Asian cinemas are no exception. They explore issues such as modernity, nationhood, and urbanization in terms of their specific experiential backgrounds. The cinemas of the eight countries that I discuss have their own distinctive trajectories of growth. While they share certain commonalities of interests and concerns, each also displays its unique preoccupations. Most moviegoers would agree that cinema is a significant social practice; that is, it has many dimensions—social, cultural, political, ideological, technological, artistic, and so on—that are closely and vitally interconnected and that constitute an important cultural discourse with considerable ramifications. It is often said that cinema mirrors social reality. However, it is equally important to recognize that cinema shapes reality, which has been the case from its beginning in the Asian countries that I have selected for analysis. In this chapter, I use the term "cinema" in its wide sense to include individual films as well as the larger social and cultural discourse within which they operated.

Concepts of Asian Cinema

At the very outset, let me share my ideas of the concept of Asian cinema, which are central to the intent of this chapter. The term "Asian cinema" appears simple on the surface, but the more we delve into it, the more we realize that it is problematic and multifaceted. For purposes of analysis, we can discuss Asian cinema at three levels of ascending complexity. The first is the geopolitical aspect. According to the imperatives of this level, we identify Asian cinemas in terms of their geographic location. This seems straightforward enough. However, even here, one runs into numerous difficulties; one has only to consider the histories and geographies of countries such as Pakistan, Bangladesh, Singapore, and Hong Kong to understand the full force of this statement. Second, we can understand Asian cinemas at the level of national cinemas. Here, the concept of Asian cinema refers to the additive collectivity of diverse national cinemas such as Chinese, Japanese, Indian, and Korean. This is the way that, for the most part, Asian cinema is being currently interpreted. However, there is a third dimension that one cannot afford to ignore—the idea of a pan-Asian cinema, which includes the commonalities that bind Asian cinema and how Asian cinema comes to signify more than its national parts. What this means is that in terms of aesthetics and discursive formations, there is a recognizable entity that can be termed "Asian cinema," which rises above the idea of an additive conglomeration of national cinemas. When we examine Asian drama, for example, we see that before the spread of Western realistic drama, the theater of different Asian countries had many things in common in terms of poetics, strategies of representation, and production of textuality. Similarly, in my work on Asian theories of communication, I have pointed out that Asian countries share certain basic presuppositions and understandings of human communication present from classical times. As we focus on the idea of Asian cinema, we need to bear in mind the complex interactions among these three levels.

Asian cinema is an open-ended and contested concept. In discussing it, we need to pay attention to continuities and discontinuities as well as synchronic and diachronic dimensions because none of the Asian cinemas discussed here present us with unproblematic and linear narratives and trajectories. On the contrary, they are driven by contradictions, ambiguities, and uncertainties. Contradictory spaces and multiple histories inform the discourse of Asian cinema. When discussing Asian cinema, we need to keep in mind that the images, meanings, and capital being produced are vitally interconnected. How cinemas draw on and forward the march of capitalism, technical innovation, and ideological issues merits close analysis. At different periods in the evolution of Asian cinema in general we have seen how the confrontations between the colonizer and the colonized, the individual and the collectivity, the local and the global, formed a central part of the cinematic discourse in Asia. Therefore, it is of the utmost importance that we are cognizant of the complexities associated with Asian cinema and not treat it unproblematically, as if there were a universal consensus regarding it, or treat it essentially, that is, historically.

There is a general tendency to treat Asian cinematic identity as transparent; nothing could be further from the truth. As with all other forms of cultural identities, Asian cinema is changing and on the move, and it cannot be contained in prefabricated categories. Our focus should be on Asian cinema not as a finished product but as an ongoing process; to speak in philosophical terms, most notably those of Heidegger, we are concerned with "becoming" and not "being." The eminent cultural critic Stuart Hall observes, "The first position defines 'cultural identity' in terms of one, shared culture, a sort of collective, 'one true self,' hiding inside the many other, more superficial or artificially imposed 'selves,' which people with a shared history and ancestry hold in common. . . . [The] second position recognizes that, as well as the many points of similarity, there are also critical points of deep and significant *difference* which constitute 'what we really are.' . . . Cultural identity, in this second sense, is a matter of 'becoming' as well as of 'being.' It belongs to the future as much as to the past."[1] This track of thought is useful when we discuss the identity of Asian cinema. Questions of globalization, post-Fordist economic transformations, the move toward coproductions in cinema, and the role of international film festivals and awards in shaping normative discourses of national cinemas demand sustained attention. At the same time, we should remind ourselves of the palimpsestic nature of Asian national cinemas and the concurrence of different models, paradigms, and aesthetic impulses inhabiting the same cinematic space. I use the term "palimpsest" to highlight that Asian cinemas contain diverse layers of historically driven significances. One has only to consider the works of Yasujiro Ozu, Akira Kurosawa, and Nagisa Oshima, in the case of Japan, to see the simultaneous existence of different cinematic models within the same national filmic space.

With the increasing velocity of cultural modernization, globalization, and transnationalization, the very concepts of national cinema and national filmmakers, which are central to the discussion of Asian cinema, become inevitably problematized. Let us consider Nagisa Oshima's film *Max mon amour* (1986), based on a story by Luis Buñuel dealing with the French bourgeoisie. It was financed by the French, and the actors and actresses in the film are French. As Oshima remarked, "This is an Oshima film," but whether it is a Japanese film is not entirely clear. Do questions regarding nationality still mean anything when we are dealing with film? Similarly, questions can be raised with regard to the work of film directors like Ang Lee and Shekhar Kapoor.

When we discuss the concept of Asian cinema, it is important to keep in mind its closer attention to the writing of film history, which is an open-ended enterprise. In writing film histories, we produce the historical objects we study. This has great implications for the study of the idea of Asian cinema. Today, when we write film histories of diverse Asian cinemas (Filipino, Korean, Vietnamese, etc.), we need to simultaneously occupy different spaces created by the past and history, by transnationalization, by the changing shapes of cultural modernities. Writing film histories is also a way of charting the course for the future. Hence, in our efforts to understand the meaning of the concept of Asian cinema, we need to pay particular attention to how film histories have been written and how they are being written today. Film histories widen the discursive domain of Asian national cinema, as is clearly evidenced in the work of Nick Deocampo with regard to the Spanish influences on early Filipino cinema. When we discuss Asian cinema, therefore, it is of the utmost importance that we keep within our sights this problematic and contested nature of the concept of Asian cinema.

The Concept of the Public Sphere

An elucidation of the concept of the public sphere is central to the intent of this chapter. As it does for the concept of Asian cinema, any discussion of the notion of the public sphere has to focus on its problematic nature. This means that we have to raise questions such as, Is there a distinctly identifiable Asian public sphere, as opposed to, say, a European public sphere? How has the nature of the public sphere in Asian countries changed over time? How do these changes affect the relationship between cinemas and the public sphere in Asia? Although the idea of the public sphere and its importance in generating public opinion was articulated in diverse ways by thinkers such as Hannah Arendt, John Dewey, and Walter Lippman, it was the German social philosopher Jürgen Habermas who in recent years was responsible for putting it into circulation in scholarly and popular discussions. *The Structural Transformation of the Public Sphere* rekindled a great interest in this concept among both specialists in the humanities and social sciences and lay intelligent readers.[2] This book, published in Germany in 1962, was translated into English in 1989. In this work, Habermas focuses on a constellation of forces and institutions that had their origins in the late seventeenth and early eighteenth centuries in Europe. According to Habermas these webs of forces and institutions are pivotal to an understanding of the dynamics of democratic societies and oppositionality that is vital to their proper functioning. He characterizes these forces and institutions as the public sphere. He is seeking to delineate a space that is separate from the government, state, and market forces and that would play a key role in democratic discussions. According to Habermas, the bourgeois public sphere was crucial to the democratically oriented social changes that occurred in the eighteenth century and the concomitant rise of the nation-states. He perceives the institutionalized bourgeois public sphere as both a nexus of interests, a space of oppositionality existing between state and society, and a rational-critical discursive practice that bears on politics in the wider sense of the term.

Habermas makes the observation that the public sphere "may be conceived above all as the sphere of private people come together as public: they soon claimed the public sphere regulated from above against the public authorities themselves, to engage them in the debate over the general rules governing relations in the basically privileged but practically relevant sphere of commodity exchange and social labor. The medium of this political confrontation was peculiar and without historical precedent: people's public use of their reason."[3] What is noteworthy about this public sphere is that it originally took shape within the world of letters. Habermas describes the ways in which the public sphere differentiated itself from the state and civil society. Here he focuses on the important part played by newspapers, journals, literary salons, coffee houses, and works of fiction. One of the great strengths of Habermas's line of thinking, according to Michael Warner, is that it conceives of the reading practices prevalent in seventeenth- and eighteenth-century Europe as a new and invigorating form of social institution.[4] The emergence of the public sphere and reading practices were imbricated in complex ways. Print discourse increasingly differentiated itself from the activities of the state and civil society. Reading practices became an important ally in the process of establishing agency and citizenship. This is, of course, not to suggest that the public sphere that took shape within the world of letters was a homogeneous formation. Far from it—it was crisscrossed and segmented by the fault lines of linguistic, religious, political, and class differences, among others.

I believe that the clearest explication of the concept of the public sphere is found in the following description by Habermas:

> By the public sphere we mean first of all a realm of our social life in which something approaching public opinion can be formed. Access is guaranteed to its citizens. A portion of the public sphere comes into being in every convention in which private individuals assemble to form a public body. They then behave neither like business and professional people transacting private affairs, nor like members of a constitutional order subject to the legal constraints of state bureaucracy. Citizens behave as a public body when they confer in an unrestricted fashion—that is, with the guarantee of freedom of assembly and association and the freedom to express and publish their opinions on matters of general interest. In a large public body, this kind of communication requires specific means of transmitting information and influencing those who receive it. Today, newspapers, magazines, radio and TV are the media of public sphere.[5]

In the eighteenth century, the print media were at the center of the public culture. Today, visual media such as film and television have become the dominant media associated with the public sphere.

There are two sets of meanings that lie at the heart of Habermas's conceptualization of the public sphere. First, he deploys the term in its historical specificity as a phenomenon that had its origins in seventeenth-century England. Second, he is keen to utilize the term in a more inclusive fashion to signify a wider social phenomenon of which the public sphere is one form. The way he has sought to describe the differences between the bourgeois and the plebian public spheres, and his general desire to extract general implications, serve to turn the public sphere into discursivity with normative resonances.

According to Habermas—a view not necessarily shared by later commentators—the bourgeois public sphere began to decline and lost its adversarial strength as a consequence of the rise of the welfare state, mass media, advertising, and public relations; he thought that these had the effect of eliminating the distinction between the public and the private. In my judgment, Habermas does not adequately explore and understand the complexities of the modern experience. There are several problematic areas in his conceptualization. First, there is a tendency to overvalorize the public sphere and underplay the historically evident tensions and conflicts within it. Second, he does not deal convincingly with the binarism of the public and the private. Third, Habermas does not pay adequate attention to the marginalized status of women in the public sphere. Fourth, he is attached to an interpersonal model of communication that cannot do justice to the complexities of modern life.

Habermas, undoubtedly, opened up an interesting and fruitful line of inquiry that was broadened by later writers. Although he does not talk of cinema as a vital adjunct of the public sphere, the German sociologist Oskar Negt and the filmmaker Alexander Kluge did precisely that. They sought to point out that workers, women, and subalterns did not find a voice in the public sphere and that the ways in which modern electronic media are shaping the public sphere have not been adequately addressed.[6] They also challenged Habermas's notion that modern media index the disintegration of the public sphere. According to Miriam Hansen, Negt and Kluge rightly focus on the salience of "social horizon of experience" grounded in "the context of living."[7]

The concept of social horizon has the merit of bringing into clearer view some of the important phenomena excluded by the public sphere that bear directly on issues of social reproduction. Hansen remarks that Negt and Kluge "do not construct this horizon in analogy to the bourgeois-liberal model—as a presumably autonomous sphere above the marketplace and particular interests—but rather trace its contours in the new industrial-commercial publics that no longer pretend to such a separate, independent status. These 'public spheres of production' include a variety of contexts, such as factory communities, spaces of commerce and consumption (restaurants, shopping malls), and, of course, the cinema and other privately owned media of the 'consciousness industry.'"[8]

What is interesting is that Negt and Kluge widened the public sphere to include the power of cinema in a way that Habermas did not. They were interested in exploring the many sides of the politics of the public sphere. According to Miriam Hansen,

> Central to his [Kluge's] film aesthetics is a concept of montage predicated on relationality—he refers to the montage as the morphology of relations . . .—a textual climbing wall designed to encourage viewers to draw their own connections across generic divisions of fiction and documentary and of disparate realms and registers of experience. A film is successful in that regard if it manages to activate (rather than merely usurp) what Kluge calls "the film in the spectator's head"—the horizon of experience as instantiated in the subject. The specific connections encouraged by the film respond to the structural blockages experience perpetuated by the dominant public sphere.[9]

Hansen makes the argument that we can productively go beyond the film aesthetics espoused by Kluge, which still carries echoes of modernism, to confront issues connected to cinema. As she observes,

> In particular, thinking of the cinema in terms of the public involves an approach that cuts across theoretical and historical as well as textual and contextual modes of inquiry, for the cinema functions both as a public sphere of its own—defined by specific relations of representation and reception—and as part of a larger social horizon—defined by other media and by the overlapping local, national and global, face-to-face and de-territorialized structures of public life.[10]

This avenue of inquiry cleared by Habermas and later enlarged and refined by such critics as Negt, Kluge, and Hansen, facilitates a more productive approach to early Asian cinema. I have discussed in some detail Habermas's notion of the public sphere because it is vitally connected to the objective of this chapter. Habermas, of course, is explicating the public sphere in terms of the European experience. In Asia, the emergence of the public sphere has had its own trajectories of growth. As one example, in the nineteenth century, newspapers and journals and, later, works of fiction emerged as a direct outcome of the face-to-face public debates related to religious issues and secularism. The arguing skills of the protagonists of novels are directly traceable to these public debates. Moreover, the structure of early journalism and fiction writing in Sri Lanka bears the imprint of public debates.

There is another aspect that invites closer analysis: Can we identify a common Asian public sphere, as opposed to a number of national public spheres? This is the same question that we discussed in relation to the idea of Asian cinema. At one level, we can talk of a common Asian public sphere because most Asian countries have had to deal with a set of common experiences related to coloniality, postcoloniality, cultural modernity, oppressive states, the Othering by the West, secularism, and so on. As a consequence of this common experience, one can see the formation of a common Asian experience. Let us, for example, consider the issue of modernity that is imbricated with the public sphere. In Western countries, modernization was part and parcel of the perceived natural growth of these countries, while in Asia modernity was and is seen as a late arrival, a game of catch-up. This is the case even in Japan, which is the most advanced and modernized Asian country. This difference of perception has great implications for the understanding of a common Asian public sphere. However, the velocities of modernization differ from country to country, giving each national public sphere a special identity.

When we talk of the public sphere, it is important to recognize its historical evolution. The way that the state, civil society, democratic polity, and mass media interact changes over time, as these elements are compelled to confront new social experiences, and provides us with important insights into the social formations of contemporary societies. The conditions under which rational-critical arguments and debates regarding public issues are conducted by public persons—a defining mark of the public sphere as defined by Habermas—also change over time. As we examine the relationship between the public sphere and cinema in Asia, these considerations should receive focused attention. The function of the public sphere in relation to cinema in the colonial period was different from that in the postcolonial period. In the colonial period, the public sphere was restricted to the educated classes, was elitist in nature, and addressed questions of national liberation, Westernization, modernization, and so on. In the postcolonial period, the public sphere expanded, became less elitist, and included criticism of the independent state as one of its functions. In the earlier period, the public sphere was allied with the aspirations of the emerging nation-state, while in the postcolonial period the public sphere was much more concerned with critiquing the nation-state and its diverse appendages. These have enormous implications for the understanding of cinema. Interestingly, in many of the Asian public spheres focused on cinema in the colonial era, the issues that dominated were modernization, nationalism, freedom, and national self-assertion. In the later postcolonial phase, the issues that received most attention were concerned with the democratic polity, cultural citizenship, freedom from state tyranny, rights of minorities and the protection of civil society, and so on.

When we examine the early cinemas and the cinematic discourses of countries such as India, Sri Lanka, the Philippines, Indonesia, Thailand, Japan, China, and Korea, we see how they were implicated in and became a vital part of the public sphere. One central theme common to these cinematic discourses was nationhood and nationalism. The construction of a national cinema was a vital animating desideratum closely connected to such issues as colonialism, modernity, technology, tradition, and cultural identity. For example, in these countries, nationalism was largely a reaction to colonialism. However, the collective response was anything but unambiguous and unified; there were diverse mutual entanglements and complicities that need to be decoded, and cinema provides us with a useful site for that purpose. These cinemas not only mirrored the then-regnant issues of nationalism and nationhood but also promoted and engaged in debates connected with these issues. In other words, cinema became a site of the construction of nationalism in its diverse forms. Cinema opens an interesting window into the topic of how people in Asia, through their early cinema, imagined the idea of nation. Arjun Appadurai observed that "the modern nation state . . . grows less out of natural facts—such as language, blood, soil, and race—and more out of a quintessential cultural product, a product of the collective imagination."[11] Benedict Anderson, who defined the nation as an "imagined community," focused on the pivotal role of newspapers and novels in this collective imagining. In more modern times, cinema has played a vital role in this collective imagining.[12]

Cinema and the Nation

In discussing the relationship between early Asian cinemas and the public sphere, nationhood looms large in the imagination of the public. Hence, it is useful to examine what this concept entails. As I remarked earlier, Benedict Anderson observed that nations should be seen as imagined communities and that the idea that nationhood exists as a system of cultural signification is one that should be pondered very carefully. He also stated that history is the nurturing basis of national narratives. The implications of this mode of thinking for the explorations of the ways in which nations have been cinematized are vast and full of productive possibilities. The discourses of history and nationhood and representational spaces carved out by films are closely related to modernity and interpenetrate each other in interesting ways.

Nationhood, as with all other kinds of identity, revolves around the question of difference—how the distinctiveness of one nation differs from the distinctiveness of another. It is useful to remind ourselves that nationhood intersects with a broad range of discourses related to history, geography, culture, society, politics, ideology, economics, religion, ethnicity, materialities, and so on. The idea of difference and the constant interaction between presence and absence are crucial to the production of nationhood. The discourse of nationhood can be most fruitfully comprehended in terms of continuities and discontinuities, boundedness and expansion, unity and plurality, the authority of the past and the demands of the present. It proceeds along two axes: space and time. On the spatial axis, the predominant issue is territorial sovereignty. On the temporal axis, the pivotal issues are the velocity of history and the connections with the past. The way these two axes interanimate each other engenders consequences that impinge directly on the idea of nationhood.

Benedict Anderson argues that nationhood should be seen as a cultural artifact of a specific kind. We can best understand its true nature and valence by examining how nationhood came into being historically and how it came to command such strong allegiances and legitimacy. Anderson redescribes nation as an imagined community—both inherently limited and sovereign. It is imagined because members of even the smallest nations cannot meet all their fellow members and know them intimately. However, in the minds of each of the members there exists the notion of communion. The nation is imagined as limited because even in the largest among them, containing a billon human beings, has boundaries. Beyond these boundaries exist other nations. It is imagined as sovereign because this concept surfaced during a period in which the divinely ordained hierarchical dynastic realms were being abolished. Finally, nationality is imagined as community because, despite the very obvious inequities and injustices that prevail within nations, it is usually regarded as a deep and horizontal comradeship. It is important, in this regard, to keep in mind that Anderson writes "imagined," not "imaginary." "Imaginary" connotes the absence or nothingness; "imagined" signifies a nice balance between real and not real. The term "imagined" is important in the way that cinema reconfigures nationhood.

Benedict Anderson's redescription of nationhood can be regarded as a potentially useful point of departure for further investigations of this topic. The critical weakness of his formulation, however, is that he pays insufficient attention to questions of materiality and overlooks discontinuities in history. It also shortchanges the political constructions of nationhood and the role religious allegiances and ethnic identifications play in the discursive production of nationhood. In addition to Anderson, there are a number of writers who have shaped contemporary thinking on nationhood. Among them, Elie Kedourie, Ernest Gellner, Eric Hobsbawm, Anthony Giddens, Partha Chatterjee, Homi Bhabha, and Arjun Appadurai deserve special mention.[13] Kedourie urges us to think of nationhood and nationalism as basically European understandings that were later disseminated throughout the world by colonialism. According to Gellner, nationhood can best be understood in terms of the close relationship between the notion of nationhood and the imperatives of modern, industrial social orders. Hobsbawm expresses the view that nationhood displays certain cunningness because it seeks to keep intact a threatened way of life enjoyed by the privileged by looking to the past for historical legitimacy. Giddens's ambition is to analyze nationalism largely in terms of the psychological aspects emerging from the transformations of human experience precipitated by forces of social modernization. Chatterjee seeks to encircle the political attitudes that are vital to understanding nationhood; it is closely imbricated with epistemology. According to him, the political emancipation of colonized countries should go hand in hand with an epistemological shift that clears a theoretical space in which the highly esteemed enlightenment regimes of value could be purposefully challenged. It is desired that people in former colonized societies would be able to produce a critically deconstructive body of knowledge about nationhood and the circumambient hegemonic discourses. Bhabha has underlined the importance of narration in nationhood. He has pointed out how notations are narrated into existence. Appadurai emphasizes the significance of imagination in producing modern nationhood. The views of Bhabha and Appadurai are of particular significance to students of cinema because they call attention to the notions of narrative and imagination, respectively.

National Cinemas

I have discussed the importance of the concept of public sphere and the idea of nationhood that figure so prominently in the public sphere as it relates to cinema. Against this backdrop, in 1896 the *Times of India* referred to film in ecstatic tones as the miracle of the century. Western filmmakers saw the importance of India as a location for filmmaking because of both its exotic cultures and natural beauty of its landscape. Such films as *Coconut Fair* (1897), *Our Indian Empire: A Panorama of Indian Scenes and Processions* (1898), and *Poona Races '98* (1898) bear testimony to this fact.

Given the potentially vast mass appeal of cinema, it is hardly surprising that Indians very quickly entered the domain of filmmaking. The first Indian to make a film was Harishchandra S. Bhatvadekhar, popularly known as Save Dada.[14] He was a stills photographer, dealer in film equipment, and film exhibitor. His innate interests naturally pointed to the art of cinema. In 1899, he produced his first film, *The Wrestlers*. A year later, F. B. Thanawala made two films: *Splendid New View of Bombay* and *Taboot Procession*. Both films generated a great deal of interest in 1901. As he entered the world of film production, he evinced a deep interest in Indian mythology and history. In 1905, a much-needed link between film production and film exhibition was forged. J. F. Madan, who had won wide acclaim in the world of theater in Calcutta, ventured to establish the Elphinstone Bioscope Company. In the ensuing years, movie theaters owned by Madan and his filmmaking activities began to influence audiences both inside and outside India. Madan was one of the earliest businessmen to realize the vast potentialities for filmmaking in India. He built a vast production empire along the lines of those in Hollywood, and he brought in well-known foreign actresses to perform in Indian films, as Indian women were reluctant to do so. The Elphinstone Company for the next few years dominated film production in the country. The geographic scope of Madan Theatre's influence was substantial; it began to influence the nascent cinemas of neighboring counties such as Sri Lanka in a fundamental way.

Indian audiences by then were becoming familiar with cinema, as they were increasingly exposed to such Western films as *Vendetta, Whirling the Worlds, The Great Train Robbery, Don Juan, Cinderella, Uncle Tom's Cabin,* and *The Sign of the Cross.* The ever-increasing interest in longer narratives coupled with the desire to see local experiences dramatized on the screen resulted in R. G. Torney's film *Pundalik.* Based on a legend about the celebrated Maharashtran saint, the movie was shown in 1912 and was widely popular among local audiences. *Pundalik* was the first feature film made by an Indian. However, it was shot by an Englishman and was never exhibited as an independent film. The honor of making the first Indian feature by an Indian goes to Dhundiraj Govind Phalke. On May 3, 1913, Phalke's film *Raja Harishchandra* was screened. It was totally Indian in terms of production and was shown as a self-contained work. Consequently, it qualified as the first Indian feature film.

Even as a child, Dhundiraj Govind Phalke was deeply interested in poetry, drama, and magic. One day he chanced to see the film *The Life of Christ.* As he watched the film, images pertaining to the life of Krishna began to well up in his mind and inspired him to make a film about Krishna. He came from a deeply religious Brahmin family and was also gifted with a strong imagination and an interest in technology. These resulted in his emergence as a pioneering film director. *Raja Harishchandra* was a fifty-minute film that dazzled audiences largely through its novel special effects. It paved the way for a flourishing film industry in India and an important genre of mythological films that made a profound impact on moviegoers down the decades. It is no exaggeration that mythological films dealing with lives and loves of gods and demons are a distinct product of Indian cinema in the way that Westerns are products of American cinema and martial arts films are products of Chinese and Hong Kong cinemas.

The success of Phalke and Madan went a long way to strengthen the foundations of Indian cinema as art, entertainment, and industry. Once cinema was established on a secure economic footing, filmmakers in other parts of India resolved to try their hand at this new medium. The first feature film in South India, *Keechaka Vadham,* based on a story from the venerated epic the *Mahabharata,* was made in 1917. Seven years after the first feature film was made, Indian cinema began to progress rapidly. In 1920, eighteen films were produced; in 1921, forty films; and in 1925, eighty films. As cinema became a popular form of entertainment as well as a lucrative industry, several highly gifted filmmakers made their appearance; among them, Suchat Singh, Dhiren Ganguly, Himansu Rai, and V. Shantaram deserve special mention.

A large number of films produced during this early phase were indebted to the two great Indian epics the *Ramayana* and the *Mahabharata.* While drawing on these two rich resources, early filmmakers sought to invest these traditional stories with contemporary meaning. They were Janus-faced—they looked back to the past longingly and aimed to reconnect with tradition. At the same time, they were interested in drawing on the resources and innovations of Hollywood films. Until now, all films made in India were silent. In 1931, the first Indian talkie, *Alam Ara* (The ornament of the world), was produced. It was a costume drama that combined realism and fantasy and was replete with melodious songs. In that year, twenty-seven talkies were made in four languages—Hindi, Bengal, Tamil, and Telugu. The introduction of sound had the effect of focusing more and more on song and music. The unprecedented success of *Alam Ara* instigated many other filmmakers to elevate it to a model worthy of emulation. Music, song, dance, and fantasy came to be regarded as significant components of the film experience.

With the increasing popularity of film as a medium of entertainment, filmmakers became more innovative and sought to explore new territory with social implications. These films formed an important part of the public sphere. The 1930s witnessed an upsurge of interest in social issues that impacted the day-to-day life of ordinary citizens. In his film *Amrit Manthan* (Churning for nectar, 1934), V. Shantaram probed into the theological absolutism and ritualistic excesses that were threatening the fabric of Indian society at the time. The highly popular film *Devdas* (1935) had as its chosen topic the ill effects of social conventionalism. Another film belonging to the early phase, *Jeevan Natak* (Life is a stage, 1935), focused on the harmful effects of modernization. Mehboob Khan, in his film *Manmohan* (1936), investigated the facets of feudal patriarchy. The film *Achut Kanya* (Untouchable maiden, 1936) took aim at the institutionalized caste system. What we see in these films is a direct involvement in the public sphere.

By the 1940s, cinema had clearly carved out a space for itself as a dominant form of mass entertainment. Although cinema as a medium of popular entertainment was obviously an importation from the West, it had been indigenized very rapidly. It began to portray characteristically Indian experiences in characteristically Indian modes of styles and performance techniques. Even in the very beginnings of Indian film production, the question of indigenizing the medium was uppermost in the minds of certain directors. Phalke expressed the view that most historians of Indian cinema have overstressed the foreignness of cinema and have not described adequately the way it was localized. As Phalke's writings maintain, commercial Indian cinema represents significant continuities with traditional Indian culture. He was constantly preoccupied with the question of absorbing Western technology into the matrix of Indian culture.

A winning formula for box-office success had been clearly established by the 1940s. This formula consisted of a mixture of song, dance, music, humor, and fantasy. A close relationship between epic consciousness and films was also in evidence. At the same time, films were playing an increasingly significant role in the public sphere—they came to be regarded as important instruments of social critique. It is against this background that the works of film directors such as V. Shantaram, Mehboob Khan, Raj Kapoor, Bimal Roy, and Guru Dutt have to be appreciated. By the end of the 1940s, Raj Kapoor had won international fame as a director and actor associated with Indian popular cinema. The foundations of Indian popular cinema were clearly strengthened in the 1940s even though it was a period of great social transformation and national trauma. Clearly, India was moving rapidly toward capitalist modernity; simultaneously, it was forced to cope with vexed issues of nationalism, ethnic and religious conflicts. The films made during this period relate interestingly to the social phenomena and changes.

The early Indian films connected in complex ways with the activities of the public sphere. The idea of India as an independent and modern nation was at the heart of these efforts. Filmmakers like Phalke were closely identified with the national liberation movement. Until 1947, India was under British rule. These filmmakers sought to instill a sense of confidence in Indians about their skills, capabilities, and visions, and their films were a means of achieving this. Later, filmmakers sought to focus on the fissures and fault lines of society, such as those represented by religious fanaticism, caste distinctions, and class conflicts, as a way of unifying the nation under the banner of social justice. The films, and the discourses surrounding them, served to propagate these ideas and raise the consciousness of the people. It is evident, as we examine the early phase of Indian cinema, that entertainment was mixed with social edification. Films were a useful site for the articulation of new cultural meanings and critiques of social injustices.

The work of Phalke is crucial to an understanding of how questions of tradition, modernity, narrative discourse, regimes of visuality, commodification of culture, and spectatorial pleasure were discussed in relation to popular cinema. Discussing the Phalke era, the film critic Ashish Rajadhyaksha focuses on the nature of neotraditionalism as a way of understanding the complex modes by which traditional forms of cultural articulation and performativities appear in modern expression as that seen in motion pictures.[15] Phalke was operating during the high point of British colonialism. He was keen to make cinema into a vital instrument of shaping public opinion. He was active in the independence movement that fiercely opposed British rule. He saw the value of cinema as an ally in the anticolonial struggle. For him, cinema was more than a means of public entertainment; his writings bear testimony to the fact that he was deeply conscious of the need to indigenize the newly acquired art of cinematography and infuse it with local modes of aesthetic understanding and evaluation. This desire, at a deeper level, was connected to his interest in making cinema into a productive instrument of consciousness raising and social critique. Similarly, when we examine the films produced in the early phase, we see a critical engagement with the vital social issues of the day. For example, during the period 1934–1939, several important films—*Chandali* (1934), *Dharmatma* (The holy soul, 1935), *Bala Yogini* (Girl saint, 1937), *Lakshmi* (1937), and *Thyagabhoomi* (Land of sacrifice, 1939)—were made, all exploring the issue of untouchability. The question of untouchability was gaining traction among social activists, so certain filmmakers' deeming it fit to tackle this theme in cinema indexes the close relationship that existed between cinema and the public sphere in India from the very beginning.

We next consider the cinema of Sri Lanka. Although there are three main languages in Sri Lanka (Sinhalese, Tamil, and English), few films are made in the latter two. Hence, I discuss Sinhalese cinema. The first Sinhalese feature film, *Kadavunu Poronduva* (Broken promise), was made in 1947, just one year prior to independence. It was directed by B. A. W. Jayamanne, who had by then gained a wide reputation as a stage-play producer.[16] To attain a deeper understanding of early Sinhalese film culture, it is important to retrace our path to a few years earlier. According to more recent research, the Sinhalese film *Rajakeeya Vikramaya* (The royal victory) was produced in 1925. However, information regarding this film is somewhat murky. It has been recorded that just nine years after Auguste and Louis Lumière initially showed their films, a film was exhibited in Sri Lanka to a select audience by a photographer named A. W. Andrew. He set up the first film company, Warwick Bioscope. Andrew constructed a theater and began exhibiting films imported from Europe. Interestingly, these appealed not only to the anglicized upper class but also to the local lower middle and working classes.

Then C. Wagner began to play a central role in showing European films, which he obtained from India. He is also regarded as the first film distributor in Sri Lanka. This period witnessed a great interest among businessmen, most notably those in India, for the commercial possibilities of cinema. One such businessman, T. A. J. Noorbai, owned two theaters in Colombo. In 1924 he established the Eastern Film Company and four years later played a pivotal role in establishing the Ceylon Theaters Company, which was to play an important role in the growth of Sri Lankan cinema.

By the 1940s, it was quite evident that there was a great interest in cinema among local audiences. In 1925, T. A. J. Noorbai made the silent film *Rajakeeya Vikramaya*, based on a traditional Indian story that dealt with the power and glory of kingship. It was first shown in Singapore and, for reasons that are not clear, was not shown in Sri Lanka. In 1936, the musician-turned-director W. John Edward made a silent film, *Pagliaganeema* (Revenge). It is generally regarded as the first Sinhalese silent film. Hence, by the time the first feature film with sound was made in 1947, the basics of a film culture were in place. There were a number of attempts made to produce a Sinhalese feature film before *Kadavunu Poronduva*, but these failed to come to fruition. This film is based on a highly popular stage play shown more than eight hundred times on the island. From the very inception of Sinhalese cinema, there was evidence of a close relationship between theater and film. *Kadavunu Poronduva* was followed by *Asokamala* (1947), *Kapati Arakshakaya* (1948), *Divya Premaya* (1948), *Weradunu Kurumanama* (1948), *Amma* (1949), *Peralena Iranama* (1949), *Gambada Sundari* (1950), and *Hadisi Vinischaya* (1950). It is interesting that most of the directors of these films were from South India. The impact of South Indian cinema culture on Sinhalese films at this time was deeply pervasive.

Kadavunu Poronduva and the films that followed were basically melodramas that contained song and dance. They did not directly address compelling social issues. However, they indirectly touched on such issues as cultural modernity, capitalism, class distinctions, and Westernization. These films, for the most part, ushered in an urban consciousness that was to spread throughout the island. The film *Amma*, directed by Sirisena Wimalaweera, who was also a well-known play producer, marks an important stage in the growth of Sinhalese cinema. At this time, the debate surrounding local cinema revolved around the question of *jathika cinamava* (national cinema). Many critics, writing in newspapers and journals, made the point that Sinhalese films were heavily under the shadow of South Indian films, and the local experiences were not convincingly portrayed. Critics contended that a national cinema could not emerge without an effort to portray such experiences. So cultural authenticity was the issue that reverberated in the public sphere regarding cinema. *Amma* is significant in that despite its weaknesses as a work of cinema, it was seen as the first step toward the creation of an indigenous cinema. Wimalaweera was perturbed by the unacceptable influence of South Indian cinema and addressed public rallies and meetings across the country, arguing for the need of an indigenous cinema and mobilizing support for it. He even solicited monetary support from those who attended the rallies. Actors and actresses who were persuaded by the novelty of his cause resolved to act free of charge. Here is an example of the vital link between cinema and the public sphere.

The dominant issue that reverberated through the public sphere is cultural authenticity in cinematic representation and the need for a truly indigenous cinema. Cultural authenticity is, of course, a highly problematic concept, as all cultural texts are always already contaminated. Second, the films associated with the early phase of Sinhalese cinema raised issues of cultural modernity, individual desire and social convention, and class divisions in societies. Interestingly, many of these films had two plots—a romantic tale dealing with the middle class and a comic tale dealing with the working class. Therefore, in a strange kind of way, these films served to focus on class divisions of society.

We turn next to Southeast Asia. The Philippines once produced the largest number of films in Southeast Asia. The region has a rich and varied tradition of filmmaking, and some Filipino filmmakers, such as Lino Brocka, Ishmael Bernal,

Kidlat Tahimik, Marilou Diaz Abaya, Mike de Leon, Nick Deocampo, Lav Diaz, Brillante Mendoza, and Raymond Red, in their different ways, have gained international acclaim.[17] There is one major problem with exploring the early cinema of the Philippines: lack of trustworthy evidence. Of the more than 350 films produced during the period 1900–1944, only a handful are in existence; many films, along with information-rich printed material that dealt with early Tagalog cinema, were destroyed during World War II. However, in recent times a number of film historians have focused on the need to excavate the films of this era.

Two Spanish businessmen are credited with introducing cinema to the Philippines in 1897, Francisco Pertierra and Antonio Ramos. Fifteen years later, two American businessmen were seeking to outstrip each other to make the first film with the life of Filipinos as its content. Edward Meyer Gross and Albert Yearsley both chose the life and times of José P. Rizal, who was shot as a martyr and later became a national hero, as the subject matter of their cinematic creations. This was indeed a subject that held a great fascination for the public at large. In 1919, José Nepomuceno made the film *Dalagang Bukid* (Country maiden), considered to be the first feature film made by a Filipino director. In the 1920s, he made a number of films, such as *Mariposa negra* (Black butterfly, 1920), *Hoy o nunca besame* (Kiss me now or never, 1920), *Estrellita del cine* (Movie starlet, 1920), and *Un capullo marchito* (A wilted rosebud, 1920). The silent era of Filipino cinema ended in 1932 when American George P. Musser directed the film *Ang Aswang* (The witch), which was shown partially with sound. In the same year, José Nepomuceno made *Sa Pinto ng Langit* (At heaven's gate), which could be described as a part talkie. The first real talkie by a Filipino director was made in 1933—Nepomuceno's *Punyal na Ginto* (Golden dagger).

By the end of the 1920s, a film industry and a film culture had taken shape, largely a result of the untiring efforts of artistically oriented filmmakers such as José Nepomuceno (Malayan Pictures Corporation), Salumbides (Salumbides Film Corporation), and Julian Manansala (Banahaw Pictures). The Philippine film industry progressed, and as was to be expected, corporations took over. In 1933, Filippine Films was established by two Americans, George Harris and Edward Tait, an event that revolutionized studio filmmaking in the country. In the following years, Parlatone Hispano-Filipino Corporation (1935), Excelsior Pictures (1937), and Sampaguita Pictures (1937) were founded, while in 1938 and 1939, LVN Pictures and X'otic Films were created. The number of films made annually began to increase. In 1931 only nine films were made; in 1932, twenty-three were produced, and the number rose to fifty-seven in 1940. At this stage, the film industry in the Philippines operated in accordance with the framework laid out by the Americans. This, of course, meant that it had to struggle against the formidable Hollywood film industry. The local films were made in Tagalog, and hence, the normal expectation was that such films would enjoy a greater measure of popularity than English-language films. However, the reality was otherwise. Because of a shortage of capital, technical know-how, and a strong industrial base, local film producers could not make films in sufficient numbers to offer a serious challenge to the continuous stream of Hollywood films. The need to create a robust film industry and culture that could boldly challenge the hegemony of Hollywood figured prominently in discussions in the public sphere. However, Tagalog films performed a vital function by disseminating the Tagalog language as a lingua franca in the country.

Another related issue that dominated the give and take in the public sphere was the deeply felt need to create a more broad-based audience for Tagalog films. Lower classes patronized the melodramatic Tagalog films, while the middle and upper classes were enamored of the technically resourceful Hollywood films. In the 1970s, Lino Brocka remarked that Filipino filmmakers should get over the hang-up of making great Filipino films and concentrate more on developing great Filipino audiences. This was indeed the feeling among serious-minded filmmakers and intellectuals during the early phase of Filipino cinema. Another issue that animated the discussions in the public sphere was the need to establish the cultural identity of the Filipinos through cinema and make movies into powerful cultural texts. Those who advocated this view underlined the need for people to get away from the blind veneration of Hollywood movies and to think in terms of indigenous films as local cultural texts. Some of the cultural critics who saw the importance of this line of thinking were focusing on both narrative content and representational style. They believed that what some film theorists refer to as the "pleasure point" in cinema has to be locally inflected. They saw a vital interconnection between production practices, industrial structure, and representational strategies. And aesthetic norms, while recognizing the appeal of cinema as a visual medium, also stressed the narrative content. The early cinemas in most countries focused on spatiality at the expense of temporality. However, Filipino cultural critics pointed out the importance of paying equal attention to the axis of time. This was indeed an issue that was imbricated with both aesthetics and epistemology—how one represents the world and understands the world in cinema.

One of the formidable challenges that early Filipino filmmakers and cultural critics encountered was to prevent Hollywood from continuing as the reference point. In terms of theme, style, and representational strategies, Hollywood exercised a profound influence on the imagination of early Filipino audiences. Hence, these films became the yardstick with which to measure the success of local films. Many filmmakers and intellectuals who were closely associated with the public sphere in the Philippines were desirous of challenging the cultural hegemony exercised by Hollywood films. Hence, when we discuss the relationship between early Tagalog cinema and the public sphere, this issue merits close and sustained analysis. When speaking of cinema in the Philippines, very often film historians tend to underplay the Spanish influence. Nick Deocampo has redressed this imbalance by demonstrating the Hispanic influence on early cinema of the Philippines.[18] The cinema of the Philippines furnishes us with a vivid example of how colonialism, modernity, nationhood, and the public sphere inflected the discourse of cinema.

We next turn to Indonesia, which is one of the most populous countries in the world. To understand the growth of Indonesian cinema over time, it is useful to think in terms of six historical stages: Dutch colonial rule and Japanese occupation (1942–1945); struggle against the Dutch (1945–1949); engagements with democracy (1950–1957); left-nationalist authoritarian rule (1957–1965); right-wing military rule (1965–1998); and the modern era (1998 to the present).[19] I concentrate on the first three stages.

The first Indonesian film, *Loetoeng Kasaroeng* (The enchanted monkey), was produced in 1926. This was a period in which Dutch colonialism was exerting a profound influence in the country, and as a consequence, feelings of nationalism were being kindled in various quarters. These two facts determined the cultural and political background of early Indonesian films. In 1928, the Wong brothers, Nelson, Joshua, and Othniel, produced *Melatie Van Java* (Lily of Java), and two years later Tan's Film, established by the Tan brothers, Khoen Yauw and Khoen Hian, produced *Melatie Van Agam* (Lily of Agam). The Wongs and Tans had come to Bandung from Shanghai and had some experience with filmmaking in China. In 1929, Tan's Film made *Njai Dasima* (Mistress Dasima), a film that dealt with the story of an Englishman and his Sundanese mistress. In the following year, the company produced two sequels to this film: *Njai Dasima 2* and *Nancy Bikin Pembalasan* (Nancy takes revenge). From the very beginning, the Chinese were closely involved in cinema and saw its importance as a lucrative business. They quickly established movie theaters. In 1929, the Wong brothers made *Si Conat*, a film dealing with a Chinese protagonist and a villain who was ethnic Malay. This film was set and made in Jakarta, which is important because Jakarta later became the center of the Indonesian film industry. This film was one of many that had Chinese or Dutch heroes battling local Indonesian villains. This trend began to decline in the 1930s with the rise of Indonesian nationalism.

The Japanese took control of Indonesia in 1945, and up until then the Chinese had maintained control over film production. In the 1930s, the Dutch government had established Algemeen Nederlandsch-Indisch Film (ANIF), which was to play a crucial role. Not only did it produce popular romantic musicals, but it was also responsible for making propaganda films. After independence, ANIF became Perusahaan Film Negara (PFN), which was to play a decisive role in the evolution of Indonesian cinema. In 1937, ANIF produced the first Indonesian sound film, *Tarang Bulan* (Full moon). Based on a Hollywood movie, it focuses on young love and the importance of overcoming traditional barriers. The story takes place in Singapore and Malaya. By this time, the nationalist movement in Indonesia had been gathering momentum, and the eruption of the war gave it added impetus. The Japanese took over Indonesia in 1942, which had a profound impact on Indonesian filmmaking. The war in Europe had the effect of curbing the flow of foreign films to Indonesia, and as a consequence local productions increased. In 1940, there were as many as forty-one films made in the country. While the Japanese took control of film production and enforced censorship, they also taught local filmmakers the newest techniques of film production. They sought to displace the influence of the Dutch and Shanghai Chinese on the Indonesian film industry and on the Indonesians who worked under the close supervision of the Japanese. The Japanese also underlined the importance of making films that carried social messages and were technically proficient.

By the 1940s, nationalism emerged as a force to be reckoned with. Several important journalists, intellectuals, cultural commentators, stage actors and actresses, and political activists saw the importance of cinema as a way of shaping public opinion. They wanted to create a nationalist cinema that articulated the aspirations of Indonesian people. During this period the interaction between cinema and the public sphere in Indonesia had important consequences. There was a concerted effort to appeal to the common man and woman in society rather than the elite, who were interested in foreign films more than inferior local products. Films such as *Sti Noerbaja* (1940), *Asmara Moerni* (True love, 1941), and *Panggilan Darah* (Call of blood, 1941) bear testimony to this fact. After the end of the Japanese rule, the Wong brothers and Tan's Film were back in business, making their trademark romances. In 1949, Usmar Ismail, who was later to make a deep mark on and is generally regarded as the father of Indonesia cinema, made two films. This was a period in which the idea of the nation-state and its relationship to the civil society was avidly discussed in the public sphere.

During the period 1910–1950, nearly 113 films were made in Indonesia, which leads to a number of justifiable conclusions. First, films became symbols of the urbanization of consciousness, and there was an uneasy relationship between city and village. While the city epitomized wealth, glamour, and modernity, it was also a site of decadence and moral decline. The village was attractive and quiet; it represented tradition but also has limited potential. Second, the idea of cultural identity loomed large. There was a deeply felt need to move away from Dutch and Japanese influences and to create a national cinema consonant with the hopes, desires, and preferred value systems of the people. Bahasa Indonesia, as the language of films, became a unifying force underlying the need to think in terms of a unified nation-state despite various efforts to the contrary. Third, the debates surrounding Indonesia focused on the need to strike a proper balance between tradition and modernity, religiosity and secularism. Indonesia is predominantly a Muslim culture that has a substratum of Indic religious beliefs and cultural practices, giving its religious discourse a distinctive local flavor.

When we discuss Southeast Asian cinema, we need to examine Thai cinema.[20] Since 1997, a new excitement has entered the Thai film industry; a Thai film won a distinguished award at Cannes, and others are generating great international interest by their bold exploration of such issues as homosexuality and transgender and transsexual issues. Like other Asian cinemas, that of Thailand has had a long history. Thais were introduced to the art of cinema in June 1897, just one year after the display of the Lumière brothers. Various mobile film troupes such as Biograph and Pathé Frères toured the country. In 1905, the first movie theater was established by a Japanese film troupe. When we discuss the evolution of Thai cinema from the beginning, a trinity of forces (monarchy, state, and Buddhism) played a pivotal role. Buddhism is the religion of 95 percent of the people and continues to play a substantial role in Thai cinema.

The film industry of Thailand had its origin during the rule of King Rama V (1868–1910). During this period the country was under total monarchy. During the rule of King Rama VI (1910–1925), members of the royal family, the nobility, and Chinese Thai founded film companies, which gained in strength and expanded activities during the administration of King Rama VII (1924–1935). The end of his reign witnessed the overthrow of the absolute monarchy. The Thai film industry during this phase was, practically speaking, in the hands of two groups: the royal family and the nobility, on the one hand, and the Thai Chinese, Indian, Japanese, and American entrepreneurs who were deeply beholden to the monarchy, on the other. This was a period that saw the country eagerly embracing modernity, and cinema was both a reflector and promoter of that modernity. In 1920, the Siam Film Company was formed. It was to play a crucial role during the next thirteen years. During this period film distribution was totally in the hands of this company, and it imported a large number of Hollywood films.

In 1923, the first Thai feature film, *Nang Sao Suwan* (Miss Suwanna of Siam), was made. The cast and crew included many Thais, although the film was produced by Henry MacRae of Universal Studios. King Rama VI was an avid connoisseur of cinema and was instrumental in fortifying the film industry and promoting the film culture in Thailand. In 1927, the first locally produced Thai feature film, *Chok Song San* (Double luck), was released; this was quickly followed by another, *Mai Kid Leuy* (The unexpected). In 1932, the first sound film, *Long Tang* (Gone astray), was made. By then, sound was the norm.

In 1932, the absolute monarchy was overthrown by the People's Party, and the tremendous power that the monarchy had exercised over the years was considerably lessened but not totally eliminated. Some members of the royal family were shrewd businessmen who became involved in cinema, while others had received film training abroad, which placed them in a decisively advantageous position. In 1930, film censorship laws were put in place. Earlier, the king himself was responsible for classifying films. The censorship laws were designed to protect Buddhism, the state, and the constitutional monarchy. For example, one of the criteria used in censoring films was whether a film was derogatory of the kingship in the country. In later years, censorship became an important issue in the public sphere. Beginning in the 1930s, propaganda films supporting the state and government were made. After the overthrow of the absolute monarchy, these movies dealt with the new politics and support of the military. The role of the military in cinema was another contentious issue that animated the Thai public sphere.

An interesting fact about the early Thai sound films is that they were for the most part musicals, and film companies also doubled as record companies, such as seen in the business activities of organizations such as the Krung Sound Film Company and the Thai Film Company. By World War II, the Thai film industry was firmly established, and there was fierce competition among film companies. Although foreign films, especially American films, began to be shown in large numbers—and this was an issue in the public sphere—gradually the local film industry was progressing. The Thai film industry, in its first two decades, reflected in interesting ways the political, cultural, social, and economic changes that were taking place in the country. As in other Asian countries, in Thailand cinema has been both a reflector and promoter of social change.

Against this background, let us consider how Thai cinema became a part of the public sphere and generated interesting and productive debates. These all centered on, in one way or another, the idea of nationhood and national cinema. The monarchy was most anxious to make Thailand into a modern nation, and it found the cinema a most useful ally for this purpose. How Thailand should be made into a modern nation, how a national cinema should be created, and what modernity implies in the Thai context were the issues discussed at the time in the public sphere. In addition, the need to clip the wings of the military, to introduce democratic values, and to create a healthy civil society were also discussed and debated in relation to cinema. Some of these issues continue to be discussed today.

East Asia can lay claim to vigorous traditions of filmmaking that enriched world cinema in important and productive ways. I focus on how the cinemas of Japan, China, and Korea interacted with and enriched the respective public spheres of their countries. Historical records indicate that the Japanese film industry was founded in 1898, three decades after the Meiji Restoration, which witnessed the country opening its doors to modernization and Western influence.[21] In most Asian countries, film was initially perceived as a purely novel and intriguing medium of mass entertainment. At that stage, it was never regarded as particularly edifying. Japan was, of course, no exception. From its inception,

Japanese cinema has generated much discussion and debate in the public sphere through intersecting discourses of tradition and modernity, values of the past and values of the present, traditional aesthetics and demands of the newer expressive form. While the art of cinematography was indeed new and imported from the West, it is quite evident that the early Japanese filmmakers sought to draw significantly on the appeal of traditional literature and drama to obtain a measure of popularity and a stamp of cultural approbation. While the rising generations displayed great interest in the possibilities of cinema, some of them resolving to be a part of the film industry in the capacity of directors, cinematographers, technicians, and so on, the older generation was somewhat skeptical about the potential social impact of cinema and its capacity to subvert the cultural identity and cultural values of the Japanese. This is a discernible response in the early phase of cinema in most Asian countries.

Japanese cinema, in its beginnings, was tethered to two popular genres: the period drama and modern social drama. The traditional Kabuki theater exercised a pervasive influence on period drama. For example, the earliest print of a Japanese film currently available is *Maple Viewing* (1898), based on a Kabuki play with the same name. It can best be described as a filmed stage play. In the period 1910–1950, except during World War II, more than one hundred period dramas were produced. These aimed to delineate the strengths of inherited social institutions, the animating relevance of the repertoires of cultural images from the past, and codes of conduct. This hankering after the past highlights an important problematic that infused the cinematic discourse and the public sphere: the way tradition could be harnessed to absorb and indigenize foreign cultural and technological forces. The second important genre was the social drama, which vied with the period dramas for the loyalty of the moviegoing public. These social dramas, for the most part, dramatized tragic and sentimental love stories that took place in modern Japan and had their roots in tradition. The social dramas were in large measure based on the traditional *shimpa* stories that dealt with the sadness, misery, isolation, dejection, and rejection encountered by young females.

At this time, Western cinema with its novel semiotics and visual strategies, was exercising a deep influence on Japanese cinematic culture. These Western films opened the door to a different cultural world, one that was novel, strange, attractive, and repulsive at the same time. Although French, Italian, and German films had some impact on the local film culture and imagination, American cinema had the most pervasive influence and promoted an interest in intercultural poetics. At this stage, among the American film directors who had a palpable impact on local audiences, Ernst Lubitsch, Frank Borzage, Frank Capra, D. W. Griffith, and Josef von Sternberg deserve special mention. The Japanese films produced in the 1920s and 1930s have generated a great deal of interest among film critics and cultural commentators for a variety of political, aesthetic, and ideological reasons. In my opinion, the golden age of Japanese cinema occurred in the 1950s with the work of such distinguished film directors as Yasujiro Ozu, Akira Kurosawa, Kenji Mizoguchi, Keisuke Kinoshita, and Heinosuke Gosho, a hugely talented filmmaker, but in many ways underappreciated. However, these directors had their roots in the earlier decades.

Of all the Asian countries, Japan was the most Westernized and technologically advanced, and hence it is not surprising that Japan progressed steadily in establishing a firm industrial infrastructure, film industry, and film culture. However, contrary to conventional wisdom, the Westernization of culture was neither smooth nor without resistance. The Meiji Restoration encouraged the influx of Western influences in the world of art and letters, and this led to the vitality of cinema as well. However, these influences were absorbed and transformed in consonance with the felt needs of Japanese culture. The growth of cinema from the 1920s to 1940s bears this out. The 1930s is a period of special importance to the growth of Japanese cinema, a period when the idea of a characteristically Japanese cinema in terms of styles, techniques, and representational strategies took root. Japanese filmmakers were, by and large, turning away from the codes, conventions, and semiotic discourses of Hollywood and carving out more indigenous paths. This trend, as is to be expected, had political and social corollaries. This was a time when society as a whole was looking back to traditional Japanese values to guide them in their march toward modernity. In addition, the bourgeois class, which had been the mainstay of cinema since the introduction of sound, increasingly identified itself as a Japanese bourgeois class that espoused Japanese values and life ways.

Japanese cinema, from its very inception, was connected closely to, and served as a vital adjunct to, the public sphere. The idea of nationhood and national cinema was the dominant theme in the Japanese discourse on cinema and the public sphere, as it was in other Asian countries. However, in the case of Japan it carried a special inflection shaped by the Japanese cultural experience. What should a modern Japan look like was the predominant question that engaged the interests of the intellectuals of the time, and it was amply reflected in the discourse of cinema as well. Some argued for a wholesale imitation of the West, and others, for a more measured approach; yet others valorized the past and tradition as unchanging entities. There were debates also among the bourgeois class, the working class, and the remnants of the feudal class. These debates had profound consequences for the growth of cinema as well.

Japanese cinema, unlike most other Asian cinemas, drew strongly on traditional theater, poetry, narrative styles, and aesthetics in its filmmaking. For example, Yasujiro Ozu, whom some would describe as the greatest Japanese filmmaker, while indebted to the West, drew fruitfully on the Japanese religious and aesthetic tradition. The influence of Zen aesthetics, in particular, is evident in his work, despite his statements to the contrary. Similarly, Gosho, in making his films, found haiku (with its extreme compression and high suggestibility) worthy of emulation. In addition, we consider the *benshi*, who was an institution of early Japanese cinema until the late 1930s. A *benshi* is a live commentator in the theater who provides voice for the characters and explanations on the film for the audience. The *benshi* problematized the filmic text that was supposed to be transparent and infused cinema with a distinct Japanese complexion. Some other cultures had commentators to explain the films but never with the intensity and organizational power displayed by the institution of the *benshi*.

In the 1920s and 1930s, the concept of modernity was in the forefront of cultural and intellectual debate, as evidenced in the writings of eminent philosophers such as Miki Kiyoshi. This was a time when the social order of an agricultural society was being transformed to one that suited the needs of an industrializing society. This was a period of panic, as pointed out by then-influential writers like Aono Suekichi, as a consequence of inexorable social change and the disappearance of stable reference points. Some turned to tradition as an eternal category. These anxieties were reflected in the public sphere. To many, the experience of the new was the experience of panic. Modernity and its concomitant developments induced a sense of unevenness into social life. Some looked to cultural memory as a stabilizing force. These tendencies were reflected in cinema as well as the public sphere of which it was a part.

The idea of a Japanese self in the modern world was another important issue in the expressive cultural forms. It was particularly important in that American and European movies shown in Japan presented a kind of self that was fragmented and subject to contradictory pulls.[22] This was most evident in the case of women. There was much discussion and debate during this period about the concept of the "modern girl" and its relationship to cinema. In journals like *Fujin Koron* and *Shufu No Tomo* (Housewife's friend) these issues were discussed at length. The entire question of cinema and its impact on society and cultural norms became a highly vexatious issue. Arguments were advanced, both pros and cons. Critics like Hatsunosuke Hirabayashi and poets like Haruo Sato underlined the importance of cinema as a gateway to modern sensibility in the 1920s and 1930s. Japanese cinema and the public sphere were intertwined extremely closely, and topics such as tradition, modernity, militarism, fascism, and national stability were avidly debated.

Next we consider Chinese cinema. Although China was exposed to the art of cinematography beginning in the year 1897, until many decades later, film was perceived as an alien and imported form of entertainment; in the early years cinema was referred to as "Western peep shows." One could observe this alienness at a number of different levels. Until the Communist Revolution in 1949, many of the films exhibited in China were of foreign origin. And most of the films shot in China were made by non-Chinese.[23] Moreover, a fairly significant number of films produced in China were based on stories by such diverse authors as William Shakespeare and Thomas Hardy, as well as Japanese and Russian writers. These factors, in combination, no doubt led to the impression that cinema and foreignness were closely connected. This, of course, had its reverberations in the public sphere, where cultural commentators and intellectuals who were dissatisfied with the current cinematic fare underlined the need to pursue alternative pathways.

From the very early days, filmmakers as well as audiences were convinced that there was a close relationship between cinema and didacticism. This conviction later led to the political significance of films. Sensing the great potential that cinema had for generating a political consciousness in most moviegoers, in 1932, the Communist Party founded the first film company. It is evident, on the basis of available historical records that the Communist Party and left-leaning intellectuals molded in very significant ways filmmaking in mainland China. This statement, of course, does not negate the fact that foreign films emanating from capitalist countries and commercial and market ambitions were totally absent.

In the 1930s and 1940s, there existed a close and valuable relationship between the art of cinema and the art of literature and drama. Most filmmakers were deeply conversant with, and at times engaged in, literary creation and theater production. The intimate linkage between cinema and literature had two important consequences in terms of the progress of cinema in China. First, literature was held in the highest regard by intellectuals and cultural critics who were associated with the public sphere, so this relationship served to legitimize the art of cinema and invest it with a greater degree of respectability. Second, until fairly recent times, a distinct feature of Chinese cinema was that the scriptwriter was valorized more than even the director, which is an important interconnection between literature and cinema. As the war with Japan began to absorb the energies of the country more and more, many writers resolved to work in the theater, which was seen as an effective means of generating patriotism. The war conditions were not propitious for film production, and people associated with cinema began to turn to theater, thereby fostering the relationship between cinema and theater. Many of the most important dramatists linked to this period, such as Xia Yan, Cao Yu, Chen Baichen, Yang Hansheng, Shi Hui, and Tian Han, came back to the world of cinema after the war.

When we examine the growth of Chinese cinema during this phase of its development, we need to focus on a number of important binarisms—commercialism and didacticism, political messaging and entertainment, mass culture and elite culture, Western-oriented audiences and local-oriented audiences. These dualities need to be understood in their proper historical and cultural context. From the 1920s onward, intellectuals linked to the public sphere were proclaiming the need for cinema to be serious and raise the consciousness of the people. At that time, cinema being a capital-intensive mass art, one could not escape the imperatives of commerce. Many felt the need to make cinema into a site where political messages could be purposefully discussed. How this could be accomplished without forfeiting its mass appeal engaged the interests of public intellectuals. The clash between elite culture and popular culture, between the Western-oriented and local-oriented audiences, was also in full evidence. It is interesting to observe that certain movie houses showed foreign films, and others showed locally made Chinese films; the price of tickets for local films was considerably lower than that for foreign films. For example, in 1920, of the nearly 500 films shown, as many as 450 were foreign, mostly American, films. These binarisms, and the conflicts they generated, traversed the discourse of Chinese cinema and the public sphere in significant ways. For example, *Zimei Hua* (Twin sisters, 1933) was a popular film that carried the stamp of authorship of artists connected to communism. It deals with twin sisters who dramatize the disparities between rural and urban living and social inequalities. At the same time, all female-oriented films operated within the framework of popular commercial melodramas.

In discussing the way that cinema figured in the Chinese public sphere in the early phase, I focus on three films. *Shennu* (The goddess, 1934) starred Ruan Lingyu, the most popular actress at that time. This film deals with the trope of prostitution, a mark of urbanization, and the character's struggles to give her illegitimate son a sound education despite severe odds. Her character stands in the film as an epitome of women who are fettered by social conventions and shackled to patriarchal norms but who are fighting for emancipation. This film has continued to generate much discussion. The second film, *Yijang Chunshui Xiang Dong Liu* (The spring river flows east), consists of two parts, shown in 1947 and 1948. It is one of the most popular films made during this period and charts the lives and loves of a single family during the war against the Japanese and the years following its aftermath. Many critics have high regard for this film because it dramatizes in epic terms the story of a family that is a metonym for the entire nation. Its political consciousness and moral imagination served to buttress its appeal among educated audiences and make it a useful topic in the public sphere. The third film, *Crows and Sparrows*, was completed in 1949, just prior to the Communist Revolution and shown in the following year. This film, which chronicles the sinister political realities of the waning years of the Kuomintang rule, is described by Chinese film historian Jay Leda as a milestone in Chinese film history, worthy to be shown alongside the best of international cinema produced in the postwar years. Leo Ou-fan Lee remarks that "Chinese films of 1945–49 may be compared to post-war Italian neo-realist films in several respects—in terms of style and mood, of social realistic content, as well as the rather primitive and unsettled conditions in which they were made."[24] Other films, such as *Baqinli Lu Yun He Yue* (Eight thousand li of cloud and moon, 1947) and *Wanjia Denghuo* (Myriads of lights, 1948), exemplify the intersection of family melodrama and the discourse of nationhood.

Earlier in the chapter, I focus on the way in which the concepts of nationhood and national cinema were vital to the cinematic discourses and the public spheres of most Asian countries; this was certainly the case with China. One can most usefully understand the growth of Chinese cinema in regard to these twin concepts in interaction. The Communist Party clearly saw the importance of cinema in the task of nation building from the inception of cinema. According to Shuqin Cui, the 1930s marked the transformation of early Chinese films from a project designed for entertainment to a socionational practice.[25] To understand the true dimensions of a nationalist cinema, one has to pay equal attention to textual and contextual aspects. Questions of production, industry, distribution, reception, and the cultural discourses surrounding cinema and the interactions with the public sphere are as important as the filmic text itself.

As stated earlier, in the early phases of Chinese cinema, the influence of American and foreign cinemas was heavy, and there was a tendency among certain segments of society to look to foreign films as norms for pleasure and meaning. However, this does not mean that there were no filmmakers at the time who were not interested in creating an indigenous representational space for cinema on the basis of traditional art and aesthetics. As Shuquin Cui points out, as a considered response to the dominance of foreign cinemas, local filmmakers sought to counter foreign competition by focusing on traditional arts.[26] China's first silent film sequence, *Ding Junshan* (The Battle of Dingjunshan, 1905), was based on a stage opera, and the first sound film made in China, *Genu Hongmudan* (Songstress Red Peony, 1930), dealt with the life of an opera singer and made use of four well-known opera arias to give structure and form to the film. The traditional theater proved to be of immense value to local filmmakers in carving out an indigenous cinematic space and investing the newly arrived art form with certain Chinese traits. Cinema, if it was to attract the attention of audiences, had to be spectacularly enticing, relevant, and interesting and should draw them into the presented experience. According to Shuqin Cui, these aspects of attraction of the films of the early period are extracted primarily from the tradition of theater. Peking opera was a form of proven popularity that film directors could deploy.[27] Discussions pertaining to the Chineseness of cinema constituted a significant part of the workings of the current public sphere.

Finally, we examine the nature of early cinema of Korea and how it interacted with the public sphere.[28] Until recent times, Korean cinema was not well known to the outside world. However, in the last fifteen years or so, Korean cinema has begun to display a new excitement and to generate international interest.

Films like *Chip Iro* (2001), *Sopyanjee* (2002), and *Shri* (2003) have enthralled national audiences, while films such as *Ch'wihwason* (2002), *Oasisu* (Oasis, 2002), *Oldu Poyi* (2003), *Pom, Yorum, Kaul, Kyoul, . . . Kurigo Pom* (Spring, summer, fall, winter, . . . and spring, 2003) have won international awards and acclaim. Im Kwon-tek, the director of more than one hundred films, has emerged as one of the most important Asian filmmakers. Today, Korean cinema is thriving with a newfound vitality and sense of purpose. It is an important constituent element of what is popularly referred to as the new Korean wave, or *hallyu.*

Korean cinema and the public sphere have had a close relationship because early Korean cinema emerged under the shadow of Japanese colonialism and government censorship has been a feature up until recently. While North Korean cinema became a part of the state propaganda machine, the South Korean cinema has had to contend with government interference and censorship. In 1876, the Choson dynasty fell, and along with it the isolationism that characterized the period. Japan compelled the Korean government to be a signatory to the treaty of peace and amity. Since then, Western goods and artifacts, along with motion pictures, began to arrive on Korean shores in large numbers. Western powers encouraged the showing of films as a part of their colonialist strategy. It was seen as an efficacious way of introducing Western cultural values and lifestyles to the Korean peninsula.

I focus on the period 1910–1945, which coincides with Japanese rule. During this period, foreign films were freely imported, and there was very little opportunity for local filmmakers to make their mark. Korean film historians debate among themselves when the first Korean film was made. Some suggest that it was Kim Tosan's *Righteous Revenge*, made in 1919, while the majority of historians believe that Yun Paengnam's *The Plighted Love under the Moon* (1923) was the first Korean film. The first sound film, *The Tale of Ch'unhyang* (1935), was directed by Yi Myongu and was a Japanese-financed production. During this period, foreign films were flooding the local market, and conditions were hardly propitious for the emergence of a local Korean cinema. During the era of silent films, Korean filmmakers had to depend on Japanese technology as well as Japanese goodwill.

The intellectuals, cultural critics, and opinion makers were fully aware that it was the intention of the Japanese colonial government to erase the Korean cultural identity and impose Japanese language, art, and culture on the Koreans. Hence, anticolonialism and the need to safeguard Korean cultural identity were the ruling concerns in the public sphere. During the early phase of Korean cinema, which was the period of Japanese rule, rigid and restrictive censorship laws were established, which had the effect of tying the hands of Korean filmmakers. Despite these adverse and inhospitable conditions, more than 160 Korean films were made during this period, and the majority were sentimental family melodramas. The Korean audiences warmed up to them, as they provided a way of escape from the sordid colonial realities surrounding them. In 1926, the film *Arirang* was produced, which was to have a significant impact on the imagination and consciousness of the people. It was a nationalistically inspired film of resistance. The title of the film refers to a popular Korean folk song. Under Japanese rule, Korean film directors were forced to make pro-Japanese films; some complied, while most did not. As a way of avoiding this situation, Korean filmmakers turned to literature. However, pro-Japanese films continued to be made, and the first pro-Japanese military film, *Troop Train*, was made by So Kwangje in 1938.

When discussing the relationship between early Korean cinema and the public sphere, we should focus primarily on nationalistic films. Ideas of anticolonialism, cultural identity, agency, and repossession of history are refigured in interesting ways in these films. Na Un'gyu is an important figure in this regard. In 1926, he directed *Arirang*. Two years later, he made *Searching for Love*, which encircles the ideas of national unity, cultural identity, and oppositionality. Film historians agree that his two films exercised a profound influence on the growth of a nationalist cinema and the deliberations of the Korean public sphere. By the time of Na's death in 1937, he had made about twenty films. The influence of Na is clearly discernible in such important films as Yi Kyuhwan's *A Boat without a Boatman* (1932) and Yun Pongch'un's *A Big Tomb* (1931). The latter dramatizes the story of anti-Japanese fighters killed by the Japanese under tragic circumstances. Yun was also a gifted actor who made his mark in about thirty films.

In our discussions of the early Korean cinema and the public sphere, the work of Na Ung'yu deserves careful study, as he pioneered the anti-Japanese and pronationalistic films. He ultimately made about twenty films. He acted in several films and founded his own production company. Surprisingly, in his later years, he made pro-Japanese films, including *To Send a Husband to a Border Garrison* (1931), which portrays a Korean couple convinced of, and committed to, the military cause of the Japanese. This led to his censure by intellectuals and cultural commentators. However, taken as a whole, his contribution to Korean cinema is indeed significant. His early work established a need to make anti-Japanese films that instilled a sense of self-confidence in the Korean people. As Hyangjin Lee remarks, "Although he was engaged in pro-Japanese activities toward the end of his career, it cannot be denied that the Korean film industry finally reached a take-off point with Na's *Arirang*. In this sense, his works marked a crucial turning point, a new phase in Korean film history."[29]

Na's *Arirang* had the effect of creating the conditions of possibility for the emergence of so-called tendency films. These films focused on social injustices and inequities and sought to eliminate class antagonisms. The Korean Artista Proletariat Federate in Esperanto (KAPFE), which consists of artists, intellectuals of an independent cast of mind, and others associated with the public sphere, was responsible for sponsoring these films. Kim Yuyong's *Wandering*

(1928) inaugurated this genre. During the period 1918–1921 five tendency films were made. The producers had to work against severe odds—lack of money, lack of technology, and government control. In 1931, KAPFE produced *The Underground Village*, which was banned by the government, and the makers of the film were arrested. After their release, some sided with the government, and these resistance-oriented tendency films faded away. However, film commentators make the point that the roots of the critical stance toward the nation-state and the identification with labor causes found in South Korean movies can be convincingly traced to these tendency films. Therefore, the relationship between early Korean cinema and the public sphere was framed by the issue of Japanese colonialism and national independence.

Modernity, Cinema, and Nation

The concept of nationhood and national cinema dominated the discussions in the public sphere in all eight countries that are the focus of this chapter. However, the trajectories of these discussions, the ways in which they were framed, and the valences attributed to them varied from country to country depending on the historical conjunctures and cultural contexts. The discursive interactions between nation and early Asian cinemas in the respective public spheres point to interesting and important social transformations taking place in those countries. Early cinema, in this regard, provides us with a valuable site, a repertoire of images, clusters of thematics that demand close and sustained analysis.

When we examine the discursive interactions among early Asian cinemas and the concept of nationhood, we see that almost invariably the concept of modernity emerges with compelling power. Nationhood in Asia was indeed a product of modernity—modernity that both reflected the desires and cultural imaginaries of nationhood and inflected them. Hence, the idea of modernity is crucial to a discussion of early Asian cinemas and the public sphere. It is generally believed that modernity represents a fundamental break with the past, and the new era can be written in entirely novel terms without reference to the past. This is indeed a myth, and even as radical a thinker as Karl Marx pointed out that it is not possible for any social order to generate social transformations that are not already inscribed. What our discussion of early Asian cinema points out is the way in which modernity arrived on the feet of the past and continued to move forward, on the same feet. There were, of course, tensions, wrong turnings, and conflicts of understandings, but these were part and parcel of the modernizing experience. Therefore, it can be legitimately asserted that the early Asian cinema opens a most useful window onto the terrain of modernization and its cultural correlates and that a careful study of these early film texts and the regimes of discourse that sustained them enables us to think afresh the processes of modernization. The early films encourage us to jettison the standard Eurocentric models of modernization (the so-called modernization theory) and think afresh the entire issue.

Any discussion of cinema and modernity in Asia must bring within its purview the concept of culture. Modernity was always mediated by culture, and, therefore, how the culture operated needs to be examined. There is generally a feeling among film historians of Asia that cinema unproblematically mirrored culture and that early cinema shows the attempt to preserve traditional cultures. This presupposes a unified, organic, essentialistic notion of culture. Culture needs to be reconceptualized not as a way of life but as a way of struggle. Culture was the site in which negotiation of meaning took place. It was not monolithic and static but plural and volatile. It consisted of numerous signifying systems and social practices that were battling each other. Questions of hegemony and allegiance, dominance and subordination, loomed large. When we look at the battles taking place in the public sphere in relation to early cinema, this becomes evident. Some opposed colonialism, while others were for it; some abhorred technology, while others embraced it; some denounced Westernization, while others were eager to embrace it; some discarded tradition, while others protected it; some enjoyed foreign films, while others wanted local products. What these divisions and fault lines indicate is that culture was the venue in which negotiation of meanings was taking place. Therefore, when discussing early Asian cinema, it is misleading to think in terms of unified and organic and unproblematic cultures. What this discussion of early Asian cinema and the pubic sphere points to is the diversity of cultural forms, formations, and institutional practices that were in contention, giving rise to heteronomous articulations and subject positions. Our discussions of early Asian cinemas, whether Japanese or Filipino, should be tempered by this understanding.

Most evaluations of early Asian cinema are premised on the conviction that early Asian films are underdeveloped or imperfectly realized Hollywood works. In other words, the Hollywood films are a template against which the worth of Asian films may be examined. The notion that these early Asian films might be straining to grow along different lines, deploying different representational strategies, never entered into the equation. However, when we investigate early cinematic productions of Asia, what we discern is the close and vital relationship between theater and cinema. As pointed out earlier, most Asian cinemas in their beginning phase drew on the theater and its strategies; many of the film directors were initially well-known stage-play producers. Whether the Peking opera in China or the *shimpa* stories in Japan and Korea or the *moro-moro* (a folk drama based on the battles between Christians and the Muslim Moro) and *sarsuwela* (musical play) in the Philippines, the theater had a profound impact on shaping early film texts, although in the Philippine case the influence of Hispanic culture was clearly evident. Not only theater but also painting, dancing, and other arts had an influence in some cases. Therefore, it is important that we look afresh at the development of Asian cinemas to determine whether incipient and indigenous forms of cinematic representation were stifled because of the cultural hegemony of Hollywood. This was not merely a question of style and technique; it was also related to the cinema industry, the public sphere, and audience reception. For example, the Indian film critic Asish Rajadhyaksha points out that D. G. Phalke deployed Indian subject matter and visuals in his cinema as a way of buttressing the development of Indian capitalism in the opening years of the twentieth century.[30] According to Rajadhyaksha, Phalke sought to build up an authentically Indian film industry to put into circulation national and indigenous imagery that would then influence the processes of production and distribution. He makes the point that tradition-based practices inflected the appropriation of technology and its reception. Cinema was inextricably linked with modernity, and this intervention on the part of Phalke into cinematic production was an effort to influence the march of modernity.

Revisiting Asia's Early Cinema

At least fifty years have passed since the production of some of the films discussed here. Hence, there is a real need to resituate these early Asian films in newer conceptual contexts, newer spaces of understanding. We now have some historical distance to see these films from a different perspective, and the recent spread of newer modes of inquiry such as poststructuralism, postcolonial theory, cultural studies, new historicism, and so on have placed at our disposal newer tools of analysis, which we can deploy productively. Therefore, it is of the utmost importance that we revisit these early Asian films, not to condemn them for falling short of the Hollywood mark but to explore their worth in seeking to forge indigenous-oriented forms of cinematic representation. For example, consider the arena of poetics of early Asian cinema. Until very recent times, it was the general practice to judge Asian cinema in terms of Eurocentric notions of realism and its accompanying codes and conventions. Both European art cinema and Hollywood were held up as the preferred norms. While the art of cinema in Asia, which emerged around the 1950s, was realistic in orientation and judged suitable for serious analysis, the popular cinemas, which were for the most part nonrealistic, were judged not to deserve such close attention. However, during the last two or three decades, once the discerning moviegoing public came to recognize that realism was just one more convention in cinema, and a bourgeois one at that, and that there were alternative ways of textualizing experiences in cinema, the stranglehold of realism began to be loosened, and film scholars were keen to explore indigenous modes of cinematic representation. Here, the work of early filmmakers assumed an importance hitherto unthinkable. The poetics of early cinema started to attract greater critical and scholarly attention.

In the case of Indian cinema, some innovative work by critics such as Ashish Rajadhyaksha, Geeta Kapur, and Anuradha Kapur have focused on aspects of traditional aesthetics as a means of mapping the poetics of popular cinema. Geeta Kapur, for example, draws attention to the importance of rethinking the posture of frontality commonly seen in early cinema. As she observes, "Frontality of the word, the image, the design, the formative act, yield forms of direct address; flat, diagrammatic, and simply profiled figures; a figure-ground pattern with only notational perspective; repetition of motifs in terms of ritual play; and a decorative mise-en-scene."[31] Anuradha Kapur remarks that "in open theaters frontality of the performer indicated a specific relationship between the viewer and the actor, turning the body toward the spectator is a sign that there is in this relationship no dissembling between the two; the actor looks at the audience and the audience looks at the actor. Both exist—as actor and audience—because of this candid contact."[32] In the Parsi theater, which influenced the early cinemas of India and Sri Lanka, while the narrative progressed in a linear fashion, the actors and actresses quite openly admitted through their performativity and way of addressing the audience that they were performers; this had the effect of subverting the linear narrative. One can clearly observe this in early Indian and Sri Lankan cinema where the frontality of the performer served to usher in a creative tension and ambiguity between narrative and performance.

Another aspect of early South Asian cinema that has continued up until present times is dance. Most Indian and Sri Lankan popular films contain dance sequences, and elite film critics almost always have dismissed them as gratuitous, pandering to the inferior taste of the masses. Some regard them as introductions of eroticism to the film text. I believe that these dance sequences perform a significant function: they are a vital segment of the meaning of these films—they usher in important creative ambiguities and tensions and focus on the production of newer scopic regimes. Dance sequences in Indian and Sri Lankan popular films generate a host of important questions connected to narrative discourse and representational strategies. What is the perceived relationship between narrative and performance and spectacle as exemplified in dance? In what ways do these dance sequences index and inflect categories of gender? What is the nature and significance of kinesthetic semiotics given expression through dance? How do the performing bodies enact their own differences from themselves? How do the bodies in dance sequences complement and unsettle the bodies in nondance sequences, and how do dances reinforce and subvert institutionalized codes of somatic representation and visuality? How do they enlarge specificities of spectatorial regimes? These and kindred questions open interesting doors to film experiences and film poetics of early South Asian cinema.

Another topic linked to early cinema that deserves scrutiny is the way spectators were constructed by cinema. In the 1970s, film scholarship came under poststructuralist thinking as evidenced by journals like *Screen*. Drawing liberally on the formulations of Louis Althusser and Jacques Lacan, film scholars aimed to highlight the production of the textual subject through cinema and ignored the empirical subject who enjoys films from different perspectives and who was located in specific historical conjunctures. These critics were more interested in the ways in which the filmic text interpellated the viewing subject in a monolithic way than the empirical subjects who displayed diversity of responses. Film critics who were influenced by poststructuralist thinking sought to redefine the embodied viewing subject in terms of the poststructuralist understanding of the subject; he or she was regarded as a product of discourse, an outcome of the signifying system. There were many film theorists who became increasingly dissatisfied with this approach to the viewing subject and began to emphasize the need to call attention to the historically situated and empirically observable subjects who were at once distinct individuals and members of an audience. This was certainly an important orientation in thinking that focused on the agency of spectatorship and a repudiation of the notion that film audiences were undifferentiated masses.

When we examine the early cinemas of Asia and audience behavior, we realize that the Althusserian notion of interpellation does not hold. Asian audiences reacted in diverse proactive ways in the movie theaters. They talked back to the screen, argued with the actors, joined in singing the songs and uttering pieces of dialogue, at times disclosed the twists and turns of the story, and freely expressed their joy and sadness and anger. There was clearly a sense of spectatorial aspect that belied the Althusserian notion of interpellation and poststructuralists' conception of the production of viewing subjects. This points out the need to explore the representational spaces of early Asian cinema against current thinking on cinema and spectatorship. The subject of cinema and spectatorship is becoming increasingly important, attracting the energies of innovative scholars. Miriam Hansen in her work has sought to examine the nature and significance of spectatorship in American silent cinema by forging an important link between the emergence of spectatorship and the historical transformation of the public sphere. It is her conviction that spectators emerged as a vital element of the Hollywood project in which an effort was made to bring together socially, culturally, ethnically, and sexually differentiated spectators into a modern culture of consumption.[33] Such an approach has deep implications for the study of early Asian cinema.

Throughout this chapter, I point out that most early Asian cinemas, in the terminology of current film criticism, can be regarded as melodramas. It is important to note in this regard that none of the Asian languages has an indigenous term for "melodrama." Classical Indian dramaturgists, for example, taxono-mized drama at great length. However, they did not come up with a category called "melodrama." It is an outgrowth of European theater. To describe these early Asian films as mere melodramas may to do them less than justice, as there are numerous issues embedded in that framework. For example, the idea of suffering is crucial to all Asian melodramatic films. At present, there is no adequate analytical vocabulary in the humanities and social sciences to conceptualize social suffering. In the domain of literature there are a bewildering variety of ways of seeing suffering. Aristotle made it (pathos) a central element of tragedy. However, he was talking of the suffering of great men and that of the nobility. Writers like Samuel Beckett regarded suffering as a manifestation of the existential absurdity. I think it is important to reconceptualize social suffering textualized in early Asian films in terms of colonialism, nationalism, and the idea of community. We need to see the suffering of ordinary men and women in everyday life that is portrayed in early Asian films as emblematic of the disruptions and conflicts brought about by colonialism. Colonialism was a harsh reality in India, Sri Lanka, the Philippines, Indonesia, and Korea and, to a lesser extent, in Thailand, Japan, and China. However, in all these countries it was a formidable and inescapable presence. The social suffering in early Asian films has to be understood in terms of colonialism and the violence unleashed by modernity. There was a hidden utopian impulse in this social suffering in that it pointed to the need for a free, national space that valued equality and justice. In an interesting way, this social suffering calls attention to the idea of citizenship in its juridical and experiential dimensions. The juridical aspect points to the protection by law by virtue of being a citizen of a nation, and the experiential dimension indexes the relationship between the power of the state and social membership.

What this chapter in general underlines is the need to subject early Asian cinemas to a deep and thoroughgoing analysis. The notion that early cinemas of Asia cannot bear the full weight of modern critical inquiry is misleading and ill founded. What is required is to subject these early Asian films to a careful materialist-historical critique. Nick Deocampo's book *Cine: Spanish Influences on Early Cinema in the Philippines*, which is the first of a planned five-volume history, exemplifies the importance of such a critique. In his book, Deocampo examines a neglected area of Filipino film scholarship, the early Spanish influence. He points out how deep and far reaching it was in terms of cinematic representation and states that even some modern films like Marilou Diaz Abaya's *José Rizal* and Laurice Guillen's *Tanging Yaman* bear the traces of that Hispanic influence.

A materialist-historical analysis of early Asian cinemas would underline the emergence of film texts and film discourses in terms of economics, property, law, class divisions, state formation, gender, ethnicity, and so on.[34] Here films are seen as not mere reflectors of society but as active shapers of social history, participating in the conflicts, struggles, and anxieties of the time. The underlying material conditions that inflect cinematic imagination figure very prominently in this type of analysis. Cinema would then be recognized as a valuable cultural space in which the evolving anxieties of the time are played out. When we explore the cultural spaces provided by early Asian cinemas, we begin to see how the disruptive and tensioned social transformations take place at diverse levels of social existence. The tragedies that are portrayed at the personal level in many of the early Asian films are indicative of wider social transformations, inequities, and injustices. The early Asian films are overdetermined by class tensions and social anxieties released by the forces of modernity, and these can be most profitably understood through a materialist-historical critique. The historical moment that is vitally inscribed in these early film texts should be explored to map the nature of the existing cultural politics.

A useful way of approaching early cinemas of Asia is by treating these films as illocutionary acts. What this suggests is that these early Asian filmmakers were desirous of participating in a national conversation, making an argument, and holding up a critical viewpoint about various tensions, anxieties, conflicts, and injustices in society with a view to changing them. Does this mean, therefore, that these early films were severely circumscribed and imprisoned in the historical moment in which they found themselves with no relevance beyond those times? Certainly not. What these filmmakers were seeking to do is to make illocutionary acts within the parameters of art and entertainment. They may not have always been successful, but it is important to view these works from that perspective. This, of course, means that we should drop our Hollywood lenses and try to understand the local poetics inscribed in these film texts on their own terms. This issue serves to focus on the context of viewing films. In what context should we view early Asian films? What are the epistemological, aesthetic, and axiological forces that shape that context? This is an aspect of inquiry that has received scant attention among historians of Asian cinema. It is hoped that this chapter will stimulate discussions underlying the importance of this context of viewing.

This discussion of early Asian cinema and the public sphere should not, of course, create the misleading impression that there were no blind spots and limitations associated with early Asian films and their commentaries. We can mobilize modern theoretical positions to identify some of them. For example, from a feminist viewpoint, one could focus on certain deficiencies in early Asian films and their discussions in the public sphere. Japanese film critics talked about the modern Japanese girl as represented in early Japanese films; Chinese critics focused on women, modernity, and the May Fourth legacy; Indian critics discussed the agency of women. These discussions, interesting as they were, transpired within the framework of patriarchal values and understandings.

In general, early Asian cinema is a terrain that invites careful and sustained scholarly attention. It has been my intention to focus on the interrelationship between early cinema and the public sphere. The chapter consists of two parts. The first is devoted to a discussion of the heuristically important concept of the public sphere. The second is devoted to a discussion of South Asian, East Asian, and Southeast Asian cinemas in terms of the concept of the public sphere. These two parts come together to underline the importance of understanding the concept of "pan-Asian cinema," which is both a descriptive and prescriptive term. Such an understanding becomes the condition of possibility for formulating Asian poetics of cinema, which is sorely lacking at present. It is descriptive because it indexes an identifiable cultural formation; it is prescriptive because it signposts an ideal toward which we should work resolutely. Clearly, there are manifold dimensions to this relationship, and within the limited space of this chapter I focus on a number of what I think are important ones. This is indeed a topic that demands a much more comprehensive treatment.

WIMAL DISSANAYAKE is Lecturer at the University of Hawaii at Manoa and a leading scholar on Asian cinema and communications. He is author of *Colonialism and Nationalism in Asian Cinema, Global/Local,* and *Narratives of Agency.* He was founding editor of the *East-West Film Journal* and served as Director of Cultural Studies at the East West Center.

Notes

1. Stuart Hall, "Cultural Identity and Diaspora," in *Identity: Community, Culture, Difference,* ed. Jonathan Rutherford (London: Lawrence and Wishart, 1990), 223, 225.

2. Jürgen Habermas, *The Structural Transformation of the Public Sphere* (Cambridge, MA: MIT Press, 1992).

3. Ibid, 27.

4. Michael Warner, *The Letters of the Republic* (Cambridge, MA: Harvard University Press, 1990).

5. Habermas, *Structural Transformation of the Public Sphere,* 71.

6. Oskar Negt and Alexander Kluge, *The Public Sphere and Experience* (Minneapolis: University of Minnesota Press, 1993).

7. Miriam Hansen, "Early Cinema, Late Cinema: Transformations of the Public Sphere," in *Viewing Positions: Ways of Seeing Film,* ed. Linda Williams (New Brunswick, NJ: Rutgers University Press, 1995), 142.

8. Ibid.

9. Ibid., 144.

10. Ibid., 145.

11. Arjun Appadurai, *Modernity at Large: Cultural Dimensions of Globalization* (Minneapolis: University of Minnesota Press, 1997), 43.

12. Benedict Anderson, *Imagined Communities: Reflections on the Origin and Spread of Nationalism* (London: Verso, 1983).

13. See Elie Kedourie, *Nationalism* (London: Hutchinson, 1960); Ernest Gellner, *Nations and Nationalism* (Oxford: Basil Blackwell, 1983); E. J. Hobsbawm, *Nations and Nationalism since 1780: Program, Myth, Reality* (Cambridge: Cambridge University Press, 1990); Anthony Giddens, *The Nation-State and Violence* (Cambridge: Cambridge University Press, 1985); Partha Chatterjee, *Nationalist Thought and the Colonial World: A Derivative Discourse* (London: Zed Books, 1986); Homi Bhabha, *Nation and Narration* (London: Routledge, 1990); and Arjun Appadurai, *Modernity at Large.*

14. K. Moti Gokulsing and Wimal Dissanayake, *Indian Popular Cinema: A Narrative of Cultural Change*, 3rd ed. (London: Trentham Books, 2004).

15. Ashish Rajadhyaksha, "The Phalke Era: Traditional Form and Modern Technology," *Journal of Arts and Ideas* 8 (1987): 14–15.

16. Wimal Dissanayake and Ashley Ratnavibhushana, *Profiling Sri Lankan Cinema* (Colombo, Sri Lanka: Asian Film Center, 2000).

17. Clodualdo A. Del Mundo, *Native Resistance: Philippine Cinema and Colonialism, 1898–1941* (Manila: De La Salle University Press, 1998).

18. Nick Deocampo, *Cine: Spanish Influences on Early Cinema in the Philippines* (Manila: National Commission for Culture and the Arts, 2003).

19. Krisha Sen, *Indonesian Cinema: Facing the New Order* (London: Zed Books, 1994).

20. Patsorn Sungsri, "Thai Cinema as National Cinema: An Evaluative History" (PhD diss., Murdoch University, 2004).

21. J. Anderson, *The Japanese Film: Art and Industry* (Princeton, NJ: Princeton University Press, 1982).

22. Wimal Dissanayake, *Narratives of Agency: Self-Making in India, China and Japan* (Minneapolis: University of Minnesota Press, 1996).

23. Jay Leyda, *Dianying: Electric Shadows: An Account of Films and the Film Audiences in China* (Cambridge, MA: MIT Press, 1972).

24. Leo Ou-fan Lee, "The Tradition of Modern Chinese Cinema: Some Preliminary Explorations and Hypotheses," in *Chinese Cinema*, ed. Chris Berry (London: BFI, 1991), 43.

25. Shuquin Cui, *Women through the Lens: Gender and Nation in a Century of Chinese Cinema* (Honolulu: University of Hawaii Press, 2003).

26. Ibid.

27. Ibid.

28. Hyangjin Lee, *Contemporary Korean Cinema: Identity, Culture, Politics* (Manchester, UK: Manchester University Press, 2000).

29. Ibid., 78.

30. Asish Rajadhyaksha, "The Phalke Era."

31. Geeta Kapur, *When Was Modernism: Essays on Contemporary Cultural Practice in India* (New Delhi: Tulika Press, 2000), 63.

32. Anuradha Kapur, "The Representation of Gods and Heroes: Parsi Mythological Drama of the Early Twentieth Century," *Journal of Arts and Ideas* 23–24 (1993): 85–107.

33. Miriam Hansen, *Babel and Babylon: Spectatorship in American Silent Film* (Cambridge, MA: Harvard University Press, 1991).

34. Raymond Williams, *Problems of Materialism and Culture* (London: Verso, 1980).

2 Nationalism, Contradiction, and Identity; or, A Reconsideration of Early Cinema in the Philippines

Charles Musser

WHEN I FIRST came to the Philippines to discuss a conference on origins of cinema in Southeast Asia with its organizer, Nick Deocampo, there was one conviction shared by my new friends and local film scholars: cinema was a fundamental aspect of Filipino culture. Certainly as someone interested in beginnings, I was curious: When, why, and how did this come about? The answers I received focused on a man traditionally seen as the Philippines' first film director: José Nepomuceno, who—among other things—directed the first movie kiss on Philippine soil.[1] Only with him did cinema in the Philippines enjoy a Filipino cinema. Before this pivotal moment, the country's motion picture practices were generally seen as impoverished and subservient to the imperial regime of the United States. Nepomuceno did not make his first feature film until 1919; this date seems rather late, and a single director likewise seems strikingly narrow as a basis for explaining this special bond between cinema and Filipino life.

The movies became deeply incorporated into American life as well, but I argue that this process was far advanced by 1919 (roughly the moment when the Classical Hollywood cinema was formed). We can already find many instances of cinema's importance in the late 1890s—in the ecstatic laughter for screen kisses, the jingoistic responses to war films, and the devotees of filmed passion plays and prize fights. One crucial turning point was undoubtedly the 1905–1907 boom in nickelodeons (storefront motion picture theaters). This rapid proliferation of specialized motion picture theaters broadened and deepened cinema's penetration into everyday life as millions of Americans went to the cinema on a daily basis. Out of this emerged the prominent role of movie stars between 1908 and 1915 (movie stars rather than directors such as D. W. Griffith fascinated most American moviegoers). Although today's movie and TV stars have played prominent roles in American life—whether Arnold Schwarzenegger as governor of California, Angelina Jolie as special envoy to the UN, or Donald Trump as president— they arguably have had an even more prominent role in Filipino culture. In regard to politics, for instance, if Filipinos are to be believed, two movie stars have won presidential elections in recent years: Joseph Estrada and Fernando Poe Jr.[2] In the United States there has been only one: Ronald Reagan (but only if we do not count reality TV stars). Moreover, at present these nations appear to be the only two whose citizens have elected actors to the position of chief executive. Obviously, some explaining is necessary.

Considering the Origins of Cinema in Southeast Asia

We still have much to learn about the first twenty-five years of cinema, as the 2005 Quezon City Conference on Origins of Cinema in Southeast Asia made evident. In many respects, this gathering of scholars from Thailand, the Philippines, Australia, Spain, and the United States was an Association of Southeast Asian Nations (ASEAN) landmark that reminded me of the now-legendary 1978 Brighton Conference on cinema from 1900 to 1906. One focused on cinema in western Europe and the United States; the other, on cinema in Southeast Asia (territories largely colonized by those same Western nations). Among the many other noteworthy differences are that more than two hundred fiction films were screened at the Brighton Conference while a handful of fragments were shown in Quezon City, making them an incidental component to this event. No fiction films made in Southeast Asia before the 1920 period survive. This open-ended, at times speculative scholarly forum went back to basics and asked, What is it that the ASEAN nations have in common regarding cinema? The answer, expressed in different ways, was colonialism. It would be far too simple, and ultimately too reductive, to say that cinema was a product of colonialism. But colonialism shaped how the cinema was introduced, how it was received, and how it became part of the cultural fabric of these geographic and political entities—only one of which avoided outright colonial status (Thailand).

Although the 1978 Brighton Conference did show a few films that took empire as their subject (whether British, American, or French Empire), conference participants were primarily concerned with charting the history of film style based on the numerous films being screened. In retrospect, we were concerned not only with cinema made in a limited number of industrialized nations; we were remarkably unconcerned about its presence and impact in Africa, Asia, and Latin America.[3] Yet we were not the only ones wearing intellectual blinders. Perhaps because colonialism had been the overwhelming historical reality for Southeast Asia during cinema's silent era, film scholars in Southeast Asia and Asia have focused their efforts on establishing the genealogy of a national, indigenous, or native cinema that broke with a colonial cinema or (to cite Louis Althusser) an ideological state apparatus that was heavily tainted and deeply problematic.[4] Wimal Dissanayake, in the introduction to his edited anthology

Colonialism and Nationalism in Asian Cinema, evokes the complex dynamics between colonialism, nationalism, and modernity.[5] This nexus has had an ongoing legacy evidenced by silences, distorted perspectives, and failures to make connections—haunting the discourses of both sides.

Let me begin with a confession. Together, and despite their differences, Clodualdo A. del Mundo's *Native Resistance: Philippine Cinema and Colonialism, 1898–1941* and Nick Deocampo's *Cine: Spanish Influences on Early Cinema in the Philippines* were revelations that have forced me to confront significant gaps and unfortunate limits in my own work. Certainly my books on early cinema discussed—briefly—the various Edison films that reenacted certain battles between American forces and Filipino freedom fighters as well as those films shot in the Philippines and shown in the United States by the Biograph company and Burton Holmes. But I failed to conceive of the Philippines as a forcibly annexed territory that had become—through no choice of its countrymen—an essential component of American film history, at least between 1898 and 1946. Cinema in the colonies (also including Puerto Rico and Cuba) remained outside my purview. This failure is all the more noteworthy because American cinema was highly nationalistic from the outset, and during the Spanish-American War the leading American producers and exhibitors effectively advocated for American intervention in Cuba and war with Spain.[6] So the fledgling American film industry clearly had quite a bit to do with the Philippines becoming an American colony, even though the various filmmakers who claimed to be present at the Battle of Manila Bay were telling fanciful, self-serving stories (we might call them lies) rather than accurate history. Nonetheless, having brutally defeated the first Philippine Republic and recolonized what Spain had essentially ceded, the United States gained not only a colony but a colony with a cinema. What was it like? Likewise, neither del Mundo nor Deocampo have fully situated cinema in the Philippines within an American or international context. We have all been guilty of a parochial, if unintended nationalism. In this regard, the Quezon City conference provided an invaluable catalyst for all of its participants.

As we seek to situate Philippine and other Southeast Asian cinemas into a regional and global framework, questions certainly abound. How useful is the periodization employed by film scholars working on cinema in Europe and the United States when it is applied to cinema in the Philippines and elsewhere in Southeast Asia? What can we learn by mapping one onto the other? Is cinema in the Philippines "the same old story" but delayed and deprived of its richness, at least until an effective national(istic) cinema emerges in response to colonial impositions? (And when does that emergence begin?) Indeed, how can our understanding of cinema in the industrialized nations provide useful insights into cinema practices in ASEAN nations during the colonial era? And how can knowledge of early cinema in ASEAN countries enrich our understanding of cinema at the center and as a whole? In this respect, it might be worth reexamining such terms as "silent cinema," "early cinema," "the novelty period," and "cinema of attractions." Certainly we know that the so-called silent cinema era was extended in some Asian nations, particularly Japan, into the mid- or even late 1930s. To some extent this is the case elsewhere in Southeast Asia as well. So what about these other, less technologically determined markers? Will cinema in Southeast Asia enrich and deepen our understanding of early cinema or underscore the limits of its utility?

Early Cinema in the United States, Europe, and Asia

What is early cinema? What time frame does it cover? In this respect, we must acknowledge that "early cinema" has been used in various ways. My first published article in the film studies field was called "The Early Cinema of Edwin S. Porter," and I was then thinking of "early cinema" as an alternative term for what was then being called the "pre-Griffith cinema"—cinema before Griffith began to direct films at the Biograph company in June 1908.[7] In his edited book *Film before Griffith*, John Fell refers to "early film" with this meaning.[8] As it turned out, mid-1908 to mid-1909 was the moment when a significant amount of cinema in the United States first conformed to familiar definitions of mass communication in terms of production (with a fledgling studio system in place), textual consistency, self-contained coherence (intertitles plus a linear unfolding of the story), and marketing (with regular release dates).[9]

Other film scholars were using the term "early cinema" more loosely and more broadly. For instance, Anthony Slide's *Early American Cinema* focused much more on the 1910s. And as more scholars began to work in this area, they often used the term to refer to cinema before the Classical Hollywood cinema as a system of production/representation and as a vertically integrated system of production/distribution/exhibition was in place. I tended to call this "preclassical" cinema and, in the American context, "the proto-Hollywood cinema" (after early cinema, before classical). It still strikes me that there is a profound shift between cinema before and after about 1908–1909; but in truth, motion picture practice was changing so rapidly between 1895 and 1920 that other crucial moments of demarcation can easily be cited as equally (or almost equally) important. What we call pre-1908–1909 cinema is now less clear. Some use the term "primitive" (from Terry Ramsaye in 1926 to David Bordwell, Janet Staiger, and Kristin Thompson in 1985)[10]—which seems problematic since cinema was at the technological cutting edge of emergent monopoly capitalism, and its articulations were naïve only to those content to stay on the surface of historical investigation. André Gaudreault has called it "le cinéma des premier temps" (the cinema of the first times) or "les debuts du cinéma" (the beginnings of cinema).[11] Employing the term "cinema of attractions," Tom Gunning argued that until about 1906, film-makers used cinema less as a way to tell stories than as a way of presenting views to an audience.[12] In a paragraph added when the essay was republished in Thomas Elsaesser's anthology, Gunning wrote,

> To summarize, the cinema of attractions directly solicits spectator attention, inciting visual curiosity, and supplying pleasure through an exciting spectacle—a unique event, whether fictional or documentary, that is of interest in itself. The attraction to be displayed may also be of a cinematic nature, such as the early close-ups just described, or trick films in which a cinematic manipulation (slow motion, reverse motion, substitution, multiple exposure) provides the film's novelty. Fictional situations tend to be restricted to gags, vaudeville numbers, or recreations of shocking or curious incidents (executions, current events). It is the direct address of the audience, in which an attraction is offered to the spectator by a cinema showman, that defines this approach to film making. Theatrical display dominates over narrative absorption, emphasizing the direct stimulation of shock or surprise at the expense of unfolding a story or creating a diegetic universe.[13]

Yet it is evident that the rise of the story film, which had become dominant by the end of 1903, meant that "cinema of attractions" had ceased to be the dominant form of cinema well before 1906, if the term as a descriptive category ever adequately characterized the cinema of any period at all. In any case, the cinema of attractions and the pre-Griffith cinema are not the same.[14]

One crucial point is that early cinema is not an alternative name for silent cinema—as a few more recent film scholars have sometimes casually employed it.[15] The term "early cinema" has become fashionable, and film aficionados and graduate students still finding their way around the discipline have often casually expanded its use. At a Society for Cinema and Media Studies (SCMS) conference, an eager graduate student remarked that he was interested in early cinema—"you know, films like *King Kong* (1932)"! In fact, Bordwell, Staiger, and Thompson note that the Classical Hollywood system of representation was essentially in place by 1917; World War I and its immediate aftermath helped produce a vertically integrated industry at home and commercial dominance abroad.[16] As a result, American films of the 1920s functioned within a well-established, mature Hollywood framework.

Certainly (and not surprisingly), an investigation of cinema in the Philippines, Thailand, China, and elsewhere in Asia reveals factors that confirm and reinforce the legitimacy of seeing the immediate post–World War I moment as an important dividing line. Two factors in the Philippines are, on the surface, contradictory. Most obviously, as Kristin Thompson details in *Exporting Entertainment*, the Hollywood majors began to establish American distribution outlets in Manila after the war, starting with Universal in 1918.[17] The Philippines was thus incorporated into the Hollywood-dominated system of world cinema. At the same time, there was the emergence of a vibrant, Filipino film industry that was producing feature films—an era that both Del Mundo and Deocampo see beginning with *Dalagang Bukid* (Country maiden, 1919), the first feature film of José Nepomuceno.[18] This suggests that it was only in the wake of World War I that Filipino cinema emerged as an independent, anticolonial force. Although these two landmarks might seem at odds with each other, they are actually dialectically related in a profound way. Likewise, scholars of Chinese cinema see a significant dividing line between the role of cinema in China before and after 1920. Jubin Hu, for example, remarks that "Before the 1920s . . . Chinese filmmakers were not highly conscious of using culture (film) to serve Chinese nationalism."[19] Such neat correspondences in terms of periodization did not happen everywhere in Southeast Asia. In Thailand, the shift from European to Hollywood films occurred after World War I, but the rise of a strong nationalist response unfolded only during the 1920s. In 1922 Prince Kambeangbejr set up a government department, the Topical Film Service of the State Railways, to make documentaries and news and publicity films. Here, as in Indonesia, the making of the first locally produced feature fiction films occurred in the mid- to late 1920s.[20] The rise—or at least the intensification and rearticulation—of nationalism in Asia was part of a complex global phenomenon.

The popularity and expansion of cinema worldwide generated the infrastructure that made possible localized cinemas even as the corresponding economies of scale facilitated and necessitated an international distribution network for Hollywood. The economic and cultural dislocations of World War I, as well as the intellectual ferment and political instabilities that followed, created opportunities both for Hollywood dominance and localized cinematic expression. In this regard, a study examining Filipino cinema in the period between World War I and World War II should consider not only the regional context of other Southeast Asian cinemas but the global context and its political, cultural, and economic position as an American colony. The emergence of the Philippines' first important director, José Nepomuceno, precisely corresponds with the appearance of African American director Oscar Micheaux with his first feature film, *The Homesteader* (1919). Both were prolific, and both were ready to foster controversy to ensure box-office success: while Micheaux feasted on interracial sex and romance, Nepomuceno made the first kissing scene in Filipino (and Asian) cinema in *Ang Tatlong Hambog* (The three humbugs, 1926).[21]

Both Filipino cinema and race cinema in the United States were criticized for their poor production values. Yet contemporary scholars in the United States have come to reassess the work of race filmmakers, Micheaux in particular. It is no exaggeration to say that Micheaux, an African American who practiced a form of black cultural nationalism, has proved to be one of the major international filmmakers of the silent era. Such an assertion can be based on the survival of three of his films (*Within Our Gates*, 1920; *The Symbol of the Unconquered*, 1920; and *Body and Soul*, 1925). The absence of surviving films by Nepomuceno from this period prevents similar (re)assessments. Yet Nepomuceno and Micheaux can be seen as part of a search for alternative national cinemas that include German expressionism, French impressionism, and Soviet montage. The lack of surviving Filipino films from the 1910s and 1920s impoverishes not only our knowledge of Filipino culture in this period but also our understanding of both American and global cinema.

Most scholarship on pre–World War II cinema in the Philippines has sought to document and construct a coherent history and to pursue that history in relation to questions of Filipino national identity. There has been a tendency to see early cinema in the Philippines as an impoverished product of American colonial rule, at least until Nepomuceno began to make films. If so, then it would seem of relatively limited interest. However, this chapter uses available historical scholarship and a modest amount of new primary source research to reassess early cinema in the Philippines. It asserts that pre-Nepomuceno cinema in the Philippines was often a center of cultural resistance to the US colonial regime and that a handful of Americans participated in this struggle—indeed, may have even played a key role. There are some serious historical issues to discuss here (and more research that still needs to be done). These debates revolve around the concepts of nationalism and colonialism, globalism and cosmopolitanism, and contradiction and resistance. In this respect, Wimal Dissanayake provides a useful starting point with the remark that national identity in Asian cinema can "most profitably be discussed at four interconnected levels: the local, national, regional, and global."[22] In this respect, it has also been helpful to break down pre-Nepomuceno cinema into four periods:

1. The novelty period—especially the role of the Lumière Cinématographe (1897)
2. The period of US military rule (1898–1902)
3. The rise of the *cinematógrafos* (cinema theaters) (1902–1909)
4. The emergence of Philippines-based filmmaking, including Albert Yearsley and then Titay Molina and Edward Meyer Gross (1909–1917)

The Novelty Period and Global Reach of Cinema, 1897

Let us start by considering the rapid, worldwide diffusion of cinema. From the outset, pioneering figures such as Auguste and Louis Lumière, Leon Gaumont, Thomas A. Edison, and R. W. Paul understood the importance of international markets and acted accordingly, establishing often attenuated but nonetheless real global networks. Compare the first showings of commercial cinema in Manila to similar premieres in other cities around the world. Cinema came to Manila (a population in 1899 that was estimated as three hundred thousand) around January 1, 1897,[23] two days after the public execution of Filipino patriot José Rizal, when Spanish businessman Francisco Pertierra showed the Cronofotógrafo, which he had acquired from Europe.[24] This introduction of projected motion pictures to a Filipino public came approximately one year after the first commercial showing of the Lumière Cinématographe in a small café in Paris, eight months after the Vitascope's premiere in New York on April 23, 1896, and seven and a half months after the first Spanish screenings on May 15, 1896. Or, from another vantage point, Manila's premiere occurred barely a month after the first motion picture showings in Harrisburg, Pennsylvania (the capital of a large industrial state in the American Northeast), on November 30, 1896, and just two weeks after cinema debuted in Lexington (a city in the state of Kentucky), on December 15, 1896.[25]

As Dissanayake reminds us, it is not sufficient to situate Manila's premiere as part of a global pattern of diffusion radiating from Paris, Lyon, London, and New York. We must also situate it regionally, in relationship to similar events in Southeast Asia and Asia. In this regard the Lumière Cinématographe played a prominent role, introducing projected motion pictures to India on July 7, 1896, at Bombay's Watson's Hotel, followed by further showings at the Novelty Theatre one week later; and to China in Shanghai on August 11, 1896, at Another Village Tea House; to Japan at an Osaka theater on February 15, 1897.[26] For Thailand, the Parisian Cinematograph (presumably the Lumière machine) provided the premiere in Bangkok on June 10, 1897, at the Crown Prince Alangkarn Theater; and, as Hassan Abdul Muthalib points out in chapter 11, cinema premiered in Singapore on August 3, 1897. The quite early date for Shanghai is noteworthy because Pertierra could have heard of this new technological novelty via Shanghai, then placed his order for the Gaumont machine with his agents in Europe, and had the equipment in Manila in time for his January 1 debut. Also important here is the first appearance of the Lumière Cinématographe in Manila on August 27, 1897. This was more than a year after its Bombay and Shanghai debuts. Given Manila's proximity to Bangkok and Singapore, it suggests the possibility of a regional circuit in Southeast Asia or at least regional affinities in regard to lagging technological and economic circumstances.

More significant than this chronology of premieres is a consideration of the ways that cinema was introduced and received in these localities. In the Philippines, Pertierra presented cinema as a scientific and communication novelty in a way that was quite American. He had been making money by giving phonograph concerts—a common and quite popular form of middle-class entertainment in the United States in the early to mid-1890s.[27] In fact, according to Agustin Sotto,

Pertierra had been to the Chicago Columbian World Exposition in 1893 and had installed a gramophone in his salon on his return.[28] In contrast to this familiar Western approach, Jubin Hu has argued that in Shanghai, "film was understood according to traditional Chinese discourses on art and entertainment rather than through modern Western discourses on science and technology."[29] Of course, this raises the question, understood by whom? Like Pertierra's audiences, members of Shanghai's European colony (approximately ten thousand people) would have understood this new phenomenon more through modern Western discourses on science and technology. Perhaps Chinese working at the economic and cultural interface with Europe would have as well. All this underscores a point made by Nick Deocampo. The audiences for Pertierra's showings were not, narrowly speaking, natives but foreign residents and Hispanicized Manileños. Unlike in China, to be literate in late nineteenth-century Manila was already to be considerably Hispanicized or Europeanized.[30]

While the Chinese were able to embrace the cinema, albeit in limited ways, by situating it within their own frame of reference, this was not possible in Vietnam where the Lumière project explicitly represented the colonizer, demonstrating the full scope of its vision and power. For the colonials in Hanoi and Saigon, this must have been a subtle but effective morale booster. They were part of this French Empire, of French culture, and technological prowess. But for the colonized, if present-day historians are to be believed, it was greeted with hostility. Thailand, in contrast to both China and Vietnam, offered another possible response. Not under Western pressure or colonial rule in the same way, Thailand greeted cinema warmly, and the royal family quickly embraced film.[31] Obviously these different responses underscore the divergent, eclectic histories of cinema in Southeast Asia (and the ways they were shaped by different colonial circumstances). The reception of cinema within Southeast Asia was much more diverse than within the regions of western Europe or Latin America.

Historians should not simply probe localized cultural responses to cinema as a new form (a new method of technological representation): we must also focus on specific films and specific programs that exhibitors construct out of them, with their distinct contents and potential meanings. Here, the Cronofotógrafo (a Gaumont-Demeny Chronophotographe) and the Cinematógrafo (the Lumière Cinématographe), which together constituted Manila's novelty era, shared many points in common. The Cronofotógrafo, however, may have been a technological curiosity more than a satisfying visual experience, since Pertierra had only four films to screen, and his screenings were characterized at one point as dark.[32] Running for less than four weeks, the Cronofotógrafo offered a taste, an appetizer, in contrast to the full-sized meal offered by the Cinematógrafo, which Spanish army officer Antonio Ramos and Swiss businessmen Leibman and Peritz brought to Manila and ran for four months.[33]

Here the cinema acted as a global phenomenon on two additional levels. First, both the Cronofotógrafo and the Cinematógrafo—despite their presentation in the Spanish language—were French machines with international pretensions. This was echoed by Pertierra's connection with the United States and the Columbian Exposition as well as Leibman and Peritz's European but non-Spanish status. Likewise, although Ramos was a Spanish officer, his wife was Russian. All of this suggests a certain cosmopolitan sophistication among the personnel involved. Second, both sets of exhibitions brought the wider world to the Philippines. Even the four films shown by the Cronofotógrafo were carefully selected in this regard. Of the three pictures that were shot in the studio, two lacked any ethnic/racial/national markings (a boxing match; a medium shot of a man changing hats), while the third was of Japanese dancers. The fourth film featured a Paris street scene of Montmartre, providing a clear French signature. Spain was notably absent from this admittedly modest selection.

Ramos's motion picture programs, reproduced in Nick Deocampo's book, detail the international, outward-looking nature of these exhibitions. In ways that were powerful—and even today quite moving—the Lumière Cinématographe showed the world to members of this aspiring nation: Arabs, Africans, French cities, the Baths of Milan, Hyde Park in London, the Brooklyn Bridge in New York, Mexico, a rural festival in Switzerland, and the Russian czar. The Russian czar proved the most extensively covered subject, with four of the thirty films on this topic—perhaps because of Ramos's wife's national heritage.[34] The Spanish influence was present, but the emphasis was on dance in *Pareja de boleros* (Bolero dancers; one of four possible Lumière films taken at the same time, possibly Lumière film no. 847, *Danses espagnoles: Bolero de medio paso* [Spanish dances: Bolero half-step]) in the first program.[35] The third program included a scene of Madrid, *Carros de la sedería de sol* (Sun silk carriages; no. 260, *Madrid, puerta del sol* [Madrid, sun gate]), but also one of a former Spanish colony, *Mercado indigena en Mejico* (Native market in Mexico; no. 355, *Marché indien sur le canal de la Viga* [Indian market on the Viga canal]). The first of Ramos's programs emphasized the exotic—a parade of Arabs at an exposition, Africans dancing in the streets, and a snowball fight (no. 101, *Bataille de neige* [Snow fight]). Several films were of former European colonies that had achieved independence, including Mexico (the Philippines had once been part of the province of Mexico) and the United States, while others were of European landmarks. This dizzying array reveals the cosmopolitan quality of these early programs, which resonated with the cosmopolitan nature of Manila's elites and middle classes—their principal audiences. Certainly the fact that the Cinematógrafo showed the world to Filipinos, many of whose countrymen would one day become overseas workers and the nation's most prized exports, has a certain poignancy. From the very first programs, Filipinos were using cinema as a window onto the world; they were already looking outward, using cinema as a way to bring the world to them.

Early film practitioners were able to establish, shape, or even completely change cultural meanings in ways that counter any notion that the cinema was essentially a technological novelty largely free of ideological resonance beyond its own expression of modernity. The first motion pictures—those made at the Edison Laboratory and shown in the Peephole Kinetoscope during 1894–1895—evidenced a strong cosmopolitan internationalism as they showed performers who came from all over the world: Austrian strong man Eugen Sandow, Spanish dancer Carmencita, Latin American tightrope walker Juan Caicedo, Mexican lasso artists, Arab tumblers, Sioux dancers with Buffalo Bill's Wild West, Irish boxers, American cowboys, and French trapeze artists. Dancing by Japanese, African American, British, Balinese, and European American performers were also popular. Peering into a small machine, one could see the entire world (or at least representative performers from different parts of the globe). The camera treated people from around the world much as it treated white, native-born Americans.

The first screenings in American theaters, nevertheless, evidenced a marked ideological shift and displayed a virulent nationalism. Why was this so? As commercial cinema was launched in the United States in April 1896, French and British exhibition services were poised to enter the American market. The first US film entrepreneurs—particularly those connected with Edison's Vitascope and the American Biograph—reconceived the kinds of films they were making and the programs they were presenting. They almost literally wrapped themselves in the American flag. One of the first films made for projection of Edison's Vitascope, which debuted on opening night at Koster and Bial's Music Hall, was titled *The Monroe Doctrine* and condemned British military posturing in Latin America. Many of the old films made for the Peephole Kinetoscope were still projected, but the selection and sequencing did much to change their meaning.[36] Among its initial subjects, Biograph filmed scenes from the all-American play *Rip Van Winkle* (August 1896), Niagara Falls (a potent symbol of America's natural grandeur), and Republican presidential candidate William McKinley.

Again, we might consider the powerful ideological message of the Lumières' project as articulated in their early France-based screenings. They celebrated the family—and in particular the Lumière family (no. 88, *Repas de bébé* [Feeding the baby]), the nation—with scenes of various national landmarks (no. 149, *Paris, Arc de triomphe*; no. 150, *Paris, bassin des Tuileries*; no. 151, *Paris, Champs-Élysées*) and the state—with numerous scenes of the French army (no. 182, *Cuirassiers: En fourragères* [Charge of the Seventh Cavalry]). Women were dutiful and adoring mothers, not performers in the theatrical world as was generally the case in early American films. "Family," "nation," and "state" would later be the call words of the Vichy government during World War II; and by 1895–1896, the Lumières had already found their cinematic equivalents. The nationalistic ideology of the Lumière programs in France stood counter to the cosmopolitan films being shown in Edison's Kinetoscope by the Continental Commerce Company. Given the Lumières' strong nationalist bent, one can understand why the appearance of their Cinématographe, which is generally treated in the most utopic terms by the international film studies community, is still greeted with overt hostility by Vietnamese scholars and archivists.[37] The Cinématographe offered an intimate view of the French Empire's heartland, French culture, and technological prowess.

The Lumière project was every bit as open to revision as its American counterparts. When the French Cinématographe appeared in the United States, its views of Europe and the world meant that the French machine assumed an internationalist and cosmopolitan position—in contrast to the local scenes and nationalistic rhetoric of the Edison and Biograph organizations. Yet the Lumières' military scenes were enthusiastically received and became crucial ingredients in their American programs. With its emphasis on charging cavalry and the military training of various European armies, the Cinématographe's internationalism was of a very particular kind. It encouraged viewers to compare the armies of different European powers and to speculate about the possible outcomes if these diverse forces were to someday clash. It is noteworthy, therefore, that such military films were almost entirely lacking from the Ramos/Leibman and Peritz screenings in Manila.[38] These offered a utopic yearning to escape the local as well as the violence and instability of war. It is hardly surprising that these films found a ready reception in the Philippines. The views constructed a phantasmatic world that Manileños could embrace. Through a careful selection of films and a change in exhibition contexts, Lumière exhibitions embodied a nationalistic discourse in one setting (France) and articulated a militaristic internationalism in another (New York), offered a colonialist agenda in French colonies (Vietnam), and provided others (Manila, perhaps Bangkok) with a cosmopolitan internationalism that might offer an implicit alternative to the colonial regimes of non-French powers. This diversity of meanings is quite a remarkable achievement, impressive in its subtlety and versatility.

The meanings generated by the Lumière Cinématographe were seldom as simple as this typology suggests. These screenings rarely had one meaning. For the Manila screenings, those still sympathetic with the Spanish cause could remind themselves of the world of European imperial powers, of which the Philippines was an outpost. For those sympathizing with the revolutionary aspirations of the Filipinos, they could imagine the Philippines joining this international array of nation-states. The emphasis on quotidian scenes (native markets in Mexico, a rural festival in Switzerland) and nonmilitaristic activities was well designed to defuse efforts to turn the screening room into a site for partisan political expression. As is often the case in capitalist systems, which try to reach the largest possible market, these film programs offered ambiguous messages in which their manifest content was contradictory and appealed to a range of potential patrons.

From its outset, the cinema in Manila was already distinct, engaging its audiences, and engaged by its audiences, in particular ways. If it was not truly Filipino cinema, it nonetheless implicitly promoted a common longing of the Filipino people toward a better future. There was a utopian component to these offerings. Certainly these exhibitions were not simply a delayed repetition of screenings at the center of ideological articulations of dominant imperial powers. The cinema was "glocalized" (a global phenomenon adapted to and appropriated for local needs and culture).[39]

Cinema in Manila under US Military Rule, 1898–1902

War fostered cinema in the United States and curtailed it in the Philippines. The nationalistic rhetoric of American cinema further intensified after the sinking of the battleship *Maine* in Havana harbor on February 15, 1898. Indeed, the American film industry boomed as images of the US Navy, American soldiers, and Cuban refugees energized the pro-war factions. Citizens flocked to vaudeville theaters, expressed their sentiments during these exhibitions, and then read about said screenings in the next day's papers. Of course, the first military action against Spain was Admiral George Dewey's victory at Manila Bay, which was quickly turned into a film, Vitagraph's *Battle of Manila Bay*, staged on a Manhattan rooftop using paper cutouts. During the most intense period of economic disruption and military warfare in the Philippines, between 1898 and about 1902, Deocampo and Del Mundo have indicated that there was little cinema in Manila—and none in 1898 or 1899.[40]

Although we have yet to find reports of films being shown in Manila during 1898, the cinematic landscape was not quite so barren as previously thought. In early January 1900, American showman Max Berol was passing through Manila and reported that "several semi-professionals with phonographs, cinematographs, etc. are coining money by showing right among the soldiers on the firing line, where several entertainments have been interrupted by a night attack of the insurgents or a false alarm. Any tent, church, barn serves as a theatre."[41] Evidence from English-language newspapers suggests that they—or newly arrived American businessmen, who serviced the needs of the troops and occupation officials—may have tried to show films in the city's commercial center. Nick Deocampo has recently found advertisements and notices for a company claiming to offer the Biograph in May 1899. According to one item, "The Biograph is giving exhibitions nightly at 18 Escolta, and a very creditable exhibition is produced."[42] Films included a "muscle dance" or "couchee couchee dance"—possibly by Fatima, which was declared "the most lively and startling spectacle ever seen in Manila."[43] A Spanish bullfight was also shown. One thing is certain. These were not 68mm/70mm films made by the American Mutoscope and Biograph Company. The exhibitor appropriated the name of a prominent film company that was well known to potential American patrons.

Efforts to show films in central Manila had a certain logic. Early in 1899, according to one American observer, "three theatres and one circus were open, and playing to fine business, considering the 'soldier boys' were kept pretty close to quarters."[44] On February 5, as warfare between Filipino patriots and American troops intensified, the military declared a curfew from 7:00 p.m. onward, ending virtually all forms of commercial entertainment. The so-called Biograph, located in a regular commercial building, was an exception. Writing in mid-August, *Clipper* correspondent D. J. Springer reported that "the only theatre open is the Colon, in which a native company is giving afternoon performances, commencing at 4 pm, consisting of gymnastic and acrobatic acts of a very inferior order, but is crowded at every performance."[45] It was announced, however, that "there will be issued an order the coming week extending the time of closing of business and clearing of the streets until 9 pm."[46] Perhaps this helps explain why the Latest Edison Novelty Company appeared to give "a wonderful entertainment" upstairs in a building at the corner of Escolta and San Jacinto Streets from August 29, 1899, until mid-September. An evening show made such an effort more commercially feasible. Show times were at 3:00 and 6:00 p.m. The Latest Edison Novelty Company included Edison's Pollyphone (though Edison never had a phonograph with that name), described as "the latest, clearest and loudest talking machine." With it was the Cineograph "with a wonderful collection of views" and illustrated songs (figure 2.1).[47] The Cineograph was not Edison's machine at all (his was the Projecting Kinetoscope) but one manufactured by Siegmund Lubin of Philadelphia—Edison's persistent and clever rival. The use of Edison's name was simply a promotional ploy. The program itself was "adapted for ladies and children, it being Clean, Crisp and Clever, and in every respect refined and up-to-date."[48]

D. J. Springer suggested that quite a few American soldiers in Manila had theatrical experience, and they were able to put together a decent vaudeville program or stag show. At the end of the year, Max Berol, manager of the Konorah company, which had toured China and come from Hong Kong to Manila, gave a more detailed report. He noted that the *New York Clipper*, a leading theatrical journal, was on sale at the American News Store and sold ten to fifteen copies weekly (though the issues were six weeks old when they arrived). The Latest Edison Novelty Company was probably one of the semiprofessional companies and may have bought its Cineograph directly from Lubin. Through the *Clipper*, Lubin was then advertising:

EVERY AFTERNOON AT 3

EVERY EVENING AT 6

Corner Escolta and San Jacinto St.—Upstairs

——THE——

Edison Latest Novelty Co

have opened as above in

A Wonderful Entertainment

introducing Edison's

POLLYPHONE

The latest, clearest and loudest talking machine. *A giant's voice but not a giant's body.* Also the . . .

CINEOGRAPH

with a wonderful collection of views. The latest

ILLUSTRATED SONGS
A HOST OF NOVELTIES

Remember this entertainment is adapted for ladies and children, it being Clean, Crisp and Clever, and in every respect refined and up-to-date

Figure 2.1. Advertisement for the Edison Latest Novelty Company. (*Manila Times*, August 29, 1899, p. 6.)

STRIKE WHILE THE IRON IS HOT! LUBIN'S CINEOGRAPH and STEREOPTICON COMBINED, with 4 Fifty Feet [*sic*] Films and 2 dozen Stereopticon Slides, all for $100.[49]

The show on Escolta Street may have been an effort to tap a civilian audience as well as a few soldiers who were not on the front lines. One wonders which films the Latest Edison Novelty Company screened. Films related to the Spanish-American War were possible, though not the *Filipino Insurgency*, at least during this particular run.[50] If patriotic military scenes were shown, how did Americans and Filipinos respond? Would Americans have consistently embraced such propaganda? Certainly an enthusiastic response from Filipinos seems unlikely. Perhaps the exhibitor showed trick and comic subjects that appealed to all sides. Or like the so-called Biograph, films of sex and violence were shown that appealed to American soldiers and young men. Rather than promote American militarism to the American military, it is quite possible that they offered escape.

American cinema in this period consistently failed to articulate an anti-expansionist/anti-imperialist stance, even though the nation's overseas adventurism was a highly contested political issue. American cinema was iconoclastic, but it was also expansionist. Shortly after making *The Battle of Manila Bay*, J. Stuart Blackton and Albert E. Smith showed it as part of a program in which Blackton claimed to be an eyewitness to Dewey's naval victory.[51] Although there were no overt antiwar films, the French (particularly Georges Méliès with his magic and fairy-tale films) continued to occupy the cosmopolitan position that offered an alternative. Cinema might spoof imperialist ideology but did not challenge it directly. A film such as *A Trip to the Moon* (1902) is particularly interesting because it retains a degree of ideological ambivalence. On the one hand, the film lampoons the use of science and technology as they are yoked to adventurism and the colonization of distant territories (the moon!). On the other hand, it could also be said to universalize this way of seeing and acting in the world. Even in the looking-glass worlds that Méliès produced, Europeans still encountered primitive and dangerous beings who attempt to capture and destroy them. By making the colonial scenario ridiculous, it also universalizes it.

Impresario Max Berol offered a detailed assessment of the possibilities for theatrical entertainment in Manila at the turn of the century. One problem was the segmented population: of the 300,000 residents, there were 180,000 natives, 50,000 Chinese, 20,000 Spaniards, 5,000 Spanish half-breeds (i.e., mestizos), 2,000 other Europeans, and 40,000 American soldiers (10,000 of which were in the city on garrison or police duty).[52] The principal languages spoken were Spanish and Tagalog (Filipino). Since Manileños who were too poor to attend commercial theaters were primarily natives, theatrical entrepreneurs were confronted with a highly fragmented audience base. As Berol explained:

The problem of advertising [to] such a mixed community is a vexing one. Anything like a house to house canvas is out of the question, owing to the size of the town and the illiteracy of the poorer classes; window display is impossible for there are no windows, all stores having their entire front open to the street for ventilating purposes. There are four English dailies, with a total combined circulation of 3,500; space rates average $4 Mex., per inch per week; but discount arrangements are easily made. Besides these are three Spanish papers, one native Tagalog paper and two Spanish Filipino papers. The bill posting in the hands of one man, being licensed ($250 Mex per annum), but is in a terrible condition. Filipinos are employed and as they cannot read they often cover paper but recently posted, while leaving some four months' old posters uncovered. No billboards are used, and of course paper don't stick well to an adobe wall. The charge is six cents Mex, per sheet, or per small poster, but only half and one sheets can be used. Possibly a very limited number of three sheets could be posted, but nothing larger. Posters in all three languages should be used, for the natives are good showgoers, especially on Sundays and holidays. All theatres run on Sundays, which is their best day. Distributing handbills on the street is permitted, but in addition to all this the Konorah Company has resorted to the plan of inclosing a different courier herald or folder every day into the English newspapers, thereby reaching Americans at their homes as well as the soldiers at the outposts and the sailors of the fleet. This service costs $5 per thousand.[53]

Newspapers were an important but not the only form of promotion, and smaller operations involving motion pictures advertised in a selective number of papers and often irregularly. Searching two or three newspapers for advertisements gives only a partial picture of local film culture. Significantly, the amusement world in Manila was already operating in three languages: English, Spanish, and Tagalog. And perhaps, though less well documented, in a fourth: Chinese.

Manila was a multiracial, polyglot society, one that was already multilingual and cosmopolitan. Even Berol's theatrical company looked to the native as well as the Spanish-speaking and American populations. The city's cultural sophistication was evident in Berol's appreciation of the native population both as showgoers and for their musical talents:

Music can be had here galore. The Filipino is the Italian of the Orient. For $2 Mex per man, one can hire at least three native orchestras, each with up to thirty instruments and each capable of reading operettas like "Merry War" or "Fatinitza" at sight and "Traviata" or "Trovatore" in three rehearsals. This may sound absurd but it is absolute fact. During the first rehearsal of a Spanish operetta, "El Re[y] que Rablo," I have myself seen that when the baritone found a certain aria too high the entire orchestra of twenty-eight pieces, at a word of their director, at once and at sight transferred the whole aria one tone lower, which few orchestras of that size would undertake in the United States.[54]

In this respect the native population was much more Europeanized than elsewhere in Southeast Asia, due to the long period of Spanish colonization and the influence of the Catholic Church. Even those who did not speak Spanish were to some degree Hispanicized. Berol also discussed the theatrical infrastructure at some length:

There are seven theatres available but only four or five would be of use to a first class company. Not one of these is more than a bamboo shed, built pavilion style, with a seating capacity of 1,000 to 1,500, generally on one floor arranged amphitheatrically. The description of one theatre would suffice for all. A bamboo fence ten or twelve feet high, unplastered except in one house, forms the wall; the roof is supported by poles eighteen or twenty feet high, leaving eight or ten feet of open space all around for ventilation, which is in keeping with the climate but makes the theatres unavailable on rainy days.[55]

Manila possessed an entertainment infrastructure and a tradition of theatergoing that both veteran and aspiring showmen sought to tap.

In this period of occupation and warfare, American exhibitors were showing a cinema intended to appeal to the colonizers more than the colonized even if their programs were "mere entertainment." Deocampo has located at least one potential exception to this paradigm. The Spanish-language press included announcements for films shown at what Berol called the best if smallest of Manila's theaters, the Teatro Filipino (capacity 925 seats), which rented for one hundred Mexican dollars (or fifty US dollars) per night. The showings commenced August 24, 1900, and were in combination with a two-act *comedia* (Spanish play in verse): *El oso muerte* (The killer bear).[56] Since nothing is known about the specific films or the play, one can only speculate the extent to which this evening's program might have already been a form of covert political and cultural resistance.[57] Here was evident the simultaneous process of both Hispanicization (Deocampo) and indigenization (Del Mundo). With Spain defeated first by the Filipinos in the Revolution of 1896–1898 and then by the Americans, who replaced them, Spanish culture assumed a new and quite different role for Filipinos. As Deocampo and others have shown, the Philippines became increasingly Hispanicized, partially in reaction to American culture. If the Philippines were to be a nation, its unity would be partially shaped by its shared (Spanish) colonial past as well as its present struggle with an upstart Anglo power. In this respect native languages such as Tagalog or Cebuano potentially articulated local rather than national aspirations. Spanish often became the language and means for national identity and (indirectly) resistance by Filipinos. Spanish represented national resistance at the expense of the local, the indigenous, and the poor.[58] To be sure, French films were international and cosmopolitan in part because they were neither American nor Spanish. To show them as part of a program that included a *comedia* was to situate them within a Hispanic culture that kept Americans at arm's length. The United States, the English language, and the colonial government were excluded from this theatrical entertainment.

The Rise of the *Cinematógrafos*, 1902–1909

The end of the Philippine-American War in 1902 (Filipino general Miguel Malvar surrendered in April while President Theodore Roosevelt declared a general amnesty on July 4) facilitated a rapid expansion of cinema and other forms of theatrical entertainment.[59] In June a Mr. Walgrah, a British national, showed the *Cinematógrafo electrico luminoso Walgrah* (Walgraph's electric light cinema) in the Intramuros.[60] The program consisted primarily of films by Méliès and Pathé.[61] *Damnacion del Fausto* and *Guillermo Tell* were almost certainly Méliès films made in 1898 (film no. 158, *Damnation of Faust*, and film no. 159, *Adventures of William Tell*).[62] *Conquista del aire* was *Conquête d'air* (Conquest of the air), a 1901 Pathé trick film that featured Ferdinand Zecca riding a bike through the sky.[63] *Bombardeo de China por los en cuadras aliadas* was likely *Bombardment of Taku Forts by the Allied Fleets* (Edison, June–August 1900). Although in some cases four years old, the films were unfamiliar to their Filipino audience and well received. Walgrah's success helped usher in a new era for cinema in the Philippines. When American occupation official Arthur Stanley Riggs published his book on Filipino drama that focused on the 1902–1905 period, he chose to reprint a program for the Walgraph (note the inserted "p") Cinematógrafo, which listed the films in three different languages: Spanish, English, and Tagalog. The first part of the program was a passion play film of almost two thousand feet (with a running time of about thirty minutes); the second, a miscellaneous group of films that included *The Arrival of King Edward at Paris*, almost certainly the Edison film *King Edward's Visit to Paris* (shot by A. C. Abadie in May 1903) but one that concealed its US source. Riggs's accompanying caption remarked, "Official Program of a mild type of unusual decorous moving picture show."[64]

According to Deocampo, European businessman Samuel Rebarber opened the Gran Cinematógrafo Parisien in 1902, with Filipino Antonio Egra as proprietor. In 1903 scenographic painter Jose Jimenez built the Cinematógrafo Rizal.[65] Nadi Tofighian has identified as many as fourteen *cinematógrafos* or cinemas in Manila during 1903.[66] Some of these must have been short-lived and/or very modest. Deocampo reports that there were seven cinemas in Manila by the end of 1904, two of which were named Filipino Cinematograph. Tofighian offers no figures for 1904 but found the same number in 1905, increasing to twelve in 1906. Moving pictures quickly found a key role in Manila's theatrical culture. The names for many of these theaters suggest that they were not extensions of the new American regime but offered an alternative public sphere.

The *cinematógrafos* often combined their film screenings with performances of plays and zarzuelas. This was the period when "seditious plays," usually written in Tagalog by Filipinos who opposed the American occupation, flourished. In many instances, writers, directors, and actors were arrested, and some writers were convicted and went to jail for violating the Sedition Act, passed on November 4, 1901.[67] Section 10 declared,

> Until it has been officially proclaimed that a state of war or insurrection against the authority or sovereignty of the United States no longer exists in the Philippine Islands, it shall be unlawful for any person to advance orally or by writing or printing or like methods, the independence of the Philippine Islands, or their separation from the United States whether by peaceable or forcible means or to print, publish or circulate any handbill, newspaper, or publication advocating such independence or separation.[68]

Resistance to the seditious act was nothing new. Actors and other intellectuals had staged subversive performances in defiance of the Spaniards.[69] These were part of an established and courageous tradition that embraced national hero José Rizal himself—who had written novels that ultimately led to his execution by the Spaniards.

How seditious were the plays and zarzuelas staged in the *cinematógrafos*? This is a question that needs further serious investigation. No doubt many merely asserted a quiet cultural nationalism, but one cannot rule out that the movies may have provided a cover for many live performances whose subversive meanings were not so transparent to the occupying forces. Overall the combination of films and plays suggests a mix of cosmopolitan sophistication that was connected to the French films and an anti-American, nationalist rhetoric that was tied to the live performances. With some of these stagings conducted in Tagalog (or quite possibly a mix of languages), *cinematógrafo* culture in Manila combined programming elements that mediated between the global, the national, and the local—while almost completely excluding elements drawn from the Philippines' new American master. Through subterfuge and/or silence, the *cinematógrafos* implicitly (at the least) rejected the nation's colonial status.[70]

Situated in a global context, the early and rapid proliferation of *cinematógrafos* in Manila was unprecedented and deserves serious recognition. The boom in nickelodeons did not begin in the United States until the second half of 1905 and reached critical mass only in 1906—three or more years after the phenomenon took off in Manila. Unfortunately, this achievement has been significantly underappreciated by Filipino historians, who have emphasized what they see as cinema's dependence on accompanying stage performances, criticizing this as a by-product of the Philippines' subservience to the United States. This chapter argues that cinema in the Philippines became a form of resistance rather than a victim of the American occupation, as it worked effectively in tandem with live performances in ways that still need further exploration. How and why was this precocious appearance in Manila possible?

A more affirming and convincing narrative that explains the early and unprecedented rise of specialized motion picture theaters or *cinematógrafos* in Manila might be that, defeated in war and forced to accept the American presence, Filipinos were looking for escape or new areas of pleasure that stood outside the realm of the new colonial regime. One such area proved to be cinema. Largely deprived of motion pictures between 1898 and 1902, Filipinos embraced Walgrah's show; and cinema became a fad. There may have been some overextension by eager entrepreneurs in 1903, followed by some reentrenchment as the reservoir of unseen films was exhausted, but Filipinos continued to embrace the cinema. Manileños undoubtedly became frustrated with the quality and freshness of all-film programs; but, as Nick Deocampo points out, the addition of musicals and other forms of live performance helped keep these cinemas going. And with these additions, a further political component could be incorporated. The *cinematógrafos* often provided a continued site of covert resistance, albeit in the cultural realm. The prevalence of multimedia programs was something other than a necessary evil: they provided a local, national, and potentially political dimension to the programs, balancing the globalism and amusement value associated with the motion pictures.[71] Certainly this is an excellent example of glocalization. While cinema was still seen as an extension of the colonizing power in Vietnam in 1904, it had become effectively integrated into Filipino culture by the same date.[72] At this moment the process of cinema becoming a central feature of cultural identity was arguably even further along in the Philippines (or at least Manila) than in the United States.

The Emergence of Philippines-Based Filmmaking, 1909–1917

In June 1909, Pathé opened an exchange on Escolta Street in Manila, offering films "Rent or Sold," with a "Fresh supply by every mail."[73] The establishment of a Pathé branch office in Manila coincided with many important changes in cinema practice, both local and global in nature. Reports suggest that Manila's cinemas began to flourish in 1909, and solving their supply problem was doubtlessly crucial in this regard.[74] Although Pathé's efforts initially strengthened the preference for French films that was already part of Filipino moviegoing, Americans were an increasing presence in the film scene, operating as theater owners, exhibitors, and even distributors. In some cases, they bought and showed American films acquired in the United States, though these were often considered junk and of poor quality.[75]

With approximately twenty to thirty theaters in Metro Manila around 1910–1914 and perhaps an equal number in other parts of the country/colony, it seems certain that one or two prints of a given subject would be sufficient for use in the Philippines. A given film would likely rotate through the theaters in Manila and be sent on to the provinces more or less quickly. Certainly in Japan the distribution of only one or two prints of foreign films was the rule. As a result, the cost of making intertitles for foreign films would have been considerable. Moreover, because the Japanese considered foreign intertitles to be part of a film's attraction and also because illiteracy was quite high, there were social, cultural, and economic reasons for not making Japanese intertitles for foreign films. This was one reason why the *benshi* or narrator became integral to the exhibition process in Japanese cinema.[76] This was not the case for the Philippines. Although there are some reports of a lecturer accompanying films in some cinemas, the practice was not widespread. A narrator working in one language would have excluded much of the potential audience. Since spectators in the same theater routinely functioned in three different languages, films featured bi- or trilingual intertitles (Spanish, English, and Tagalog). To handle these developments, local distributors (including but not limited to Pathé) had basic production capabilities so they could shoot, develop, and print intertitles for the local market. For this and other reasons, production capabilities became available in Manila in the 1909–1911 period.[77]

By the early 1910s, Manila film culture was vibrant. Italian as well as French films were popular. *Dante's Inferno* (1911) was a hit. Louis Feuillade's *The Maid of Argos* (*La vierge d'Argos*, Gaumont, 1911) was playing in Manila even before it opened in the United States.[78] Fight films were widely promoted. By 1912, movie theaters were frequently advertising screenings of multireel feature films. American films were beginning to be shown with some regularity, but this penetration of the Filipino market was sometimes more fraught than might first appear. The Grand Opera House showed Thomas Ince's *General Custer's Last Fight* (1912) for five days. A full-page advertisement elaborately described the subject matter of this four-reel feature as "The Massacre of the Little Big Horn. The Entire Action Taken on the Scene of the Most Disastrous Catastrophe of U.S. Troops in Western Warfare."[79] Filipinos flocked to the theater to see the American military suffer defeat. The screenings produced "an outbreak of enthusiasm" that had obvious political implications.[80]

According to Kristin Thompson, many of the men operating movie houses in this period were American,[81] often former members of the US military who decided to stay. Although historians have tended to characterize these showmen as pro-imperialist and an extension of the American colonial regime, they represented a range of ideological and political perspectives. Many Americans (including some who were then in the Philippines) had opposed the Philippine-American War and the continued subjugation of the Philippines to a colonial regime. Of course, American showmen benefited from the American colonial regime even as they met resistance from elements of a local film culture that had been a counterweight to the American occupation. A few of these exhibitors sought to overcome this resistance by appealing to Philippine sentiments, for instance, by keeping a lively Filipino presence in their program's stage performances. In what might be seen as a logical extension of this practice, restaurant-manager-turned-exhibitor Albert W. Yearsley quickly began to produce local news films with a Filipino emphasis: according to Agustin Sotto, this began with the filming of Rizal Day celebrations at the Luneta on December 30, 1909. These were followed by news films such as *The Manila Carnival of 1910* and many other subjects designed to appeal to Filipinos through their local and national identities.[82] This was a sustained and quite stunning commitment. Certainly they differed from earlier efforts by Australian Herbert Wyndham to shoot local scenes and show them to local audiences in 1905.[83] Yearsley's subjects were newsworthy events and national in scope (including, for example, *Cebu before and after the Typhoon*) (figure 2.2).[84] The point to be emphasized here is that Yearsley, while perhaps an adventurer, was not the shock troops of a colonial agenda—quite the contrary. His films gave visual recognition to local Filipino events rather than provide scenes of the US military (though there were, admittedly, some exceptions to this tendency). Yearsley's efforts more than met his audiences halfway. If nothing else, this illustrates the contradictions of capitalism: to win over patrons, an American shows films that appealed to Filipino identity and cultural nationalism.

Edward Meyer Gross (1869–1946), born in New York City, was the American who most clearly embraced Filipino life and the Philippine aspiration for independence.[85] Having been in the US Navy and fought in the Spanish-American War, Gross came to the Philippines in 1902. A chemist, he started a coconut plantation in Laguna and manufactured coconut oil (figure 2.3).[86] His American wife did not like their new life and returned to the United States. He remained, they divorced, and Gross eventually met and married Titay Molina, a mestizo star of the Zarzuela theater. Her brother (or possibly cousin) was Antonio J. Molina, a well-known Filipino composer and conductor. (The Molina Orchestra was periodically advertised—playing at the Metropole Hotel on Thursdays and Sundays and also based at the Grand Opera House.)[87] Gross loved books, and he and his wife had a salon that attracted musicians, artists, and intellectuals. While running his business, Gross bought a theater and in 1905 wrote a play about the

AMAZING MAGNIFICENT WONDERFUL

EDUCATIONAL

THE MARVEL OF STAGE CRAFT

2000 PEOPLE IN THE CAST

Has Received the Stamp of Approval of the Clergy --- Far Greater Than the Passion Play

DANTES INFERNO

AT THE **EMPIRE** FOR BALANCE OF WEEK

DON'T MISS IT

AT THE MAJESTIC

Cebu Before and After the Typhoon

This Combination of Pictures--Makes a Very Interesting Film of the Disaster.

Figure 2.2. Movie theater advertisements. (*Manila Times*, October 31, 1912.)

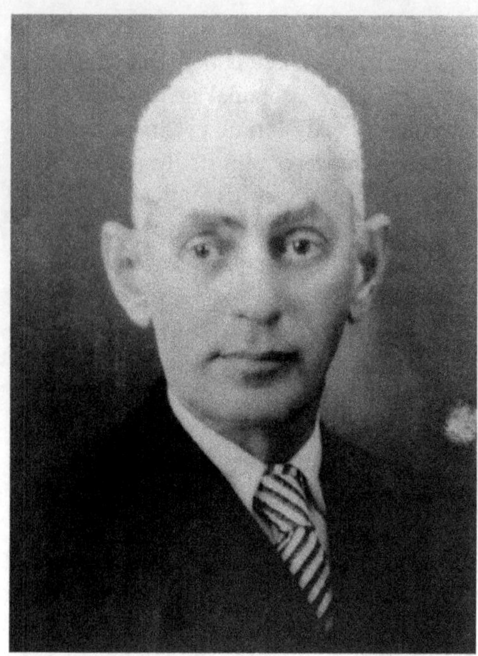

Figure 2.3. Edward Meyer Gross. The photograph was probably taken after his incarceration in the Philippines during World War II. (Courtesy of Victor Gross, son of Edward Meyer Gross.)

national hero of the Philippines, José Rizal. One wonders if under other circumstances this would have qualified as a seditious play. Had he been Filipino, would the play have been banned and the playwright thrown in prison? He was protected by his American citizenship and could have served as a useful front for his Filipino colleagues.

Gross moved into the theater and eventually into filmmaking as a joint venture with his beloved wife.[88] They made the first acted film on Filipino soil, with Americans Harry Brown, owner of the Gaiety movie theater, as producer and Charles Martin, a government photographer, as cinematographer.[89] Its title reflected a topic of historical and nationalistic importance: *The Life and Death of Dr. José Rizal* (*La vida de José Rizal*, 1912). This five thousand–foot feature film was based, in part, on Gross's play and relied on him as an authority of Rizal's life. The film starred writer Honorio Lopez as Rizal, while the actress Chananay (Valeriana Mauricio), whom Rizal had featured in his novel *Noli me tangere* (Touch me not, 1886) as an embodiment of Filipino culture, played Rizal's mother. Titay Molina assumed the role of Maria Clara, Rizal's wife, and other actors came from Severino Reyes's Gran Compania de la Zarzuela Tagala.[90]

Rizal, a national hero and intellectual who sought Filipino independence, was then a contested figure—appropriated by the American regime as someone who supported its democratic values and embraced by many Filipinos who still yearned for an independent nation. The colonialist perspective was doubtlessly expressed by the illustrated lecture *The Life of Rizal*, which was presented at Manila's Grand Opera House on December 27 and 28, 1911. It was indebted for its illustrative material to Austin Craig, who had already published *The Story of José Rizal: The Greatest Man of the Brown Race* and would soon complete *Lineage, Life and Labors of José Rizal, Philippine Patriot* (1913)—the latter putting him in a line of "heroes of the free Philippines," which began with Magellan and ended with US president William McKinley.[91] The first chapter heading labeled Rizal as "America's Forerunner." But as Filipinos were preparing to observe the fifteenth anniversary of his death, the *Manila Times* acknowledged that "the ardent advocate of immediate independence" believed that they represented "the true ideals of Rizal."[92] Not surprisingly, the newspaper also editorialized against this interpretation.

Gross's assessment of Rizal's political legacy obviously differed from that offered by Craig. The Brown-Gross-Molina film included scenes titled "The Emissary of the Katipunan" and "The First Cry of Liberty at Balintawak"—the latter a scene in which Andrés Bonifacio fled to the mountains and issued the Grito de Balintawak on August 26, 1896, which began the revolution and led to Rizal's arrest.[93] One news item remarked that the film's depiction of the "raid of the tulisanes" (the term for "bandits" that the Spanish applied to the Filipino revolutionaries) was true to life, intensely dramatic, and especially good (figure 2.4).[94]

The efforts of Brown, Gross, and Molina were imitated by Yearsley, who rushed out a shorter film, which was shot in one day, August 21, 1912, and then premiered at his Majestic Theater the next day.[95] Its title varied but was initially called *The Life and Death of Dr. José Rizal*.[96] It was a hastily assembled affair, which employed some of the same actors as the Brown-Gross production, which did not open until August 24. The Yearsley film was shown on a longer program that included two dramas, a comedy, and the Kinemacolor film *Swiss Alps in Winter Time*. It ran for ten days, until September 1. The Brown-Gross-Molina film was the sole film on its program and ran until Thursday, September 5.[97]

Agustin Sotto has remarked that "the filmmakers, despite being Americans, cashed in on prevailing sentiments of the native population and produced films with historical themes."[98] Yet a stronger appreciation for contradiction makes this less surprising and less opportunistic. Moreover, with the US presidential election barely two months away, the Democratic Party had a platform that called for Filipino independence.[99] Although Woodrow Wilson, who had supported the US occupation of the Philippines, backtracked from this position once elected, some Americans, including Gross, used this as an opportunity to support independence-minded Filipinos and their cause. At the same time, we should not give undue authorial importance to the Americans behind the camera. They must have deferred to a considerable degree to the Filipinos in front of the camera. This

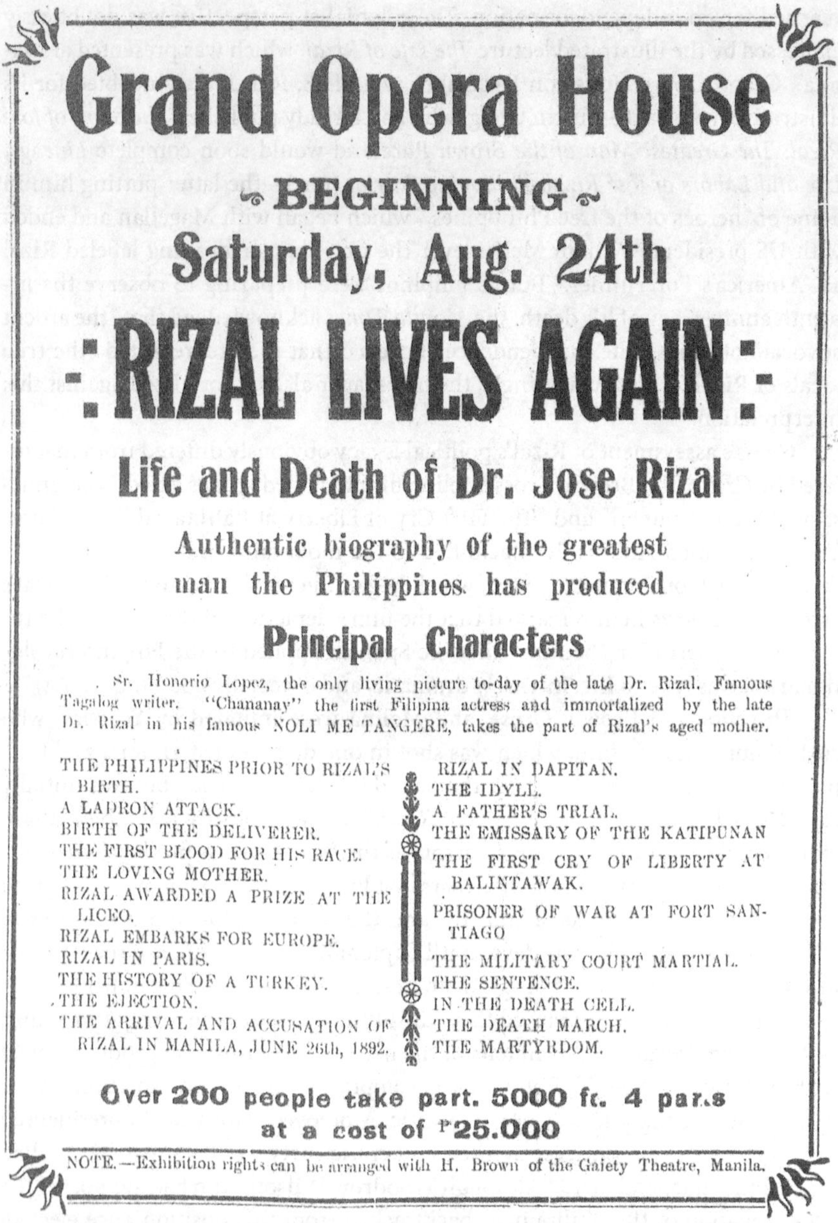

Figure 2.4. Advertisement for the Edward Meyer Gross, Titay Molina, and Harry Brown feature film *The Life and Death of Dr. José Rizal*. (*Manila Times*, August 22, 1912.)

was their history, after all. These Filipinos not only knew that history; they knew how Filipino audiences would want it to be represented. Filipino theater had long been a center of resistance to the colonial regime. So it seems unlikely that these Filipinos would have participated in a project in which they did not believe. Although, in the end, the content, as well as the range of political interpretations elicited by both Rizal films, is difficult to pin down with precision, it is clear that the issue of nation and the political status of the Philippines were overtly presented, to the discomfort of many both then and now.

The Brown-Gross-Molina version of *The Life and Death of Dr. José Rizal* was significant for another reason: Putting Filipino actors on the screen was an important moment in the nation's cultural history. This must have been particularly true for Titay Molina, who starred in a number of their subsequent productions. Moreover, hers was almost certainly not a small, supporting role. She played a forceful, independent national heroine: Josephine Bracken, who was born in Hong Kong of Irish parents and was Rizal's lover. (Because he had rejected Catholicism, they were not given dispensation to marry by the church.) Although the facts are in some dispute, they were said to have finally married less than two hours before his execution, and she stayed by his side while he was shot. Later that day, she left Manila and joined the Filipino revolutionaries, opening a field hospital to care for the wounded. The year that Molina played Rizal's wife and the legendary Chananay played Rizal's mother also saw the appearance of Sarah Bernhardt in *Queen Elizabeth* (1912). Other prominent stage stars in the United States such as James O'Neill and James Hackett also began to make films of their theatrical vehicles. American actresses such as Mary Pickford, Florence Turner, Marian Swayne, Mabel Norman, and Mary Fuller were also becoming movie stars. Molina gave to the Philippines its *own* film star. If the movie star—rather than the director—has proved to be the face of a nation and central to its citizens' sense of identity and self, then 1912 more than 1919 was a decisive moment in Filipino political, social, and cultural history.

A feminist reassessment of cinema in the 1910s has shown that many actresses (e.g., Gene Gauntier, Lois Weber) assumed prominent roles in shaping not only their own performance but the overall achievement of the films in which they appeared. *Tess of the Storm Country* (Famous Players, 1914) was essentially codirected by Edwin S. Porter (who was behind the camera) and Pickford (who performed in front of it). Of course, other actors besides Molina were in a position to contribute, but her close relationship with Gross put her at the center of this production. Why should we not assume that the first fiction film made in the Philippines was spearheaded by a woman, the great actress Titay Molina? To say otherwise merely combines a certain knee-jerk anti-Americanism with a traditional male-centered view of history.

The move to generate a nationalist cinema that echoed the Tagalog theater of the previous decade moved ahead rapidly after the success of the Rizal films. Yearsley's Majestic Theater showed *Walang Sugat* (Not wounded, 1912), a forty-five-hundred-foot feature film for four days in late October. Advertisements claimed it was the "First Philippine Drama reproduced in motion pictures."[100] By early November Gross, Brown, Martin, and Molina had made their second feature, *The Three Martyrs* (*Los tres martires*, 1912), about the three Filipino priests whom the Spanish executed for fostering Filipino rebellion (the Cavite Insurrection of 1872) and to whose memory Rizal dedicated his second novel, *El filibusterismo* (Subversion, 1891). Perhaps it was not coincidence that a few days after the Philippine Assembly met and agreed to a ban on "immoral films," the censors refused to permit the screening of *The Three Martyrs*, or at least a section of the scene where the priests were executed.[101] There was grave concern that the film would "tend to excite the Filipino people" in ways that "can lead to no legitimate social end."[102] *Walang Sugat* also seems to have dropped from sight, and the absence of any press coverage in the *Manila Times* suggests that its subject matter was also controversial. All this was developing as Woodrow Wilson was running for president on a platform calling for Filipino independence. Was it coincidence that the day that Yearsley showed *Demonstration in Honor of Wilson's Election* at his Majestic Theater was also the day that the ban on immoral films was passed?[103]

Edward Gross and Titay Molina then made a series of films celebrating Filipino nationalism. These included feature-length adaptations of Rizal's novels: *Noli me tangere* (1915) and *El filibusterismo* (in two parts, 1916). Most if not all of their other films showed a strong sense of Filipino culture—as well as a feminist perspective in such films as *Nena la boxeadora* (Nena the boxer, 1916), starring actress Marie de la Tronqued (not Molina) in the title role. To be sure, these films did not explore Filipino resistance to American colonialization, but it goes without saying that the American government would never have allowed such films to be shown. These were perhaps compromises but also displacements. It did not take a genius to make a substitution for, or the connection with, a more recent ongoing struggle: Filipinos could easily interpret these films allegorically, as part of a nationalist agenda that extended into the American era.

Agustin Sotto writes, "The early American colonizers found film to be a lucrative investment. However, their primary objective was to make as much money [as possible] and then pack their bags for home."[104] Deocampo likewise wonders about Gross's "personal knowledge and historical competence as an American who was newly-settled in a country he hardly knew."[105] But it seems that Yearsley gave up filmmaking not because he wanted to go home but because his film business went badly and he was forced to turn to carnivals for a living. Gross also never left the Philippines. After Titay Molina died from heart failure at the age of forty-three, Gross did not just give up moviemaking; he gave up on life—losing his plantation as well. Eventually he regrouped and acquired a plantation and business in Davao (Mindanao) with a Japanese partner. He eventually remarried—Zoima Loma—and had children, including Maria Salomé (born in 1938), named after one of the heroines in Rizal's *Noli me tangere*. After the Japanese occupied the Philippines, his partner returned to Japan while Gross was sent to a concentration camp. By the time he was liberated, the former filmmaker was dying of tuberculosis. His continued ties to the Molina family are evidenced by the fact that he arranged for his daughter Maria Salomé to live with Antonio Molina to study music.[106]

Perhaps Gross could be seen as the Alexander Korda of the Philippines. Korda, who was Hungarian, established himself in Great Britain and made numerous films that celebrated the British Empire in terms that his domestic audience often adored. He was even more British than the normal gung-ho Brit. Gross was Korda inside out in that his Filipino nationalism was also anti-imperialist. In this respect we must reflect carefully on the nature of a nation's cinema. If we consider real "American films" to be only those made by native-born Americans rather than recent (often Jewish) immigrants, then American film history would be drastically reduced in size. American cinema was international in its roots as well as its orientation. Many of the film pioneers had been born and/or raised in Europe, including W. K. L. Dickson, J. Stuart Blackton, and Albert E. Smith. Charles Chaplin was British; Mary Pickford and Mack Sennett were Canadian; Siegmund Lubin, Carl Laemmle, Erich von Stroheim, and Ernst Lubitsch were German and Eastern European Jews (like many others); Alice Guy Blaché and Maurice Tourneur were French; and Greta Garbo was Swedish. Whether in the silent or sound era, the honor roll of Hollywood cinema is filled with the names of people who were born and often trained elsewhere. It is what made Hollywood cinema great—or at least what enabled Hollywood cinema to be Hollywood cinema. Why cannot one say the same for the Philippines, particularly when non-Filipinos were working closely and extensively with Filipinos in key roles?

This chapter has depended on Filipino film historians for much of its data and information. Its value comes from emphasizing interpretive perspectives that are increasingly familiar in the international study of early cinema. The first is to situate early cinema in the Philippines within a global system that characterizes motion picture practice. This requires a reassessment not only of Philippine cinema but of world cinema (the whole as well as an individual part). Such a global contextualization allows for comparison and judgment on the regional, national, and local levels as well as an assessment of the dynamics between colonizer and colonized. This requires a strong appreciation for contradiction and irony. Moreover, it requires greater respect for those working in this early period, an approach I like to call "critical sympathy." It is not only in the Philippines that early cinema and its creative personnel have been consistently underevaluated, even maligned over the years. For many years American historians insisted that Edwin S. Porter, America's first filmmaker, had an important insight—that films could tell a story. Yet they also believed he did not know how to go about such a task. He was a lousy storyteller. It was only D. W. Griffith who learned how to tell stories on film and made cinema a great art. Again, Oscar Micheaux was considered noteworthy as the major black filmmaker working in the period between World War I and World War II. Scholars generally thought he was an important symbol but was a better showman and self-promoter than a filmmaker. Such conclusions were reductive and wrong in both cases. Porter and Micheaux were so radical in their filmmaking that historians, judging their films against Hollywood standards, could not recognize their remarkable achievements.

The prominent role of women in the American and European film industries of the 1910s is being reassessed and appreciated by new studies of Lois Weber, Alice Guy Blaché, Gene Gautier, and Mary Pickford, among others.[107] Weber and Guy Blaché likewise worked with their husbands. Their work encourages us to see the actress Titay Molina as something more than a dutiful and subservient wife (in the mythic Filipino style) to an American playwright, screenwriter, producer, and showman. Molina was a "New Woman" and well suited to help pioneer a new Filipino cinema. Filipino film historians, concerned that their early cinema reflected their colonial status in a negative way, have been predisposed to minimize its extraordinary vitality in this period before the Hollywood majors arrived and before José Nepomuceno bought Gross's film equipment and then, in 1919, made his first feature film. Under- or unequal development, according to Clyde Taylor, has its constraints and its pressures, but it can also create a space that enables powerful and creative alternative discourses.[108]

If cinema and other forms of theatrical culture played a crucial role in the Filipino imaginary, as film scholars argue, it came to assume that role at a very early stage. This role was already present, in inchoate form, during the 1897 novelty period (particularly the Cinématographe screenings of Ramos, Leibman, and Peritz). It emerged more clearly in the cinema and theatrical programs of the 1900s and reached initial cinematic expression in terms of local productions by the early 1910s. To make sense of this history of Filipino cinema also means, I think, immersing it within a broader and older history of theatrical entertainment. The nationalist, independence-minded films of 1912 came out of and were often reworkings of the nationalistic plays of the previous decade.

The Quezon City conference began with the assumption that cinema in a given Southeast Asian political entity/culture/colony was quite different from that people's cinema. Clearly, early cinema in Vietnam was not Vietnamese cinema. It was a colonizer's cinema. A similar assessment seemed applicable to the Philippines. That was our working principle. Although such instances occurred in the Philippines, these seem to have been of limited scope and efficacy. Far more often, the cinema embraced the cultural and political aspirations of Filipinos, including those seeking a quick end to American colonial rule. In the pre-1919 period, cinema in the Philippines was not a pure Filipino cinema. But the search for such an ethnically and culturally pure cinema made after 1919 may prove highly elusive, and if found, the results are likely to be reductive. American "impurities" of various sorts would thus compromise the contributions of both Isabel Rosario "Dimples" Cooper and Fernando Poe Sr. Even if scholars can identify a group of films that meet the most rigorous criteria, they functioned in a much larger system that cannot. Cinema in the Philippines has never been purely Filipino, but then it is not clear that the Philippines has been purely Filipino since soon after Lapu-Lapu killed Magellan in 1521 (and perhaps much earlier). Much of the cultural vitality of the Philippines comes from its polyglot cosmopolitan culture. In this sense, cinema in the Philippines was remarkably and distinctly Filipino from the outset. That is, it was unique, and that uniqueness came out of the specific cultural, political, and economic conditions in which it operated, as it was remade by audiences (from 1897 onward), exhibitors (from 1902 onward), and filmmakers (from 1910 onward). Filipino cinema, like American cinema, has been an impure cinema from the outset. This creative tension between the local and national, on the one hand, and the global, on the other, has been one of its greatest strengths.

Afterword

After reading this chapter, Nick Deocampo responded with the following generous comment:

> While I very well admire your contributions, especially in defining the early cinema in the Philippines, I wonder what thoughts you may have regarding early cinema in Asia when this cinema will be seen from a regional vantage point? I felt your jump from the global to the national/local skirted the regional issue, which is at the heart of this anthology. I would be so grateful if you can share some thoughts that would help us conceive of early cinema in a way that is more regional in definition.[109]

Deocampo's concerns are well taken, though at this stage I doubt I can respond with much specificity to his request. Certainly there are different regions of the world, but in what sense are there regional cinemas? In respect to these regional cinemas, we might ask: When and how were they constituted? How strong is the regional pull in relation to other considerations (local, national, global)?

There are at least two obvious ways to define a regional cinema. First, we might look at what entities and qualities bind together the different cinemas within the region. Are films made in one part of the region shown in another? Do personnel from one part of the region circulate and work in another part? Do they share a more broad-based culture in literature, theater, and so forth? Ramos moved from the Philippines to Shanghai, but did he send films from China back to Manila? Certainly Titay Molina and Edward Meyer Gross seem to have made films for the Philippines, not for export either to other parts of the region or to the United States and Europe. This is only a hypothesis, based on the nature of their material. Was this also the case with José Nepomuceno? Nepomuceno, for instance, was the first Filipino to shoot a film outside the Philippines—in Japan in 1923.[110] As this suggests, it might be easier to construct a more viable regional cinema when focusing on a later stage in cinema's history. Perhaps this visit also involved purchases and sales of films. We may find that Nepomuceno's films were sold to other territories in the region. At least we find films of his counterpart, Oscar Micheaux, in Europe. So this is something that historians might investigate. Would it not be ironic that the person credited for initiating Filipino cinema can be more accurately credited with contributing to the creation of a Southeast Asian or Asian cinema?

A second way to define the strength and qualities of a region's cinema is simply to contrast it to other regional cinemas. For instance, we might compare Southeast Asian cinema before 1920 to Latin American cinema of the same period. I suspect the Latin American region had many more elements in common than Southeast Asia because it boasted two closely related languages and cultures as a result of its colonial heritage (Iberian—Spanish and Portuguese), as well as a common religion (Catholic). In this respect, one might recall a remark by the Japanese film critic Tadao Sato (offered by Deocampo) that Filipino cinema reminded him of Mexican cinema more than Asian cinema (by which I suppose he meant Japanese and Chinese). There are historical antecedents that make this rather peculiar regional unity compelling, notably a shared heritage based on Spanish colonialism. Nonetheless, affinities are not static, and they are always multidirectional.

Deocampo has posed an immensely challenging question, in effect: To what extent was there a regional, Southeast Asian cinema in the period before 1920, before 1930, or perhaps even before the onset of World War II? Certainly in the period 1902–1912, there were extraordinary differences between cinema in the Philippines and elsewhere in Southeast Asia. According to Kristin Thompson, around 1912 there were three theaters in Singapore but twenty-five in Manila. Manila was already a center of modest production; Singapore, apparently not. By the 1920s, these discrepancies may have been reduced. Perhaps we still need to know much more about these individual cultural communities and their cinema activities before offering any sweeping conclusions. I feel confident that this will happen eventually, but it requires substantial historical investigations at the local level. When did films made in China begin to be shown to the Chinese communities in the Philippines? Nevertheless, Southeast Asian cinema may also prove to be most interesting for its internal differences rather than its shared elements. Seeking to understand how different religions, different languages and cultures, and different if related political histories have produced different cinema histories within the region seems to me a legitimate outcome and even a legitimate goal of this project. Because they share a regional history, we will find Filipino cinema more interesting as a cultural response to its twentieth-century circumstances when compared to Thai cinema within the same time frame, and vice versa. In the course of exploring these different responses, commonalities may well become more apparent.

What I have done is quite modest but perhaps also a significant step toward a shared regional history. I have argued that cinema in the Philippines was, with one brief exception (1898–1901), never simply the cinema of the colonizer (Spain, the United Sates). Indeed, it played an integral role in Filipino culture. Was it a "Filipino cinema"? Perhaps it simply depends on how one defines the term. From 1902 onward, many Filipino *cinematógrafos* were run by Filipinos. The performances inside those theaters were also Filipinos. And after 1912, Filipinos sometimes appeared on Filipino screens. One thing is clear: Filipino cinema in the period before 1920 should not be seen as a retarded version of the cinema created by the industrialized center but was both different from and sometimes even in advance of those of Europe and North America. This is, I think, an important step; and if we use the Philippines as a model, it suggests that agency for cinema in Southeast Asia will often be located in Southeast Asia itself. But again, as the case of Vietnam suggests, not always. Within the region, cinema played a wide range of roles as its practitioners responded to opportunities framed by a diversity of colonial circumstances and local cultures.

CHARLES MUSSER is Professor of Film and Media Studies and American Studies at Yale University. He is author of *The Emergence of Cinema: The American Screen to 1907* and *Politicking and Emergent Media: US Presidential Elections of the 1890s*, as well as the documentary feature *Errol Morris: A Lightning Sketch*.

Notes

1. For scholarship on Nepomuceno, see Joe Quirino, *Don Jose and the Early Philippine Cinema* (Quezon City: Phoenix, 1983); and Nadi Tofighian, "The Role of Jose Nepomuceno in the Philippine Society: What Language Did His Silent Films Speak?" (master's thesis, Stockholm University, 2005).

2. Movie star Joseph Estrada was elected president in 1998 with Gloria Arroyo as vice president. When Estrada was forced to step down, she replaced him. Arroyo became president in her own right in 2004, defeating Fernando Poe Jr. It is widely believed that her opponent

actually won the election. (Poe's father was also a movie star; his mother was an American.) Political life in the Philippines currently boasts numerous governors (e.g., Vilma Santos) and senators (e.g., Jinggoy Estrada) who have had careers in motion pictures and television.

3. The examination of more than two hundred American and European films was a compelling starting place for a new investigation of the pre-Griffith cinema. The overriding interest of this group was in its mode of representation.

4. Louis Althusser, "Ideology and Ideological State Apparatuses (Notes towards an Investigation)," in *Lenin and Philosophy and Other Essays*, trans. Ben Brewster (New York: Monthly Review Press, 1971), 127–186.

5. Wimal Dissanayake, "Nationhood, History and Cinema: Reflections on the Asian Scene," in *Colonialism and Nationalism in Asian Cinema*, ed. Wimal Dissanayake (Bloomington: Indiana University Press, 1994), xiii.

6. This statement could use unpacking. Edison-licensed cameraman William Paley was essentially working with William Randolph Hearst, using his news yachts as a platform for filming.

7. Charles Musser, "The Early Cinema of Edwin S. Porter," *Cinema Journal* 19, no. 1 (1979): 1–38.

8. John Fell, ed., *Film before Griffith* (Berkeley: University of California Press, 1984), 3.

9. For a discussion of this decisive moment in film history, see Charles Musser, *Before the Nickelodeon: Edwin S. Porter and the Edison Manufacturing Company* (Berkeley: University of California Press, 1991) .

10. Terry Ramsaye, *A Million and One Nights* (New York: Simon and Schuster, 1926), 268, 320, 347, 430–431; David Bordwell, Janet Staiger, and Kristin Thompson, *The Classical Hollywood Cinema: Film Style and Mode of Production to 1960* (New York: Columbia University Press, 1988), 158.

11. André Gaudreault, Germain Lacasse, and Jean-Pierre Sirois-Trahan, *Au pays des ennemis du Cinéma: Pour une nouvelle histoire des débuts du cinéma au Québec* [In the land of the enemies of cinema: For a new history of the beginnings of cinema in Quebec] (Quebec: Nuit Blanche, 1996); André Gaudreault and Tom Gunning, "Le cinéma des premiers temps: Un défi à l'histoire du cinéma?" [The cinema of the first times: A challenge to the history of cinema], in *Histoire du cinéma: Nouvelles approches* [History of cinema: New approaches], ed. Jacques Aumont, André Gaudreault, and Michel Marie (Paris: Sorbonne, 1989), 49–63.

12. Tom Gunning, "The Cinema of Attraction(s)," *Wide Angle* 8, no. 3–4 (1986): 64.

13. Tom Gunning, "Cinema of Attractions," in *Early Cinema: Space, Frame, Narrative*, ed. Thomas Elsaesser (London: British Film Institute, 1990), 58–59. Unless otherwise noted, I cite this version of Gunning's article.

14. For a discussion of "cinema of attractions," as well as "early" and "primitive" cinema, see Wanda Stauven, ed., *Cinema of Attractions Reloaded* (Amsterdam: Amsterdam University Press, 2006), particularly the essays by André Gaudreault, Tom Gunning, and Charles Musser.

15. See, for instance, Jennifer Bean and Diane Negra, eds., *Feminist Reader in Early Cinema* (Durham, NC: Duke University Press, 2002), which includes numerous articles on cinema of the 1920s.

16. Bordwell, Staiger, and Thompson, *The Classical Hollywood Cinema*.

17. Kristin Thompson, *Exporting Entertainment: America in the World Film Market, 1907–34* (London: British Film Institute, 1985), 72.

18. Clodualdo A. del Mundo, *Native Resistance: Philippine Cinema and Colonialism, 1898–1941* (Manila: De La Salle University Press, 1998); Nick Deocampo, *Cine: Spanish Influences on Early Cinema in the Philippines* (Manila: National Commission for Culture and the Arts, 2003).

19. Jubin Hu, *Projecting a Nation: Chinese National Cinema before 1949* (Hong Kong: Hong Kong University Press, 2003), 29.

20. Chalida Uambumrungjit, "Cinema in Thailand: 1897–1970," in *Film in South East Asia: Views from the Region: Essays on Film in Ten South East Asia-Pacific Countries*, ed. David Hanan (Hanoi: SEAPAVAA, Vietnam Film Institute, and National Film and Sound Archive of Australia, 2001), 124.

21. "Hambog" is a word that was itself adopted or adapted from the American word "humbug." Dimples Cooper, the star of *Ang Tatlong Hambog*, was half Filipina, half American.

22. Wimal Dissanayake, "Nationhood, History and Cinema: Reflections on the Asian Scene," in Dissanayake, *Colonialism and Nationalism in Asian Cinema*, xiii.

23. Letter from D. J. Springer to *New York Clipper*, August 18, 1899, in *New York Clipper*, October 14, 1899, p. 667. Letter from Max Berol to *New York Clipper*, n.d., in *New York Clipper*, February 10, 1900, p. 1047.

24. Del Mundo, *Native Resistance*, 48; Deocampo, *Cine*, 37–44, 62–67. In *Native Resistance*, Del Mundo identifies this machine as the *kronophotografo*, and this is the spelling that first appeared in newspapers. Deocampo points out that the spelling was quickly changed to *cronofotógrafo* in subsequent *anuncios* (advertisements). Deocampo, *Cine*, 337n7.

25. Pennsylvania was the home state to traveling exhibitor Lyman Howe (Wilkes-Barre), producer Siegmund Lubin (Philadelphia), and pioneering nickelodeon owner Harry Davis (Pittsburgh). See Greg Waller, *Main Street Amusements: Movies and Commercial Entertainment in a Southern City, 1896–1930* (Washington, DC: Smithsonian Institution Press, ca. 1995), 24–27.

26. Hiroshi Komatsu, "Le Cinématographe Lumière et la production du cinéma au Japon dans ses premiers temps" [The Lumière Cinématographe and the production of cinema in Japan in its first time], in *Les frères Lumière et le Japon, 1895–1995* [The Lumière brothers and Japan, 1895–1995], ed. Futoshi Koga (Tokyo: Asahi Shumbun, 1995), 41.

27. Del Mundo, *Native Resistance*, 48. Quite a number of early motion picture exhibitors in the United States had begun their careers as phonograph showmen. See, in particular, Charles Musser and Carol Nelson, *High-Class Moving Pictures: Lyman H. Howe and the Forgotten Era of Traveling Exhibition, 1880–1920* (Princeton, NJ: Princeton University Press, 1991).

28. Agustin Sotto, "A Brief History of Philippine Cinema," in Hanan, *Film in South East Asia*, 32.

29. Hu, *Projecting a Nation*, 30.

30. As Threese Serana notes, "Manila was the bastion of colonizers who had to have many *inquilinos* (overseers), native right hands who also behaved as if they were Hispanic. This group would like[ly] read a Manila newspaper in Tagalog, which had begun publication in 1892. Assuming it (or other subsequent publications of this kind) survives, it would be important for film scholars to examine their coverage of cinema." Threese Serana, e-mail to the author, August 25, 2005.

31. Sam Ngamsnit, "Thailand," in *The Films of ASEAN*, ed. Jose F. Lacaba (Quezon City: ASEAN Committee on Culture and Information, 2000), 165; Uambumrungjit, "Cinema in Thailand," 119–120.

32. The Cronofotógrafo used a 60mm film format that made the costs of pictures considerably more expensive compared to Lumière and Edison pictures.

33. Deocampo, *Cine*, 45–46, 66–67. The role of Spanish officer Antonio Ramos has proved somewhat controversial, with Agustin Sotto claiming, "There is no evidence that he participated in any aspect of the film business in the Philippines." Sotto, "A Brief History of Philippine Cinema," 32. Erik Barnouw had asserted that Ramos was "one of the first to buy a Lumière cinématographe," which the French firm placed on the market in March 1897, and

"inaugurated the motion picture era in the Philippines." Erik Barnouw, *Documentary: A History of the Non-fiction Film* (New York: Oxford University Press, 1974), 20. There are several reasons why Ramos might have been a silent partner, given the revolution then being waged in the Philippines and his military status.

34. Deocampo, *Cine*, 47.

35. Film numbers and French titles are taken from Jacques Rittaud-Hutinet, *Auguste et Louis Lumière: Les 1000 premiers films* [August and Louis Lumière: The 1,000 first movies] (Paris: Philippe Sers Editeur, 1990), 160, 170, 210.

36. Charles Musser, "Nationalism and the Beginnings of Cinema: The Lumière Cinématographe in the United States, 1896–1897," *Historical Journal of Film, Radio, and Television* 19, no. 2 (1999): 149–176.

37. Pham Ngoc Trung, "A Brief History of Vietnamese Films," in Hanan, *Film in South East Asia*, 59; Nguyen Van Tinh, "Vietnam," in Lacaba, *The Films of ASEAN*, 193.

38. Militaristic scenes seem to have been absent from the first Lumière screenings in India, which, like the Philippines, was the colony of a rival European power. It may have been a commercial strategy of the Lumières to neither show nor encourage sales of such films for screenings in these types of venues.

39. Nick Deocampo foregrounded the idea of glocalization for the Quezon City conference. The term, involving the ability to think globally but act locally, was popularized by Roland Robertson and others in the 1990s. See Roland Robertson, "Glocalization: Time-Space and Homogeneity-Heterogeneity," in *Global Modernities*, ed. Mike Featherstone, Scott Lash, and Roland Robertson (London: Sage, 1995), 25–44.

40. Del Mundo, *Native Resistance*, 48–52; Deocampo, *Cine*, 59, 99. Deocampo builds substantially on the number and kinds of film exhibition documented by Del Mundo.

41. Letter from Max Berol to *New York Clipper* [early January 1900], in *New York Clipper*, February 10, 1900, p. 1047.

42. "A Wonderful Exhibition," *Freedom*, May 25, 1899, p. 5. I thank Nick Deocampo for sharing this item and also for the suggestion that American entrepreneurs not in the US military may have already taken on the role of showmen in Manila.

43. Ibid.

44. D. J. Springer to *New York Clipper*, August 18, 1899, in *New York Clipper*, October 14, 1899, p. 667. Max Berol to *New York Clipper* [early January 1900], in *New York Clipper*, February 10, 1900, p. 1047.

45. D. J. Springer to *New York Clipper*, August 18, 1899, in *New York Clipper*, October 14, 1899, p. 667.

46. Ibid.

47. Advertisements, *Manila Times*, August 29, 1899, p. 6, and September 6–12, 1899, p. 6.

48. Advertisement, *Manila Times*, September 5, 1899, p. 6.

49. Advertisement, *New York Clipper*, April 22, 1899, p. 160.

50. Edison began to advertise its films "illustrating movements of our troops in the Philippine Islands" in June 1899. See *New York Clipper*, June 10, 1899, p. 297. Lubin made plenty of films related to the Spanish-American War but not of the Philippine-American War. Throughout the second half of 1899, he was focusing on making and selling fight reenactment films (see, e.g., advertisement, *New York Clipper*, August 19, 1899, p. 502).

51. Vitagraph Company, "At the Martha's Vineyard" [broadside], August 3 and 4, 1898, reproduced in Musser, *The Emergence of Cinema*, 260.

52. Max Berol to *New York Clipper* [early January 1900], in *New York Clipper*, February 10, 1900, p. 1047. The Mexican dollar was in fact the peso.

53. Ibid.

54. Ibid.

55. Ibid.

56. Deocampo, *Cine*, 99.

57. Doreen G. Fernandez, *Palabas: Essays on Philippine Theater History* (Quezon City: Ateneo de Manila University Press, 1996), provides a useful discussion of the *comedia*.

58. The question of resistance goes to the heart of the issue between Deocampo and Del Mundo. It does seem that the term "native resistance" suggests a variety of potential meanings that can create some confusion. Deocampo sees "native" as a term referring to the local or indigenous cultures (Tagalog, Cebuano, etc.) and inappropriate to apply to the elite Hispanic culture of the colonizer. However, after the defeat of Spain, Spanish could become the language not only of the old elites but of cultural nationalism. What language was a Filipino from Cebu to use when speaking to a Manileños to signal an equal, shared national identity? Spanish was certainly one option; and for this reason, the middle classes began to adopt Spanish. At the same time, Hispanic culture was not, as Deocampo emphasizes, neutral. It implied a certain class position and cultural outlook. Some Filipinos prided themselves on their ability to operate in multiple local languages. Leon Kilat, a Filipino revolutionary who fought the Spanish, operated in both Cebuano and Tagalog. The question we often asked ourselves during the Manila conference was when did English eclipse Spanish in this role? One possible answer is that it occurred in the late 1930s as American withdrawal and the Japanese threat became increasingly proximate.

59. Fernandez, *Palabas*, 97.

60. Advertisement, *El Comercio* [The trade], June 14, 1902, cited in Deocampo, *Cine*, 99–100. Walgrah might have come from Hong Kong, a British colony and nearby port with strong shipping ties to Manila.

61. Deocampo, *Cine*, 100.

62. Paul Hammond, *Marvellous Méliès* [The marvelous Méliès] (New York: St. Martin's, 1975), 137–138.

63. Georges Sadoul, *Histoire du cinema* [History of cinema], vol. 2, *Les pionniers du cinema* [Pioneers of cinema], *1897–1909* (Paris: Editions Denoël, 1948), 183, 186.

64. Arthur Stanley Riggs, *The Filipino Drama, 1905* (Manila: Intramuros Administration, 1981), 30. Evidence suggests that this program was from the Lenten period of 1904.

65. Deocampo, *Cine*, 100–101.

66. Nadi Tofighian, e-mail to the author, September 19, 2005.

67. Fernandez, *Palabas*, 97–103; Vincente L. Rafael, *White Love and Other Events in Filipino History* (Quezon City: Ateneo de Manila University Press, 2000), 39–51; Riggs, *The Filipino Drama, 1905*, 40–350; Tomás C. Hernández, review of *The Filipino Drama, 1905*, by Arthur Stanley Riggs, *Journal of American Folklore* 17, no. 67 (1904): 279–285.

68. *Public Laws Annotated*, quoted in Tomas Hernandez, *The Emergence of Modern Drama in the Philippines (1898–1912)* (Honolulu: University of Hawaii Press, 1976), 82.

69. Macario Sakay, who was later executed by the Americans for his revolutionary activities, regularly performed in *comedias* in Manila and elsewhere. Reynaldo Clemeña Ileto, *Pasyon and Revolution: Popular Movements in the Philippines, 1840–1910* (Quezon City: Ateneo de Manila University Press, 1979), 214–215.

70. For examples of live performances in Spanish and Tagalog, see Deocampo, *Cine*, 131–132. Today it is quite common for Filipinos to move back and forth between English and Tagalog or English and Cebuano

71. In contrast to Deocampo, who suggests that the mounting of Spanish zarzuelas "contributed to the delay of the ascendancy of films" (*Cine*, 128, 147), I argue that these live performances played a positive, indeed crucial role. The cinemas may well not have survived without

them. Nor should we assume that the theaters were closed when they were not advertising in *El Comercio*, though certainly it appears that live acts merited the additional expense of newspaper promotion. At least in the United States, small movie theaters often advertised irregularly (or not at all). With so many movie houses and limited supply, live performances may have provided a crucial diversity of programming that kept up attendance and kept the cinemas operating. Also, they helped create the multifaceted cultural mix that was the basis of their popularity.

72. Panivong Norindr, "Vietnam," in *Encyclopedia of Early Cinema*, ed. Richard Abel (London: Routledge, 2005), 678.

73. *Cable News American*, June 12 and 13, 1909.

74. Sotto, "Philippines," 33. Sotto's assessment of the pre-1909 period is even more negative than Deocampo's. Sotto remarks that "except for a brief period in 1905, the shows were too few and far between." Ibid.

75. Thompson, *Exporting Entertainment*.

76. Charles Musser and Hiroshi Komatsu, "Benshi Search," *Wide Angle* 9, no. 2 (1987): 72–90.

77. Deocampo has identified a number of Pathé actuality films that were made in the Philippines around 1909–1911, including *Recolte et preparation des noix de coco aux Philippines* (Gathering and preparing coconuts in the Philippines, 1911). Nick Deocampo, *Film: American Influences on Philippine Cinema* (Mandaluyong: Anvil, 2011), 136.

78. Ideal Theater advertisement, *Manila Times*, December 6, 1911, p. 10. *The Maid of Argos* was released in the United States on December 23, 1911. See "Calendar of Licensed Releases," *Moving Picture World*, December 23, 1911, p. 996.

79. Advertisement, *Manila Times*, December 12, 1912, p. 3.

80. "Custer's Fight Stirs Audience," *Manila Times*, December 13, 1912, p. 8.

81. Thompson, *Exporting Entertainment*, 45.

82. Sotto, "Philippines," 34; Deocampo, *Cine*, 82–83. These cameras may have also been used to film intertitles in multiple languages.

83. Nadi Tofighian has located newspaper documentation indicating that at least one Filipino-operated cinema in Manila was involved in the production and exhibition of local actuality films in 1904–1905. Nadi Tofighian, *Blurring the Colonial Binary Turn-of-the-Century Transnational Entertainment in Southeast Asia* (Stockholm: Stockholm University Library, 2013), 211–212. For instance, the Cinematografo Walgraph, under the management of M. E. Quintaro, was showing a film of the Taft Committee in late 1905. "En el cinematografo insular" [In the island cinematograph], *El Tiempo* [Time], December 4, 1905, p. 3.

84. Deocampo, *Cine*, 83.

85. His parents were Jewish: his father from Germany, his mother from Hungary. Maria Salomé (Gross) Coke, telephone conversation with the author, November 4, 2006.

86. For more on the role of coconuts in Laguna, see "Cocoanut King in La Laguana," *Manila Times*, September 26, 1912, p. 5.

87. Advertisements, *Manila Times*, December 7, 1911, p. 10; and September 7, 1912, p. 7.

88. Coke, telephone conversation with the author.

89. "Rizal's Death Will Be Shown," *Manila Times*, August 22, 1912, p. 23.

90. Sotto gives the title of the Brown-Gross-Molina film as *The Life of Rizal*, but this is not a title ever assigned to the film in the *Manila Times*. Sotto also suggests that the film opened one day after the Yearsley film, though it did not open until August 22, two days later. See Sotto, "Philippines," 34.

91. Austin Craig, *The Story of José Rizal: The Greatest Man of the Brown Race* (Manila: Philippine Education, 1909); Austin Craig, *Lineage, Life and Labors of José Rizal, Philippine Patriot* (Manila: Philippine Education, 1913), 13.

92. "If Rizal Had Lived," *Manila Times*, December 30, 1911, p. 4.

93. These two sections are among the twenty-two delineated in an advertisement for the film. See Advertisement, *Manila Times*, August 22, 1912, p. 10.

94. "Rizal's Death Will Be Shown," 23.

95. "Rizal Killed at Cementerio" and "Rizal's Death Will Be Shown," *Manila Times*, August 22, 1912, p. 3.

96. Advertisement, *Manila Times*, August 22, 1912, p. 3; See also Sotto, "Philippines," 34; Del Mundo, *Native Resistance*, 57; Deocampo, *Cine*, 82; and "The Moving Picture," *American Cablenews*, August 25, 1912, 6.

97. Advertisement, *Manila Times*, September 5, 1912, p. 10.

98. Sotto, "Philippines," 34.

99. Paul A. Kramer, *The Blood of Government: Race, Empire, the United States and the Philippines* (Chapel Hill: University of North Carolina Press, 2006), 344–363.

100. Advertisement, *Manila Times*, October 24, 1912, p. 12.

101. "Put Ban on Immoral Films," *Manila Times*, November 15, 1912, p. 5; "Censors Forbid Film Display," *Manila Times*, November 19, 1912, p. 1.

102. "Censors Forbid Film Display," 1.

103. Advertisement, *Manila Times*, November 14, 1912, p. 10.

104. Sotto, "Philippines," 35.

105. Deocampo, *Cine*, 240.

106. Coke, telephone conversation with the author.

107. See, for instance, Alison McMahan, *Alice Guy Blaché: Lost Visionary of the Cinema* (New York: Continuum, 2002); and Jane Gaines, Radha Vatsal, and Monica Dall'Asta, eds., *Women Film Pioneers Project* (New York: Columbia University Libraries, 2013), https://wfpp .cdrs.columbia.edu.

108. Clyde Taylor, "Black Silence and the Politics of Representation," in *Oscar Micheaux and His Circle: African American Filmmaking and Race Cinema of the Silent Era*, ed. Pearl Bowser, Jane Gaines, and Charles Musser (Bloomington: Indiana University Press, 2001), 3–10.

109. Nick Deocampo, e-mail to the author, July 17, 2006. This request recalls the title of a popular textbook edited by David Joel Steinberg: *In Search of Southeast Asia: A Modern History*, rev. ed. (1971; repr., Honolulu: University of Hawaii Press, 1987).

110. Tofighian, "The Role of Jose Nepomuceno in the Philippine Society," 3.

3 Film's Initial Reception in China during Its Period of Infancy

Ritsu Yamamoto

WHEN FILMS WERE first introduced in China, when, where, and to whom were they shown? Before the Spaniard Antonio Ramos built the first movie theater in Shanghai,[1] which was called Hongkou Huodong Yingxi Yuan, films were mostly screened at tea gardens and amusement parks like Xu Yuan.[2] This is confirmed by advertisements in newspapers such as *Shen Bao* (Shanghai news).[3] However, there is still much information about film screenings of the early period that remains unknown.

A large number of films and materials from the silent film era were lost during the three defining periods in modern Chinese history: the Sino-Japanese War (1937–1949), the formation of the People's Republic of China (1949), and the Cultural Revolution (1966–1976). During those times, many of the films and the materials about them were lost, leaving behind only a few historical data to prove whether the established theory that the first film screening in China happened on August 11, 1896, is indeed fact.

Until now, everything narrated about Chinese film history up to the 1920s has been based on the 1963 book *Zhongguo Dianying Fazhan Shi* (History of the development of cinema in China), edited by Jihua Chen. It was the first comprehensive history of films made in the People's Republic of China. The government criticized the book because it did not follow the policy of the central government. However, after the Cultural Revolution, it was reevaluated and then reprinted in 1981.[4] Up to the present, it is recognized as the fundamental source of the history of films made in China.

According to *Zhongguo Dianying Fazhan Shi*, films at the time were referred to as *Xiyang Yingxi* and were shown for the first time in Chinese film history at Xu Yuan in Shanghai on August 11, 1896. This became the accepted theory that has been used by scholars to establish the beginning of motion pictures in China. However, there are a few film researchers who have raised objections to this date. I have discovered documents revealing facts different from the ones presented in Chen's book. Using newly discovered materials, I can now claim that the films were shown in China for the first time on May 22, 1897, at the Astor House Hotel.

To prove my claim, I have identified two Chinese researchers who investigated the dates when films were first shown in China. Hongshi Lu found that films were first shown on August 2, 1896, whereas Dequan Huang found that films were first shown in May 1897 but did not specify the date.[5]

Huang wrote that the *Xiyang Yingxi* shown on June 30 and August 11, 1896, were slides. On the basis of advertisements printed in *Xinwen Bao* on June 2–4 and June 8–13, 1897,[6] Huang surmised that the film first shown in China in May 1897 at the Astor House Hotel could have been for a non-Chinese audience and that the first time a film was shown to Chinese people was at Zhang Yuan on June 4, 1897. Furthermore, from the advertisements printed in the *North-China Herald* dated May 28, 1897, Law Kar and Frank Bren concluded that films were first shown in China on May 22, 1897, at Astor Hall (in the Astor House Hotel) in Shanghai.[7]

Other sources that document my claim are the influential Chinese newspapers *Shen Bao* and *Xinwen Bao*; a typical city paper, the *Youxi Bao*; and the English-language newspaper *North-China Daily News*.[8] *Xinwen Bao*'s column related to movie viewing, "Yingxi Qiguan," and articles in the *North-China Daily News* have never been mentioned in previous research into Chinese film history.

First, I discuss the first day that a movie screening took place in China. Second, I focus on the composition of the audience for movie screenings at the time. Third, I examine the background of the first film screening.

The First Film Screening in China

Previously, the date on which the first film screening took place in China was believed to be August 11, 1896. The evidence for this are advertisements in *Shen Bao* on August 10, 1896, and in *Xinwen Bao* on August 11 that report that *Xiyang Yingxi* was shown. The advertisements read as follows:

> Wenfu tunes still being performed on evening of the 3rd
> Western shadow plays and improvised dramas
> Guaranteed to produce exotic electric light and fiery flames.
> "Qin Huai Showboat"
> "Flooding of the Golden Mountain"
> "Battle of the Toads"
> "Fiery Word Silver Flower"
> "Prosperity in the Jade Hall"
> "Legendary Fish transforms into Dragon"
> "Nezha in Battle"
> "Five colors Ripples"
> During Double Seventh Festival on the 7th, there will be a display of old curiosity artifacts and exotic flowers, with songs for your enjoyment.
> Admission is 20 cents each.[9]

Starting from the 20th from evening till midnight, this Garden will provide performance of Wenfu small tunes, children improvised dramas, French western shadow plays for the random enjoyment of our patrons. In the past, the uneven roads near the areas of the Old Gate and North Bridge that obstructed the entrance to the Garden have been smoothed, carriages can now drive right up to the entrance of the Garden. Whether you take a leisurely stroll to visit, or come with your horse, you are most welcomed. As usual on the night of the 23rd along the banks of River Huai, there will be fireworks displays. Admission is 30 cents each.[10]

According to these advertisements, we can see that on August 11, *Xiyang Yingxi* was shown. However, some advertisements show that *Xiyang Yingxi* had been shown prior to August 11, such as those on June 30 and August 2 in *Shen Bao* and *Xinwen Bao*. One can see that on all three days, *Xiyang Yingxi* was shown to visitors along with other performances, and they all happened before August 11. It is possible to deduce from these advertisements that the spectacle called *Xiyang Yingxi* was first shown on June 30, 1896. However, there is a problem regarding whether *Xiyang Yingxi* refers to films or not. In China, there have always been shadow plays called *Yingxi*. The name *Xiyang Yingxi* was used to differentiate itself from shadow plays. Thus, *Xiyang Yingxi* may not refer to films but probably refers to slides. It will take knowing exactly what was shown under the name *Xiyang Yingxi* to determine the date of the first film shown in China.

Huang's article mentioned that *Xiyang Yingxi* were indeed slides, for these reasons. First, if *Xiyang Yingxi* were indeed what was later known as the *Jiqi Dianguang Yingxi* (films), the newspapers would surely have had a strong reaction, since they were new. However, both in *Shen Bao* and *Xinwen Bao*, no clear descriptions were given in the advertisements about *Xiyang Yingxi*, and no audience has written anything about the screenings. Second, the advertisements for both *Xiyang Yingxi* and the *Jiqi Dianguang Yingxi* appeared in the newspapers on the same day, which suggests the possibility that they were completely different from each other. Third, from July 1898 onward, a string of articles—"Meiguo Xindao Huodong Dianguangxi," "Liusheng Dianguangxi," "Faguo Huodong Yingxi," and "Ying Fa Xingdong Yingxi"—began to appear in advertisements printed for Xu Yuan.

From Huang's article, it is difficult to conclude that *Xiyang Yingxi* were slides. The terms used to refer to films or slides in newspaper advertisements at the time were not the same. Following are a few examples of words found in advertisements for Xu Yuan in the nineteenth century, which could refer to films or slides. These can be read from microfilms of articles in *Youxi Bao* found at the Shanghai Library.

- *dianguang yingxi* (February 18–19, 1899; March 20–29, 1899; August 23, 1899)

- *xingdong yingxi* (September 24–October 1, 1898; July 25, 1899; August 2, 1899)
- *dianguang xingdong yingxi* (August 4–5, 1899; August 11, 1899)
- *huodong yingxi* (February 11, 1900; October 23, 1900)
- *dianqi yingxi* (August 12, 1899)
- *dianguang jiqi dayingxi* (September 2, 1899)
- *ying fa yingxi* (June 11, 1899; July 8, 1899)[11]

There is obviously not a unified vocabulary in the use of words referring to slides or films; thus, it is difficult to judge from these advertisements which word refers to which medium. It is also difficult to determine whether *Xiyang Yingxi* refers to a film just by looking at the advertisements.

However, I have discovered another advertisement in the *North-China Daily News* dated May 22, 1897, which clearly showed that the first actual film screenings took place on that date. Research into the history of Chinese cinema up until now has not mentioned this advertisement, but having read through articles and advertisements in the *North-China Daily News* starting from January 1, 1896 (looking at dates following the December 28, 1895, public screening of the Lumière films in Paris, reputed to be the "birth" of cinema) confirms that this article is the first to be printed about films in China. The advertisement reads:

THE ANIMATOSCOPE
GRAND OPENING NIGHT! TO-NIGHT
THE ANIMATOSCOPE will be opened to the public on SATURDAY EVE-NING the 22nd instant, at the ASTOR HALL. THE WONDER OF THE 20th CENTURY THE RAGE OF LONDON, PARIS, NEW YORK, SYDNEY, ETC. *EDISON'S Latest Marvel. FOR THE FIRST TIME IN CHINA.*
The Animatoscope reproduces scenes of everyday life with the exactest fidelity and it is difficult to realize that the incidents represented are not actually taking place.
ONE CAN SEE
The waves breaking on the beach. A church parade of British Soldiers. Serpentine dancing. The Czar in Paris. Bicyclists in Hyde Park, Gondolas Gliding in Venice, and many other wonders.
The Band will also be in attendance
Doors open at 8.30 P.M.
Exhibition commences at 9 o'clock.
Price of Admission......$1.00
Reserved Seats......$1.50
Tickets may be obtained from W. Brewer & Co. or at the Door.
HARRY WELLBY-COOK
Sole Manager
Shanghai, 22nd May, 1897[12]

This advertisement announced that the Animatoscope will be on show by Harry Wellby-Cook on May 22, a Saturday night, at Astor Hall, located inside the Astor House Hotel built by the British in 1846. It was originally called Richard's Hotel but was renamed in 1860. The Chinese name was Licha Yuguan but is now the Pujiang Fandian.

After the May 22 screening, a special feature article about the screening in the *North-China Daily News* dated May 24 and 27 was published. The article dated May 24 is reproduced here.

> In the Astor Hall on *Saturday night residents* were afforded *the first opportunity in Shanghai* of witnessing the demonstration of the wonderful machine which under a variety of names has become so popular at home. *The Animatoscope as it is called in the present instance is a marvelous advance upon the familiar optical lantern inasmuch by the extremely rapid reproduction of photographs taken at a high rate of speed*, the eye is deceived so surprisingly that the life of bustling thoroughfares at home, the arrival of a railway train, and the picturesque [view] of the turbulent sea, are presented to us with a fidelity that is little short of marvelous. But this high praise must not be taken to mean that the machine—at least the one now being shown in Shanghai—is mechanically perfect. The chief defect is the presence of a certain amount of vibration, but whilst there is room for improvement in this respect, the correctness and vividness of the pictures were so marked that again and again the spectators burst into hearty applause, and were gratified with repetitions. Altogether some twenty pictures were projected upon the screen, besides a number of pleasing *lantern slides*. All were very good, but special notice was won by those representing the arrival of a train, the Czar's procession in Paris, workmen leaving Portsmouth Dockyard, King's Road, Brighton, conjuring, sea-bathing, and the vanishing lady trick.[13]

In this article, it is clear that "Saturday night" refers to May 22, 1897, and "the first opportunity in Shanghai" could mean that the Animatoscope was shown in Shanghai for the first time on this day. With the focus now on the Animatoscope, one begins to wonder what the Animatoscope is. The article states that the Animatoscope was a "marvelous advance upon the familiar optical lantern" due to "the extremely rapid reproduction of photographs" that were taken at high speed. (It is significant to know that near the end of the nineteenth century in London, an optical instrument maker called J. Ottway and Son used to make film projectors called Animatoscopes.)[14] One can infer that the Animatoscope was definitely a film projector used to show moving pictures. Also, one can see that the Animatoscope was mainly shown to the hotel guests, as the article commented that the "residents" got to enjoy the Animatoscope. Since it merited a special feature article, one can infer that the showing of the Animatoscope was big news in China at the time. In short, the article suggests a convincing possibility that a moving picture was first shown in China on May 22, 1897, at the Astor

House Hotel, and its first audiences were foreign guests. Even more interesting is an article in the *North-China Daily News* dated May 27, 1897, which has not been cited in previous accounts.

> ANIMATOSCOPE at the Astor Hall, 9.00 p.m.
> THE ANIMATOSCOPE
> Another exhibition of the Animatoscope was given at the Astor Hall on Tuesday evening. The same views were exhibited as on the previous occasion, but in a different order. The fidelity to life of the pictures is really marvelous and it is hard to realize that the figures shown are not endowed with life. Especially good is the series "Rough Sea Waves." One can almost imagine that the sound of the breakers can be heard. "Workman leaving Portsmouth Dockyard" and "Sailors of H. M. S. Excellent" are also exceedingly good. Another exhibition, at which some new pictures will be shown, will be given in the Astor Hall this evening.[15]

The details of the films shown by the Animatoscope on May 22, 1897, can now be determined. The article also mentioned that five days later, on May 27, another film was shown, which further leads one to infer that what was shown on May 22 was indeed a film and the first movie to be shown in China. In an article from the *North-China Daily News* on September 10, 1897, we find that this film screening was very successful. (After Wellby-Cook's film screening, Johnson and Charvet's screening for foreigners followed in Shanghai on September 8, 15, and 18.) This article is reproduced here.

> There was a very full house on Wednesday night when Messrs. Johnson and Charvet gave their first exhibition of the Cinematograph, all parts of the house being crowded, and the entertainment gave, in some measure, great satisfaction. This was, no doubt, principally due to its comparative novelty in Shanghai, for previously this modern and clever adaptation of photography has only had one exhibit. And the Lyceum was probably crowded on Wednesday because *Messrs. Johnson and Charvet promised that in their exhibition the vibration so noticeable and trying to the eyes at Mr. Wellby-Cook's entertainments would be entirely eliminated, but this, unfortunately, was not the case.* The program contained twenty views, amongst which were some recent and very excellent ones of the jubilee procession in London, that were received with most enthusiastic applause by the audience, which culminated when the last picture thrown on the screen showed the Queen's carriage passing in the procession, so that before it had faded from view the audience rose and broke out with the English national anthem. This was the most striking incident of the evening, and went far to compensate for defects in the exhibition that had been too apparent during the course of completing the program, while some of the plates were new and good, many were somewhat worn-out and defective, and the vibration was too plainly and disagreeably in evidence. Some of the comic views that were shown pleased the audience immensely, amongst which may

be particularized the "Love Scene, Columbine and Clown," the "Nurse Maid," the "Lightning Artist," "The Haunted Castle," and "A Troubled Dream." The cleverest in design of these was the "Lightning Artist," who drew a very good likeness of Thiers by a few bold lines, but owing to want of proper adjustment the name of the French statesman was written backwards: so also the troops in the procession carried their awards in their left hand. The great drawback to the entertainment was the difficulty in focusing the pictures on the screen, the delay in many instances being very tedious and if the proprietors intend to give further exhibition of the Cinematograph they should practice manipulation of the plates, so as the moving views. Would it not be possible, by means of curtain at the back of the screen, to arrange the proper focusing out of view of the audience, and even to throw the picture on the screen as it commences to move? It is so done in London, where the pictures are never shown in a stationary condition even for a moment. But if want of experience on the part of the exhibitions would excuse the delays that took place, nothing can excuse the gross mismanagement that was shown as regards the seating arrangements. Many people booked reserved seats well in advance, only to find that they could not obtain those seats when they arrived at the theatre. A paper ticket without a pass check was made to do duty for several seats, and as this had to be given up at the door the owners had no means of proving their right to the seats they had booked. And which they were occupied by others, so had to content themselves with such seats as were vacant. The custom of booking and reserving seats at the Lyceum is well understood here, and if the most ordinary care had been exercised no difficulty whatever would have occurred.[16]

When did the Chinese people first see a film? I have obtained materials that are an important key to answering this question.

The First Account of a Movie Viewing Written by a Chinese

Until now, the first written account about movie viewing by a Chinese was "Guan Meiguo Yingxi Ji," printed in *Youxi Bao* on September 5, 1897. However, while looking through articles from 1896 onward in *Xinwen Bao*, *Shen Bao*, and *Youxi Bao*, I discovered that an earlier article, "Yingxi Qiguan," was published in *Xinwen Bao* on June 6, 1897. Furthermore, as Huang has pointed out, we can confirm that a detailed account of movie viewing, "Weichun Yuan Guan Yingxi Ji," was printed in *Xinwen Bao* on June 11 and 13, 1897.

Clarification needs to be made concerning some of the names in the article. What Huang refers to as "Weichun Yuan," the place where the screening was held, was officially Zhang Shi Weichun Yuan, and it was commonly known as Zhang Yuan. According to Xiong Yuezhi, Zhang Yuan was a mansion with a garden, built by the British between 1872 and 1876. Shuhe Zhang then became the owner of the residence in 1882 and named it Zhang Shi Weichun Yuan. In 1893, Shuhe Zhang constructed a Western-style building, named An Kai Di, within the compound of the residence . It was a two-story building and could accommodate up to a thousand people. Zhang Yuan was formally opened to the public in the spring of 1885. Admission was at first free. However, from January 1886, a fee of one *jiao* per person had to be paid for admission into the compound. Then no admission was charged beginning in 1893. From its opening in 1885 and over the next twenty years, Zhang Yuan became well known as Shanghai's largest public space.[17]

The article "Yingxi Qiguan," printed in *Xinwen Bao* on June 6, 1897, contained the following item, an article that has never before been mentioned by any film historian: "On the day of the Boy's Festival, a rare Western film was shown at the Weichun Yuan. The film was brought by a Western friend. At 10 o'clock, Western and Chinese gentlemen, together with the ladies, gather together at the An Kai Di."[18] Boy's Festival falls on May 10, using the old calendar of the Da Qing Guangxu era, which was June 4, 1897, in the modern calendar. An advertisement titled "ANIMATOSCOPE at Chang Su-Ho's Garden, 9.00 p.m." announcing the film screening at Zhang Yuan was printed in the column "To-Day's Doing" in the *North-China Daily News* on June 4, 8, 9, and 10, 1897. "Chang Su-Ho's Garden" refers to the garden owned by Shuhe Zhang, which was commonly known as Zhang Yuan. From this notice and the "Yingxi Qiguan" mentioned earlier, we can see that the film screening at Zhang Yuan on June 4, 1897, was shown to both Chinese and Western viewers.

The following passage is from "Weichun Yuan Guan Yingxi Ji," printed in *Xinwen Bao* on June 11, 1897:

> According to *Ferris*, a friend from the West, the newly arrived Dianji Yingxi was like a work of God. *A few days earlier at the screening at the Astor House Hotel*, it was praised by all the Westerners. In the upcoming holidays at An Kai Di of the Zhang Yuan, a screening will also take place.[19]

From this account, it is clear that after the first screening at the Astor House Hotel, the screening at An Kai Di of the Zhang Yuan followed immediately, and the films shown were exactly the same as the ones shown at the Astor House Hotel. The newspaper articles "Yingxi Qiguan" and "Weichun Yuan Guan Yingxi Ji" recorded the place of screening as An Kai Di. Also, as mentioned in Huang's article, audiences numbered about a few hundred. From this, we can form a picture of the scale of the screenings that took place at Zhang Yuan. Furthermore, "Yingxi Qiguan" notes, "Tonight, too, a different film will be shown at this place. Isn't it an outing to be enjoyed, to participate in this film screening?" Given that a film was first shown in China at the Astor House Hotel on May 22, 1897, and that a similar film was first shown to the Chinese people at Zhang Yuan on June 4, one can infer that later on June 6 a different movie was shown. The screenings at Zhang Yuan could have possibly been the first chance for the Chinese people to view films after the initial hotel screenings. Additionally, in Shanghai, Johnson showed films for a Chinese audience at Tianhua Chayuan (July 26, 1897, until August 27, 1897) and in Qi Yuan (August 14, 1897, to September 12, 1897).[20]

Background to the Movie Screening at Zhang Yuan

What is the background for the first film screening at Zhang Yuan for an audience of Chinese and Western people? Shuhe Zhang, owner of Zhang Yuan, was the biggest investor in *Xinwen Bao* when it was first published. Furthermore, Ferris, mentioned as "a friend from the West" in the June 11, 1897, article "Weichun Yuan Guan Yingxi Ji," was president of *Xinwen Bao* when it started operation. Advertisements for the movie screening at Zhang Yuan were always first printed in this paper, and a special feature article was printed about the screening, which demonstrated the social relationship between the entertainment venue owner and the publisher. The special feature article was never printed in the other newspaper, *Shen Bao*.

Xinwen Bao was first published in 1893. Unlike *Shen Bao*, which was first published in 1872, it initially experienced difficulties attracting advertisements for performances such as plays. This account of the situation was written by Ma Guangren, chief editor of *Shanghai Xinwen Shi*.

> Ferris also had his mind on the field of advertising. At the time, the advertisements for the screening schedule of the various theaters in Shanghai were printed only in the *Shen Bao*. The owners of the various theaters were also willing to spend only a small sum on advertisements. After *Zilin Hu Bao* was first published, money spent on advertisements became nonexistent. When *Xinwen Bao* was first published, Ferris "sent people to every theater to copy down the programs every day and printed them in the newspapers. Owners of the theaters refused and tried to keep the programs a secret. Ferris was furious about this. He asked the typesetter to make up programs anyway and put them in the newspapers every day, confusing the people visiting the theaters. The various theaters, fearing the doings of Ferris, pleaded for him to stop. After they had written down the programs of their theaters, they sent them to Ferris and also started to pay their advertising fees shortly after. Before long, to attract the attention of the people, not only advertisements giving details of the programs were being printed, but special advertisements were also being printed, for example, when a famous actor came to Shanghai to perform a new play." The behavior of Ferris, which could certainly be called an act of intimidation, showed that adventurers of the early times would resort to any means possible when they wanted to have their news published.[21]

Even if this passage is not entirely true, one can tell how much effort was being put into advertisements at the time by *Xinwen Bao* and its president. When the first film program, which was shown to foreigners at the Astor House Hotel in

May 22, 1897, was shown immediately to the Chinese people at Zhang Yuan on June 4, 1897, *Xinwen Bao* printed a notice about the event.

Based on the *North-China Daily News* on August 3, we can see Wellby-Cook selling his Animatoscope. And from the *North-China Daily News and North-China Herald*, after August 14, 1897, we cannot confirm Wellby-Cook's film screening in Shanghai. However, many foreigners were involved in the first film screening in China, including the owner of the Astor House Hotel and Ferris, president of *Xinwen Bao*. Considering the events leading to the screening of films to native audiences, interpersonal relations in Shanghai between foreigners and natives were close and played an important role. Through such relations, Chinese people slowly began to play a big part in the motion picture business in China.

Conclusion

The history of Chinese cinema written by Chen Jihua in *Zhongguo Dianying Fazhan Shi*, became the established theory of this history, especially before the 1920s, and has never been reexamined until now, mainly because many resources on the silent movies made in China have been lost. Furthermore, *Zhongguo Dianying Fazhan Shi* was the first book in the People's Republic of China to be written comprehensively on the history of Chinese cinema.

The year 2005 was assumed by many to be the one hundredth anniversary of the day films were first made in China by the Chinese people. Although many researchers have tried to reexamine the date that the first film was *made*, there has been no reexamination of the date when a movie was first *shown* in China. Newspaper articles at the time reveal that the date was not August 11, 1896, but rather May 22, 1897. Film was first shown mainly to foreigners who were guests at the Astor House Hotel. A film screening was then held for both Westerners and Chinese people at Zhang Yuan on June 4, 1897.

That Shanghai was a concession where Western colonial powers gathered to do business also played a part in the first film screening in China, making Shanghai the place where motion pictures would most likely be introduced. However, until now, even though we know that Westerners in Shanghai were the first to introduce films in China and that Shuhe Zhang in cohort with Western businessmen strongly influenced screenings at the time, these accounts of film's early beginnings have been historically overlooked.

RITSU YAMAMOTO is a doctoral student studying film arts and cultural studies of contemporary China at the Graduate School of Letters, Arts and Sciences at Waseda University, Japan. She works as a research assistant for the Global COE Program at the Tsubouchi Memorial Theatre Museum at the same university.

Notes

This chapter was informed by trips to Shanghai December 20–26, 2008, and February 8–17, 2009. The trips were made under a research grant from the Chinese Project in the Film Arts course of the Global COE Program offered by the Tsubouchi Memorial Theatre Museum of Waseda University.

1. According to Nick Deocampo, Antonio Ramos was in Manila before he left for Shanghai and started the movie industry there. See Nick Deocampo, *Cine: Spanish Influences on Early Cinema in the Philippines* (Manila: National Commission for Culture and the Arts, 2003).

2. Xu Yuan was built by Xu Hongkui as a mansion with a Chinese-style garden in 1883 at Zhabei Tangjia Nong (present-day Fujian Lu). Not long after, it was opened to the public. The beautiful seasonal views and the events held in the park made it a famous public space in Shanghai. According to an article printed in the *Xinwen Bao* on February 20, 1896, visitors to the park were required to register their names in both Chinese and English.

3. *Shen Bao*, first published by the English merchant Ernest Major on April 30, 1872, was discontinued on May 27, 1949. From the final days of the Qing dynasty to the period of the Republic of China, it was the most influential newspaper. The newspaper included advertisements for shops and goods and for plays and movies. About thirty advertisements were printed on just half a page of the newspaper. Thus, it was normal for each of the advertisements to be very small, and not much information was printed. I researched articles such as advertisements and accounts printed in the newspapers from January 1, 1896, to December 31, 1897.

4. The two editions are the same except for a new preface in the reprint. Jihua Chen, ed., *Zhongguo Dianying Fazhan Shi* (Beijing: Zhongguo Dianying Chubanshe, 1963).

5. Hongshi Lu, *Zhongguo Dianying Shi 1905–1949* (Beijing: Wenhua Yishu Chubanshe, 2005); Dequan Huang, "Dianying Chudao Shanghai Kao," *Dianying Yishu*, no. 314 (2007): 102–109.

6. *Xinwen Bao* was first published on February 17, 1893, and contained many advertisements. The chairman of the board of directors was the Englishman A. W. Danforth. Another Englishman, F. F. Ferris, was the president. Shuhe Zhang, a Chinese merchant, was the biggest investor when it was first published. It was discontinued in the year 1949. I researched articles such as advertisements and accounts printed from January 1, 1896, to July 19, 1897.

7. Law Kar and Frank Bren, *Hong Kong Cinema: A Cross-cultural View* (Lanham, MD: Scarecrow, 2004). Law Kar (b. 1941) is a Hong Kong film historian; Frank Bren (b. 1943) is an Australian film historian, actor, playwright, and producer.

8. *Youxi Bao* was a typical city paper during the final days of the Qing dynasty. It was first published by Boyuan Li on June 24, 1897. Until it was discontinued in 1910, five thousand issues were published. It caused widespread interest and resulted in similar papers being published one after another. I researched articles such as advertisements and accounts from August 5, 1897, to January 24, 1908, which were made available for reading on microfilm at the Shanghai Library.

The Chinese name of the *North-China Daily News* was *Zilin Xi Bao*. First published on June 1, 1864, it was discontinued in 1951. When first published, articles printed in the paper were mostly about the relations between China and other countries. Other articles included information on ship schedules and commerce, along with various advertisements. I researched articles such as advertisements and accounts printed from January 1, 1896, to December 31, 1987.

9. Advertisement, *Shen Bao*, August 10, 1896 (translated by Bede Cheng).

10. Advertisement, *Xinwen Bao*, August 11, 1896 (translated by Bede Cheng).

11. These can be read on microfilms of *Youxi Bao* at the Shanghai Library.

12. Advertisement, *North-China Daily News*, May 22, 1897 (emphasis added). An advertisement about the Animatoscope was first printed on May 15, 1897, but that advertisement lacked detail.

13. "The Animatoscope," *North-China Daily News*, May 24, 1897 (emphasis added).

14. For a detailed illustration of the movie projector Animatoscope, made by J. Ottway and Son, see John Barnes, *The Beginnings of the Cinema in England* (London: David and Charles, 1976), 1:146–147.

15. "To-day's Doing," *North-China Daily News*, May 27, 1897.

16. Untitled article, *North-China Daily News*, September 10, 1897 (emphasis added).

17. Yuezhi Xiong, "Wang Qing Shanghai Siyuan Kaifang yu Gonggong Kongjian de Tuozhan," *Xueshu Yuegan* 8 (1998): 73–81.

18. "Yingxi Qiguan," *Xinwen Bao*, June 6, 1897.

19. "Weichun Yuan Guan Yingxi Ji," *Xinwen Bao*, June 11, 1897 (emphasis added).

20. See *Youxi Bao*, September 5, 1897.

21. Ma Guangren, *Shanghai Xinwen Shi (1850–1949)* (Shanghai: Fudandaxu Chubanshe, 1996), 92, quoting Hu Daojing, "Xinwen Bao Sishi Nian Shi," *Baoxue Zazhi* 1, no. 2 (1948).

4 Hong Kong's Cinematic Beginnings, 1896–1908

Wai-ming Law

When Did Cinema Enter Hong Kong?

The cinematic histories of many countries are riddled with uncertainties that need resolution. The main one is the question of when cinema began or was brought into the respective countries. Such uncertainties abound in Hong Kong. The historical orthodoxy states that in 1896, the Lumière brothers, Auguste and Louis, dispatched their operators throughout the world to show their films and, at the same time, to photograph views and scenes of the countries they visited. For a long time, it was believed that the operators visited Hong Kong. Hong Kong film historian Yu Mo-wan, in his books *Anecdotes of Hong Kong Cinema* and *Eighty Years of Hong Kong Cinema*, subscribes to this view without offering any annotation of sources. Hence, there is no way to authenticate the claim.

In June 1994, someone at the Hong Kong Film Archive wrote to the National Film Center in France to ask about the Hong Kong films shot by the Lumière operators. Michelle Aubert at the center replied, "I must tell you that the Lumiere operators never went to China at all, only Indochina and Cambodia."

There is no reason to suppose that the Lumières did not send their operators to China, but there are no literary sources, including Georges Sadoul's *History of World Cinema*, to suggest that they ever did.[1] Sadoul's *Louis Lumière* stated that the brothers sent their operators to various Asian countries between 1896 and 1901, and the book lists a filmography of films shot in Asia.[2] There is no listing of films shot in China or Hong Kong.

However, these early Lumière films, shot on five continents, were recently included in a documentary made by French filmmaker Jean Chapot.[3] There were indeed scenes of Beijing, but Chapot cannot ascertain that these scenes were shot in 1896. Taiwanese critic Daw-Ming Lee has voiced the same doubts that Lumière's operators ever went to China in 1896.[4] Lee writes that one of the operators, Maurice Sestier, exhibited the Lumière films in Bombay on August 15, 1896 (the date was in fact July 7, 1896), and then went on to Australia. On September 28, the Lumière films were shown in Sydney. Another operator, Francis Doublier, went to China, but only in 1899. Thus, more research must be done concerning the exact dates when the Lumière operators entered China.

There are scant materials to provide further authentication for Hong Kong. The only resources available of Hong Kong's early experience with cinema are old editions of the *Chinese Mail* and the English-language *China Mail*.[5] Reading through the 1896 and 1897 editions of the *Chinese Mail*, I found no record to show that there were film showings in Hong Kong at the time. The *Chinese Mail* is a thin newspaper, but it is not lacking in reports of new inventions and curiosities. In 1896, it reported an exhibition of war paintings at the Old Victoria Hotel in Central,[6] and it also reported a public exhibition of the new X-ray technology the following year. Thus, it would not have missed reporting an event such as a film showing. No such report is carried in the *Chinese Mail*, but that does not necessarily mean the event did not happen. The truth of history awaits more research.

Lumière aside, what is known for certain is that Hong Kong's earliest recorded filmmaking activities occurred in 1898, when the Thomas Edison team came to the territory to film scenes of Hong Kong. The Edison film strips, lasting four minutes in total, included scenes of Government House, the Sikh Artillery, the Hong Kong Regiment, the harbor, and street views. The two cameramen were James Henry White and Frederick Blechynden. The twelfth and nineteenth editions of the Hong Kong International Film Festival included these films in its retrospective programs. The fact that the Edison cameramen were in Hong Kong would also presuppose that they showed the Edison films in the territory. Edison's motive in sending his operators to various parts of the world was the same as that of the Lumières—to show off their inventions to the world. Unfortunately, no historical records are presently available of their film showings.

The resources currently available are recorded in Yu Mo-wan's books, where it is mentioned that in 1899, an American, MacDunn, had built a venue for film showings on the site opposite the Central Market. The film magazine *Yilin* reports that he had opened a cinema twenty years ago, situated in the old football field in Kowloon (where an ice factory then stood).[7] Apart from this, no other materials are available.

The *South China Morning Post*'s column "Old Hong Kong" (which ran between 1933 and 1935) states that the first films ever exhibited were in Central's Zetland Street and in Kowloon's YMCA site. At the time, the YMCA site was an empty lot on which a wooden makeshift theater, the Palisades, was built, which was run by an Australian named Daniels. However, in 1908—the time that this information referred to—film performances were quite abundant in Hong Kong. Therefore, the two sites reported in the *South China Morning Post* could not possibly be the first to show films in the territory.

Records of Hong Kong's Early Film Activities in the *Chinese Mail*

The most reliable documented evidence to date of the first showing of a film in Hong Kong states that on February 20, 1900, "Exotic Western Pictures" were projected at the Chungking Theatre in Central's Dai On Terrace.[8] The program was mounted after a Cantonese opera troupe, the Hang Tong Chun, had finished their performance. This event was mentioned in Yu Mo-wan's *Anecdotes of Hong Kong Cinema*, but he dates this event to February 23. However, in the *Chinese Mail* edition of February 19 an advertisement stated that the Hang Tong Chun opera troupe would be putting on a program of Western moving pictures on February 20. The opera troupe performed for seven days, each day putting on a different program with the added attraction of the "Exotic Western Pictures." There is no record of what films were shown.

Apart from the Chungking Theatre, the *Chinese Mail* advertised the Ko Sing, a theater situated on Des Voeux Road West. It alternated opera programs and film shows with the Chungking Theatre, so the two theaters did not compete with each other except on New Year days and other festival dates. At the time, there were many opera troupes in the territory, but only a handful put on "Exotic Western Pictures" in their theaters. These troupes included the Wing Tong Chun and the Pu Tong Chun. The Wing Tong Chun included film showings in their program on June 28–29, 1900, with an extra performance on July 2 at the Ko Sing theater. The Pu Tong Chun performances took place on September 22 to October 1 at the Ko Sing. Then they moved to the Chungking for performances from December 10 to 14.

Apart from this handful of opera troupes, only the Kwok Feng Nin put on film shows at the Ko Sing, on January 22, 1901. All other troupes concentrated on opera. Not until 1903 did film shows become a regular part of opera shows, a format adopted by such troupes as Chuk Shou Nin, Chuk Yiu Nin, Chow Feng Nin, and Sheung Feng Yi.[9]

The only independent operator showing movies, according to the *Chinese Mail*, was the Hei Loi Garden situated at Number 18, Hollywood Road. Yu Mo-wan writes that the Hei Loi started showing films on January 16, 1901. However, the *Chinese Mail* carried an advertisement for the Hei Loi Garden on November 5, 1900. The advertisement reads, "Magical and Exotic Shows; from 8 p.m. to 10 p.m. every evening; tickets at 25 cents, concession rates for children." The advertisement announces that the show would go on for three days, and then it would tour the towns. It is most likely that the theater never observed the three-day limit since its advertisement appeared in the *Chinese Mail* until December 27 and reappeared on January 15, 1901. The dates of the performances were "every Tuesday, Thursday and Saturday." The times were from 7:00 p.m. to 9:30 p.m. The shows lasted half an hour, and tickets cost ten cents for first class and five cents for second class with half rates for children. Each show included twenty "Western pictures."

On January, the Hei Loi Garden moved to another location near the cricket ground in Central. They advertised programs until February 8 after which no more advertisements were seen. Advertisements reappeared on February 21 but were not seen again until October 24, 1902. At that time, the theater had moved to 140 Hollywood Road.

In 1902, another theater, the Kok Sun Garden, started showing films on December 3. The theater was located in Tsimshatsui, near the Ta Lap Chi Park. The program included *The Coronation of King Edward VII* and the film views of foreign countries. Chinese and Western songs and music were played on a phonograph. Admission prices were much more expensive: a first-class ticket cost one dollar; second class cost sixty cents; and hard seats cost twenty cents. Regarding *The Coronation of King Edward VII*, the *Hong Kong Telegraph* reported that a company called 21st Century Projectscopic showed the film at City Hall on October 11 and 14, 1902 (the City Hall was then located at what is now the Hong Kong and Shanghai Bank headquarters in Central). The performance dates were close to that of the Kok Sun Garden, but it is not known whether the two different venues were organized by the same company. The Kok Sun Garden eventually moved to Hong Kong to compete with the Hei Loi Garden. On December 16, it moved to a venue near the Central Market. On December 27, a new theater opened, the New Hei Loi, making the market even more competitive. However, advertisements for the Kok Sun appeared only once and vanished from sight. The New Hei Loi resumed performances on February 7, 1903. Other theaters putting on operas also added film showings to their programs.

Films were shown only sporadically in 1902. There were no theaters putting on regular film programs. This situation changed in 1903, when film showings became a regular part of theater life in the territory. The Chungking, under new management, specialized in showing films. Under the management of the Wah Kei group, the theater showed films produced by England's Stephenson Company between January 21 and February 26. The show times were from 8:00 p.m. to 10:00 p.m. each night. It also put on film programs in other theaters after the opera performances had finished at 9:00 p.m. Advertisements appeared for the theater on December 16, 1904, when it came under the management of the Yu Kei Group. Other theaters putting on regular film shows included the Ko Sing and the Tai Ping.

Because of the lack of materials, there is no way of knowing who the responsible people were who ran the film showings or the circumstances of distribution at the same time. However, from the advertisement sections in the *Chinese Mail*, we can form a picture of some of the foreign and Chinese distributors and businessmen dealing in films. On March 8, 1904, a Chinese distributor named Yu

Fung-shun advertised in the paper canvassing for rentals of films and projection equipment. The ad also announced that he could arrange film showings in cinemas, teahouses, and private homes. Yu's company was located at a Tsimshatsui address. On April 5, this address shifted to the Ko Sing Theatre, probably because Yu programmed films for the theater. On June 25, 1908, he showed films at the Tai Ping Theatre.

In the years ahead, many film advertisements became more elaborate since they had to explain the contents of their programs to attract audiences. From these advertisements, we know that Georges Méliès's *A Trip to the Moon* (1902) was shown in Hong Kong on April 7, 1906, at the Chungking. In 1904, film advertisements appeared once every two or three days. These ads were printed by one or two theaters, which alternated their programs. By 1907, advertisements appearing on the same day were put there by two or three theaters, each with its own independent programs. All these advertisements were printed on the same page. On this evidence, 1907 was a watershed year for film in Hong Kong. That year, both the Chungking and Taiping were still active players in the local film distribution scene, which had expanded greatly to include many other theaters. It was during this period that the Bijou Theatre was established[10]—regarded by most anecdotal historians as the first theater established in Hong Kong. However, Yu Mo-wan thinks that the Bijou was renovated from the auditorium of the Wiseman Hotel, but the advertisements in the *Chinese Mail* do not denote the Wiseman Hotel auditorium as the Bijou Theatre. This advertisement first appeared on September 7, 1907. Another theater called the Hong Kong Film Show—later changed to the Hong Kong Film Theatre[11]—was situated opposite the Central Market. It started business on December 5, and it was reported that French performers were hired to perform onstage.

Another cinema located near the junction of Des Voeux Road Central and Pottinger Road was called the Victoria New Style Motion Picture. The theater's selling point was its new, advanced equipment. Its pictures, when projected, would not shake terribly. It opened for business on November 7. Yu Mo-wan in his book regards this as Hong Kong's "first real cinema."

These two cinemas, together with another specializing in American movies, took out advertisements on April 16, 1908—a sign of intense competition among the cinemas. The cinema showing American movies was run by an American and was situated at 37 Queen's Road Central. It opened on April 13, 1908. Show times were from 12:00 noon to 10:00 p.m. The cinema was equipped with phonographs for music. However, this theater did not break the record for long show times established by the Jebsen Company, which showed French films. Between December 29, 1907, and January 1, 1908, the Jebsen Company showed seven films from 11:00 a.m. until 11:00 p.m. It was the first cinema to program so many performances in one day. However, the first cinema to put on day programs was the Chungking. On April 5, 1906, it started shows at 1:00 p.m.

Apart from American, French, and English film merchants, there were the Italian Film Company and the South Seas Film Company. The former had a cinema located on Possession Street. It opened on August 19, 1907, showing films from all countries. The latter had a cinema located at Sek Tong Tsui, 496 Queen's Road West, showing films taken in the South Seas. It opened the same year on August 12. A Japanese company opened a cinema in 1905 at 14 Des Voeux Road Central, showing documentary footage of the Russo-Japanese War.

The film market was in bustling condition when Hong Kong's first film was made in 1909, thus opening the first chapter in the development of Hong Kong's film industry.

WAI-MING LAW is a writer, film critic, and film director. He is the previous chief editor of *Film Biweekly* magazine, a previous research officer at the Hong Kong Film Archive, and a former programmer of the Hong Kong International Film Festival.

Notes

This chapter was originally written as part of research undertaken for the Hong Kong Film Archive and published as Wai-ming Law, "Hong Kong's Cinematic Beginnings, 1896–1908," trans. Stephen Teo, in *Early Images of Hong Kong and China*, ed. Law Kar (Hong Kong: Urban Council, 1995), 20–26. Special thanks go to the Leisure and Cultural Services Department for allowing the reprint of this essay and also to the Urban Council of Hong Kong.

1. See Georges Sadoul, *Histoire générale du cinéma*, 6 vols. (Paris: Denoël, 1946–1975).

2. See Georges Sadoul, *Louis Lumière* (Paris: Seghers, 1964).

3. *Les annees lumière* [The Lumière years], directed by Jean Chapot (Filmanthrope, 1972).

4. Daw-Ming Lee, "How Cinema Came to China: Some Theories and Doubts," in *Early Images of Hong Kong and China*, ed. Law Kar (Hong Kong: Urban Council, 1995), 33–36.

5. The *Chinese Mail* was founded in 1864. It published its last edition on Christmas Day 1941 but was briefly revived for a short period in 1946 (from June 10 to July 1).

6. The advertisement printed in the January 18 edition of the *Chinese Mail* reads, "From the various European countries come the paintings and images of war. Viewers will be gripped by the solemn depiction of war and view the stories that emanate from hundreds of paintings, ten will be exhibited each day and alternatively changed each evening." A *Chinese Mail* reporter wrote of the exhibition, "Amazing images: the Old Victoria Hotel is exhibiting oil paintings depicting armies in war. The viewer will be transported to the battleground. Those who wish to know more should not miss the opportunity to view these paintings."

7. *Yilin* [Art land], no. 3 (1937).

8. Wong Yin-ching, *Hong Kong Anecdotes* (1958). Wong states that the Chungking Theatre was larger than the Ko Sing.

9. Wong states that a famous Cantonese opera star named Liang Tsiu-tsai returned from America with films and projectors. Apparently, the actor incorporated film images in his on-stage opera performances, the effect of which amazed the audiences. Such integration of film with real-life theater performances was known as *lianhuan xi* (chained plays), which were popular for a while. However, because there is little historical material, no further details of such plays are known. Ibid., 18.

10. It was situated at Wyndham Street, next to today's Entertainment Building.

11. Wong, *Hong Kong Anecdotes*, 18. Another Hong Kong Film Theatre was built, located at today's Queen's Theatre site. Wong does not state when the theater was built, so there is no way of knowing whether the two theaters were one and the same.

5 How Cinema Arrived and Stayed in Taiwan

Daw-Ming Lee

In 1894 TAIWAN was ceded to Japan by the Chinese Qing government after losing the First Sino-Japanese War. The Japanese army took over Taiwan the next year and, after the June 17 inauguration ceremony of the first Taiwan governor-general in Taipei, began a half century of Japanese colonial rule. Around the same time, the French Lumière brothers, Auguste and Louis, showed the first short films on their invention, the Cinematograph, such as *La sortie des usines* (Workers leaving the Lumière factory, 1895). It may be coincidence that 1895 marked both the coming of the age of cinema and the coming of the age of modernity in Taiwan under Japanese colonial rule. However, the Cinematograph, used for filming, printing, and projecting motion pictures, was not introduced to the isolated Taiwan island until 1900, later than in many other parts of the world. Why is that?

Since cinema did not arrive in Taiwan until it was ruled by the Japanese, and the arrival of cinematic apparatus in Japan did not occur until 1896, it is reasonable to deduce that the origination of early film exhibition in Taiwan came from Japan proper. The Cinematograph was brought to Japan by Katsutaro Inabata and first used in February 1897. Inabata was a schoolmate of Auguste Lumière in France and thus was able to buy a few machines to bring back to Japan one year before Lumière started to sell them to the outside world.[1] Before that, only their appointed cameramen/projectionists were allowed to travel throughout the world with the Cinematograph.[2] Inabata also purchased about fifty films from the Lumière collection before setting sail to Japan in November 1896 with François-Constant Girel, the Lumières' representative and cameraman/projectionist.

Inabata showed the Lumière films early the next February to a selected theater audience in Osaka and Kyoto. On February 15, the Cinematograph was officially introduced to the Japanese public in an Osaka theater. Inabata soon sold the Cinematograph and the Lumière library distribution rights to Einosuke Yokota. In March 1897, Yokota screened the films theatrically in Asakusa, Tokyo, in direct competition with the Tokyo opening of Thomas Edison's Vitascope, called "moving photographs" in Japan. To distinguish itself from Vitascope, Yokota called the Cinematograph "automatic magic pictures."[3]

The Lumières' Cinematograph was publicly introduced in Taiwan on June 21, 1900, at Juji-kan (Cross Theater) in Taipei. It was brought in by Putaichi Oshima, a Japanese restaurant owner and businessman living in Taipei.[4] Oshima obviously solicited help from the French Automatic Magic Pictures Association, presumably the same organization set up by Yokota when he screened Lumière films in Tokyo in 1897. On June 16, at the sneak-preview screening in Tamsui-kan, a private club for government officials, Japanese businessmen, and their families, the Cinematograph was overwhelmingly welcomed by the audience, many of whom were female. It is interesting to note that Shozo Matsuura, a projectionist sent by the French Automatic Magic Pictures Association, was so enthusiastic in commenting on the films that he was criticized by a local reporter for showing off.[5]

After the ten-day showing of films to a predominantly, if not completely, Japanese audience at Juji-kan, Oshima and Matsuura moved their exhibition to the northern part of Taipei City in quest of a mostly local Taiwanese audience. Screenings were in a makeshift public hall and said to be extremely successful and highly profitable to the partners.[6] Three months later, they traveled with a group of Japanese magicians and dancers across the Taiwan Strait to Fuchow (Fuzhou) to entertain Japanese residents living in southern China. The Lumière films won applause from Japanese council officials and the Japanese navy stationed in Amoy (Xiamen). Oshima stayed on in Amoy, renting a local foreign-operated hotel for screenings.[7] This was probably the first commercial film exhibition in the area.[8]

The Lumière's Cinematograph was not the first film system to arrive in Taiwan, however. Newspaper articles and advertisements that year indicate that Edison's Vitascope was brought to Taiwan in September 1899. *The Spanish-American War* and other titles were shown for ten days in Juji-kan.[9] It is very likely that audiences were mostly Japanese, since Taiwanese at the time did not usually visit the Japanese government and business area in central Taipei, where Juji-kan was located. Moreover, film, called "western electric shadow play," had already been introduced to local Taiwanese in Taipei a month earlier by Poqi Zhang, a Cantonese projectionist.[10] There is no information regarding his origin or the system used for those electric shadow plays.[11] The exhibition was inside a house, with four screenings daily. It must have attracted local populace from all over Taipei, because after a month, the box office dropped rapidly when Zhang moved the exhibition to Monka, a Taiwanese area in the southern part of Taipei City.[12]

It is very possible that the Vitascope used in the September 1899 Taipei screenings came from Japan. This speculation is based on circumstantial evidence, because the films were shown to a mostly Japanese audience at a theater located in the Japanese business area. Since there were at least two sources of the Vitascope system imported to Japan in 1896, it is not easy to determine the precise origin of the Vitascope system used in Taiwan. In February 1897, the Vitascope was simultaneously introduced to Japan in Osaka and Tokyo. Kazuichi Araki, an Osaka import/export merchant, purchased the Vitascope and a package of films from the Edison Company in 1896 and showed them at an Osaka theater in late February the next year. Around the same time, Saburo Arai, a Japanese gardener working in the United States, bought two Vitascopes and a dozen films from the Edison Company, hiring Daniel Grimm Krouse as projectionist and commentator for screenings.[13] The Arai screenings began in early February in Asakusa.[14]

According to Jun'ichiro Tanaka, Kōyō Komada was the only major traveling film exhibitor in Japan before 1900,[15] who used the Vitascope that Arai purchased from the Edison Company. Komada was an employee of Hiromeya, an advertising agency responsible for propagating Arai's Vitascope screenings in Tokyo and for showing films for Arai's company in Yokohama in 1897. After screenings in Yokohama, Arai sold his Vitascope business to Hiromeya. Komada decided to purchase the Vitascope from Hiromeya to start his own film exhibition business.

With twenty to thirty reels of film at hand, Komada's team, consisting of a manager, a projectionist, two commentators, three to five musicians, and an accountant, started to travel throughout Japan in 1897 and continued to do so for the next ten years. In the late nineteenth century in Japan, there was no permanent theater devoted entirely to films, which were mostly shown by traveling exhibitors who stayed at each location for about one week. Screenings were accompanied by a live band, and the films were explained to the audience by a commentator. Each screening usually lasted two to three hours, with up to thirty reels of film.[16]

Before 1903, Komada's source of prints was mainly from the Yoshizawa Company, which had established a branch office in London. Films about the Spanish-American War were among the first it purchased.[17] Because of the lack of stability in the supply of films from abroad, film exhibition in the latter days of nineteenth-century Japan became increasingly less popular in urban areas. Traveling exhibitors were thus forced to move their screenings to remote rural areas.

Although Taiwan was already under the rule of the imperial Japanese government when cinema became popular in Japan, only the most adventurous Japanese civilians would venture their lives to visit the newly acquired colony. During the first few years of colonial rule, countless revolts by the local Taiwanese populace against Japanese military forces erupted.[18] The unstable political and social situation might have deterred any bold attempt to bring expensive electricity-based film projectors to the newly acquired colony. Poor sanitary conditions in Taiwan might also have discouraged Japanese film exhibitors from traveling to Taiwan. More Japanese soldiers died from contagious diseases than on the battlefield when Japan took over Taiwan in 1895.[19] It should be noted, however, that assorted forms of traditional Japanese entertainment, such as bow-lift (*ageyumi*) and air-gun (*kukiju*) games, telling comic stories (*rakugo*) and military stories (*gundan*), and puppet shows (*gitaifu* and *joruri*), arrived in Taiwan within a year after the inauguration of the governor-general's office in Taipei.

There is a likely connection between Taipei screenings and the Japanese traveling exhibitors when cinema did arrive in Taipei's Juji-kan in September 1899, because there was at least one Spanish-American War film in the Taipei program.[20] Also, in view of the great effort Komada's team, Nihon Sossen Katsudo Shashin Kai (Pioneer Japanese Motion Pictures Association), made in May 1905 to travel all the way to Hong Kong to show films about the Russo-Japanese War,[21] it is very possible that before 1905 (possibly in 1899) the exhibitor might have already visited the empire's newly acquired Taiwan colony.

After 1900, film screenings became increasingly regular events in theaters around Taiwan. Traveling exhibitors were also showing films in both urban and rural areas throughout Taiwan, even after 1915. Until then, there were only four permanent movie theaters in Taiwan: two in Taipei and one each in the southern cities of Tainan and Takao (Kaohsiung). In comparison with other parts of the world, the cinema business developed rather slowly in the early twentieth century in Taiwan. Most film exhibition was conducted by businessmen and technicians from Japan.[22]

Huang Liao may be the first, and one of the few, Taiwanese to be involved in the film business during the first decade of the twentieth century. He went to Tokyo to learn projection skills and returned in 1903 to Miaoli, his hometown in central Taiwan, with a projector and some twenty-five titles, which included films about wars in northern China (the Eight-Nation Alliance against the Qing government) and South Africa (the Second Anglo-Boer War), as well as Japanese films, such as *Geisha no Teodori* (Geisha's hand dance, 1899), *Asakusa no Kyokugei* (Asakusa acrobatics), and *Jujutsu Shiai* (Jiu jitsu match). His film entertainment business was extended into the Taiwanese areas of Taipei in 1904.[23] To some Taiwanese elite, however, cinema was also considered a possible tool for advocating modern concepts.

In 1907, Heshou Lin, an heir of one of northern Taiwan's richest landlord families, was invited to attend the sixth Osaka Exposition. A Western family occupied the hotel room next to his. Lin was so envious of them that he began to consider ways he could use cinema to help end the Chinese custom that prohibited women from traveling with their husbands. He brought back a motion picture machine (presumably a projector) to help do so. However, Lin was not sure of the role of film education in the colonial society or whether it would be successful.[24]

The first genuine movie mogul in Taiwan was, ironically, a labor-movement activist from Japan. Toyojiro Takamatsu became famous in the late 1890s for using projected motion pictures to enhance the agitation aroused by speeches he gave while traveling throughout Japan with his fellow union organizers.[25] Such an innovative use of motion pictures soon caught the attention of Prime Minister Hirobumi Ito, who persuaded Takamatsu to hold film exhibitions in Taiwan to benefit colonial rule ("to educate the ignorant Taiwanese" in support of Japanese colonial rule), while also developing his show business career on that recently annexed island. Ito promised to support Takamatsu and told him not to worry about his socialist speeches.[26]

With the support of the central (and colonial) government, Takamatsu soon became not only owner of more than eight theaters in major cities devoted mainly to cinema screenings but also the first filmmaker in Taiwan. *Taiwan Jikkyo Shokai* (Introduction to the actual conditions in Taiwan, 1907), a two-hour-long information film accurately showing conditions in the colonial administration (with a staged scene about subjugating an aboriginal tribe), industrial development, civilian lives, and landscapes in more than one hundred locations around Taiwan, was commissioned by the governor-general's office to Takamatsu's company, Taiwan Dojinsha. It was said the film was used by the colonial government as supporting evidence before the Imperial Diet budgetary subcommittee to demonstrate the excellent results of twelve years of colonial rule.[27] Circumstantial evidence, however, suggests that the film was most likely made mainly for screenings in Taiwan Hall at the 1907 Tokyo Industrial Exposition and for the subsequent seven-month exhibition tour throughout Japan.[28]

To the Japanese colonizer, the film was proof of the modernization and progressive results of Japanese colonization in Taiwan. It also served as an introduction to mainland Japanese about the excellent outcome of the colonial government's acculturation and industrialization policies. Since early colonial rule, Japanese officials and residents had been frustrated by the misunderstandings about Taiwan, and prejudices against people from Taiwan, by mainland Japanese. A reporter listed the things about Taiwan that mainland Japanese found distasteful and feared: summer heat, rampant epidemics, dirty streets, and lack of clean drinking water.[29] To clear up such prejudices, the newspaper urged the colonial government to introduce guests from the mainland to the actual conditions in the colony, using means at its disposal, such as newspapers, magazines, and even government reports.[30] Throughout its rule in Taiwan, the colonial government used film for education and propaganda purposes.[31]

Before his return to mainland Japan in 1917, Takamatsu had made more than twenty information films for the colonial government and its affiliated organizations. To make up for his absence, the governor-general's office was forced to establish its own filmmaking unit in the Taiwan Education Society (TES), one of its affiliated organizations, and hired professional cameramen from Tokyo to take over Takamatsu's role as "communicator" for the government. TES would continue to be the most prominent producer, distributor, and exhibitor of "educational" information films in colonial Taiwan, despite competition from other private filmmaking organizations, such as the Film Unit of *Taiwan nichi nichi shinpo* (Taiwan daily news), established in 1923, that was primarily involved in making and showing newsreels and commissioned "documentaries" for various governmental departments.

By 1915, feature films screened in Taiwan theaters came mostly from Japan. Competition between the two movie houses in Taipei was fierce, which, in essence, was an extension of the competition between Nikkatsu and Tenkatsu, the two major studios in mainland Japan. Distribution deals, regardless of their country of origin and print condition, were made between Taiwan theaters and Kyushu branch offices of major Japanese studios. Such a distribution system had been established in 1908 by Toyojiro Takamatsu.[32] European and American films, especially action-adventure features from Pathé Frères, were very popular among adult male audiences, while Japanese comedy films were the favorites of female audiences. Entertainment was the main reason for working-class audiences to go to the movies. Not until sound was introduced in films did people who had social esteem in Taiwan start to attend the cinema.[33]

The first cinema study organization, Eiga Kenkyu-kai (Film Research Association) emerged in Taipei in 1926. It held monthly meetings and published a film journal, *Film Comments*. Its core members included well-known film commentators, music performers in cinemas, and government officials. Serious film magazines, such as *Movies*, *Shadow Garden*, *Southern Films*, and the *Light of Cinema*, had been published much earlier, around 1920.[34]

A film-club movement erupted on the island in 1931 with the founding of Taihoku (Taipei) Cinema League in Taipei by a group of high school, college, and university faculty and students, as well as staff from various departments in the governor-general's office.[35] Working with local film distributors and cinemas, the league held monthly screenings of quality foreign films, mostly from Hollywood and Europe, and was instrumental in promoting film art in colonial Taiwan. Membership expanded rather quickly in one year, from fifty in late 1931 to more than a thousand in late 1932. Similar film clubs were formed by cinephiles in other major cities, such as Taichu (Taichung), Kiryu (Keelung), Pingdong, Tainan, and Shinchiku (Hsinchu).[36] In 1935, an island-wide cinema study organization was formed. It held a film culture exposition and invited famous Japanese film critics Akira Iwasaki and Matsuo Kishi to hold conferences and give speeches in Taiwan.[37] Following the trend, some local branches of Zen Taiwan Eiga Kenkyu-kai (All Taiwan Film Research Association), such as the Takao (Kaohsiung) Cinema League, were formed after 1935. The film club movement lasted for seven or eight years until the outbreak of the Sino-Japanese War in 1937. Among all the local film clubs on the island, only Taihoku and Takao Cinema Leagues published their own journals. Most of the editors, writers, and members of these cinema leagues were Japanese intellectuals who loved to watch and talk about European and American quality (art) films. However, they did not become involved in any filmmaking activities.

Meanwhile, other cinephiles, led by colonial government officials, their families, and children of local wealthy families, were enthusiastically making small-gauge films (i.e., 16mm, 17.5mm, 9.5mm, 8mm), using amateur movie cameras to produce their own home movies and art films. Amateur cine clubs were set up in the 1920s for sharing experiences and showing one another's work. The first screening of the first such cine club in Taiwan, the Don Club, was held in October 1928 in Taipei.[38] By late 1929, ads selling small-gauge movie cameras, such as the Pathé Baby, started to appear in local newspapers. The fashion continued in the 1930s. Koyokai and Lumière Club were two active clubs during this period. Koyokai devoted itself to the study of Pathé 9.5mm filmmaking techniques and was the only Taiwan amateur cine club to join the All Japan Pathé Cine Association. Because of its achievements, the club was commissioned by the Taiwan Military Headquarters to make a 9.5mm documentary film, *Taiwan Special Exercises*. Among all Taiwanese amateur filmmakers in the 1930s, Nanguang Deng, a professional photographer who had developed his skills in Tokyo, was one of the most prolific, and his work won many awards in Japan.

Feature-film production in Taiwan during Japanese colonial rule was sporadic. The Taiwan colony, which had mysterious head-hunting tribes, fascinated many Japanese filmmakers, and a few features, made in a studio in Japan, exploited the subject.[39] Yet before 1941, there were only eight theatrical features made in Taiwan that were either originated by local filmmakers or were about (and shot in) Taiwan. There were also a couple of feature films made mainly for educational use. In the 1940s, during the Pacific War, two "national policy" films were initiated by the colonial government and made in association with major film studios from mainland Japan (and Manchuria).

The first feature film to be photographed on the island was *Butsuda no Hitomi* (Buddha's pupils). Edward K. Tanaka's 1924 period film was a revenge story set in Nanking, ancient China's capital. Tanaka aimed to export the six-reel "mood film" to the United States to propagate the theme of Buddha's ubiquitous love. The film was shot entirely on location in Taiwan and included several temples in Taipei and beaches on the northern coast.[40] Nevertheless, all the main actors and crew members came from mainland Japan. Some local Taiwanese, however, did get a chance to be film actors for the first time. The title was changed to *The Trail of the Gods* when Tanaka brought the film to Los Angeles in May 1925. He showed it to Douglas Fairbanks, his boss for seven years before Tanaka returned to Japan in 1920 to become the consultant (and film director) for newly established Shochiku Studios.[41]

The making of *Butsuda no Hitomi* created an obvious ripple effect. Xiyang Liu, one of the Taiwanese actors playing a bit part in the film, formed an organization the following year, Taiwan Eiga Kenkyu-kai (Taiwan Film Research Association),[42] to prepare for making the first Taiwanese feature. After soliciting support for more than a month, Liu was able to gather moral and budget support from thirty-one young men and two young women (mostly local Taiwanese). After the inauguration of the Film Research Association in mid-May, Liu started working with his cast and crew, members of the association, deciding how to turn his script into a film.[43] The film, *Whose Fault Is It?*, was shot entirely on location in and around the Taipei metropolitan area. The simple love story was shot by amateur cameraman Shu Li, who had taught himself cinematography by reading books, as well as trial-and-error practice with a Universal 35mm camera purchased by mail order from Chicago.[44] The film received quite a favorable newspaper review, which pointed out impressive acting by the leading actress and the cinematography.[45] Despite the review, the box office in theaters, which catered mostly to local Taiwanese audiences, was not very good. However, this may have been due to the film's very limited distribution.

The box-office failure led to the disintegration of Taiwan Eiga Kenkyu-kai but did not dissuade Li from continued efforts to make another feature. In 1929, Li and his partners founded Baida Productions. They made a very popular action-romance film, *Blood Stains* (1930), produced and directed by Yunhe Zhang, one of the directors of *Whose Fault Is It?* Box office during the three-day premiere equaled almost half of the production cost, establishing *Blood Stains* as the first "blockbuster" film in Taiwan history.[46] Even so, the Taiwanese film business did not progress smoothly after 1929, mainly because of the arrival of sound films. The demand for good scripts, reliable technicians, sufficient funding, and support from the government all worked against local filmmakers.[47] The influx of Chinese movies from Shanghai also helped squeeze the very few local productions out of the small domestic market.

The early years of the Showa era, between 1925 and 1937, were the first golden age of filmmaking and film exhibition in Taiwan. The Second Sino-Japanese War abruptly ended the good old days of cinema in Taiwan. From then on, until the end of the Second World War, Taiwan cinema was almost entirely in the service of Imperial Japan. Film and politics were also mixed in Taiwan after the war, until the emergence of Taiwan New Cinema in the 1980s.

DAW-MING LEE is Professor and Chair of the Department of Filmmaking at Taipei National University of the Arts, which he founded. Lee is a veteran filmmaker and a scholar who has written extensively on film history, documentary aesthetics, and film digitization, including *Historical Dictionary of Taiwan Cinema* and *Documentary: History, Aesthetics, Production, Ethics*. He has been a member of the Editorial Board for *Studies in Documentary Film* since 2007.

Notes

1. Jun'ichiro Tanaka, *Nihon Eiga Hattatsu-shi* [Developmental history of Japanese film] (Tokyo: Chuokoronsha, 1975), 1:38–39.

2. Erik Barnouw, *Documentary: A History of the Non-fiction Film*, rev. ed. (Oxford: Oxford University Press, 1983), 11.

3. Tanaka, *Nihon Eiga Hattatsu-shi*, 44–46.

4. "Denki ōyō katsudō dai shashin" [Electricity-applied big motion pictures], *Taiwan nichi nichi shinpo* [Taiwan daily news], June 21, 1900.

5. "Katsudō shashin" [Motion pictures], *Taiwan nichi nichi shinpo*, June 19, 1900.

6. "Kaiyan huandeng" [Performing shadow play], *Taiwan nichi nichi shinpo*, July 11, 1900.

7. "Amoyi no katsudō shashin" [The motion pictures of Amoy], *Taiwan nichi nichi shinpo*, December 26, 1900.

8. Xiaolei Liu, *Zhongguo Zaoqi Huwai Diqu Dianyingye de Xingcheng, 1896–1949* [The beginning of the film business in areas outside Shanghai in the early years of China, 1896–1949] (Beijing: Zhongguo Dianying Chubanshe, 2009), 20. Liu cites the noncommercial exhibitions in 1909 in Fuchow's Lianjiang County as the beginning of film exhibition in the area, much later than Oshima's activity in Amoy.

9. "Jūji kan no katsudō shashin" [The motion pictures of Juji-kan], *Taiwan nichi nichi shinpo*, September 8, 1899.

10. "Xiyang yanxi da huandeng" [Western big shadow play performance], *Taiwan nichi nichi shinpo*, August 5, 1899.

11. My speculation is that the machine might have come from Hong Kong. However, Poshek Fu, renowned American scholar on Chinese film history, suggested to me that Poqi Zhang might have been a Cantonese residing in Japan.

12. "Diandeng yingxi" [Electric lamp shadow play], *Taiwan nichi nichi shinpo*, September 5, 1899.

13. Thus, Krouse, who was born in Philadelphia, became the first film commentator (*katsuben* or *benshi*) in Japan. He was an employee of the Edison Company sent to Japan not only to help the Japanese project films but also to supervise the box office.

14. Yoshinobu Tsukada, *Nihon Eigashi no Kenkyu* [Studies of Japanese film history] (Tokyo: Gendaishokan, 1980); Jun'ichiro Tanaka, *Hiroku: Nihon no Katsudo Shashin* [Secret minutes of Japanese motion pictures] (Tokyo: Wides Shuppan, 2004).

15. Tanaka, *Nihon Eiga Hattatsu-shi*, 94–96.

16. Ibid.

17. These films about the Spanish-American War were shown in a Tokyo theater beginning on June 1, 1899. Presumably, these films were made either by the Edison Company or by American Mutoscope and Biograph Company.

18. May 30, 1902, was pronounced by Governor-General Komada as the "recovery day of public order on the island." Before then, countless revolts erupted across the island. It was estimated that more than seventy-seven hundred Taiwanese rebels were executed and eight thousand more jailed between 1897 and 1902. See Yusuke Tsurumi, *Goto Shinpei Den* [The biography of Shinpei Goto] (Tokyo: Fujiwara Books, 2005), 2:149.

19. Ming-cheng M. Lo, *Doctors within Borders: Profession, Ethnicity, and Modernity in Colonial Taiwan* (Berkeley: University of California Press, 2002). Lo points out that only 164 Japanese died in battle when Japan took over Taiwan, but 4,642 Japanese soldiers died from malaria and various contagious diseases, and an additional 26,094 contracted other diseases.

20. "Jūji kan no katsudō shashin" [The motion pictures of Juji-kan], *Taiwan nichi nichi shinpo*, September 8, 1899.

21. Shuk Ting Yau, *Honkon Nihon Eiga Koryu Shi* [Interrelations between the Japanese and Hong Kong film industries] (Tokyo: University of Tokyo Press, 2007), 9.

22. Dietrich (or Letrich), manager of a Paris film company in France, was one of the few European traveling exhibitors to come to Taiwan. He arrived in the Far East after a trip to Berlin, London, New York, Boston, and San Francisco. The exhibition route took him to Hong Kong, Macau, and Fuchow but was discontinued in Shanghai due to national mourning for the deaths of Emperor Guangxu and Empress Dowager Cixi. His film screenings in Taiwan started in Taipei in early December 1908 and lasted more than two weeks. Most of the films were from Pathé Frères. *Taiwan nichi nichi shinpo*, December 6, 1908.

23. "Katsudō shashin" [Motion pictures], *Taiwan nichi nichi shinpo*, January 7, 1904.

24. "Lin Heshou shi no naichi miyage (ka)" [Mr. Lin Heshou's souvenirs from mainland Japan (II)], *Taiwan nichi nichi shinpo*, May 18, 1907.

25. Kappei Matsumoto, *Nihon Shakai Shugi Engeki Shi: Meiji Taisho Hen* [History of Japanese socialist theater: Meiji Taisho period] (Tokyo: Chikuma Shobo, 1975), 71.

26. Ibid.

27. Sai Ichikawa, *Ajia Eiga no Sozo Oyobi Kensetsu* [Creating and developing an Asian cinema] (Tokyo: International Movie News Service, 1941), 89.

28. The following reports stated that the film would go directly to the Tokyo Exposition after screenings in Taiwan: "Katsudō shashin satsuei no shūryō" [The end of shooting motion pictures], *Taiwan nichi nichi shinpo*, April 12, 1907; "Taiwan shōkai katsudō shashin" [Motion pictures to introduce Taiwan], *Taiwan nichi nichi shinpo*, May 12, 1907; "Taiwan shōkai katsudō shashin" [Motion pictures to introduce Taiwan], *Taiwan nichi nichi shinpo*, May 21, 1907; "Tainan no takamatsu katsudō shashin" [Takamatsu's motion pictures in Tainan], *Taiwan nichi nichi shinpo*, June 4, 1907; and "Tainan zhi gaosong huodong xiezhen" [Takamatsu's motion pictures in Tainan], *Kanbun Taiwan nichi nichi shinpo* [Chinese edition of *Taiwan Daily News*], June 15, 1907.

29. Hashishika An, "Zappō: Shokan ichi ni" [Miscellaneous report: Some feelings], *Taiwan nichi nichi shinpo*, August 19, 1899.

30. Uhaku, "Naichi jinshi shōchi no kōki" [Good opportunities to invite people from mainland Japan], *Taiwan nichi nichi shinpo*, October 10, 1901.

31. The governor-general's office produced several such films, commissioned to a local production company owned by Takamatsu or made by government-affiliated organizations, in the first half of the twentieth century.

32. Daw-Ming Lee, "Taiwan Dianyingshi Diyi Zhang: 1900–1915" [Chapter one of Taiwan film history: 1900–1915], *Film Appreciation* 13, no. 1 (1995): 29–44. See also Daw-Ming Lee, "You Dianying Keneng Zi Xianggang Chuanlai Taiwan Kan Shijiu Shijimo Dianyingren Zai Taiwan Xianggang Riben Zhongguo yu Zhongnanbandao jian de Liudong" [Movement of manpower in the film exhibition business between Taiwan, Hong Kong, Japan, China, and Indochina in the late nineteenth century: Speculation that Hong Kong was the origin of cinema in Taiwan], in *Proceedings of the Conference on History of Early Chinese Cinema(s) Revisited* (Hong Kong: Hong Kong Film Archive, 2009), 126–143.

33. Daw-Ming Lee, "Taiwan Dianyingshi Diyi Zhang," 43.

34. "Eiga hyōron hakkō eiga kenkyūkai te" [Film research association publishes film comment journal], *Taiwan nichi nichi shinpo*, September 4, 1926.

35. Masao Takahashi, "Shinema Rigu to Kogyo Mondai" [Cinema League and the issue of exhibition], *Eiga Seikatsu* [Movie life] 3, no. 4 (1932): 2–8.

36. Ibid., 8.

37. "Eiga jidai no senku zen Taiwan eiga kenkyū kai naru na hen 'yumemiru kuchibiru' 'yado naki shōnen gun' kōkai eiga bunka ten o mo hiraku" [Pioneer of the film era, all Taiwan film research association was born: Open screening of famous films "Der träumende Mund" and "Wild Boys of the Road"; Thus commences film culture exposition], *Taiwan nichi nichi shinpo*, March 27, 1935.

38. "Shirōto no eiga satsuei-netsu taihoku ni umareta Don kurabu daiichikai sakuhin wa daitai seikō" [Amateur filmmaking fever: Don club was born in Taipei; Its first exhibition is generally a success], *Taiwan nichi nichi shinpo*, October 7, 1928.

39. For example, dealing with the issue of class difference through a melodramatic story set in the deep mountains of Taiwan and involving the aborigines, Yoshiro Edamasa's *Awaremi no Kyoku* (Sad songs, 1919) was shot entirely in a studio in Japan. See Tadao Sato, *Zohoban Nippon Eiga* [History of the Japanese cinema], vol. 1, *1896–1940*, rev. ed. (Tokyo: Iwanamishoten, 2006), 163–166.

40. "Eiga-kai: Taiwan o haikei ni budda no ai o shudai to shi yushutsu eiga seisaku no Tanaka Kinshi shi" [Film circle: Using Taiwan as background, Mr. Tanaka Kinshi of the export film productions will produce a film with the theme of Buddha's love], *Taiwan nichi nichi shinpo*, March 30, 1924.

41. "Japanese Film Star Here: Producer Brings Leading Man over for Study of Hollywood Methods; Was Fairbanks Pupil," *Los Angeles Times*, May 10, 1925; Tanaka, *Nihon Eiga Hattatsu-shi*, 311–314.

42. This is not to be mistaken with Eiga Kenkyu-kai, the film study organization established a year later, or the 1935 film study organization Zen Taiwan Eiga Kenkyu-kai. Similarities in organizational names occurred quite often during the colonial period.

43. "Eiga-kai: Taiwan eiga kenkyū-kai tanjō" [Film circle: Taiwan film research association was born], *Taiwan nichi nichi shinpo*, May 28, 1925.

44. G. Y. Sheng, "Taiwan eiga-kai no kaiko (ue)" [A retrospective of the Taiwan film circle (I)], *Taiwan shinminpo* [Taiwan new people's news], January 30, 1932.

45. "Shei zhi guo yingpian shangying" [Film *Whose fault is it?* released], *Taiwan nichi nichi shinpo*, September 11, 1925.

46. Sheng, "Taiwan eiga-kai no kaiko (ue)."

47. G. Y. Sheng, "Taiwan eiga-kai no kaiko (ka)" [A retrospective of the Taiwan film circle (II)], *Taiwan shinminpo*, February 6, 1932.

6 One Print in the Age of Mechanical Reproduction

Film Industry and Culture in 1910s Japan

Aaron Gerow

THE SEPTEMBER 1917 journal *Katsudo no sekai* (Movie world), containing probably one of the first attempts at a broad factual overview of the Japanese film industry, is a valuable resource to those studying the early Japanese film industry. For instance, in the corner of one page, the journal summarizes the average budget of a four-reel, four-thousand-foot *shinpa* or *kyuha* film (*shinpa*, literally "new school," were the films set in the contemporary era and often based on the contemporary stage genre of the same name; *kyuha* were "old school" period dramas).[1] In itemizing the expenditures of a typical movie that would take four days and cost 2,270 yen to make (in the conversion rate of those days, about US$4,500), *Katsudo no sekai* lists some numbers that must strike some as curious:

Negative film:	¥360
Positive film:	¥360
Location costs:	¥200
Costume/props:	¥350
Script:	¥100
Filming rights:	¥150
General costs:	¥650
Miscellaneous:	¥100

According to the magazine, "filming rights" (*satsuei shoninryo*) was the gratuity paid to the author when filming one of his or her works; "general costs" included studio salaries and other costs and were calculated by considering the proportion of four days of work out of the studio's monthly costs. But the figures for the cost of film stock stand out, not simply because the price for the two accounted for 32 percent of the total budget: note that the amount for negative and positive stock is the same. While *Katsudo no sekai*'s numbers must be taken with a grain of salt (for instance, they probably did not take into account the slight difference in cost between positive and negative film at the time),[2] they seem to reflect a film industry that not only rarely reshot a scene but considered making only one positive print from a negative the norm. This assumption about prints is backed up by other sources:[3] Up until the early 1920s, Japanese studios rarely made more than one or two prints of a film.[4] If a film had more prints than that, such as the five of *Ikeru shikabane* (The living corpse, 1918),[5] it was treated as a sign of success, not regular practice, one worth noting in movie journalism.

Almost anyone with a basic knowledge of early film industry practice outside Japan might find this situation odd. The first movie producers elsewhere made their money less by renting than by selling prints, and thus the mass production of prints was essential to business. Even after film exchanges helped make rentals more central to industry commerce, multiple prints were a matter of course for an increasingly international business, with prints traveling throughout the country and the world. Theorists like Walter Benjamin in Germany and Yasunosuke Gonda in Japan focused on the technological potential of the moving pictures to fundamentally change conceptions of art (e.g., "aura" and "originality").[6] Why then did the Japanese film industry go against what seemed to be not only common business practice but the capacity of the technology?

One print in the age of mechanical reproduction could potentially be an example of those idiosyncrasies that have served as fodder for studies of Japanese cinema both inside and outside Japan. The most famous idiosyncrasy is the *benshi*, the narrator who stood next to the screen and explained the film to the audience during the silent era in Japan, which lasted well into the 1930s. That apparent anachronism has, in the work of Noël Burch, Joseph Anderson, and others, been a marker of difference that guides explorations of the cultural contrasts between Japan and the West. While the ways scholars have used these idiosyncrasies vary, the tendency has been, as it is with Burch and Donald Richie, to have them represent the cultural uniqueness of Japan and its cinema rooted in cultural tradition.[7] That trend, however, often obscures specific historic industrial factors, as well as the precise conflicts over forming the modern nation—and thus a culture. In this chapter, I use the idiosyncrasy of one print in the age of mechanical reproduction to elaborate historical appropriations of mechanical reproduction in a specific context and thus explore the relations of industry and culture in a modernizing Japan. I investigate the problem of one print less as a form of cultural resistance against modernity than as an articulation of cinema as event through an alternative, hybrid form of modernity that problematized the contemporary formation of the nation. This case can provide a fascinating example to those studying early cinema of the particular historical problems of structuring the nation and the modern in a non-Western context subject to the pressures of universalization and globalism; it is also an example of the varied, local articulations between industry and culture that shape cinematic experience. I consider how the three fields of economy, power, and culture offer various explanations for this seemingly aberrant practice.

Economy

One of the economic impetuses behind the development of technological means of reproduction was the capitalist pursuit of cost reduction, labor savings, and rational efficiency, conditions that in the motion picture world led not only to the mass production of prints but to the creation of styles and forms of storytelling conducive to Fordist production. The Japanese film industry's practice of one print in the 1910s seems to go against such modes of economic rationalism, a suspicion that is initially justified by a look at the numbers.

If we accept *Katsudo no sekai*'s figures as reasonably accurate for the time,[8] it is clear that film costs accounted for a major portion of the budget in the late 1910s. It would take striking only six more prints for a film's budget to double, mainly because the price of film stock, which was a wholly imported product (and would remain so until Fuji began domestically producing 35mm film in the mid-1930s), rose dramatically after the start of World War I. It also reflected that, with an industry limited in production facilities (the Tenkatsu Company, for instance, still did its filming on a rickety open-air stage) and without an established star system (with most being third-rate traveling players, actor salaries were relatively low), other elements in the budget were not costly. But while the rise of the price of film may help explain why prints were not mass-produced,[9] it does not account for the practice of only one print, a situation that existed before the war.

Scarcity of film, which was occasionally lamented in the trade journals, could have also served to check the large production of prints, but as a cause it does not quite square with the contemporary volume of production. From the mid-1910s, most Japanese theaters changed their bills once every week or ten days and showed programs averaging sixteen reels (about four hours long), composed of one foreign film, one *shinpa* or *kyuha*, and several comedy or actuality shorts.[10] Although foreign movies were in the majority, Japanese studios still had to produce a considerable number of titles to keep up with the pace. In 1918, Nikkatsu's Mukojima studio (specializing in *shinpa* films) was making four to five pictures a month, and Nikkatsu's Daishogun studio in Kyoto (for *kyuha*), about seven to eight, which for just one company amounts to about eleven to thirteen titles a month—most about four thousand feet in length.[11] Amid this flood of products, Nikkatsu and Tenkatsu took a variety of measures to save costs, ranging from rereleasing old films either as is or under new titles or remaking films by using old footage and just adding a few newly shot scenes. It must have been more cost efficient to organize distribution such that a few more prints at 360 yen each could substitute for producing an entirely new 2,270-yen film, but studios did not pursue that option.[12]

Financial instability also seems not to have been a factor. Even though Nikkatsu would continue to be plagued by the debts it incurred at its inception when four companies (Yoshizawa, Yokota, M. Pathé, and Fukuhodo) merged in 1912 to form a trust, after the initial shock of the increase in film costs had passed and the wartime economy began to boom, the companies after 1915 were reporting phenomenal profits: Nikkatsu in the first half of 1918 reported a gross profit of 185,155.03 yen on inlays of 1,250,243.45 (14.8 percent),[13] and Tenkatsu reported a gross profit of 227,436.84 yen on an income of 292,431.13 yen (an amazing 77.8 percent) for the same term.[14] One could speculate that the preference of a new film over extra prints of an existing one was the product of a luxury mind-set brought on by excess profits, but given that Nikkatsu gained these profits in part by engaging in such notorious practices as cranking at eight frames per second or selling worn-out films to fairground dealers who would cut them up and peddle them one frame apiece to fans, these studios were not known for their largesse.

One economic factor behind the low number of prints may lie in the structure of the exhibition circuit. Both Nikkatsu and Tenkatsu possessed large theater chains, about 247 and 134, respectively, at the end of 1918,[15] but neither owned many of those theaters. Although each company had different ways of categorizing its relationships with chain theaters, in general cinemas were divided between *chokuei* (directly operated), *tokuyaku* (special contract), and *buai* (percentage) houses. The studio had to pay all the costs of *chokuei* theaters, which need not have been directly owned, but in exchange could take all the proceeds. *Tokuyaku* houses were owned by others, who contracted with the company to show only company-distributed films—in essence, this was a block-booking contract. The theater owner paid a set amount each month for a guaranteed supply of films, but the studio had to bear the cost for at least the projectionist and one clerk (to make sure the company was not being cheated), and sometimes the *benshi* and the projector.[16] The theater owner usually bore all the costs of *buai* theaters (although companies would still send a clerk to check receipts) and simply paid a percentage to the movie company (50-50, 40-60, 60-40 being the usual options). Importantly, *tokuyaku* far outnumbered the other kinds of houses—accounting, for instance, for 146 of Nikkatsu's 247 chain theaters (what Nikkatsu called *kyodo* and *chintai* houses)—but in this period provided the least income: only 136,217.750 yen (10.9 percent) of Nikkatsu's total income of 1,250,243.450 yen in the first half of 1918, a figure less than half of the 345,370.115 yen in income Nikkatsu's sixty-five *buai* houses generated.[17] Clearly, *chokuei* houses, while being the fewest in number, brought in on average the most income for the company: Nikkatsu's thirty-six theaters in 1918 provided 684,777.610 yen (54.8 percent) in inlays, or 19,021.6 yen per theater for a six-month term. Whether *chokuei* houses were the most profitable is another matter, considering the company had to bear all the costs. That Japanese studios refrained from maintaining more than a few dozen *chokuei* houses until the late 1930s indicates that only the small number of central urban cinemas were profitable enough to be maintained as *chokuei*. This possibly reflects that Japanese theaters in the silent era, while on average large, also maintained sizable staffs, sometimes numbering more than seventy. Given these conditions, it is conceivable that the small number of prints was made because the more prints made available, the more they had to run at theaters that were less profitable.[18] Making a limited number of prints and concentrating them at their higher-grossing houses before sending them on to second-run theaters made good economic sense.

This, however, does not explain why the companies made only one or two prints. Nikkatsu, after all, had far more *chokuei* houses and chain theaters than that. The structure of the exhibition circuits thus provides only one element in why the number of prints was small, but it, like the other economic determinants mentioned here, does not sufficiently account for such an absolutely low number. For an explanation, we have to combine the economic factors with a consideration of the power structure in the industry.

Power: Exhibition over Production

It is interesting to compare the average return between *tokuyaku* and *buai* theaters. Using the Nikkatsu numbers given earlier, the difference between the two is clear: an average of 933 yen per *tokuyaku* theater versus 5,313 per *buai* house. The gap is almost too wide to believe: given that the average *tokuyaku* rental rate was 300 yen per month, one would imagine a figure closer to 1,800 for this six-month term. Perhaps theaters themselves deducted the salaries of those sent from the company before paying rentals. Nonetheless, it is true that for Nikkatsu, *buai* income exceeded that from *tokuyaku* theaters for the first twelve years of its existence. The reasons are complex, but *buai* houses were generally less powerful theaters in the countryside and could not demand lower rental fees.[19] Conversely, companies could not exact more from *tokuyaku* theaters precisely because they did not have a dominant position at the bargaining table. *Tokuyaku* contracts involved block booking, but they could be broken easily (for a penalty), and it seems many were. Although Nikkatsu was formed in 1912 as a supposed monopoly, upstarts like Tenkatsu and later Kobayashi Shokai had little problem in acquiring theaters (although not always in the best places) because of the relative freedom of choice theater owners had.[20] Allegiance of theater owners to a company was thus weak; it was not uncommon for an owner of two or more theaters, such as Keiji Ono, who ran the Daiichi Kofu-kan and Daini Kofu-kan in Kofu, Yamanashi, to have each contract with a different company.[21]

The struggle for dominance between producers and exhibitors is certainly one of the central issues in early Western film history, but it remains a crucial framework for narrating the structural transformations in Japanese industry history even after World War II. In general, one can argue that in the Japanese film industry strong exhibitors dominated weak producers up until the 1950s.[22] The reasons for this condition are multifold. First, and stressed by Naoki Sanjugo in his critiques of the industry in the 1920s,[23] regardless of the amount of capital companies reported, they were actually capital poor, which made them vulnerable to the demands of the more-monied exhibition interests. Second, there is the reality that, partially due to prolonged police regulation of theater construction (which started from the Edo era—for Kabuki theaters—and continued with varying degrees of restriction until the end of World War II), there were far fewer theaters per capita than in other major film-producing nations; the houses that did exist thus tended to be sizable enterprises that could use their size as leverage against the capital-weak producers.[24] Third, and most important, most of Japan's early film producers were exhibitors who began making films simply to fill their programming. Although Yoshizawa Shoten was originally a supplier of photographic equipment, Yokota Shokai, M. Pathé, and Fukuhodo, while possibly obtaining their capital from elsewhere, were all at first exhibition companies; exhibitors, or those who started out as exhibitors, such as Einosuke Yokota, Kisaburo Kobayashi, and Yoshitaro Yamakawa, continued to dominate later companies such as Nikkatsu and Tenkatsu. The production studios themselves, more than being companies creating a product to sell on the market or factories producing commodities for their sales outlets, the theaters, were like subcontractors hired by exhibitors to maintain film supply, a tendency that colored the film industry until well into the 1930s. This relationship was reflected in at least two dimensions: the power of individual theaters and the loose structure of the film companies.

First, in the 1910s, it was not uncommon to see individual theaters, usually the flagship houses of a company, specifically order the production of films. This was not simply the case regarding theaters running *rensageki*, the "chain-drama" combination of scenes acted out onstage with those presented in film, which by definition could be made only for a theater and its resident acting troupe. For instance, the *tokuyaku* Taishokan in Asakusa specifically ordered *kyuha* films from Tenkatsu's Nippori studio; on average three films a month were made for that theater.[25] *Benshi* in such cinemas were also known to write up or suggest film stories. Seemingly then, relations between producers and exhibitors were such that one twelve hundred–seat theater in the central location of Asakusa such as the Taishokan—a theater not even owned by the company—could dictate over half of what the Nippori studio produced.

This was possible in part because film companies in the 1910s were not centrally organized entities that dominated the individuals in them. It might strike some as odd that Nikkatsu, which was formed by buying out four companies, did not also as a result acquire the Asian rights to Kinemacolor, Charles Urban and G. Albert Smith's early color-film process, even though Fukuhodo had bought those rights and applied for a Japanese patent well before it agreed to the merger. This may have been possible only because Fukuhodo's employees, whether legally or illegally, had power over the rights that the company itself did not.[26] Most other companies were in similar situations. On the one hand, this characteristic facilitated the kind of one-man businesses that were prominent in the industry until World War II; on the other hand, often companies had little central control over the powerful individuals within them, especially when they had strong ties to exhibitors. For better or for worse, the Japanese film industry was far from being a business run on modern accounting and centralized management principles: money was handled in a *donburi kanjo* manner (where precise books are not kept and fooling with the figures is a persistent problem); fraud and cheating were not uncommon; and relationships with organized crime often influenced the status of individuals, theaters, and companies.

A good example is the decentralized, if not unorganized, company Tenkatsu.[27] A year and a half after it was formed in March 1914, the company effectively subcontracted its operations to Kobayashi and Yamakawa, two power brokers who either owned or had influence over many central theaters (Kobayashi in Tokyo, Yamakawa in Osaka). The two resigned from Tenkatsu's board but effectively ran the company behind the scenes, being in charge of both production and exhibition. After a year, Kobayashi, always the maverick lone wolf, pulled out of the contract to start Kobayashi Shokai, but Yamakawa, more conservatively calculating, remained at Tenkatsu even after the contract ended, essentially ruling autonomously over the company's Osaka operations. Although Tenkatsu had an Osaka branch office located in the office of Kada Shokai, a company owned by Kinzaburo Kada, a powerful financial backer of Tenkatsu, there was a separate *chokueibu* (directly operated theater office) in Yamakawa's home that was largely independent of the branch office. The branch office handled film rentals for *tokuyaku* and *buai* theaters west of Nagoya, but the *chokueibu* was in charge of the *chokuei* houses in the region, most of which were owned or operated by Yamakawa. Importantly, the Osaka studio was under the jurisdiction not of the branch office but of the *chokueibu*. At first, the studio was on the grounds of the country villa of a relative of Yujiro Yamamatsu, a powerful Osaka exhibitor close to Yamakawa, before a new one was completed in January 1917. Even then, the studio essentially concentrated on producing films for Yamakawa's theaters, especially *rensageki* for the Rakutenchi.[28]

Given this example of how exhibitors exerted considerable control over production companies, it is less difficult to understand why only one or two prints of each film were being made. When a single theater or its owner was powerful enough to order a film from a company, or to exert influence over production, the production of other prints that could be shown at other houses at the same time was out of the question. Even figures like Yamakawa or Kobayashi, who had control over several theaters, were not likely to demand more prints for their own theaters, because both were involved with *rensageki*, itself a form that required only one print, and because the power of their individual theaters, and the hierarchy of exhibition, depended largely on location (Tokyo's Asakusa was the prime spot) and status as a *fukirikan* (less a first-run than a premiere theater)—that is, as a theater that was the only one to show certain films first.

Culture

A consideration of the structure of power in the industry does much to help us understand the background of one print in the age of mechanical reproduction, but it should be clear that the realm of culture—the meanings attached to these practices—has already entered the picture. The power of certain exhibitors, for instance, was based not only on their economic strength or influence on production companies but also in an audience practice of placing value in seeing unique films first at *fukirikan* in special locations like Asakusa or Sennichimae.[29] While it is difficult, given the paucity of primary source materials that still limits research on early Japanese film history, to locate evidence to elaborate on these spectator attitudes, contemporary magazines do offer indications of the importance of the local *fukiri* house. The value of *fukiri* status, for instance, is evident from theater ads that promoted film programs as not yet being shown anywhere else in Japan; the importance of single theaters is apparent from trade journals, such as the early *Kinema rekodo* (Kinema record), that introduced less the recent films than the new bills showing at particular houses. Magazines continued to print introductions to famous theaters into the 1920s, emphasizing their atmosphere and unique programming. Sections in *Kinema rekodo* and other journals, usually supplied by local fans, reported in every issue on conditions in cities away from Tokyo, often lamenting the time it took films to reach their towns, while also emphasizing, for better or worse, local differences in programming, *benshi*, audiences, and theater conditions.

This emphasis on the cinematic experience as local, as a form of event or performance, was more visibly associated with institutions such as the *benshi* or *rensageki*, but I argue it was also reinforced by the industrial practice of producing only one print of a film. Films in 1910s Japan retained some of their aura as unique objects, as originals that could be viewed anywhere only in a certain time and place. We, however, should take care when attempting to theorize this culturally.

It would not be hard to consider the practice of making only one print as part of an effort to appropriate cinema within premodern cultural traditions such as Kabuki, Bunraku, or other performance or narrative traditions. This echoes Burch's point, but other scholars such as Anderson and Hiroshi Komatsu have also emphasized how the *benshi*, for instance, carried on traditions of verbal narration, in part, as with *kowairo* (voice imitation of famous actors) renditions of *kyuha* films, to perfect an illusion of Kabuki theater.[30] I hesitate, however, to call this practice traditional or premodern. While I believe this research tells us much about the textual relationship between *benshi* and film, or even between *benshi* and audience, it has to be contextualized within both larger industrial and exhibition practices and contemporary discourses on class and the nation. I argue that, far from representing the traditional culture of the nation, the practice of one print represents a hybridity that renders problematic notions of culture and nation itself within the modern.

Consider first the critical discourses generated around the practice of making only one print. *Kinema rekodo*, from soon after the journal's inception, was editorializing against the practice on basically two fronts: industrial and national. First, the problem of one print was cited within a discourse calling for modernization of the industry. In several editorials, the practice was taken as an example of an industry that failed to rationally distinguish the roles of production, distribution, and exhibition and instead allowed exhibition to rule over the rest.[31] That failure was in part related to differences in class. Showmanlike exhibitors (note the frequent use of the epithets *kogyoshi* and *yashi*—the latter literally meaning "charlatan") were seen as different in taste and worldview from producers, not only catering to the lowest denominator but also lacking the modern business acumen of the new industrialist. I have noted that this picture was not without foundation—people like Yamakawa did not exactly fit in high society—but to attack the practice of one print was to attack a wide range of industrial methods that were seen as crass, vulgar, and unfitting for a rising industrialized nation, an assault that was not unrelated to contemporary criticisms of dirty and smelly theaters, bare-chested laborer spectators, or audience tastes as being those of children and nursemaids.[32] Eliminating the practice was then one part of a larger effort to institute a clear division of labor in the industry, introducing to Japan such new independent businesses as distributors and exhibitors that were related to the studios only through renting films, and to reverse the existing power structure in light of modern commercial practice and capitalist society. The reformer Norimasa Kaeriyama's model for the film business was the publishing industry, where publishers/studios would create the product that was distributed to the readers/spectators, creating a situation in which "exhibitors are retail book stores."[33]

The problem, however, was not simply industrial. The first mentions of the one-print practice in *Kinema rekodo* go alongside discussions of foreign-made films featuring stories set in Japan and sometimes starring transplanted Japanese actors such as Sessue Hayakawa. Criticizing these works, the editors lamented an industry that, far from eyeing the international market by mass-producing prints, could not even make more than one print for its home market. By their reasoning, prints had to be reproduced so that truer images of Japan could be sent abroad and understood. In a related argument, that meant, however, that Japanese films must abandon such practices as having the *benshi* bear narrative information and adopt the international language of cinema already found in the globally successful films of Hollywood and Europe. Both the mass production of images and the adoption of a universal language were thus, in some ways paradoxically, seen as the means by which Japanese cinema could represent the nation—in effect become a national cinema expressing a national culture.

In the eyes of intellectual reformers, industry practices such as making only one print were representative, first, of a business culture that was economically unsound and socially vulgar and, second, of a form of local experience that did not further the interests of national or universal culture. Given this criticism, there is the temptation to consider the persistence of these kinds of practices as a sign of resistance against such class-based efforts to modernize the nation. One wonders, for instance, whether this situation is not similar to that in Quebec described by Germain Lacasse, who argues that the longevity of the lecturer (*bonimenteur*) in more plebeian venues was a sign of local resistance against both the dominant high culture that criticized them and the universal pretensions of cinema.[34] The situation in Japan in the 1910s does resemble that which Lacasse details in Quebec, to the extent that divisions between class-related cultures overlapped somewhat with the opposition between the local and the national/international spheres. However, there are crucial differences that make one hesitate to call the practice of one print a form of resistance. First, while reformers of a socially higher class did strongly criticize these localizing practices, they were in the minority: the culture of the *benshi* narrating solely existing prints was the dominant one in the Japanese film world (though one that would come under increasing pressure toward the end of the decade, not just from reformers but from censorship officials). Second, I still think there is insufficient evidence that any of these practices, such as using a *benshi* or making one print, was operating specifically in opposition to other practices. Hiroshi Komatsu has presented evidence of audience discourse that defended such institutions as the *onnagata* (the male actors who played female roles) against the attacks of reformers, in part by using nation-based reasoning (i.e., arguing that practices such as the *onnagata* are good for the Japanese while those promoted by the reformers are good for Westerners).[35] But while he rightly notes that the presence of such discourses indicates a multiplicity of conceptions about cinema at the time, when he uses the term *teiko* (resistance, opposition) in describing these discourses, he does not relate them to any culture-wide hegemonic linking and thus does not show them to be anything more than cases of individual defense. It has yet to be sufficiently argued that the institutions themselves were, in conjunction with modes of reception, specifically operating in opposition to Western film cultural practices.[36]

There are several reasons for arguing that such forms of opposition were unlikely. Non-Japanese films were still in the majority numerically and were not yet subject to any significant nationalist discourse rejecting their presence or influence (this became significant only after 1920 in reaction to the Yellow Scare in the United States. A discourse resisting Western film culture coalesced in the 1930s in conjunction with the rise of militarism). The greater part of film programs were a mixture of Japanese and Western movies, and thus the latter could not be easily avoided by viewers.[37] This then cautions us about concluding that, because *benshi* working with a *shinpa* or *kyuha* film may have depended on Japanese narrating traditions, the spectators were engaging in a cinematic experience rendered traditionally Japanese. While they might have expected the *benshi* to fill in for the image in a *kyuha* film, they were enjoying another, possibly different kind of semiotic experience with the Western film that invariably played before or afterward. No research has yet shown that there were discourses existing within reception that clearly demarcated these experiences and marked any as non- or antiforeign.

The same is true with the issue of the modern. While it is certain that traditional stories, narrative structures, acting styles, and forms of verbal narration were used by the films and the *benshi* that were narrating them, sometimes to the extent that *kyuha* films were presented like traditional theater, they were often offered on the same bill with Charlie Chaplin or Pearl White; at a speed unlike that of Kabuki; in a space darker than any Kabuki hall; with benches in a building with a Western architectural style, especially in Asakusa; and in amusement centers like Asakusa that featured not only neon, noise, and the mass, anonymous urban crowd but also Asakasa Opera and other Westernized entertainments. In other words, the cinematic experience as a whole in Japan was still participating in some of the modern transformations of time, space, and perception that have been noted of film in Western nations and that Yasunosuke Gonda claimed as early as 1914 in his writings on film in Japan.[38]

The fact that only one print was made does imply that film culture in 1910s Japan was less subject to the destruction of the aura of the art object, but it does not mean that this practice was either pre- or antimodern. Rather, I contend it was situated in a more complex temporality, mixing modern and premodern elements. This included an alternative or competing modern experience occasioned less by massification and Fordism than by the combinations made possible by new technologies and forms of transportation: the unique experience of spatial juxtapositions and mixtures occasioned by international commerce and the photographic image; the new flows and encounters concomitant with the urban crowd and mass transport; and the hybridity that arises in a country rapidly transforming in an imperialist world system. Spectators who went to see early film stars like Matsunosuke Onoe or Teijiro Tachibana probably did enjoy the pseudo theatricality of their *kyuha* and *shinpa* films, but they also were attracted to the mixtures of films, people, spaces, and, in some ways, temporalities of which these works were only a part.

The best way to understand this culture of combination is to recall that what disturbed reformers about contemporary Japanese cinema and its industry was not as much its noncinematicity as its hybridity. The appellation *jun'eiga* (pure film) underlines their advocacy of nonmixture, one defined less as a modernist pursuit of cinematic essence than as a modern advocacy of rationalized divisions and orders. The prospect of cinema imitating theater, of films being shown between theatrical acts (*rensageki*), of silent images being spoken for by a *benshi*, of male actors playing women, of Japanese films playing with Western ones, of a mechanical reproductive technology being used to make only one print—all these implied border crossings that upset the rational organization of perception, experience, and meaning production. They were, however, precisely what many audiences in Japan in the 1910s enjoyed.

The practice of making one print provides an interesting focal point for analyzing these issues. On the one hand, a one-print film, by not having a transcendental—national or transnational—character through reproduction (where it is the same in different places at the same time), becomes easier to mix and manipulate at the local level because it had no competing existence elsewhere. At the same time, it truly made that mixture an event because no other space could have that same component at that time. Advertising and modes of exhibition made audiences aware of the singularity of the event such that, even if one cannot easily prove how conscious spectators were of the lack of other prints, the combination of few prints with recognized local and regional differences in *benshi* style, program length, social milieu, programming, and other factors helped shape modes of reception that had unique and local dimensions.

On the other hand, the uniqueness of the text provided a check on the total chaos mixture could bring. It has been said that the practice of the *benshi* undermined text-based meaning because two *benshi* in different theaters showing the film at the same time could offer different meanings. That, however, was largely untrue because films were rarely subject to different readings at the same time. From week to week, a film's meaning could shift, as it was combined with different *benshi*, different theaters, and different programs, but for any given time, its status was relatively secure in a unique local combination of reception factors. One print enabled a film to belong to a local space for a time as a singular entity; thus, while it helped local theaters provide unique mixtures, it managed that hybridity by making it more intimate and possibly more human.

Its localism, however, did not make the practice of one print sit well with those attempting to construct a national culture or cinema. Whether it represented a form of resistance to these nation builders is a matter worth pursuing, but at the least it exemplified that Japanese popular entertainment culture had not been rendered national as of the 1910s. Yet just as the *benshi, onnagata, rensageki*, and canned theater came under attack from reformist critics and government and educational elites, the practice of one print was subject to reform as industry practices changed in the 1920s. New studios like Shochiku and Taikatsu, by announcing their intention to aim for the international market—an aim one must admit was never realized—signaled their desire to move away from one-print culture and enter the realm of a national cinema operating through universal forms of signification and industrial rationality. It was at this time that companies actually began producing more than one print as a matter of regular business practice.

Yet just as the *benshi* took a long time to disappear (although the institution was subject to change and reform in the meantime), the number of prints stayed low until World War II, as studios still persisted in opting for mass production of titles over mass production of prints.[39] This persistence of the local—of cultural and industrial hybridity—was probably one reason cinema would remain socially inferior in the eyes of government and cultural elites; its practices, after all, did not represent the nation well. And it also provides a background for why, after the Film Law in 1939, the attempt to construct a nationalist cinema was conjoined with an industrial reform aimed at reducing the number of titles and increasing the number of prints.[40] If one accepts that the material conditions for the formation of a cinema capable of serving a national imagined community include a centralized, top-down industrial structure; the availability of theaters for most of the populace; a large number of prints for each film; and a film language understandable not only by the national citizenry but by noncitizens (who then recognize those films as a product of that nation), I argue that most of these conditions were met—and only then contradictorily met—in Japan only during and after World War II. Only after this time could one imagine a Japanese national cinema finally being mechanically reproduced.

AARON GEROW is Professor of East Asian Cinema at Yale University. He is author of *Visions of Japanese Modernity: Articulations of Cinema, Nation, and Spectatorship, 1895–1925, A Page of Madness: Cinema and Modernity in 1920s*

Japan, and *Kitano Takeshi*. With Abé Mark Nornes, he authored *Research Guide to Japanese Film Studies*. His current research is on the history of Japanese film theory. He also runs his own Japanese film website, Tangemania (www.aaron gerow.com).

Notes

A shorter version of this chapter was presented in English at the annual conference of the Society for Cinema Studies, Chicago, Illinois, March 10, 2000. A Japanese version, "Fukusei gijutsu jidai no wan purinto," was later presented at the conference of Nihon Eigashi Kenkyukai at Meiji Gakuin University, Tokyo, April 25, 2000. I thank the participants of both sessions for their questions and comments. After receiving comments from some anonymous readers, I published a revised version as Aaron Gerow, "One Print in the Age of Mechanical Reproduction: Culture and Industry in 1910s Japan," *Screening the Past* 11 (2000). This chapter is a slightly expanded version of that article.

1. "Shin-kyuha eiga no satsuei nissu to satsuei hiyo" [The filming costs and production duration of new and old school films], *Katsudo no sekai* [Movie world] 2, no. 9 (1917): 55.

2. The June 1917 *Katsudo no sekai* gives the price per foot as 8.5 sen for negative and 7.8 sen for positive: "Honpo ni okeru hirumu no yu'nyu to kako" [The importation and processing of film in Japan], *Katsudo no sekai* 2, no. 6 (1917): 32. Note that such numbers underline the fact that for a four thousand–foot film, very little film was shot that was not used (4,000 × 7.8 = 31,200 sen or 312 yen).

3. For instance, Jun'ichiro Tanaka quotes the pioneer director Shozo Makino describing the practice in the days of Yokota Shokai (before 1912) in *Nihon eiga hattatsushi* [The history of the development of Japanese film] (Tokyo: Chuo Koronsha, 1975), 1:176, and an editorial laments the same practice in 1914; see "Obei gekidan to Toyo no geki" [Oriental dramas and drama troupes in Europe and America], *Kinema rekodo* [Kinema record] 2, no. 9 (1914): 2–3.

4. The subcontracting agreement between Tenkatsu and Kisaburo Kobayashi and Yoshitaro Yamakawa specified three prints per film; see Tanaka, *Nihon eiga hattatsushi*, 238. It is not certain whether this term of this short-lived contract was obeyed.

5. "Mukojima satsueijo kenkyu" [A study of the Mukojima Studio], *Katsudo no sekai* 3, no. 10 (1918): 29. The article does not mention whether the extra prints were made at the time of the film's release or after the film's success.

6. See Walter Benjamin, "The Work of Art in the Age of Mechanical Reproduction," in *Film Theory and Criticism*, 6th ed., ed. Leo Braudy and Marshall Cohen (Oxford: Oxford University Press, 2004), 791–811; and Yasunosuke Gonda, "The Principles and Applications of the Moving Pictures," trans. Aaron Gerow, *Review of Japanese Culture and Society* 22 (2010): 24–36.

7. See Noël Burch, *To the Distant Observer: Form and Meaning in the Japanese Cinema* (Berkeley: University of California Press, 1979); J. L. Anderson, "Spoken Silents in the Japanese Cinema; or, Talking to Pictures: Essaying, the Katsuben, Contextualizing the Texts," in *Re-framing Japanese Cinema*, ed. Arthur Noletti Jr. and David Desser (Bloomington: Indiana University Press), 259–311; and Donald Richie, *A Hundred Years of Japanese Film: A Concise History* (Tokyo: Kodansha International, 2001).

8. Even *Katsudo no sekai* would give different numbers in 1918 in its more specific reviews of Nikkatsu (in October) and Tenkatsu (in December). They, however, still confirmed that the

cost of film stock accounted for a significant portion of the budget. See "Mukojima satsueijo kenkyu"; "Nikkatsu Kyoto satsueijo kenkyu" [A study of Nikkatsu Kyoto Studio], *Katsudo no sekai* 3, no. 10 (1918): 30–35; "Tenkatsu Kaisha no genjo" [The present state of Tenkatsu Company], *Katsudo no sekai* 3, no. 12 (1918): 5–9; and other articles in these issues.

9. The increase in price is one reason Tenkatsu, which was founded to produce films in Japan using Charles Urban's Kinemacolor process, abandoned producing Kinemacolor pictures, since the process used twice as much film as a regular camera.

10. In August 1918, *Katsudo no sekai* reported twelve-reel programs as the norm for high-class theaters, sixteen for lower-ranking city and Japanese-film-centered cinemas, and phenomenal five- to six-hour programs (up to twenty-four reels) as the fad in Osaka and the countryside. "Naigai katsudo josetsukan no bangumi" [Programs at movie theaters in Japan and abroad], *Katsudo no sekai* 3, no. 8 (1918): 30–31.

11. See "Nikkatsu Kyoto satsueijo kenkyu," 34; and "Mukojima satsueijo kenkyu," 27. According to a 1915 *Kinema rekodo* report, this incredible rate of production left little time for staff to rest (there was only one day off a month) or even see their own work. Akatsuki Hashio, "Nikkatsu Kyoto satsueijo no kigen oyobi enkaku: Daigo-shin, soshiki oyobi genjo" [The origins and history of Nikkatsu Kyoto Studio: Part five, the organization and present state], *Kinema rekodo* 30 (December 1915): 14.

12. Nikkatsu was making more *kyuha* films per month than any single theater could show, since even theaters that concentrated on Japanese films at best showed one *kyuha* and one *shinpa* in any program.

13. *Nikkatsu shijunen-shi* [Forty-year history of Nikkatsu] (Tokyo: Nikkatsu Kabushiki Kaisha, 1952).

14. "Tenkatsu Kaisha no genjo," 8.

15. See "Nikkatsu no genjo" [The current state of Nikkatsu], *Katsudo no sekai* 3, no. 10 (1918): 11; and "Tenkatsu Kaisha no enkaku" [The history of Tenkatsu Company], *Katsudo no sekai* 3, no. 12 (1918): 4. Other companies like M. Kashii and Universal, as well as independent operators, made up the remaining number in the total of about five hundred theaters in the country (including Korea, Taiwan, and other possessions) as of July 1918. "Zenkoku katsudo shashin josetsukan ichiranhyo" [List of moving picture theaters in the country], *Katsudo no sekai* 3, no. 8 (1918): 75–89.

16. The September 1917 issue of *Katsudo no sekai* adds the *benshi* and equipment to the costs the company sometimes had to bear, while the journal's December 1918 issue states the company was responsible for only one projectionist and one clerk. See "Eigyojo ni okeru josetsukan to kaisha to no kankei" [The business relationship between theaters and companies], *Katsudo no sekai* 2, no. 9 (1917): 67; and "Tenkatsu Kaisha no genjo," 7.

17. "Nikkatsu no genjo," 11.

18. It is important to remember that the income a company received for a program of films it provided, regardless of which kind of contract, had to in effect be divided among several films, since the average bill consisted of several features and shorts.

19. One other reason is that two of Nikkatsu's top theaters, Tokyo's Chiyoda-kan and Osaka's Ashibe Kurabu, were *buai* houses. Thus, not all *buai* theaters were less-powerful rural houses.

20. *Katsudo no sekai* uses the case of Kobayashi, which was able to acquire some fifty theaters within a year of its inception, to illustrate the weakness of other producers and the mobility of theaters. See "Eigyojo ni okeru josetsukan to kaisha to no kankei," 68.

21. See "Zenkoku katsudo shashin josetsukan ichiranhyo," 84. That Kofu had only those two theaters in 1918 probably made that a smart business decision, even though it was also not uncommon at the time to see a town with only two or three theaters that were all contracted to Nikkatsu.

22. This observation is echoed both by contemporary critics of the industry—for instance, in "Kaku arubeki katsudokai" [The way the movie world should be], *Kinema rekodo* 20 (February 1915): 2—and by later historians, such as in Tanaka, *Nihon eiga hattatsushi*, 225. Kanae Imamura, following Yoshio Shibata, cites the post–World War II democratization of stock holdings as one of the crucial factors enabling production to free itself economically of the demands of exhibitors. Kanae Imamura, *Eiga sangyo* [The film industry] (Tokyo: Yuhikaku, 1960), 64; Yoshio Shibata, *Eiga no keizagaku* [The economics of film] (Toyohashi-shi: Eigakai Kenkyujo, 1954), 13.

23. See, for instance, Sanjugo Naoki, "Nihon eiga oyobi eigakai" [Japanese film and film world], in *Naoki Sanjugo zenshu* [Complete works of Sanjugo Naoki] (Tokyo: Kaizosha, 1935), 31:208–216.

24. This situation changed after World War II when inflation sparked a boom in the construction of theaters, which were now less regulated. The resulting surplus of theaters, putting suppliers in the better bargaining position, was another factor in enabling producers to finally dominate exhibitors. See Imamura, *Eiga sangyo*, 152.

25. See "Tenkatsu Nippori kyuha satsueijo kenkyu" [Study of the Tenkatsu Nippori old-school film studio], *Katsudo no sekai* 3, no. 12 (1918): 14.

26. Technically, Nikkatsu did not end up with Kinemacolor because Fukuhodo did not reveal that it had bought the rights secretly. But the rights must not have been purchased by the corporate entity Fukuhodo, which was bought by Nikkatsu, but by the individuals who later used Kinemacolor at Tenkatsu.

27. For more on Tenkatsu, see Hiroshi Komatsu, "From Natural Colour to the Pure Motion Picture Drama: The Meaning of Tenkatsu Company in the 1910s of Japanese Film History," *Film History* 7, no. 1 (1995): 69–86.

28. See "Tenkatsu Osaka satsueijo" [Tenkatsu Osaka Studio], *Katsudo no sekai* 3, no. 12 (1918): 20–23.

29. This value was not just ascribed to Japanese films. The term *fukiri* was first attributed to imported films shown just after being unloaded from the boat and unpacked or unsealed (*fukirareta*). In general, there was usually only one print of foreign films as well, although there were exceptions with pirated films or in cases when different companies bought prints of the same film from different foreign dealers (conflicts over exhibition rights would plague the industry until the nationalization of censorship in 1925 helped regulate exhibition rights).

30. See Anderson, "Spoken Silents in the Japanese Cinema"; and Hiroshi Komatsu and Frances Loden, "Mastering the Mute Image: The Role of the *Benshi* in Japanese Cinema," *Iris*, no. 22 (Autumn 1996): 33–52.

31. See "Kaku aru beki katsudokai," 2; and "Kaku aru beki katsudokai (shozen)" [The way the movie world should be (continued)], *Kinema rekodo* 21 (March 1915): 2.

32. For more on the class issues involved in film reform in the 1910s, see Aaron Gerow, *Visions of Japanese Modernity: Articulations of Cinema, Nation, and Spectatorship, 1895–1915* (Berkeley: University of California Press, 2010).

33. Norimasa Kaeriyama, "Katsudo shashin no shakaiteki chii oyobi sekimu" [The social status and responsibility of the moving pictures], *Kinema rekodo* 41 (November 1916): 479.

34. See Germain Lecasse, "Du bonimenteur quebecois comme pratique resistante" [The Quebecois bonimenteur as practical resistance], *Iris*, no. 22 (Autumn 1996): 53–66.

35. Hiroshi Komatsu, "Hisutoriogurafi to gainen no fukususei: Taikatsu o rekishikasuru tame ni" [Historiography and conceptual multiplicity: Historicizing Taikatsu], *Eigagaku* 13 (1999): 2–11.

36. The discourse of censors at the time reveals a concern for the possibility of class-based readings of films (by *benshi* or spectators) that were antagonistic to status quo values. This is

an important issue worthy of more study, but it clearly is not one reducible to the opposition between traditional and modern or Japan and West.

37. In the mid-1910s, a small number of what were considered high-class urban theaters began offering foreign-film-only programs, partially in response to the desire of some audiences to avoid the vulgar Japanese fare. In this way, the manner by which Western films were shown at certain venues could serve as a marker of social divisions within Japan.

38. Gonda, for instance, saw in film the end of art as "quiet, excellent, calm, rare, unique, or the non-practical" and the beginning of a beauty that is "mobile, stupendous, majestic, organized, and practical." Gonda, "The Principles and Applications of the Moving Pictures," 35. For my analysis of his conception of film, see Gerow, *Visions of Japanese Modernity*, 72–93; and Aaron Gerow, "The Process of Theory: Reading Gonda Yasunosuke and Early Film Theory," *Review of Japanese Culture and Society* 22 (2010): 37–43.

39. While Home Ministry censorship records show an average of five to ten prints for films in the 1930s, by the late 1930s, the industry as a whole was producing more than five hundred titles a year, a figure that in some years made it the top producer in the world. This was not a source of pride for industry observers and government regulators, who considered the overproduction of cheap films a sign of the backwardness of the industry.

40. During the war, government officials used both the Film Law and their monopoly over film stock to consolidate the industry, reduce the number of films made, and increase the quantity of prints. The September 1941 agreement between regulators and the industry that merged the ten existing companies into three also stipulated a total production rate for the industry of six films a month, with thirty prints per film (doubling the average figure at the time).

7 Distributing Scandinavia

Nordisk Film in Asia

Nadi Tofighian

THE SINO-JAPANESE WAR in 1894–1895, the Boxer Uprising in China near the turn of the century, and the Russo-Japanese War in 1904–1905 brought the so-called Far East to the political foreground in the West. Asia was a vast market, and Western trade with Asia steadily increased near the turn of the century. Ports in Asia, such as Colombo, Bombay, Calcutta, Rangoon, and Singapore, were of a very high standard and equaled the large European ports. Ships increased their capacity, and new shipping lines continuously opened, both within Asia and between continents. Scandinavian companies and governments also wanted to be involved in this trade. In 1897 the Danish East Asiatic Company was formed to pursue trade, shipping, and industrial activities in East Asia.[1] Ten years later the Swedish East Asiatic Company was formed with the motto "Trade follows the flag" and with the aim to increase trade and find new markets for Swedish products.[2] The path of Scandinavian trade to Asia was thereby opened.

This chapter assesses the Asian film market during the first decades of the 1900s, with a focus on the 1910s, by examining trade and distribution patterns of Scandinavian films to Asia, particularly Southeast Asia. I concentrate on the distribution of films by the Danish company Nordisk Films Kompagni (Nordisk Film), as they represent about 80 percent of the Scandinavian films that were distributed to Asia during the silent film era. Nordisk Film was founded by Ole Olsen (1863–1943) in Denmark in 1906 and was a major film-producing company during its first ten years of existence. Its trademark of the polar bear standing on a globe with "Copenhagen" written inside the globe was almost as well known as the Pathé rooster. In the *Moving Picture News* the company promoted itself as "the 'King Pin' of Quality Films" and by stating, "The Bear-on-the-Globe trade mark is the emblem of high quality."[3] And its ambitions were high; in an interview in February 1915, Ole Olsen said, "Nordisk Films Kompagni will now become the biggest in the world. We are already the finest."[4]

Nordisk Film made films with the international market in mind from the outset; in 1906, only 7 percent of its film copies were for the domestic market, the following year it was 4.5 percent, and later it was only 2 percent.[5] It started exporting films to Europe and the United States the year after its inception and had branches in Berlin, London, and Vienna by 1907. The following year the company opened a subsidiary, the Great Northern Film Company, in New York. Censorship rules in other countries were considered from an early stage, and special endings for different markets were made for more than fifty films.[6] Nordisk Film never opened any branches in Asia, yet I have identified more than three hundred films that were exported from Denmark to the Philippines, Hong Kong, China, Japan, Federated Malay States and Straits Settlements (colonial Malaysia and Singapore), Dutch East Indies (colonial Indonesia), Indochina (colonial Vietnam, Cambodia, and Laos), Siam (Thailand), and British India (colonial India and Burma) from 1908 to 1928.[7]

The chapter consists of three sections. The first section gives a brief overview of the development of early film distribution in Asia, including the role of Pathé and US companies, regional distribution centers, and dealers of secondhand films. The second section assesses Nordisk Film's distributors and the corresponding financial contracts. It also examines whether distribution of Scandinavian films in Asia led to increased trade in other goods between countries or if the films followed already-established trade paths. The final section examines the exhibition and reception of Nordisk Film productions in Asia, particularly Southeast Asia.

Film Distribution in Asia

The first decades of cinema in Asia saw the development from traveling exhibitors to agents to established film companies such as Pathé and US companies, and the gradual rise of permanent movie houses. In Southeast Asia moving pictures were exhibited for the first time in 1896 and 1897: in Batavia (colonial Jakarta) through the Scenimatograph in October 1896;[8] in Manila through the Kronofotografo in January 1897;[9] in Singapore through the Ripograph or Giant Cinematograph in May 1897;[10] in Bangkok through the Cinematograph in June 1897;[11] and in Hanoi through the Cinématographe in September 1897.[12] During the following years a steady flow of traveling cinemas went from country to country; elsewhere I have discussed how seating and pricing arrangements in the exhibition halls created a division based on social class and ethnic background (with the cheapest gallery seats being reserved for "natives").[13] After ten years of film exhibition in Southeast Asia, an editorial about cinema in the *Malay Mail* stated, "The cinematograph in the East became a permanent institution long ago. It appeals very strongly to the native mind." It then warned about the risk of showing "the shady denizens of the underworld of crime and poverty and filth" to the "impressionable Asiatics."[14]

Permanent movie houses were established in business districts, in residential areas, near markets, and on the outskirts of cities. Japan was the Asian country where cinema was most popular, and reports stated that "the country is flooded with moving picture shows."[15] Tokyo was reported to have almost a hundred cinema houses, Osaka about fifty, and Kyoto about fifteen. Many of these cinema halls were said to be "handsome modern buildings equal to the best London halls."[16] Cities in Southeast Asia with a significant number of cinemas in the early 1910s were Manila, which had more than twenty; Batavia, which had about fifteen; and Singapore and Bangkok, which each had about ten.[17] The actual figures were likely higher, as new movie houses were surfacing everywhere. An editorial in the *Bangkok Times* stated that "there are far more cinematograph shows flourishing in this town than the average foreign resident has any idea of. One substantial building is known to everyone, but cinematograph shows are also given in canvas erections and in buildings from which there would be little hope of escape if anything serious were to happen."[18]

Asian countries, with the exception of Japan and India, did not have any domestic film production during the first decades of cinema. There was thereby a risk of cementing the worldview of the colonizer, as mostly Western films were exhibited. Colonial discourse and Orientalism were prevalent in early newspapers, films, and trade journals. In Asia, Cinematographs and other technological inventions were in some cases introduced as a way of highlighting Western progress and contrasting it to Asian backwardness.[19] The so-called Oriental, or native, was often portrayed in the local press as irrational, ignorant, primitive, and lazy.[20] The *Moving Picture World* also described native Asians, with the exception of those of Japan and Java, as stupid and hostile. Particularly, the Malay people were negatively portrayed: "The Malay is a warlike fellow, ready to draw his knife at the slightest provocation."[21] In 1918, the *Moving Picture World* called Asia ("the Orient") "one of the most difficult markets of the world" and claimed that it was difficult to penetrate, since Western films "are made from the standpoint of Western peoples, setting forth their religious, sociological, ethical and political views, with which the East has so few points of contact." It continued by declaring that the diffusion of Western ideas was mainly due to the power of cinema: "It is encouraging, however, to note that in a very short time, largely through the medium of motion pictures, Western ideas are rapidly being assimilated by our Oriental brothers."[22]

Before World War I, European film companies, particularly Pathé, dominated the Asian market. The vertically integrated Pathé was involved in production, distribution, and exhibition and opened branch offices in most major cities around the world. Pathé opened offices in Singapore and Calcutta in 1907, Manila in 1909, and Shanghai in 1911. Singapore was a large free port, a center for trade and storage, and a focal point for the trade to British Malaya, the Dutch

East Indies, Siam, and Indochina. Since the Pathé office located there, Singapore strengthened its position as a regional film distribution center, and the company distributed films from there to Burma, Java, Sumatra, Hong Kong, the Philippines, and Siam.[23] Many films were thus first exhibited in Singapore and then distributed to other countries in the region. More than 70 percent of films imported to Siam in 1916–1917 came from Singapore.[24]

Hong Kong was another distribution center for films because of its location. Many film exchange and rental companies had offices there and used the location as a hub to distribute films to the Philippines, Indochina, British Malaya, Siam, Burma, and North China.[25] European and US film companies frequently distributed used film copies to Asia. The strategy of Variety Film Exchange Company, with offices in Hong Kong, Shanghai, Harbin, Tokyo, and Yokohama, in the Chinese market was to send cheap, used films there, since sending new film reels to China was like "casting pearls before swine." The company's view changed when it realized that "junk film does not get the money in the Orient."[26] Secondhand films were, however, still common in China in 1917, and a report in *Moving Picture World* claimed audiences had low demands and accepted films that were seven to eight years old, defective, and difficult to watch because of scratches.[27] The following week the film exporter Charles Margelis, who had just returned from a seven-month trip to Japan, China, the Philippines, Straits Settlements, and the Dutch East Indies, warned film production and distribution companies (maybe for self-serving purposes) about the large amount of film duping in Asia.[28]

Nordisk Film also experienced problems with duping and secondhand dealers around the world. In 1911, Brandenburgh, a film trader in Philadelphia, unlawfully bought the Nordisk Film production *Ved Fængslets Port* (Temptations of a great city, 1911) from a trader in London. Claiming copyright laws, Great Northern pursued the case, and both Brandenburgh and the exhibitors were fined.[29] And in 1913, *Moving Picture News* reports that Nordisk Film "effected the seizure of a film which had been surreptitiously brought into the United States against the provisions of our copyright law, and in violation of said company's rights."[30] Santos y Artigas, Nordisk Film's agents in Cuba, wrote to Nordisk Film in 1913 warning about secondhand dealers: "Mess. Baer & Co., of London, are repeatedly sending lists to this country [Cuba] in which they offer your films. We have written to you before regarding this and beg to insist that this be avoided, as it harms our business here."[31]

It was therefore important for film producers to register their brands and trademarks in foreign countries to avoid film piracy. Despite these difficulties, not until the early 1920s did Nordisk Film try to get its trademark registered in about thirty countries. In Asia, it registered its trademark only in Japan and India, most likely because the colonized countries were considered part of the colonizing country. In India the trademark was accepted in 1920.[32] In Japan, however, the trademark of the polar bear sitting on a globe was rejected in 1921, as it resembled another trademark with a tiger sitting on a globe.[33]

Before World War I Britain had a major share of the transit trade, including the film trade, and London was seen as an infallible market, where correct prices were given. The role of London decreased during the war, however.[34] US film companies frequently gave away exporting rights for Asia and Africa when trading with Europe. David P. Howells, exporter of American films, claimed US film manufacturers were forfeiting much profit by trading with London instead of trading directly with Asia.[35] Kristin Thompson opines that US film companies started dominating the world market after the war because they implemented new distribution procedures, such as opening offices in foreign markets instead of distributing through agents in London. Universal Pictures was the only US company that opened offices in Asia before doing so in other parts of the world. In 1916, Universal opened branches in Japan, India, and Singapore, followed by branches on Java and in Manila the following two years.[36]

The connection of film and trade was explicit in the United States, where the Department of Commerce and the Motion Pictures Producers and Distributors of America (MPPDA) aimed to exploit opportunities for trade that followed from export of films. The Department of Commerce claimed that trade in commodities followed the films and estimated that every exported foot of film could render exports of one dollar in other goods.[37] And the Philippines, as a US colony, played an important role, since it was "a natural gateway to the markets of the Orient. . . . Manila is but a few days' ocean travel from all of the great ports of eastern Asia, and is thus in a position geographically to quickly supply the trade of this section of the world."[38] The Philippines was also the country in Asia where most Nordisk Film productions were distributed.

Distributing Nordisk Film

Kristin Thompson describes three different ways of exporting film in the first two decades of cinema: (1) through an agent, who paid the producer a certain price for the rights of the film, and the agent would in turn reap all profits or losses; (2) through a licensing agreement in which producer and distributor shared profits; and (3) through direct sales by opening either an office abroad or a subsidiary.[39] Initially it was more common to use agents or distributors than to open foreign offices. Nordisk Film did not open branch offices in Asia and chose to export films via agents or through licensing agreements. Yet Nordisk Film wanted to promote its brand in Asia, and a condition in all its contracts was "to use the name of Nordisk Films Kompagni prominently in all advertisements."

The US trade press wrote very positively about Nordisk Film's subsidiary in the United States, Great Northern Film Company: "The work of the Great

Northern is par excellence. Why cannot some of our American firms aspire to a like perfection of theme and production?"[40] Ron Mottram shows that the description of the trade press was too positive, and in effect there were constant tensions between Ingvald C. Oes, the manager for Great Northern, and Nordisk Film, mostly because of lack of profitability and trust.[41] For instance, Oes created a separate distribution company, the Great Northern Special Feature Film Company, which focused on long feature films, without the authorization of Nordisk Film.[42] The *Moving Picture News* reported about the "entirely new and novel [distribution] scheme" of the Great Northern Special Feature Film Company: "It sells its films at a much lower rate than any other feature film company, which enables its customers to have several big features on hand at one time, allowing theatre managers to follow up one feature after another."[43]

The most important markets for Nordisk Film were Germany, Russia, and Austria-Hungary.[44] Particularly in Germany, it had a very strong position as both a distributor and an exhibitor. World War I affected Nordisk Film, and the company gradually lost its position as markets became inaccessible. The level of production decreased from one hundred films per year during 1911–1916 to eight productions per year in 1920.[45] Previously, contracts and incomes from Russia, Germany, and Austria-Hungary earned the company twice the amount of the production costs of the films. Now there was no income from Russia and minimal income from Austria-Hungary due to the exchange rate, and the income from the German market was dependent on German importers because of import restrictions. The importance of markets in the rest of the world thus increased.[46] The increased importance of Asia for Nordisk Film can also be illustrated by an eight-page special on Asia, written by Marie Luise Droop, that Nordisk Film published in the late 1910s in *Der Eisbär*, Nordisk Film's German newsletter to branches in Budapest, Vienna, and Prague.[47]

Places in Asia printed in the distribution protocols of Nordisk Film in the 1910s (where films were most frequently exported) were the English colonies (primarily referring to India), East Asia, Japan, the Philippines, and Dutch East Indies.[48] Table 7.1 shows the distribution of Nordisk Film productions in Asia based on the distribution protocols and contracts of Nordisk Film. I have divided the distribution of the films of Nordisk Film to Asia into four phases: For the first phase, 1906–1910, distribution protocols of Nordisk Film do not exist. The distribution protocols indicate that films started being distributed to Asia in 1912; however, film advertisements show that films had already been screened in Singapore as early as 1909.[49] The second phase, 1911–1915, coincides with the period frequently referred to as the golden age of Nordisk Film. During this period the Philippines was the Asian country where most films were distributed; in the financial accounts of Nordisk Film, Manila was often one of the first ten places

Table 7.1 Distribution of Films by Nordisk Film in Asia

	1906–1910	1911–1915	1916–1920	1921–1928	Total
Philippines	—	91	31	0[†]	122
Dutch East Indies	—	2*	38	27	67
Japan	—	4	24	13	41
India	—	0	12	7	19
China	—	0	2	6	8
Siam	—*	0*	3*	1	4*
Straits Settlements	—*	0*	4*	0	4*
Burma	—	0	1	2	3
Ceylon	—	0	0	2	2
Hong Kong	—	0	0	2	2
Total	—	97	115	60	272

Source for data: Distribution protocols of Nordisk Film, XI, 7 and XII, 33–43, Nordisk Film Special Collection, Danish Film Institute, Copenhagen, Denmark; Isak Thorsen, "Isbjørnens anatomi: Nordisk Films Kompagni som erhvervsvirksomhed i perioden 1906–1928" [Anatomy of the polar bear: Nordisk Films Kompagni as a business enterprise in the period 1906–1928] (PhD diss., Copenhagen University, 2009), 40.
Note: The years refer to the year of distribution, not the year of production. No distribution protocols exist until spring 1912.
*My research in Southeast Asian archives has found more films than the listed number.
†No specific film titles have been found, but there is a contract between Nordisk Film and Rudolph G. Riis from this period.

in the list of places where the films were sold. The third phase, 1916–1920, was the period when the effects of the war hit Nordisk Film hard. In 1916 Nordisk Film had to close its New York office, and in 1920 it closed its last foreign branch, in London. The Philippines and Dutch East Indies were the countries where most films were distributed. In the fourth phase, 1921–1928, Nordisk Film was no longer a major film producer; the company produced a total of twenty-five feature films during that period.[50] The decline continued, and in 1928 the company was liquidated (but in 1929 it was reconstructed).

The actual number of films exported to Asia is considerably higher. My archival research in Asian newspapers shows that many more films were exported to the Dutch East Indies, Straits Settlements, India, British Malaya, and Siam, particularly before 1920. I have identified more than fifty Nordisk Film productions exhibited in Singapore, Malacca, and Kuala Lumpur before 1920. Furthermore, many early films were based on subjects and stories produced by several different film companies, such as Sherlock Holmes (Nordisk Film made five films on the character between 1908 and 1909), William Tell, Robinson Crusoe, and Hamlet.

Thus, even more Nordisk Film productions were exhibited in Southeast Asia, since, with a few exceptions, the manufacturer of these films is not listed in film advertisements. In addition to the feature films, Nordisk Film made many travelogues, especially in Norway, Sweden, and Denmark. The international outlook of the company was thus combined with representations of Scandinavian nature, as exemplified by most of the companies' travelogues.[51] I have found several film advertisements with Scandinavian travelogues exhibited around Southeast Asia. These films, however, could have been produced by Pathé, Nordisk Film, or other manufacturers.

Before World War I, distribution contracts of Nordisk Film were on a long-term basis: the distributor bought the rights for films for several years. The Nordisk Film contracts in the Danish archives are mostly from 1915 and later. A possible reason for the lack of contracts and systematic documentation of the distribution of films to Asia during earlier phases could be the profitability and the large quantity of exported films to other parts of the world during that period. Another reason early contracts with Asia are not found is that the Nordisk Film branches in Europe also exported films to other parts of the world. The Berlin branch sold films to Russia, Hungary, Switzerland, and China, and the London branch sold films to Brazil, Australia, Africa, and Singapore.[52] In some rare cases, the headquarters in Copenhagen also sold individual films directly to smaller markets, such as Bangkok.[53] The translation of intertitles to major languages was initially made at Nordisk Film's copying lab in Copenhagen, but as the quality of the translations varied, Nordisk Film's branches and agents became responsible.[54]

Nordisk Film's distribution statistics can be juxtaposed with the trade of Denmark in Asia, as well as that of the Danish East Asiatic Company. Denmark exported most goods to China, British India, the Dutch East Indies, Straits Settlements, Japan, Siam, and the Philippines.[55] There thus seems to be no positive correlation between trade in commodities and trade in films. The Danish East Asiatic Company considered Bangkok, Yokohama, Shanghai, Hong Kong, and Singapore the best places in Asia for business.[56] Its most common trade route was Copenhagen to Shanghai via Antwerp, an English port, Marseille or Genoa, Port Said, Suez, Colombo, Penang, Singapore, Bangkok, and Hong Kong. Its ships did not stop in the three countries in Asia where most films were exported. Denmark's exports to Asia and the trade route of the Danish East Asiatic Company illustrate the independence of the distribution of Nordisk Film and its strong brand name. As a contrast, the export of films from Svenska Biografteatern AB (Svenska Bio) during the silent era was correlated with the export of Swedish goods to Asia. The films of Svenska Bio were distributed to Japan (about forty films), China (about thirty), British India (about ten), and the Dutch East Indies (about ten),[57] and the Asian countries where most Swedish goods were exported between 1906 and 1927 were Japan, British India (including Straits Settlements), China, and the Dutch East Indies.[58] For the smaller Svenska Bio, film trade seemed to follow the trade in commodities.

Denmark had closest contact with Siam in Asia. In the early 1900s Danes were the third-largest Western population in Siam after the English and the French, and eleven Danish businesses operated in Bangkok in 1920, outnumbered only by fifty British ones.[59] King Chulalongkorn of Siam was well disposed toward Denmark and sent his young relatives to Denmark to be trained in Danish schools and at the royal court.[60] In Bangkok, the first electrical tram, the electric power plants, and the first railway (Bangkok–Paknam) were run or initiated by Danes.[61] Hans Niels Andersen founded the Danish East Asiatic Company and became its chairman. The company took over his trade company, Andersen and Co., which had operated in Bangkok since 1884. He was also the general consul of Siam in Denmark from 1898 to 1932. The company was successful in Siam and expanded its shipping line with several new steamers. It started a mail, passenger, and cargo line on the eastern side of the Gulf of Siam, subsidized by the Siamese government.[62] It also owned the popular Oriental Store in Bangkok, which explains the number of advertisements for Danish goods in the local press.[63] An editorial in the *Bangkok Times* stated that the Danes had been crucial in connecting Bangkok to Europe and that without "political ambitions to serve, nor political influence to back them, the Danes have quietly and steadily built up their commercial influence in this country till now they have a position of assured importance in the expanding shipping trade of the Far East."[64]

Nordisk Film sent the traveling film photographer Ludvig Lippert to Siam in late 1908 to film the fortieth anniversary of King Chulalongkorn's reign, the sacred white elephants, and ordinary street scenes.[65] He shot the travelogues *Bangkok* (1909), *Siamese Actors and Actresses Play a Siamese Drama* (1909), *Streetlife in the North of Siam* (1909), *The Grand Procession at the King of Siam's Jubilee* (1909), and *Crossing Siam on the River Menam* (1909).[66] Considering all this, it is surprising that Danish trade with Siam was limited and that so few Danish films were exhibited in Siam; a total of only five advertisements featuring Nordisk Film productions have been found in the local press.

Film production companies that did not own local cinemas were dependent on distributors. The better movie houses often had exclusive contracts with certain distributors or manufacturers, which made it harder for Nordisk Film to get a strong permanent position in Asia. Nordisk Film distributed new film copies to Asia, although used films most likely also found their way there, even if they were not directly exported to Asia. For instance, several Nordisk Film productions were exhibited in British Malaya and Indochina, yet no contracts have been found with any distributor. It is, however, a possibility that they were distributed there via one of Nordisk Film's branches. During the early 1910s, Nordisk Film's

London branch was in charge of distribution of films to India, China, Japan, and East Asia; and J. B. Turull Fournols, Nordisk Film's agent in Barcelona, was the distributor for the Philippines.[67]

Nordisk Film used both private agents and distribution companies to find markets for its films. Nordisk Film's network was limited in certain areas of Asia, and many of its Asian contracts were with agents in London. In the late 1910s and 1920s Nordisk Film worked with the distribution companies Publio Alliata and the Calcutta-based Alliance Trades Agency for British India, Burma, and Ceylon; it worked with P. R. van Duinen, Hoenson's Film Exchange, and the Netherlands Trading Society (N. V. Nederlandsche Handel-Maatschappij) for the Dutch East Indies. The distributors handled all profits or losses; only the contract with the Netherlands Trading Society was based on commission. The contract in 1919 with the Amsterdam-based film distribution company P. R. van Duinen gave the company the rights for thirty-six films in the Dutch East Indies.[68]

Almost half of the contracts were with private entrepreneurs. Most foreign film entrepreneurs in Southeast Asia were citizens of the colonizing country who had moved to the colonies, where they saw opportunities, creating colonial extensions of their home countries. Many were traders who imported various commodities; thus, there was an early connection between trade in film and other goods. The agents Nordisk Film employed for exporting films to Asia were the Danish-born American Rudolf G. Riis and J. A. Rojas de Torra in the Philippines; C. Boisen in China and Hong Kong; Sonne Schmidt (of the Danish East Indian Export Company based in Batavia) in the Dutch East Indies; Arthur G. Gregory, who previously had been in charge of opening an office for Fox in Copenhagen,[69] in China; Jacob Usunian in China; and J. S. Reynell (of the Central Film Distributing Company based in Tokyo) in Japan. Nordisk Film also gave C. Boisen, the distributor in China and Hong Kong, the rights to show films for buyers in Japan as well, and if he sold them, he was entitled to one-third of the net price.[70]

These contracts were license agreements through which the agents and Nordisk Film shared the profits. In its financial report to stockholders in 1924, Nordisk Film claimed that licensing agreements usually rendered more income, but the income was received after the exhibition of the films.[71] The contract between Nordisk Film and Rudolph G. Riis in the Philippines was on a long-term basis and not connected to specific films. The contract gave Riis the rights of "the films which Nordisk might place at his disposal," which are those that "Nordisk shall deem suitable for the said territory." Riis paid Nordisk DKr 0.50 per meter, and they split the profit. The contract was indefinite and could be canceled with three months' notice.[72]

Information in the distribution contracts of Nordisk Film, for instance, the date and price of film rights, illustrate which markets were most lucrative. The rights for *Klovnen* (*The Golden Clown*, 1926) were sold for USD 5,000 to the United

States, USD 2,500 to Italy, and USD 450 to China. For Japan, GBP 100 was paid when the contract was signed and an additional GBP 80 in London when shipping documents were presented.[73] As the marginal cost of every new copy of a film is limited, it was profitable to sell export rights to other markets, such as Asia, even at a low price. During the second phase, most films were sold at a fixed price. The prices for the films sold to the Philippines in 1913–1915 ranged between DKr 900 and DKr 2,200. During the third and fourth phases, most films were sold on a commission-based contract in which risks and profits were shared. Selling rights in advance later became part of the strategy of Nordisk Film because the company needed capital.[74] The rights to *Maharajahens Yndlingshustru* (The maharaja's favorite wife/Oriental love, 1926) for British India, Burma, and Ceylon were sold to Alliance Trades Agency in Calcutta for GBP 100 two months before the film premiered.[75]

Most Nordisk Film productions were sold on average six months after they premiered. In some cases it could be up to three or four years from the time they premiered in Europe until the films were distributed to Asia, especially during World War I.

Exhibition of Nordisk Film in Southeast Asia

The earliest mention of the exhibition of Danish films in Asia was in an advertisement for the New Japanese Cinematograph in the *Straits Times* in 1908, in which "Danish pictures" are most likely Nordisk Film productions.[76] Newspaper advertisements suggest that Nordisk Film quickly became an established brand, and it was renowned for and advertised by its name. Nick Deocampo names Nordisk Film as one of six film companies whose films were shown in Manila in the early twentieth century, and it was described as doing "brisk business" in the country.[77] A 1909 article in the *Straits Times* presents the cinema programs in three cinema houses in Singapore, and Nordisk Film is the only company mentioned by name: "Some new Nordisk films will be presented, and promise to be high-class productions."[78] And a front-page advertisement for the Grand Cinematograph in Harima Hall states, "New Programme. Trial show of Nordisk's new films."[79]

Two early international successes by Nordisk Film were *Isbjørnejagt* (Polar bear hunt, 1907), which sold 191 copies around the world, and *Løvejagten* (The lion hunt, 1907), which sold 285 copies.[80] *Isbjørnejagt* was exhibited at Alhambra in Singapore in January 1910, but there was no mention of it being a Nordisk Film production.[81] *Løvejagten* was the first Nordisk Film production named in an advertisement in Asia. It was exhibited as *Hunting the Lion* at Krung Thep Cinematograph in Bangkok in January 1909.[82] In the film, two white-clad, cigar-smoking white men are on a safari, hunting lions with the assistance of a light-clad, dark-skinned man. The film ends with the men shooting two lions and posing in front of them, evoking images of US president Theodore Roosevelt hunting and posing with his prey.

The film can be read as part of a colonial tradition in which the white man shows he can handle exotic climates and wild animals, and it contrasts the sophisticated Westerner with the primitive dark-skinned man. Considering that most early films were made in Europe and North America, there was a distinct Eurocentric worldview reproduced in early film images, and other parts of the world were portrayed as exotic, strange, and sometimes uncivilized.[83] Denmark was not a colonizing country like most other early film-producing and film-exporting countries. Yet it can be argued that Danish films are part of the same Eurocentric worldview, and hence the films of Nordisk Film serve as a prism of colonial culture. Danish companies, moreover, contributed to the social segregation in Southeast Asia, as reported by the *Bangkok Times*: "The [Danish] East Asiatic Co., Ltd, are to give a dance on board the a/s Siam on Monday evening, and they are following high precedent and good sense in putting the word 'white' on the corners of the cards of invitation."[84]

The Nordisk Film criminal series Dr. Gar el Hama (five films from 1911 to 1916) had an Oriental story line in which the main character portrayed an Oriental master criminal. The nationality of Dr. Gar el Hama is never revealed, but considering his name and the fez/peci/songkok he is wearing, he is supposed to come from somewhere in the Orient (or the Ottoman Empire). The first film, *Dr. Gar el Hama* (1911), was advertised and exhibited as *The Oriental/Dr. Gar-El Hama* at Ideal in Manila forty days after it premiered in Denmark.[85] The same film was exhibited two months later, in March 1912, at Olympia in Cebu,[86] which means the film was likely screened in several other movie houses in the Philippines in between those two exhibitions. In May 1912 it was exhibited at the Globe Bioscope in Batavia, and in February 1913 it was shown at the Oranje Bioscoop in Medan.[87] It was exhibited three and a half years later, in October 1915, as *The Dead Man's Child* at Casino Cinema in Singapore, where the film was promoted through Dr. Gar el Hama's antagonist: "Introducing the Famous Private Detective 'Newton.'"[88]

The Dr. Gar el Hama films were exhibited throughout Asia: for instance, at Phathanakorn Cinema in Bangkok in October 1913 and August 1914, at Bioscoop De Ster in Makassar (on Sulawesi) in June 1914, and at La Scala Picture Theatre in Kuala Lumpur in June 1915.[89] They were all marketed as *Dr. Gar el Hama*, so it is hard to determine which film was actually exhibited. In the 1913 exhibition in Bangkok, a newspaper notice described the film's protagonist as "a criminal who caused quite a sigh of relief when at last he was seen securely in prison."[90] We can thus conclude that the exhibited film was the second in the series, *Dr. Gar el Hamas Flugt* (Dr. Gar el Hama II, 1912), as that one ends with his imprisonment. The sequel was also exhibited at the Oost-Java Bioscope in Bandung in January and December 1914,[91] and other sequels were exhibited at Elita Biograph in Bandung in April 1916.[92]

Another Nordisk Film production with an Oriental feature is *Maharajahens Yndlingshustru* (Oriental love, 1917) and its two sequels, cowritten by the previously mentioned Marie Luise Droop, and one remake. It was exhibited at the Royal Standard Biograph in November 1920 in Batavia, where it was promoted as "an Indian love novel."[93] And the 1926 remake was called a "romantic-mysterious love story" in the Batavian press in October 1927.[94] The film is about an officer's daughter who falls in love with an Indian maharaja in Europe and runs away with him to India, where she becomes part of his harem. The film uses the trope of the Oriental harem as a way to exotify the East, the so-called Orient, and objectify women. Ella Shohat and Robert Stam write about "the imaginary of the harem" and how that idea offers a voyeuristic male gaze into a forbidden Orientalist fantasy.[95] It is, moreover, a theme that Nordisk Film had used earlier, for instance, in *Et Haremsæventyr* (An adventure in a harem, 1915).

Film advertisements suggest that most distributors purchased several films, as multiple Nordisk Film productions were exhibited within a matter of weeks or months. Ideal Theater in Manila exhibited *Den Sorte Kansler* (The black chancellor, 1912), *Dødsspring til hest fra cirkuskuplen* (The great circus catastrophe, or The great attraction, 1912), and *Seamen Trade* within a month in 1912.[96] *The Black Chancellor* was exhibited two months after it premiered in Denmark, whereas *The Great Circus Catastrophe* was exhibited a mere two weeks after its Danish premiere. The latter film, one of Nordisk Film's most successful productions, sold 245 copies around the world.[97] In Manila, it was called "one of the far-famed Nordisk art series of films" and promoted as "a film of the highest merit backed by the reputation of the Nordisk Film Company."[98] *Seamen Trade*, in turn, was described as "another of the famous Nordisk films" and "the chief attraction of the program."[99]

In Kuala Lumpur, the earliest mention of Nordisk Film I have found is a 1911 advertisement for the traveling Auxetophonoscope ("the only true and perfect synchronising machine touring the World"), which exhibited films from major film companies: "American Biograph Co., The Ambrose Co., Gaumont Co., Pathe Freres, Eddison [sic] Co., Vitagraph Co., Nordist [sic] Co, Lux Co."[100] Two years later, four Nordisk Film productions were exhibited within three weeks. Cinematograph Française marketed *Dødens Brud* (The bride of death, 1911) as a "great special feature film [that] appeals to all tastes" with "magnificent acting and staging."[101] The following week it showed *Jernbanens Datter* (The little railroad queen, 1911), whereas another movie house in the city, Kuala Lumpur Kinematograph, exhibited one of Nordisk Film's Sherlock Holmes features.[102] And the third week, Cinematograph Française exhibited *Livets Løgn* (The fatal lie, 1911), which a short review described as "exceptionally good" and a film that "amused and interested the audience from start to finish."[103] A month later, *The Black Chancellor* was promoted as a "powerful drama, well acted and beautifully tinted, a feature in a thousand; Nordisk's masterpiece."[104] The following year, Estana Hall Kinema exhibited *Mormonens Offer* (A victim of the Mormons, 1911), promoted as "the greatest sensational drama ever produced," and the travelogue *Life and People South of the Equator* (1911).[105]

How, and if, Nordisk Film productions moved between countries in Asia is yet to be discovered. *The Little Railroad Queen*, for instance, was exhibited at Gaiety Picture Palace in Singapore in August 1914,[106] more than a year after it was exhibited in Kuala Lumpur. *The Great Circus Catastrophe* was exhibited in Manila in September 1912 and at Globe Bioscope in Batavia three months later, but it did not reach Singapore until January 1917, when it was exhibited at Gaiety Picture Palace.[107] *The Bride of Death* was exhibited at the Oost-Java Bioscope in Bandung on Java in May 1914,[108] more than a year after its Kuala Lumpur exhibition. *A Victim of the Mormons* was exhibited at the Oranje Bioscoop in Medan on Sumatra in December 1914,[109] four months after its Kuala Lumpur exhibition. *Manden med Kappen* (The man in the white cloak, 1913) was exhibited at the Gaiety Picture Palace in Singapore in September 1915 and again at Cinema Casino in the same city a year and a half later.[110] *Fæstningsspioner* (The spy, 1913), with its "thrilling motor car chase," was exhibited at Cinema Casino in March 1916 and at Deca-Park in Batavia in February 1917.[111] *Evangeliemandens liv* (The candle and the moth, 1915) was exhibited at the Alhambra in Singapore in October 1916 and again at the Royalty in Malacca in March 1920.[112] In none of these cases have I been able to follow the movement of the films between the exhibitions or establish whether they were the same or different film copies. The only exception, besides *Dr. Gar el Hama*, is *Staalkongens Villie* (The steel king's last wish, 1913), which was exhibited at Cinema Casino in Singapore in July 1915 and at Deli Bioscoop in Medan two months later.[113]

In Singapore, Nordisk Film productions were exhibited in at least six different movie houses: in late 1915, *Den tredie magt* (The stolen treaty, 1913) was exhibited at Palladium one week and at Theatre Royal the next;[114] *Bristet Lykke* (Paradise lost, 1913) was exhibited at Cinema Casino in October 1916 and at Empire Cinema in May 1917;[115] and *Children of the Circus* was exhibited at Alhambra Cinematograph in October 1916 and at Gaiety Picture Palace in June 1917.[116] In January 1916, *Atlantis* (1913), adapted from Nobel Prize–winner Gerhard Hauptman's novel, was exhibited at Gaiety Picture Palace. The film was advertised as "the Nordisk Co.'s stupendous production: recalling the great 'Titanic' disaster."[117] It had cost USD 60,000 to produce, and it sold for DM 2,500 to the Philippines and for DM 2,545 to the Dutch East Indies. It was such a large and important production that Ingvald C. Oes wrote an article, "The Exclusive Program," about it in the *Motion Picture News*.[118]

There were, yet again, periods when several Nordisk Film productions were exhibited in the same cinema. The Alhambra Cinematograph exhibited seven films within six months, including three films within three weeks in October 1916.[119] In a matter of weeks in June and July 1915, Cinema Casino showed *Af Elskovs Naade* (Was she justified, 1914), *Prinsesse Elena* (Princess Elanor's prisoner, 1913), *Hammerslaget* (In the hour of temptation, 1914), and *Staalkongens Villie*. The films were advertised as "Produced by the Famous Nordisk Company," "Produced by the well-known Nordisk Co," "A Nordisk Special," and "The Great Nordisk Exclusive."[120] In the first few months of 1917, another group of Nordisk Film productions was screened at Cinema Casino. The first was *I Farens Stund* (The fortunes of war, 1915) in January 1917,[121] and for five weeks in March–April 1917, the cinema showed a Nordisk Film feature every week. The exhibited films were *The Man in the White Cloak, Endelig alene* (Alone at last, 1914), *Out of the Deep, Hvem er Gentlemantyven?* (Who is the gentleman's lady?, 1915), *Om kap med døden* (A race with death, 1915), and *Den Blinde Skæbne* (Blind fate, 1915).[122]

The Phathanakorn Cinematograph in Bangkok also exhibited two Nordisk Film productions in consecutive weeks in late 1916: *Fiskeren og hans Brud* (Saved from the sea, 1911) and *Satans Datter* (The devil's daughter, 1913).[123] In the Dutch East Indies, the West-Java Bioscope in Batavia had regular successful exhibitions of Nordisk Film productions as early as 1912,[124] and several other cinemas throughout the Dutch East Indies exhibited Nordisk Film productions. When Nordisk Film features were exhibited at Nederlands-Indische Electro Bioscope in Surakarta (Solo) in 1913, the name of the company was written three times in bold font in the sparse advertisements, as if the strength of the brand name would suffice to attract the crowds.[125]

I have not been able to identify the Danish titles of several exhibited films. In some cases it is hard to ascertain which Nordisk Film production was exhibited, as the films could be screened under different titles or described in similar ways. The two-reel *Den Mystiske Fremmede* (A deal with the devil, 1914) exhibited at Casino Cinema in Singapore in July 1916 and the four-reel *Revenge and After* screened there in February 1917 were both described in the same way in the advertisements: "[The film] tells a story which grips the imagination in the first reel and keeps its grip unloosened throughout the two [four] reels of superb artistry of which it consists. The story is based on a theme which strikes a note of intense human passion, and is played by the principal artistes in startingly [*sic*] realistic fashion. The whole production has been staged with the greatest care and skill."[126]

The aforementioned Great Northern Special Feature Film Company also seems to have distributed films to Southeast Asia. When *The Man in the White Cloak* was exhibited at the Gaiety Picture Palace in Singapore in September 1915, it was promoted as "a superlative dramatic production by the Great Northern Special Feature Film Co. of America."[127] *Verdens Undergang* (The end of the world, 1916), on the other hand, was promoted as a film from the Great Northern Film Company.[128] I have found only one instance in the local press where it is mentioned that Nordisk Film is a Danish company. When *Expressens Mysterium* (Alone with the devil, 1914) was exhibited at Cinema Casino in March 1915, a short review described it as "a modern mundane drama of considerable power, in three reels, produced by the Nordisk (Danish) Company."[129]

This chapter illustrates how a major European film company viewed and acted toward the Asian market, particularly Southeast Asia. It examines the distribution and exhibition of Nordisk Film productions through analyzing distribution protocols and contracts of Nordisk Film as well as contemporary Southeast Asian newspapers and trade data. From as early as 1908 Nordisk Film productions were exhibited throughout Asia to a much greater extent than the 272 exported films found in the archives of the Danish Film Institute. In my archival newspaper research, I have found more than fifty occasions when the films of Nordisk Film were exhibited, without finding corresponding contracts. Distributors often bought or rented several of their films and exhibited them at a cinema within a time frame of a few weeks. The films created their own trade paths independent of the influential Danish East Asiatic Company and Danish commodities exported to Asia. I have, however, not been able to trace individual film reels because of insufficient data. This kind of mapping increases our understanding of early film trade between Europe (or North America) and Asia, but more research is needed.

NADI TOFIGHIAN is Lecturer in the Department of Film and Literature at Linnaeus University in Sweden. He was previously Lecturer at Stockholm University and De La Salle University Manila and a postdoctoral research fellow at Yale University. He has published on early cinema, colonial history, and Southeast Asia.

Notes

1. Denmark has a long history of trade with Asia; in 1616 the Danish East India Company (Dansk Ostindisk Kompagni) was formed, and in 1620 it bought land and established a colonial port in Tranquebar (East India), which remained a Danish colony until 1845.

2. Swedish East Asiatic Company Stiftelseurkund (memorandum of association), April 30, 1907, in Fritz Scheel, *A.-B Svenska Ostasiatiska Kompaniet, dess tillkomst och verksamhet under 20 ar* [The Swedish East Asiatic Company, its establishment and operation during 20 years] (Gothenburg, Sweden: Wald. Zachrissons Boktryckeri AB, 1928), 51–52. In 1732–1813, its precursor, the Swedish East India Company (Svenska Ostindiska Companiet), operated and traded particularly with China. These trade companies were politically powerful; during the First World War, the chairman of the Swedish East Asiatic Company, K. A. Wallenberg,

became minister of foreign affairs, and its CEO, Dan Broström, became naval minister (during which period they resigned from the company). See Scheel, *A.-B Svenska Ostasiatiska Kompaniet*, 126.

3. Nordisk Film advertisement, *Moving Picture News*, April 1, 1911, p. 2. The advertisement (with changing films) also appears in subsequent issues for over a year.

4. Isak Thorsen, "Nordisk Films Kompagni Will Now Become the Biggest in the World," *Film History* 22, no. 4 (2010): 466.

5. Isak Thorsen, "Isbjørnens anatomi: Nordisk Films Kompagni som erhvervsvirksomhed i perioden 1906–1928" [Anatomy of the polar bear: Nordisk Films Kompagni as a business enterprise in the period 1906–1928] (PhD diss., Copenhagen University, 2009), 39–40; Isak Thorsen, "Rise and Fall of the Polar Bear," in *100 Years of Nordisk Film*, ed. Lisbeth Richter Larsen and Dan Nissen (Copenhagen: Danish Film Institute, 2006), 59.

6. Isak Thorsen, "'We Had to Be Careful': The Self-Imposed Regulations, Alterations and Censorship Strategies of Nordisk Films Kompagni, 1911–1928," in *Evaluating the Achievement of One Hundred Years of Scandinavian Cinema: Dreyer, Bergman, Von Trier, and Others*, ed. John Tucker (Lewiston, NY: Edwin Mellen Press, 2012), 146–169.

7. I have consulted the archives of Nordisk Films Kompagni at the Danish Film Institute in Copenhagen and visited archives in all Southeast Asian countries. I thank Isak Thorsen and Lisbeth Richter Larsen for their help at the archives in Copenhagen.

8. Advertisement, *Java-Bode*, October 9, 1896, cited in Dafna Ruppin, *The Komedi Bioscoop: Early Cinema in Colonial Indonesia* (New Barnet, UK: John Libbey, 2016), 42.

9. Advertisement, *El Comercio* [The trade], January 2, 1897.

10. Advertisement, *Straits Times*, May 12, 1897, p. 2.

11. Advertisement, *Bangkok Times*, June 9, 1897, p. 2.

12. Advertisement, *L'Avenir du Tonkin* [The future of Tonkin], September 1, 1897, p. 3.

13. Nadi Tofighian, "Blurring the Colonial Binary: Turn-of-the-Century Transnational Entertainment in Southeast Asia" (PhD diss., Stockholm University, 2013), 155–198.

14. Editorial, *Malay Mail*, November 8, 1910, p. 6.

15. H. F. H., "A Visitor from the Orient: Present Conditions of Moving Picture Industry in China Undergoing Many Changes for the Better: First-Hand Information," *Moving Picture World*, May 18, 1912, p. 620.

16. "Great Film Industry: Theatres in the East," *Siam Observer*, June 18, 1914, p. 5.

17. H. Frankel, "The Apolo Theater, Manila," *Moving Picture World*, December 3, 1910, p. 1304; various film advertisements in local papers of Southeast Asia.

18. Editorial, *Bangkok Times*, January 15, 1908, p. 2.

19. Nadi Tofighian, "Watching the Astonishment of the Native: Early Audio-visual Technology and Colonial Discourse," *Early Popular Visual Culture* 15, no. 1 (2017): 26–43.

20. "The Unsophisticated Malay," *Bangkok Times*, June 16, 1897, p. 2; "The Blind Faith of the Oriental," *Bangkok Times*, January 16, 1903, p. 3; "The Malazy People," *Times of Malaya*, August 15, 1908, p. 4; "One Way of Governing Malays," *Perak Pioneer*, August 26, 1908, p. 4; "The Interior of Siam: A Primitive and Indolent Population; The Simple Life," *Malay Mail*, December 9, 1909, p. 2.

21. Doré Hoffman, "The Melies Company in Java: The Round-the-World Picture Makers, Doing a Good Educational Work, Pause at an Interesting Island," *Moving Picture World*, June 21, 1913, p. 1234.

22. Horace T. Clarke, "Film Trade Difficulties in the Orient: Brief Resume of Conditions in Japan, China, Strait Settlements, India, and Dutch East Indies—Australasia Partial to American Product," *Moving Picture World*, October 19, 1918, p. 428.

23. Advertisement, *Straits Times*, August 17, 1907, p. 3.

24. Kristin Thompson, *Exporting Entertainment: America in the World Film Market, 1907–34* (London: British Film Institute, 1985), 76.

25. "Pictures Invade China: American Materials and Supplies in Demand in Celestial Kingdom," *Motion Picture News*, December 20, 1913, p. 20.

26. H. F. H., "A Visitor from the Orient," 621.

27. G. P. Harleman, "Motion Pictures in the Orient," *Moving Picture World*, August 25, 1917, p. 1225.

28. Hanford C. Judson, "Big Possibilities for Pictures in the Orient: Charles Margelis, Back from a Seven Months' Trip from Yokohama to Java, Believes There Is Great Chance for Picture Promoters in the East," *Moving Picture World*, September 1, 1917, p. 1357.

29. "Brandenburgh of Philadelphia, in the Toils," *Moving Picture News*, November 4, 1911, p. 6.

30. George William Miatt, "Miatt-Patents Department," *Moving Picture News*, January 4, 1913, p. 23.

31. Letter from Santos y Artigas to Nordisk Film, November 19, 1913, XII, 88:27, Nordisk Film Special Collection (NF), Danish Film Institute (DFI), Copenhagen, Denmark.

32. Registration of the trademark in India, June 8, 1920, I, 61:8–9, NF, DFI.

33. Registration of the trademark in Japan, September 30, 1920; July 25, 1921; and September 24, 1921, I, 61:155–162, NF, DFI. In Norway, the trademark application was denied in 1914, as Bio Film had a trademark with a reindeer standing on a globe. See registration of the trademark in Norway, May 30, 1914 to October 27, 1914, I, 61:163–181, NF, DFI.

34. Thompson, *Exporting Entertainment*, 61–71.

35. "We Sacrifice Markets in East, Says Howells: Americans Should Deal Direct with Antipodes and Not through London, Declares Exporter," *Moving Picture World*, May 5, 1917, p. 769.

36. Thompson, *Exporting Entertainment*, 71–76.

37. Ibid., 122–123.

38. "Resources of Philippines: Natural Gateway to Markets of the East," *Straits Times*, December 11, 1908, p. 7.

39. Thompson, *Exporting Entertainment*, 2–3.

40. "Our 'Roving Commissioner': Interesting Facts from Abroad, Gleaned from an Interview with Mr. I. C. Oes, Manager of the Great Northern," *Moving Picture News*, September 23, 1911, p. 11.

41. Ron Mottram, "The Great Northern Film Company: Nordisk Film in the American Motion Picture Market," *Film History* 2 (1988): 71–86.

42. "Our 'Roving Commissioner'"; "Great Northern Special Feature Film Co.," *Moving Picture News*, January 6, 1912, p. 12; Mottram, "The Great Northern Film Company," 79–80.

43. "Great Northern Special Feature Film Co.," *Moving Picture News*, March 2, 1912, p. 21.

44. Nordisk Film even gave the distribution rights of their films in Denmark and Norway to Fotorama, another early Danish film producer. The agreement, in 1910–1911, was reached after Nordisk Film made *Den hvide Slavehandel* (The white slave trade, 1910), a rip-off of Fotorama's *Den hvide Slavehandel* (1910). Marguerite Engberg, "Plagiarism, and the Birth of the Danish Multi-reel Film," in Larsen and Nissen, *100 Years of Nordisk Film*, 73–79; Casper Tybjerg, "An Art of Silence and Light: The Development of the Danish Film Drama to 1920" (PhD diss., University of Copenhagen, 1996), 73–74.

45. Lisbeth Richter Larsen and Dan Nissen, "100 Years of Nordisk Film," in Larsen and Nissen, *100 Years of Nordisk Film*, 14, 19, 21.

46. Annual report of Nordisk Film, 1920–1921, III, 37:15–16, NF, DFI.

47. Marie Luise Droop, "Asien, wir grussen Dich" [Asia, we salute you], *Der Eisbär* [The polar bear], nos. 3, 4, and 10 (1917), nos. 19, 20, 33, and 34 (1918), no. 51 (1919), I, 29:1–7, NF, DFI.

48. Distribution protocols of Nordisk Film, 1912–1914, XII, 33, NF, DFI; distribution protocols of Nordisk Film, 1914–1924, XII, 40, NF, DFI; distribution protocols of Nordisk Film, 1916–1919, XII, 43:1, NF, DFI.

49. Advertisement, *Straits Times*, February 25, 1909, p. 1; "Cinematograph Shows," *Straits Times*, February 25, 1909, p. 7.

50. Larsen and Nissen, *100 Years of Nordisk Film*, 21.

51. The issue of the "Nordicness" of Nordisk Film, as well as other early Scandinavian film companies, is discussed in detail in Anne Bachmann, "Locating Inter-Scandinavian Silent Film Culture: Connections, Contentions, Configurations" (PhD diss., Stockholm University, 2013), 47–130.

52. Thorsen, "Isbjørnens anatomi," 72, 75.

53. Ibid., 79.

54. Ibid., 45–46.

55. Trade data, 1905–1928, Danish Office of Statistics, National Library of Denmark, Copenhagen, Denmark.

56. Chr. Erichsen, *Siam som Handelsland og "Det Ostasiatiske Kompagni"* [Siam as a trade country and "The East Asiatic Company"] (Copenhagen: H. Hagerups Forlag, 1900), 92.

57. Svenska Bio archives, Swedish Film Institute, Stockholm, Sweden. For more on the global distribution of Svenska Bio, see Laura Horak, "The Global Distribution of Swedish Silent Film," in *A Companion to Nordic Cinema*, ed. Mette Hjort and Ursula Lindqvist (Oxford, UK: Blackwell, 2016), 457–484.

58. Statistiska Centralbyrån (Central Bureau of Statistics), *Statistisk Årsbok för Sverige, 1928* [Statistical yearbook for Sweden, 1928] (Stockholm: Kungliga Boktryckeriet och P. A Norstedt and Söner, 1928), 171.

59. C. Sjögren, "Siams näringsliv" [Siam's business community], *Kommersiella Meddelanden* [Commercial messages], February 25, 1921, appendix, 31–32.

60. Erichsen, *Siam som Handelsland*, 14.

61. Ibid., 16–18.

62. "The East Asiatic," *Bangkok Times*, November 27, 1906, p. 2; "East Asiatic Company: The Bangkok Branch," *Bangkok Times*, May 9, 1908, p. 3.

63. In the 1910s there were frequent advertisements for Danish sterilized milk, beer, tinned vegetables, butter, account books, pens, brushes, and cigars. The press in neighboring countries also featured regular advertisements for Danish beer and the Danish East Asiatic Company.

64. Editorial, *Bangkok Times*, February 16, 1900, p. 2.

65. Bachmann, "Locating Inter-Scandinavian Silent Film Culture," 85.

66. "Comments on Film Subjects," *Moving Picture World*, April 17, 1909, p. 476.

67. Thorsen, "Isbjørnens anatomi," 356.

68. Nordisk Film, contract with P. R. van Duinen, December 5, 1919, XII, 31:81, NF, DFI.

69. "Wm. Fox Opens Offices in Copenhagen to Supply Entire Scandinavian Field," *Moving Picture World*, April 9, 1921, p. 608.

70. Nordisk Film, contract with C. Boisen, April 20, 1925, XII, 46:27, NF, DFI.

71. Nordisk Film, financial report to stockholders, 1923–1924, III, 37:22, NF, DFI.

72. Nordisk Film, contract with Rudolph G. Riis, September 1, 1925, XII, 46:36, NF, DFI.

73. Nordisk Film, contract with Central Film Distributing Company, February 11, 1929, XII, 46:85, NF, DFI.

74. For instance, the agent Axel H. Geermann was given the distribution rights for *Maharajahens Yndlingshustru* and *Klovnen* in Mexico (five and three months, respectively, before the films premiered). "Axel H. Geermann: Ansat som agent i Mexico" [Axel H. Geermann: Employed as agent in Mexico], May 10, 1926, I, 4:54, NF, DFI.

75. Nordisk Film, contract with Alliance Trades Agency, June 24, 1926, XII, 46:41, NF, DFI.

76. "One Verdict: 'No Comparison.' Present programme outshines all. Crowded nightly. English, American, German, Dutch and Danish pictures. Never exhibited and never can be exhibited by any other show out East." Advertisement, *Straits Times*, February 26, 1908, p. 1.

77. Nick Deocampo, *Cine: Spanish Influences on Early Cinema in the Philippines* (Manila: National Commission for Culture and the Arts, 2003), 104. The other companies were Pathé, Gaumont, Messter Film, Edison, and the American Mutoscope and Biograph Company. Ibid., 151.

78. "Cinematograph Shows," *Straits Times*, February 25, 1909, p. 7.

79. Advertisement, *Straits Times*, February 25, 1909, p. 1.

80. Ebbe Neergaard, *Historien om dansk film* [The history of Danish film] (Copenhagen: Gyldendal, 1960), 25; Thorsen, "Isbjørnens anatomi," 32–33.

81. Advertisement, *Straits Times*, January 29, 1910, p. 6.

82. Advertisement, *Bangkok Times*, January 2, 1909, p. 5.

83. See Alison Griffiths, "'To the World the World We Show': Early Travelogues as Filmed Ethnography," *Film History* 11, no. 3 (1999): 282–307; Jeanette Roan, *Envisioning Asia: On Location, Travel, and the Cinematic Geography of U.S. Orientalism* (Ann Arbor: University of Michigan Press, 2010), chap. 1; and Jennifer Lynn Peterson, *Education in the School of Dreams: Travelogues and Early Nonfiction Film* (Durham, NC: Duke University Press, 2013).

84. Notice, *Bangkok Times*, June 4, 1898, p. 2.

85. Advertisement, *Cablenews-American*, December 27, 1911, p. 7.

86. Advertisement, *Cebu Chronicle*, March 2, 1912, p. 2.

87. Advertisement, *Bataviaasch Nieuwsblad* [Batavian newspaper], May 28, 1912, p. 7; advertisement, *De Sumatra Post* [The Sumatra post], February 3, 1913, p. 11.

88. Advertisement, *Straits Times*, October 23, 1915, p. 11.

89. Advertisement, *Siam Observer*, October 25, 1913, p. 8; "The Phathanakorn," *Bangkok Times*, October 26, 1913, p. 5; advertisement, *Siam Observer*, August 18, 1914, p. 3; advertisement, *Pemberita-Makassar* [Makassar reporter], June 27, 1914, p. 3; advertisement, *Malay Mail*, June 16, 1915, p. 2.

90. "The Phathanakorn," 5.

91. Advertisement, *De Preanger-Bode* [The Preanger], January 16, 1914, p. 9; advertisement, *De Preanger-Bode*, December 5, 1914, p. 3.

92. Advertisement, *De Preanger-Bode*, April 8, 1916, p. 8.

93. Advertisement, *Het nieuws van den dag voor Nederlandsch-Indië* [The news of the day for the Netherlands Indies], November 6, 1920, p. 6.

94. Advertisement, *Bataviaasch Nieuwsblad*, October 24, 1927, p. 6.

95. Ella Shohat and Robert Stam, *Unthinking Eurocentrism: Multiculturalism and the Media* (London: Routledge, 1994), 161–165.

96. Advertisement, *Manila Times*, August 22, 1912, p. 5; "Offerings at the Cines," *Manila Times*, September 5, 1912, p. 5; "Offerings at the Cines," *Manila Times*, September 19, 1912, p. 5. I have not been able to identify the Danish title of *Seamen Trade*.

97. Larsen and Nissen, *100 Years of Nordisk Film*, 13.

98. "Offerings at the Cines," *Manila Times*, September 5, 1912, p. 5; advertisement, *Manila Times*, September 5, 1912, p. 5.

99. "Offerings at the Cines," September 5, 1912, 5.

100. Advertisement, *Malay Mail*, April 21, 1911, p. 4.

101. Advertisement, *Malay Mail*, April 16, 1913, p. 5.

102. Advertisement, *Malay Mail*, April 23, 1913, p. 5; advertisement, *Malay Mail*, April 26, 1913, p. 5.

103. Notice, *Malay Mail*, May 5, 1913, p. 6.

104. Advertisement, *Malay Mail*, June 14, 1913, p. 5.

105. Advertisement, *Malay Mail*, July 16, 1914, p. 3; Advertisement, *Malay Mail*, August 13, 1914, p. 3. The latter film was advertised as *Amid Raging Beasts*, with the following description: "A marvellous Realistic Picture of Wild life under the Equator. The Animal Sensation of the Season. Something entirely different—episodes and scenes that beat anything ever attempted before." I have not been able to find the corresponding Danish title. Advertisement, *Malay Mail*, July 16, 1914, p. 3.

106. Advertisement, *Singapore Free Press*, August 12, 1914, p. 1.

107. Advertisement, *Het nieuws van den dag voor Nederlandsch-Indië*, December 16, 1912, p. 7; advertisement, *Malaya Tribune*, January 5, 1917, p. 1.

108. Advertisement, *De Preanger-Bode*, May 11, 1914, p. 8.

109. Advertisement, *De Sumatra Post*, December 12, 1914, p. 4.

110. Advertisement, *Straits Times*, September 18, 1915, p. 11; advertisement, *Straits Times*, March 1, 1917, p. 5.

111. "At the Cinemas," *Malaya Tribune*, March 29, 1916, p. 9; advertisement, *Bataviaasch Nieuwsblad*, February 9, 1917, p. 4.

112. Advertisement, *Straits Times*, October 23, 1916, p. 8; advertisement, *Malaya Tribune*, March 17, 1920, p. 3.

113. Advertisement, *Straits Times*, July 14, 1915, p. 11; advertisement, *De Sumatra Post*, September 7, 1915, p. 4.

114. Advertisement, *Malaya Tribune*, November 25, 1915, p. 6; notice, *Straits Times*, December 2, 1915, p. 6.

115. Advertisement, *Malaya Tribune*, October 26, 1916, p. 9; advertisement, *Singapore Free Press*, May 17, 1917, p. 3.

116. Advertisement, *Malaya Tribune*, October 14, 1916, p. 3; advertisement, *Malaya Tribune*, June 22, 1917, p. 1. I have not been able to identify the Danish title of the film.

117. Advertisement, *Straits Times*, January 21, 1916, p. 5.

118. Ingvald C. Oes, "The Exclusive Program," *Motion Picture News*, October 25, 1913, p. 35.

119. The exhibited films were *Soul's Awakening, Children of the Circus, The Candle and the Moth, Mr Young's Love Affair, The Stolen Heiress, Black Britta,* and *The Opera Singer's Triumph.* I have not been able to identify the Danish titles of six of these films. Advertisements, *Straits Times*, July 22, 1916, p. 6; *Malaya Tribune*, October 14, 1916, p. 3; *Straits Times*, October 23, 1916, p. 8; *Malaya Tribune*, October 28, 1916, p. 3; *Straits Times*, December 16, 1916, p. 8; *Straits Times*, January 13, 1917, p. 8; *Straits Times*, January 29, 1917, p. 8.

120. Advertisements, *Straits Times*, June 10, 1915, p. 8; *Malaya Tribune*, June 26, 1915, p. 1; *Malaya Tribune*, June 30, 1915, p. 1; and *Straits Times*, July 14, 1915, p. 11.

121. Advertisement, *Straits Times*, January 24, 1917, p. 11.

122. Advertisements, *Straits Times*, March 1, 1917, p. 5; March 7, 1917, p. 11; March 14, 1917, p. 7; March 24, 1917, p. 11; April 2, 1917, p. 11; April 7, 1917, p. 11; and April 12, 1917, p. 9. I have not been able to identify the Danish title of *Out of the Deep.*

123. Advertisements, *Bangkok Times*, November 22, 1916, p. 5; *Siam Observer*, November 22, p. 3; *Bangkok Times*, December 1, 1916, p. 5.

124. Ruppin, *The Komedi Bioscoop*, 227.

125. Advertisement, *De Nieuwe Vorstenlanden* [The new principality], April 1, 1913, p. 4.

126. Advertisement, *Straits Times*, July 12, 1916, p. 11; advertisement, *Straits Times*, February 12, 1917, p. 11.

127. Advertisement, *Straits Times*, September 18, 1915, p. 11.

128. Advertisement, *Malaya Tribune*, September 12, 1917, p. 1.

129. "Singapore Amusements," *Straits Times*, March 20, 1915, p. 10.

8 The Civilizing Cinema Mission
Colonial Beginnings of Film in Indochina

Tilman Baumgartel

Marguerite duras's semiautobiographical novel *Un barrage contre le Pacifique* (The sea wall, 1950) contains one of the most evocative descriptions in world literature of a cinema visit during film's early period:

> The light went out. Now Suzanne felt invisible, invincible and began to cry with glee. This was an oasis, the black hall of the afternoon, the night of the lonesome, the artificial and democratic night, the great, egalitarian night of cinema, more real than the real night, more beautiful, more comforting than all the real nights, the chosen night, open to everybody, offered to everybody.[1]

The oasis that Duras describes is the Cinema Eden in colonial Saigon, a *locus amoenus* (pleasant place) that the French novelist repeatedly revisited in articles, interviews, and literary works.[2] It is one of the few places in which her troubled protagonist, raised by an abusive mother left to her own devices in the French colony of Indochina after the death of her husband, finds temporary peace of mind. Duras's infatuation with the cinema on the tree-lined rue Catinat—which Graham Greene immortalized in his novel *The Quiet American*—went as far as to claim that her mother worked as a pianist in this cinema to supplement her meager income as a schoolteacher.[3]

Although the year in which the narrative of *Un barrage contre le Pacifique* takes place is 1931—when the period of "early cinema" was historically over—I feel that the quotation is a fitting introduction to this chapter on early cinema in Indochina. It provides a personal testimony to the awe-inspiring novelty that cinema continued to cast more than three decades after its invention. The description of the screening seems to suggest that Duras's protagonist was watching a silent movie, and it is likely that silent films were still in circulation at that time in Indochina, five years after Alan Crosland's *The Jazz Singer* (1927) heralded the commercial ascendance of the talkies.[4]

Some readers might take issue with the fact that I have chosen a description of a cinema visit of a *colon*, a French inhabitant of the colony, Indochina, as a starting point to this chapter. There are two reasons for doing so: First, no similar account of "going to the movies" by a member of the autochthon population has surfaced so far from the archives. Second, as will become abundantly clear, early cinema in Indochina was a predominantly colonial enterprise, and the indigenous population of Indochina started to participate in the production and distribution of films only very late in the period of early cinema. Early cinema in Indochina was colonial cinema, first and foremost, often not just made by French citizens in the colony but actively supported by the colonial administration.[5]

According to a Vietnamese source, the first article on cinema written by a local did not appear until 1921 in the Vietnamese press; although given the number of newspapers and magazines printed at that time, this claim may be hard to believe. The claimed pioneering article was written by Truc Dinh, a student, who argued in the magazine *Nam Phong* (South wind) that "movies can replace daily news, books. It is possible for movies to display within five minutes the world's great events that newly took place this week."[6] For Cambodia and Laos, no similarly early writing has so far been found.

Early Cinema in Indochina: A Colonial Enterprise

It seems important to note at the very beginning of this chapter that the films that came out of the Asian colonies of France were but a tiny fraction of the total film production made in the entire French colonies. Indochina was at the very periphery of "la plus grande France," the "Greater France" of colonial times. The colonies in Africa—including Tunisia, Algeria, and Morocco—were closer to Europe and therefore paid more attention to the "motherland" than to the remote colonial holdings in faraway Asia, where even at the peak of colonization, only a relatively small number of French citizens resided. (A maximum of thirty-four thousand Frenchmen lived among the over twenty-two million indigenous people of Indochina. In Algeria alone, there were one million Europeans and nine million Algerians in 1954.)[7] Such numbers are reflected in the film production of Indochina. According to Eric LeRoy, *chef de service* (head of service) of the film archives of the French Center national du cinema (CNC), among the colonial documentaries that the CNC had restored until 2001, only 15 percent were from Indochina.[8]

One has to keep these numbers in mind when trying to assess the significance of cinema within the French colonial project and its self-prescribed mission. That is not to say that the filmmakers of the early twentieth century did not see themselves as important arbiters of the French *mission civilisatrice*, the "civilizing mission," that was the official rationale for French colonization, a concept that French republican political leader Jules Ferry had started to champion in the 1880s. The French felt that they contributed to the spread of civilization among the "backward" inhabitants of the colonized countries. Rather than merely govern colonial subjects and exploit the raw materials and cheap labor of their colonies, the French asserted their desire to develop the countries that they had conquered.[9]

However, historians like David Chandler have frequently pointed out that this mission was nothing more than a benevolent myth meant to obscure the fact that French colonialism was driven almost exclusively by self-interest. Chandler writes, "In all issues that mattered, France in Indochina placed the interests of the colonizers above those of the colonized."[10] There were strong profit-oriented motivations for the French conquest of Indochina, and economic exploitation and political oppression were dominant features of French colonial rule. At the same time, the French *did* support the founding of schools and universities in Indochina and took an active interest in researching the history of the countries they occupied, as well as preserving ancient monuments, most famously the ancient temple city Angkor Wat.

It is within this framework that film production in Indochina attains its significance. The great majority of films produced there during the colonial period were documentaries and educational films. Many of them were produced for the various colonial exhibitions in France that presented alluring images of the colonizing country's foreign possessions to the French people.

These films were part of the far-reaching project to "faire connaitre la France en Indochine et l'Indochine en France" (make France known in Indochina and Indochina in France), according to the famous slogan of Albert Sarraut, governor-general of Indochina from 1911 to 1914 and 1917 to 1919 and later minister of colonies.[11] This slogan became so popular that it was repeated time and again in essays and articles that sought the support of the colonial administration for the film productions made in the colony.[12] However, a sober historical analysis has to differentiate between the pompous claims and high-flying ambitions of those who wanted to use cinema as a way to propagate French culture and way of life (and who often had a strong economic interest in making those films) and the reality of actual film production in Indochina.

Only a handful of narrative films were made in Indochina during the silent period. Of those, so far only one has been rediscovered in a French film archive: the charming *Sous l'oeil de Boudha* (Under the eye of Buddha, 1923) by André Joyeux. No major French production was shot in Indochina, even though Jacques Feyder studied the possibilities to film a follow-up to his enormously successful movie *L'Atlantide* (Atlantis, 1921)—with its spectacular scenes set in the North African desert—in the temple ruins of Angkor Wat. However, the project did not push through. For Indochina, there is no equivalent to *L'Atlantide* or to films like Julien Duvivier's *La bandera* (Escape from yesterday, 1935) and *Pepe le Moko*

(1936), two movies from the heyday of French colonialism that used French Algeria and Morocco, respectively, as exotic and colorful settings for these two internationally successful films.

The French and Indochina

To understand the policies that shaped French colonialism and to find out how they made an impact on colonial film production, a very brief overview about the history of French colonialism in Asia is in order. French traders and missionaries have been active in today's Vietnam since the seventeenth century. When two Spanish Catholic missionaries were executed by the troops of the Vietnamese emperor Tu Duc, the French used this event as a pretext to attack. Napoleon III of France authorized Admiral Rigault de Genouilly to send a punitive expedition to Vietnam. The first attack against Tourane (today's Da Nang) was unsuccessful, but in 1859, French and Spanish troops captured Saigon, an important source for food for the Vietnamese troops.

It took the French troops almost a decade to expand their control over all six provinces on the Mekong Delta and to form a colony in 1867, which they named "Cochinchina," a term originally invented by Portuguese traders in the sixteenth century. From this military base, they slowly conquered the rest of Vietnam. They took northern Vietnam (which they called Tonkin) in 1873, captured Ha Noi in 1882, and after the Sino-French War (1884–1885), they took control of all of Vietnam. The process through which French Indochina was pieced together played a vital role for the administrative structure of the colony (including its film policies), as different parts of the colony each had a different status: Cochinchina in the south was a colony, Annam (Trung Ky, or central Vietnam) was a protectorate where the dynasty of the Nguyen emperors still ruled from the imperial city of Hue, and Tonkin (Bac Ky, or northern Vietnam) had a French governor with a local government partly run by Vietnamese officials.

While Vietnam was taken by force, both Cambodia and Laos became part of Indochina because they sought French protection against their overbearing neighboring countries. The small and militarily and economically weak Cambodia had been a victim of the whims of its two larger and more powerful neighbors—Thailand and Vietnam—for centuries when King Norodom Sihanouk signed a treaty with the French in 1863 in the Cambodian capital, Udong. The French offered Cambodia protection from attacks by Vietnam and Thailand, for which Norodom rewarded its French protectors with timber concessions and mineral exploration rights. Access to raw materials was one of the two prime motivations for the French colonial enterprise in Indochina, with rice, tea, timber, coffee, cocoa, sugar, corn, and, in the twentieth century, rubber as main export commodities. (The other motivation was the chance to use the Mekong as a direct passage into China's Yunnan Province with its vast mineral resources.)[13] The French also used the name "Indo-China" (later, Indochina) for their new colony, which included Laos, Vietnam, and Cambodia, a term that has stuck despite its not being descriptive.

Consciously or not, many of the early French filmmakers in Indochina acted like aspiring custodians of the culture of the country that France had conquered. They trained their lenses on the very traditions that made the colony unique from a Western point of view: first and foremost Angkor Wat and the other temples of the celestial city of the ancient Khmer kings, the Cambodian emperor, his palace, the Royal Ballet, the royal elephants, the Water Festival in Phnom Penh in Cambodia, the pagodas, temples, market scenes, rice planting and harvesting, silk weaving, and other traditional activities and genre-scene-like vignettes in all of the colony. If signs of modernity enter the picture at all, they are typically depicted in association with the colonial project, often represented by French administrators.

Coolies in Saigon: The Beginnings of Filmmaking in Indochina

The first filmmakers in Indochina defined the canon of subjects in colonial film production that would further develop in the following years. The first film that was shot in Indochina, *Coolies in Saigon*, was made by a camera operator of the Lumière brothers on December 30, 1896, almost exactly one year after the first films of Auguste and Louis Lumière were shown in Paris at the Salon Indien du Grand Café. The film was taken by François-Constant Girel (1873–1952) during a brief stopover on the way from France to Japan.[14] Girel traveled with Katsutaro Inabata, a Japanese businessman, who had bought two Cinématographe camera projectors and some film stock and secured the performing rights for the new invention from the Lumière company during his latest visit to France. Inabata had been a fellow student of Auguste Lumière at the polytechnic school in Lyon in 1878, where the two had become friends. He had been sent back to Europe as a representative of a spinning company based in Kyoto. But when Girel's old friend presented his new invention to him, Girel decided to spend his budget on the new technology to start his own business.[15]

Girel was only sixteen years old when he shot what was probably the first film, not only in Indochina but most likely in all of Asia. He had studied pharmacy in Lyon, where his brother-in-law was working at the Lumière factory. He was among the first group of camera operators deployed by the Lumière brothers to introduce their invention to the world[16]—the *chasseurs d'image* (image hunters), as one of the cameramen, Felix Mesguich, would later refer to himself in his autobiography.[17] (Among them, Girel was not the only one with a background in pharmacy or chemistry, an experience in working with chemicals that was essential for the traveling cinematographers, as they had to develop their films themselves.)

Apart from showing the Cinématographe to dignitaries, opinion makers, and the public throughout the world, these operators were charged with the task of sending back to France moving images from the foreign countries they visited for international distribution.[18] Girel was first sent to Germany, then to Switzerland, and on December 6, 1896, he left for Japan. Girel filmed extensively in Japan, and many of his films ended up in the Lumière catalogue. After a year, he was replaced by Gabriel Veyre, another French cameraman sent by the Lumière company, and returned to France. Girel's ability as a cameraman has been questioned, which may be why he failed to find further work in film and returned to the field of pharmacy.[19] Veyre made hundreds of films for the Lumières and others, many of which survive today.

Coolies in Saigon shows a group of twelve laborers in traditional Vietnamese attire who slowly drag a compressor from the right to the left of the frame, apparently to even out a street in the city of Saigon. It is a strange subject for the first film made by a young European during his first encounter with the Orient. Like the Lumières, who in their first films trained their camera on symbols of modernity—their own factory, the steam train—Girel also chose to film a scene that seems to indicate progress rather than to document a stereotypical image of Asian traditions (pagoda, market, dragon dance, etc.): a street is identified with the need for faster and more efficient transportation.[20]

Still, the coolies in this shot do cater to Orientalist ideas about Asia: These slavelike manual laborers, who did backbreaking work for little reward, fascinated early European visitors to Asia, and they frequently appeared in travelogues and photographs in the nineteenth and early twentieth centuries.[21] The coolies in this short film clip—seen with their robotic movements and bereft of any individual traits—may be read as examples of the low regard for the individual typical of Asia at the time. Or they may be considered as harbingers of modernity who turned Saigon into one of those oft-quoted phrases, "Pearl of the Far East." Despite their dire working conditions, they exemplify the advancement that the French rule of Indochina brought to the colony. "What is most compelling in this film," writes Panivong Norindr, "is the fact that it documents the unheralded labor of the Vietnamese people. . . . Although the identities of these 'coolies' will remain unknown forever, they have nevertheless left a filmic trace that must be accounted for if we are to give a fuller and more nuanced account of early cinema production."[22]

There is always the danger of reading too much into these few extant works of early filmmaking in Asia. (After all, how many hours did Girel spend on his stopover in Saigon during his voyage to Japan? How much opportunity did he have to film other street scenes?) Informed by the memoirs of another Lumière camera operator, Felix Mesguich, Martine Astier Loutfti has pointed out bluntly, but irrefutably, that the traveling Lumière operators were looking for two things in the *vues* (views) they filmed: exotic scenes and movement. "Capturing movement was the great innovation, the technological breakthrough brought out by the Lumière machine, and movement was what the viewers were demanding."[23]

Every overtly ideological analysis of films from the earliest period should take this plain but profound observation as a warning. But at the same time, Girel's choice of the subject matter for his first film after weeks on a ship is so peculiar (and seems so much at odds with my remarks about the focus on the "traditional" in early filmmaking in Indochina) that it does warrant some reflection. Yes, the small army of *Metropolis*-like work drones that drag the compressor over the screen is alluringly cinematic and had the advantage of not requiring any kind of staging on the part of the filmmaker. Yet it seems to me that it is precisely the tension between the transformation of an Indochinese city (that was most likely decreed by the French colonial administration) and the atavistic methods with which this development was achieved that make this film not only a fascinating document of French colonialism but also a fitting introduction to the major themes in colonial filmmaking in Indochina: the traditions and culture of the region, on the one hand; the French *mission civilisatrice*, the progressive and "civilizing" impact of colonialism, on the other hand.

Gabriel Veyre, the First Documentarist of Indochina

The first person who produced a serious body of cinematic work in Indochina was also a Lumière camera operator, Gabriel Veyre (1871–1936). He was a chemist from Saint-Alban-du-Rhone, a small village in l'Isere, France. He became one of Lumière's most widely traveled camera operators. The Lumière brothers sent him to the United States, Mexico, Guadeloupe, Cuba, Venezuela, Martinique, and Colombia in 1896. On his second trip, which began in October 1897, he set out for Japan, traveling via Canada. In October 1898, he arrived in Japan and replaced Constant Girel. From Japan, he went to China, and on April 28, 1899, he arrived in Hanoi. He stayed in Indochina for eight months until late December 1899 before returning to France.[24] Dean Wilson has identified 119 films that Veyre shot in Indochina. There is also a good number of other films in various archives, whose director is not known but could be Veyre's works.

Since the letters he wrote to his mother during his travels have been published, we are relatively well informed about his activities and even about the production of some of his films.[25] He took on the job as a camera operator because he was looking for adventure and because he wanted to earn money, with which he planned to purchase a pharmacy after his return to France. Yet he was genuinely interested in the countries that he visited; he tried to learn the languages of his host countries and develop a good understanding of their customs and traditions. While his film work is intimately connected to the colonial project, they often transcend the framework of colonial ideology.

Veyre arrived in Indochina when Paul Doumer was governor-general of the colony (1897–1902). Doumer, a firm believer in progress by means of culture and science, was tasked with giving the rather loosely organized Indochinese Union a well-organized colonial administration.[26] He moved the capital from the imperial city of Hue to Hanoi, brought in hundreds of French administrators, founded a number of colonial enterprises, started the construction of a train route network, supported education, and made Hanoi the first city with electricity in all of Asia. At the same time, he introduced a strict taxation system, with high tariffs on salt, opium, and alcohol, to make the Indochinese colony a profitable, rather than money-losing, enterprise.

In 1899, Doumer commissioned Veyre to make five hundred films for the Exposition Universelle, according to a letter by Veyre to his mother: "The Governor of Indochina was very nice to me. He did give orders to help me in all of my travels and asked me to take as many shots as possible for the Paris Exhibition *to make Tonkin known in France as it is.*"[27] With the support of the governor, Veyre was able to travel throughout Vietnam and Cambodia. Two Vietnamese carried his equipment in a sedan when it was not possible to use ox carts or other more comfortable means of transportation.

"To make Tonkin known in France as it is"—this sloganlike phrase would reverberate not only through Veyre's work but in all documentaries made with the support or as direct commissions of the administration of a colony whose French inhabitants often saw themselves at the margins of Greater France. To make Tonkin known in France as it is included showing the accomplishments and merits of the colonial administration. Veyre dutifully complied with this briefing: two of his films, *Baignade de chevaux et pont Doumer* (Horse bath at the Doumer Bridge, 1899) and *Dechargement d'une barque et pont Doumer* (Unloading a ship and the Doumer Bridge, 1899), show the Pont Doumer in Hanoi, which had been named after the governor-general while he was still in office. *La garde d'honneur du gouverneur-general* (Honor guard of the governor-general, 1890) has Doumer himself surveying his soldiers. Six films show Doumer performing various official duties, from inspecting soldiers to attending a boat race.[28] Many films show the French military parades in honor of Prince Valdemar of Denmark, who visited Indochina in January 1900, demonstrating the discipline and the glory of the French army.

A good number of films depicted the industrial progress that the French had brought to Indochina, including nine films showing the Hon Gay coal mines, such as *Les mines de charbon de Hon Gay* (The coal mines of Hon Gay, 1899). There is even a remake of *La sortie des usines Lumière* (Workers leaving the

Lumière factory, 1895), the very first film of the Lumière brothers, as *Sortie de la briqueterie Meffre et Bourgoin a Ha Noi* (Leaving the Meffre and Bourgoin Brick Factory in Ha Noi, 1899). Many of these films were shown at the World Fair in Paris in 1900.[29] Taken as a whole, they depicted the work of the colonial administration positively and stressed the progressive (and, for France, profitable) dynamic that colonialism had brought to Indochina.

The majority of films, however, are dedicated to more exotic aspects of native life. Veyre filmed dragon dances and other festivities during Tet (the Vietnamese New Year), mandarins greeting the Vietnamese emperor, opium smokers, a Vietnamese funeral, and people eating. In Cambodia, he filmed King Norodom in his coach, the Royal Ballet, the royal elephants during a walk in Phnom Penh, and the road to Angkor Wat. With all of these films, Veyre defined a canon of subjects to which later documentary filmmakers working in Indochina would return time and again: "Subsequent French reportage filmmakers . . . reproduced the themes first documented by Veyre with fidelity," writes Dean Wilson.[30]

For all of Veyre's efforts to document native scenes, these films were not particularly popular when they were screened at the World Fair in Paris in 1900 as an attraction in the Indochinese pavilion. Compared to the splendor of the Japanese pavilion and the dance performances there, the Asia that Veyre showed looked "poor and disorganized," argue Philippe Jacquier and Marion Pranal. His films simply did not cater to the glossy exoticism that was in vogue in Europe.[31]

Yet an important precedent was set with Veyre's films. The "idea to export images of Viet Nam for propaganda and publicity started with Doumer," declares Wilson.[32] In the following years, the colonial administration considered film as a means both to popularize Indochina in France and to inform their new subjects in Indochina about their new "mother country," France. As a result, the French had far-reaching control over the films that were produced, distributed, and screened in Indochina. They introduced a strict system of censorship to control what people in the colony were allowed to watch.[33] In fact, they also commissioned and paid the production costs of a good part of the few films that were made in the colony. They were likewise involved in their export, thereby controlling the images of Indochina that appeared on French and other international screens.

The Mission Cinématographique

While Paul Doumer might have been the first to regard film as a means of colonial propaganda when he commissioned Gabriel Veyre to make films for the Paris World Fair, Albert Sarraut (1872–1962), twice the governor-general of French Indochina, turned film into the centerpiece of his political strategy. Programmatically, he had declared, "it was absolutely indispensable that a methodical . . .

propaganda by word and visual image, journal, conference, film, and exhibition be activated in our land among adults and children" to overcome their ignorance of the colonies.[34] He set up a film and photography department in the colonial Economic Service to systematically produce photos and shorts on Indochina for distribution in France: Mission cinématographique (Cinematography Mission).

During his second term, he launched what may have been the most spectacular cinema activity of the colonial government: a mobile cinema that traveled through Indochina and showed patriotic short films to an audience of tens of thousands, as a publication on this endeavor claims.[35] The Mission was originally set up by the French army. In a treatise that Andre Touzet, *chef du cabinet et des affaires politiques et indigenes* (chief of the cabinet and political and indigenous affairs) in the colonial administration, published in the popular *Revue indochinoise* (Indochinese review)—and later had it reprinted as a small brochure, supposedly for wider circulation—he quotes Sarraut's statement about his goal to "make France known in Indochina and Indochina in France." The Mission cinématographique was set up to turn that purpose into practical reality: to show films on France in Indochina and to create photographs and films on Indochina for distribution in France.

Its first major project, however, was an extended tour with mobile projection with its primary goal to sell war bonds to the French in Indochina and the Annamites (the Vietnamese) to support the French war effort against Germany during the First World War. The cinema had been used for that purpose before. Touzet wrote in a report on the war bonds issued in 1917 about the Mission's successful marketing in cinemas: The Mission cinématographique, "which has already rendered such excellent service in terms of recruitment of workers and sharpshooters and whose documentary films will soon be sent to France, has provided the means to effectively reach all segments of peoples of Indochina."[36]

The Mission had used various methods to propagate its objectives. According to Touzet, anti-German propaganda cartoons, drawn by André Joyeux, the *directeur des ecoles d'art Annamite de Cochinchine* (director of the Annamite Art School in Cochinchina), with captions in French, Chinese, and Vietnamese, were shown in "all theaters of Cochinchina, Tonkin and Cambodia: in Saigon, Cholon Baclieu, Cantho, Mytho, Sadec, Vinh Long, Phnom Penh, Haiphong, Hanoi and Nam Dinh."[37] And they had distributed three French propaganda films made the previous year with some local scenes added. As a result of these films and other measures, the inhabitants of Indochina signed war bonds for more than sixty-six million francs.

Financially, the tour of the Mission cinématographique through Indochina was even more successful. Some 144 million French francs were raised in the territory during the Mission's traveling shows. For that purpose, a group of around two dozen men toured the colony with the equipment to show films. A projector, an enormous screen ten meters across, a generator, and other machinery were moved about the colony with the help of oxcarts, boats, and coolies. The leaders of this enterprise were two French military photographers, Gaston Brun and René Tétard. Brun was in charge of shooting films, while Tétard, who led the tour, took photos and worked as a projectionist. The project was financed by the French government, and for two years the group traveled through most of the colonial holdings in Indochina.

After the end of World War I, the Mission produced more short documentaries that it made available to French film companies such as Gaumont and Pathé, adding to the newsreels that both companies produced. An entry in the *Annuaire general de l'Indochine* (General directory of Indochina) of 1925 still listed Tétard as *chef contractual* (head contractor) and Alexis Mesrouze as *operateur* (operator) of the laboratory of the Service photographie–cinématographie (Photographic and Cinematographic Service), a division of the Direction des affaires economique (Directorate of Economic Affairs).[38] In the following year, the photography and film service of the colonial government was privatized, and the task of "making France known in Indochina and Indochina in France" was farmed out to the company of a man who had created and systematically expanded his cinema empire since 1908: Joseph de la Pommeraye. He was among the first entrepreneurs who turned the presentation of movies in Indochina into an apparently highly profitable business venture.

Indochina Films and Cinemas and Their Competitors

The *Annuaire general de l'Indochine* of 1908 lists one "Cinématographe" business in all of Indochina, operated by "J. de la Pommeraye et Cie" on rue d'Ormay, no. 63 in Saigon.[39] The *Annuaire* was a yearly publication of the colonial administration providing extensive information on Indochina. With well over one thousand pages during its heyday in the 1920s, the *Annuaire* is an impressive document of the desire of the colonizers to re-create their territories in Southeast Asia in their own image by measuring, ordering, organizing, and indexing them in the most rigid and systematic fashion. The almanac provides everything—from city maps to listings of addresses and telephone numbers of businesses and private persons; from directories of the offices of the administration with the names of the officials down to the lowest clerk to the timetable of trains, including fares; from tips for visitors to reports on the latest accomplishments in the colony. The Indochina depicted in the *Annuaire* is one where everything is organized according to French wishes and desires, a true "France on the Mekong," to use John Tully's term.[40]

The picture of de la Pommeraye that emerges from the pages of the *Annuaire* is that of a "well-connected businessman." He is first mentioned in the 1905 edition as an engineer by profession with addresses on rue Paul Bert, no. 38,[41] and on the adjoining rue Dong Khanh, no. 16,[42] probably his shop and his private residence. (The house on rue Dong Khanh was most likely an apartment building, as the street directory lists eighteen names under this address.) He was the proprietor of the Société française Indo-Chinoise de l'eclairage par l'acytelene (French Indochinese Society for Acetylene Illumination) in Hanoi that had branches in Saigon, Haiphong, and Tourane.[43] In the early twentieth century, carbide lamps (which used the acetylene that de la Pommeraye imported from France) were widely used for illumination, for example, in street lighting, in torches, and in the headlights of early automobiles, occasionally even in early film projectors. An article on the development of the industry in Tonkin in the 1908 *Annuaire* reports that his company had installed carbide street lights in some of the inner cities of the colony.[44] In the 1920s, he added a rubber and coffee plantation to his portfolio, where a Guy de la Pommeraye, most likely a relative, was a manager and also served as president of the Chamber of Commerce.[45]

In the following years, he systematically expanded De la Pommeraye et Cie.[46] In 1908, his company was selling car parts, gasoline engines, and typewriters and ran an *agence generale de publicité*, an advertising company, that sold advertising spaces on train wagons, train stations, and water reservoirs.[47] He was now "agent for the Pathe Brothers for Indochina" in Hanoi (business address: boulevard Francis-Ganier),[48] a position that he held for more than two decades. A Cinématographe, run by "S. de la Pommeraye et Cie," is listed at Rue d'Ormay, no. 63, in Saigon.[49] The 1910 *Annuaire* lists a Cinématographe Pathé frères at the same address, with a M. Lebreton as the director.[50] This might very well have been the first permanent cinema in Indochina. (The Cinématographe Louvet, located on rue Richaud, no. 56, appearing in the same edition of the *Annuaire* was rather short-lived and disappeared from the colonial annals after two years.)[51]

This does not mean that there were no other places for regular film screenings in Indochina at that time. A request for permission to the *resident superieur*, the French ruler over the Protectorate of Cambodia, indicated that a Monsieur Brignon had set up a cinema on the riverbanks of the Tonle Sap in Phnom Penh in 1909. These screenings were mostly "frequented by the European population."[52] This cinema was probably not more than an outdoor sitting area, where films were screened at night.[53] The program of a screening for schoolchildren from 1915 mentions the cinemas Royal and Casino in Phnom Penh. As the screenings were organized for more than seven hundred schoolchildren, these must have been stationary cinemas, probably of considerable size.

The businessman De la Pommeraye was the most successful among a number of entrepreneurs who, about 1910, started film businesses in Indochina. His strongest competitor, an A. Messner, also began as an importer of lamps and other electric equipment and gradually diversified into cinema, with theaters in some of the major cities of Indochina. Even in the mid-1920s, when he had a number of cinemas, he also ran a couple of ice factories and power and water plants in the Mekong Delta.[54] (Messner might have thought about investing in cinema because he lived on rue d'Ormary near de la Pommeraye's Cinématographe Pathé frères in the year when it opened.)[55] In 1911, the *Annuaire* lists three other cinemas in Saigon: the Leopold on boulevard Charner, the Casino on rue Pellerin, and the Bassora on rue Catinat, most likely an earlier incarnation of the Cinema Eden, which Marguerite Duras immortalized in *Un barrage contre le Pacifique.*

Film Distribution, Reception, and Censorship in Indochina

In all likelihood, none of these places were cinemas in the sense that we think of them today. Early films in the West were typically screened in small storefront shops with chairs on an even floor without any amenities, or they were part of other businesses. It is unlikely that this was very different in Indochina. For instance, the Casino was located in the official casino of Saigon. Hotels occasionally had their own cinemas, too—such as the Hotel Metropol in Hanoi, which boasted of its café, restaurant, bar, and cinema in an ad from 1916: "Very beautiful films of Tonkin. New Programs every week."[56]

But most theaters at the time were not located in fancy hotels or casinos but seemed to have been found in more mundane, if not downright sordid, places. An account of the cinemas in Hanoi in the 1930s mentions that many second-run movie houses had shows without any intermission, leaving no time to clean out the garbage between screenings. The cheaper theaters of that time—and there is no reason to believe that this was substantially different in the 1910s and 1920s— were crowded, smelly (smoking inside theaters was allowed), dirty, and bug ridden.

There were, however, more elegant cinemas. One source mentions the Majestic and the Eden in Hanoi as belonging to first-class cinemas that showed international films first in Indochina.[57] Then the films were screened in second-class movie theaters and then in third-class cinemas. As there was typically only one copy of any film available in all of Indochina, it took up to one and a half years for them to make the rounds throughout the entire cinema circuit in the colony.

In the 1910s and 1920s, cinemas opened in most of the major cities and many of the smaller towns of Indochina. A telephone book from 1933 lists twenty-four cinemas in twelve cities, which are most likely just a small group of more sophisticated cinemas that already had telephones.[58] There were also a number of cinemas showing Chinese-language movies that apparently were not included in the *Annuaire.* A tourist guidebook from 1930 provides this information: "The only European cinema in Phnom Penh is the Excelsior besides which there are two or three Chinese-owned picture houses in town."[59] In addition, there must have been a good number of mobile cinemas touring the countryside, as numerous requests for business licenses in the colonial records show.[60]

Owners of these theaters were typically businessmen who started cinemas as a sideline to their other businesses. Some of them imported their films themselves: De la Pommeraye distributed Pathé films both to his own cinemas and to Leopold Bernhard, who owned Casino and Leopold and opened a number of other cinemas in Cochinchina; Bernhard occasionally imported films from the United States.[61] Messner showed films from different companies in his own cinema and rented them out to others, including movies from Gaumont, Eclipse, Film d'art, Films Lardier, and Films Harry from France; Pascali, Cines, and Gloria from Italy; and Vitagraph, Triangle, and Keystone from London. Most of these companies had offices in Paris, and the majority of the prints were sent through the intermediary firm l'Agence generale cinématographique in Paris.[62]

But what did these cinemas show? A flyer for a screening at the Cinema des nouveautés à Phnom Penh for the program from April 16 to 22, 1918, gives us an idea: There were two screenings, one from 7:00 to 9:00 p.m., one from 9:00 to 11:00 p.m., in what the flyer calls "the most beautiful cinema hall in Indochina."[63] (Again, the cinema is not listed in the *Annuaire*, which means that there were probably other cinemas without any record in its directory.) "Electric Ventilation is available on all seats" and "the projecting is very clear and stable" are two other advertising claims made that give us an idea what film screenings in lesser theaters might have been like at that time. There were eight price brackets for seating; for example, seats in the loge cost one piastre, while regular seats were sixty cents, and the cheapest were thirty cents.

The first program began with three short films, one of which was the Gaumont *Actualités* no. 34 newsreel. The main attraction, however, were two acts of Giovanni Pastrone's *Cabiria* (1914), followed by the short comedy *Les exploits de Joseph* (The exploits of Joseph), starring Charlot (a.k.a. Charles Chaplin). The second screening started with two short comedies, and then the next two acts of *Cabiria* before the program ended with another short comedy.

The colonial administration apparently had little faith in the "media literacy"—to use a contemporary term—of the local film audience. Governor-General Albert Sarraut himself warned the *resident superieur* of Cambodia, in a letter dated June 23, 1917 (under a letterhead proclaiming "Liberté, Egalité, Fraternité"), that in Indochina "people are easier to impress" and that one had to be "careful with films that show bad people who perform smart tricks, as it sets a bad example." In France, people are more educated and more intelligent, he pointed out, but in the colony, "because of the many mixed-race people, most of them are not able to understand that movies are fiction, not the reality."[64]

Two and a half years later, the matter of cinema seemed urgent enough to require swift action. In December 1920, Sarraut's successor, Maurice Long, sent a telegram to all administrators of French Indochina, warning them of the damage that films could do to the unprepared minds of the local population and asked them about the situation in their respective territories. From Cambodia, the *residents* of Kratie, Battambang, Prey Veng, and Kampong Thom replied dutifully and described the state of film distribution in their respective communities.[65] On the basis of their statements, Long set up a broad system of censorship in Indochina, with two commissions in Hanoi and Saigon to give out visas (screening permits). Only films with visas were allowed to be shown in Indochina, and importers of films had to register with the colonial administration.[66]

The lists of films presented to the *resident superieur* of Tonkin and the governor of Cochinchina in Saigon gave a good impression of the films that were imported into Indochina in the 1920s. The lists of films that went through censorship between 1926 and 1928 and have survived in the National Archives of Cambodia show a surprisingly international selection. Films brought into the country were from France, the United States (from companies such as Paramount and United Artists), China, and occasionally even from India.[67] The censorship board banned some films that were submitted for review, mostly for their violence, sometimes for formal errors (no subtitles), but occasionally also for political reasons. A movie about the funeral of Sun Yat-sen was not granted permission to be shown in the colony because the censorship board regarded the film as communist propaganda.[68]

One other important stipulation of Long's film decree from 1921 was that a tax of 20 percent was exacted on movies that did not come from France. Wilson argues, based on archival documents, that this tax was introduced because of the lobbying of de la Pommeraye.[69] As he was the official importer of Pathé films for Indochina, these machinations would have made sense for him on a business level. However, de la Pommeraye's company, Indochina Films and Cinemas (IFC), would also import films from US companies such as United Artists in the 1920s.[70]

The First Feature Film in the Colony: *Sous l'Oeil de Boudha*

IFC became the leading film company in Indochina in the 1920s. De la Pommeraye, the former salesman of acetylene and typewriters, imported the bulk of films shown in cinemas throughout Indochina. He also owned a chain of cinemas in the colony, as well as shops that sold photography and film equipment and records. Significantly, IFC was the first company that produced feature films in Indochina. IFC took over documentary film production from the Mission cinématographique de l'Indochine in April 1924, essentially privatizing the film production of the colonial government. When IFC took over film production, it was required to produce a minimum of twenty-seven hundred meters of film per year, according to a contract with the French administration, an effort for which the company was handsomely rewarded. The company received a substantial fixed income to set up its operations as well as an annual budget for film production.

The resulting films, the production of which was already paid for by the colonial administration, were then bought by the Agences economique for comparatively high rates. IFC also paid the film companies Gaumont or Pathé to include its material in their newsreels. Finally, the company was to show its films in its theaters and in traveling cinemas in Indochina.[71] It is hard not to see this deal between the colonial administration and de la Pommeraye—at this point, with almost two decades of experience in Indochina, a textbook example of the well-connected colonial "old hand"—as an instance of the cronyism that was rampant in French Indochina.

There are relatively few surviving examples of documentary films that the IFC produced for the colonial administration, even though its materials might be included in some of the Pathé and Gaumont newsreels about Indochina in the 1920s. However, the greatest accomplishment of the company was the production of three feature films that can be considered the first narrative films shot in Indochina. Relatively little is known about the first of them, an adventure film called *Sous l'oeil de Boudha*, coproduced by the Cinematography Service of the colonial administration and IFC in 1923, apparently as a maiden offering of the company. Since the film has surfaced only in 2004 from the archive of the French CNC, no research has been done on it so far, and we know almost nothing about the circumstances of its production.

The forty-minute film tells the story of young Ly (Le Van Bang), a theater actor, who falls in love with the daughter of a high-ranking official. He is arrested and exiled to prevent the marriage. An elephant hunter finds him in the jungle and helps him save a Vietnamese general from the palace of the Cambodian king, the scene shot in Angkor Wat. The cameraman was René Tetard, a veteran of the Mission cinématographique five years earlier and the head of the Cinematography Service of the colonial administration. The director was André Joyeux, who had been involved in the activities of the Mission cinématographique as early as 1916.[72] His attachment to the indigenous arts is clearly evident in the film, as he included impressions of the traditional arts of Indochina in the scenario—Ly's father is depicted as a wood carver. With Ly himself an actor in the story, this gave the director an opportunity to include dramatic performances in his film. The climax of the film takes place in Angkor Wat, for many of the French historians and archeologists working in Indochina at that time, *the* pinnacle of culture in the region, which prominently figured in much French colonial propaganda.

Sous l'oeil de Boudha was an ambitious production that was clearly made to be shown in theaters—in Indochina and probably even in France. That so far no review or article has surfaced mentioning the film makes it uncertain if it was ever shown. In any case, the film seems to have been produced with Sarraut's intention of making Indochina known in France in mind. Even though the plot is not based on historical events or local folklore, there is a clear effort to give the audience something representative of the cultures of both Vietnam and Cambodia. The film highlights the landscapes, art, architecture, and traditional dress of the region. The actors are all Vietnamese, whereas the parts of the "natives" in French films that took place in the North African colonies were typically played by French actors in blackface.

The film's introduction points out this pursuit of authenticity:

> The Asian drama that we present here aims at making the customs, habits, life of the Annamite and Cambodian races known, who fought each other for centuries but now enjoy under the protection of France, mother of the people, a laborious peace. To make the documentation as faithful and as sincere as possible—in addition to the costumes, the weapons, the furniture, and the houses that are all extremely faithful to reality—we wanted the actors to be all of Cambodian or Annamite race, from the protagonist to the last extra.[73]

In the following year, IFC embarked on an even more ambitious project to make a film that was a faithful representation of the authentic culture of the colony: a movie version of *Truyen Kieu* (Kieu's story), an epic poem by Nguyen Du (1766–1820) first published in the early nineteenth century as a criticism directed toward Confucian morals. It describes the life of Kieu, a virtuous young woman, who cannot marry the man who loves her and has to agree to being sold into prostitution to save her family. It is considered the national epic of Vietnam. The choice of this story signaled that the IFC was set to create a film with cultural relevance to the colony.

In a letter to *La revue du Pacifique* (The Pacific review), a nameless writer (most likely de la Pommeraye himself) claims that he was inspired to undertake this production after visiting the Colonial Exhibition in Marseilles in 1922, where he noticed "gross errors." The film was supposedly conceived in conversations with Maurice Long, then governor-general of Indochina. The letter also makes it clear that the film was made with the audience in France in mind, when the writer cheerfully invites Leon Archimbaud, editor of *La revue du Pacifique*, "to, hopefully in a few months, attend a movie composed of shots made and edited entirely in Tonkin." He also mentions that he has set up "a studio equipped with modern appliances," which, if he is correct, was probably the first film studio set up in Indochina.[74]

As apparently no print of the fifty-five-minute film *Kim Van Kieu* has survived, we have to rely on a couple of printed articles to appraise the film. Most of the French-language press in Indochina enthusiastically supported the movie. *L'avenir du Tonkin* (The future of Tonkin) praised, in a brief piece published on March 7, 1924, the "scenes shot outdoors in rural Tonkin, without studio trickery, without electricity under skies that are far less favorable than those of the Cote d'Azur, for instance" and points out the many other obstacles during eight months of production: rain, fog, and flood. Nevertheless, the newspaper opines, the final result compares favorably with American productions that are "currently invading" the colony.[75] At the same time, the Vietnamese-language newspapers were very critical of the film, pointing out inconsistencies and misrepresentations of the original epic.[76]

Even in the colonial press, there was criticism of the film: "While the large majority of the European audience welcomes the film, because they do not know any better, the whole of the Vietnamese audience laughs, because they know better," writes Maurice Koch, himself a colonial official, in the magazine *Les pages indochinoises* (The Indochinese pages), and then he ridicules the "Chinese" sets "from the time of Sun Yat-sen." His final judgment is that "in our times, it is neither good to demonstrate such regrettable ignorance before the eyes of our protégés, nor is it necessary to pull the wool over the eyes of the French public."[77]

Some Vietnamese sources mention the film *Su tich Ba De* (The legend of Ba De), a "French production" from 1929 that might be another IFC creation, as it repeated the formula of using a folk tale as the basis for its plot.[78] However, no more information on this film is available. What is certain is that IFC produced one more fiction film, apparently in 1925, a thirty-minute comedy called *Toufou se marie* (Tu Phu gets married), apparently borrowing heavily from the movies of Charlie Chaplin. Because the film lost money (apparently all entertainment films of IFC did), the company seems to have stopped making fiction films after this movie.[79]

There were no productions from France shot in Indochina. Some filmmakers tried but failed. Director Jacques Feyder traveled to Indochina in 1925, looking for a location for his next movie after the success of *L'Atlantide*. The film, based on a novel by Pierre Benoit, is about two French officers who discover the legendary kingdom of Atlantis in the Sahara. The entire film was shot over a period of eight months on location under grueling conditions in the Aures Mountains in Algeria, then part of the French colonial empire.

As a follow-up to this film, Feyder considered another novel by Benoit, *Le roi lepreux* (The leper king), which was set in Cambodia. He traveled with his cameraman, his assistant, and his wife to Angkor Wat and shot some footage there. However, the project never came to fruition, probably because of the huge budget the production would have required.[80] Instead, Feyder edited the material he had shot in Cambodia into a short documentary, *Au pays du roi lepreux* (In the land of the leper king, 1926). It contains some of the most lyrical materials that had been shot in the colony apart from the rushes that Leon Busy took for Albert Kahn.

Leon Busy and Albert Kahn's *Archives de la Planète*

The short films that Leon Busy (1894–1951) made for Albert Kahn's visionary *Archives de la planète* (Archives of the planet) occupy a special position among the documentaries shot in French Indochina, as they were conceived outside both the colonial propaganda apparatus and the realm of commercial filmmaking.[81] Arguably, they are the films where the desire to "show Tonkin as it is," to use Doumer's phrase, was complemented most successfully by an intimate knowledge of his subject by the filmmaker. Busy shows quotidian life in the colony with patience and in great detail, even though with an almost nostalgic touch.

Archives de la planète was an ambitious and visionary attempt to create a visual atlas of the world.[82] Influenced by the ideas of French philosopher Henri Bergson, Kahn, a Parisian banker and philanthropist, spent a good part of his fortune to sponsor photographers and filmmakers to create visual records of humankind's existence.[83] Between 1908 and 1931, the eleven cameramen in his service visited forty-eight countries and brought back seventy-two thousand autochrome color plates, four thousand stereoscopic views, and almost 183,000 meters of film.[84] The geographer Jean Brunhes, supervisor of the project, also acquired newsreels and scientific films from commercial film companies. The goal of this collection was to contribute to world peace by furthering the mutual understanding between nations. Ironically, as the pictures and films from the collection were shown to only a select group of friends, confidants, and occasional visitors to Kahn's villa in Boulogne, a suburb of Paris, the collection failed to realize its utopian goal. Kahn, a highly secretive man, lost his fortune during the Great Depression, bringing an end to the project. His collection survived, however, and can be viewed today in a museum in Kahn's villa.[85]

Kahn's collection presents an astonishing panorama of the world in the early twentieth century: sumo wrestlers in Japan and fishers in Newfoundland, the signing of the Briand-Kellogg Pact in 1928, and A. J. Balfour visiting Zionist colonies in Palestine in 1925, most of them mere rushes rather than complete documentaries. The collection contains sixteen scenes from Vietnam and eleven from Cambodia for a total of fifty minutes of footage. They were commissioned for the Kahn collection, and the semiprofessional photographer Leon Busy was hired to produce the films.

Busy was a graduate of the École polytechnique. An officer in the colonial army, he had been stationed in Tonkin since 1898. He was also a photography enthusiast and a member of the French Photographic Society from 1913 to 1924. His films are among the oldest in Kahn's collection. All of these films must have been made about 1921, although no precise dates are available. Their lengths vary from a couple of seconds up to fifteen minutes. The longer films contain several shots, which set them apart from the *vues* of the period made by the Lumière brothers.[86]

Unlike the films made for the colonial administration, these were under no pressure to foreground the colony's *mise en valeur* (economic utilization), as Albert Sarraut had called it. The Indochina in Busy's film shows a predominantly agrarian society and its traditions: fishing, rice planting, paper making, a wedding, and various theater and dance performances that include a fifteen-minute piece on the Royal Ballet of Cambodia. In Busy's films, it almost seems as if Indochina had not been colonized at all. Only a few films, such as those on the fishers in the Tonle Sap river near Siem Reap and on the archeological work of the École française d'Extreme-Orient (EFEO; French School of the Far East) in Angkor Wat, show French officials supervising the work of their colonial subjects. (As it was part of the philosophy of the *Archives de la planète* to present its films in a "raw" manner, none of these films carried any title.)

The best-known and most controversial film from Busy's collection is a one-minute scene that shows a young Vietnamese woman taking off her traditional dress until she is completely naked, before putting it on again. Film critics influenced by a certain brand of postcolonial theory had a field day with this film. They condemned it as voyeuristic and degrading to the woman, who was presented as a mere object, even though Busy discreetly pulls his lens out of focus when his protagonist gets naked.[87]

Viewed in the context of Busy's other works, the brief scene seems representative of his cautious approach as a filmmaker. Most of the films he made for the Kahn archive may be characterized both by his familiarity with his subject (at the time when he made the films, he had lived in Indochina for two decades and spoke fluent Vietnamese), as well as by the attempt to give the viewers a close understanding of what he saw. Busy allowed events in front of his camera to unfold patiently. In one film lasting almost eight minutes, he documents the whole process of rice farming from the tilling of the soil to the selling of rice dishes at a food stand. In his film on the Cambodian Royal Ballet, he spends a good part of the film showing the preparations for the performance rather than the performance itself. In the same spirit, the film with the young woman taking off her dress seems more like a demonstration of the convenience of traditional Vietnamese dress rather than a sexually charged striptease. This wariness and the informality of his films set him apart both from the perambulating camera operators such as Veyre and the filmmakers in the service of the colonial administration.

Colonial Misadventures

A pattern may be found in Busy's unseen films, the unpopular shorts of Gabriel Veyre, the unproduced leper king film by Feyder, and the unsuccessful feature films by IFC. The lack of good fortune of all these productions might have had many causes: absence of funds, absence of talent by those involved, or plain bad luck. But this seems to be only half the story. The French colony in Indochina might have been simply too far and not spectacular enough to command continuous interest in France. Whereas East Asian countries like Japan and China had managed to capture the attention of the European audience in the late nineteenth and early twentieth centuries, Indochina was probably too unimportant or simply too miserable to fascinate the public back home. Sarraut's formula of making France and the colonies known to each other was not working. The colony tried to make itself known to France, but France seemed not to care, with one exception: Angkor Wat, the ancient temple city in Cambodia that never failed to fascinate the public.

At the World Exhibitions in Paris in 1878, 1889, and 1900 and in the Colonial Exhibitions in Marseille in 1906 and 1922 and in Paris in 1931, replicas of Angkor Wat were consistently among the most popular exhibits. (Providing the 1922 Colonial Exhibition and the showrooms on Indochina with replicas of Angkor Wat through photos and films was one of the most challenging tasks that Tétard and his Service photo-cinematographique de l'Indochine had to undertake during the existence of the service.)

Nevertheless, the attraction of Angkor Wat did not lead to further film production in the colony. (In fact, after the IFC productions, only one other French fiction film was shot in Indochina during the colonial period: Rene Barberis's *Ramuntcho*, 1938.) It would take another quarter of a century after the production of *Sous l'oeil de Boudha* until Angkor Wat became the set of another narrative film—Wilhelm Dieterle's *Die Herrin der Welt* (The mistress of the world, 1960), using the spectacular temple landscape as a backdrop for its climactic final scenes. International productions that followed were Marcel Camus's *L'oiseau de paradis* (Bird of paradise, 1963), a veritable encyclopedia of all things Khmer, and Richard Brooks's *Lord Jim* (1965). The latter movie drew the ire of King Norodom Sihanouk, then head of state of Cambodia, who was angered by remarks made by actor Peter O'Toole to a film magazine depicting Cambodia as "a primitive state."[88] To show a different, developed, and modern Cambodia, Sihanouk made his first film the following year and consequently became one of the most prolific filmmakers in Southeast Asia. (Angkor Wat continues to fascinate filmmakers even today, and it was used in blockbuster productions such as Simon West's *Lara Croft: Tomb Raider* [2001] and Jean-Jacques Annaud's *Deux frères*

[Two brothers, 2004), as well as in art-house films such as Wong Kar-Wai's *Fa yeung nin wa* [In the mood for love, 2000]).

In France, Indochina became a full-blown subject of cinema only in the 1990s with films such as Jean-Jacques Annau's *L'amant* (The lover, 1992) and Regis Wargnier's *Indochine* (1992), a phenomenon that—to some critics—signaled a nostalgia for former colonial glory among the French. These films have been labeled "Indo-Chic" by Panivong Norindr.[89] They emerged at a time when a debate on how to judge France's past colonial records emerged in the country. Some conservative forces argued that there was much to admire in France's colonial past, consciously or not returning to the trope of the French *mission civilisatrice* in the colonies, which had informed much of the discourse around early filmmaking in Indochina. The films that have survived from the period of early cinema in French Indochina tell their own story of this mission, of its lofty goals, but also of its hubris and shortcomings. But in their best moments, as in some of the films by Gabriel Veyre and the work by Leon Busy, they do show some of the realities of quotidian life in colonial Indochina, transcending their colonial pedigree.

Beginnings of a National Cinema

Vietnamese film history in most cases dates the beginning of a national cinema on March 15, 1953, the date when Ho Chi Minh signed a decree establishing a National Cinematic and Photographic Enterprise,[90] even though it took until 1958 for the first Vietnamese feature film to be made. While it might be understandable that Vietnamese film historians have little interest in the filmmaking activities of their former colonizers, a colonial version of Vietnamese film history as written in this chapter may ignore the incipient productions that were made earlier by Vietnamese people. (As stated previously, there was no Cambodian film industry before the 1960s.) But I address this issue by pointing out that while local filmmaking activities took place at the very end of the period of early cinema, they are worth mentioning here because they initiate the transition from a colonial to a national cinema in Indochina, a process that was delayed by the Second World War.

Tracing film's transition from colonial to native hands, one discovers that a man named Nguyen Lan Huong (a.k.a. Huong Ky) quietly entered the scene and produced a couple of reasonably successful short films, while the French filmmakers associated with IFC used funds from the colonial administration to produce high-minded flops. This marked the beginning of the national cinema of Vietnam. Nguyen had learned filmmaking with an unnamed Frenchman and ran a photo studio in Hanoi. He started his film production with a short comedy, *Mot dong kem tau duoc ngua* (A penny for a horse, 1924), based on a fable by La

Fontaine. In 1926, he filmed the funeral ceremony of Emperor Khai Dinh and the coronation of his heir, Bao Dai. The films played in Vietnamese cinemas for almost a month, and the short documentaries were sold to Gaumont and Pathé, respectively. Few accounts of the country's film history mention these films as the first Vietnamese movies.[91]

The first feature-length film made by a Vietnamese director was *Canh dong ma* (The haunted field, 1937–1938), written by Dam Quang Thien and directed by Tran Phi. This was a ghost film shot in a Hong Kong studio with Vietnamese actors. This film, as well as *Tran phong ba* (Storm of anger, 1938), another production by the same group done in Hong Kong right after *Canh dong ma*—apparently to cover the costs of the production of the first—was not positively received according to accounts in Vietnamese sources.[92]

Other Vietnamese films that are occasionally mentioned in Vietnamese accounts of early cinema are *Tron voi tinh* (Devoting whole life to love) and *Co Nga di dao thankh thi* (Mrs. Nga's walk around the city) by a collective that called itself Asia and was headed by the artist Nguyen Phoung Danh, as well as a number of other short-lived film production ventures. But these films are all lost (if they were finished at all), and details such as production year, content, cast, and distribution are not available.[93] The beginnings of autochthon filmmaking in Indochina were modest, as these accounts suggest. It would take more than another two decades until both Vietnam and Cambodia started to build their respective national cinemas, while Laos never developed a film industry to speak of.

TILMAN BAUMGARTEL is Professor of Media Theory at the University of Applied Sciences, Mainz. A German media critic and journalist, he has published on independent cinema in Southeast Asia, media piracy, internet art, and the German director Harun Farocki. He is editor of *The Pirate Essays: A Reader in International Media Piracy* and *Southeast Asian Independent Cinema*.

Notes

1. Marguerite Duras, *Un barrage contre le Pacifique* [The sea wall] (Paris: Livre de poche, 1968), 165 (my translation).

2. See, for instance, Marguerite Duras, *L'Eden Cinema* [Cinema Eden] (Paris: Mercure de France, 1977); and Marguerite Duras, *L'amant de la Chine du nord* [The lover of northern China] (Paris: Gallimard, 1991).

3. Duras, *L'amant de la Chine du nord*, 179–180. The old Eden Cinema was torn down in late 2010 to be replaced with—what else?—a shopping center. See "Saigon: L'Eden Cinema n'est plus" [Saigon: The Eden Cinema is no longer], *Gavroche* [Newsboy], July 4, 2010, http://www.gavroche-thailande.com/actualites/viet-nam/182-saigon-l-eden-cinema-n-est-plus.

4. Interestingly, *Un barrage contre le Pacifique* was made into a film twice, first by René Clément in 1958 and then by French-Cambodian filmmaker Rithy Pan in 2008, who stressed the anticolonial thrust of Duras's novel.

5. For the most authoritative account of early filmmaking in Vietnam, see Dean Wilson, *Colonial Viet Nam on Film: 1896 to 1926* (New York: City University of New York, 2007). For accounts on Cambodia, see Ingrid Muan and Ly Daravuth, *Cultures of Independence: An Introduction to Cambodian Arts and Culture in the 1950s and 1960s* (Phnom Penh: Reyum Institute, 2001), 141–190; and Ingrid Muan and Ly Daravuth, "A Survey of Film in Cambodia," in *Film in South East Asia, Views from the Region: Essays on Film in Ten South East Asia-Pacific Countries*, ed. David Hanan (Hanoi: SEAPAVAA, Vietnam Film Institute and National Film and Sound Archive of Australia, 2001), 93–106. For accounts on Laos, see Bounchao Phichit, "Lao Cinema," in Hanan, *Film in South East Asia*, 83–92.

6. Xuan Lam and Dao Xuan Chuc, "Movie Activities in Viet Nam prior to the August Revolution," in *Vietnamese Cinematography: A Research Journey*, by Xuan Lam and Dao Xuan Chuc (Hanoi: Gioi, 2007), 12–23.

7. Beate Weghofer, *Cinema Indochina: Eine (post-)koloniale Filmgeschichte Frankreichs* [Cinema Indochina: A (post-)colonial film history of France] (Bielefeld, Germany: Transcript, 2010), 19.

8. Eric LeRoy, "Le fonds cinematographique colonial aux Archives du film et du depot legal du CNC" [The Colonial Cinematographic Fund at the CNC Film and Legal Deposit Archives], *Journal of Film Preservation* 63 (2001): 55–59.

9. The most detailed account of French colonialism in all of Indochina so far (but with a focus on today's Vietnam) is Pierre Brocheux and Daniel Hemery, *Indochina: An Ambiguous Colonization, 1858–1954* (Berkeley: University of California Press, 2009). For a comprehensive account of the colonial period in Cambodia, see John Tully, *France on the Mekong: A History of the Protectorate in Cambodia, 1863–1953* (Lanham, MD: University Press of America, 2002).

10. David Chandler, review of *Indochina: An Ambiguous Colonization, 1858–1954*, *Contemporary Southeast Asia: A Journal of International and Strategic Affairs* 32 (August 2010): 302–304.

11. Peter J. Bloom, *French Colonial Documentary: Mythologies of Humanitarianism* (Minneapolis: University of Minnesota Press: 2008), 127.

12. See, for example, an unsigned letter to the *Revue du Pacifique* by a representative of the newly founded production company Indochina Films and Cinemas (IFC) (mostly likely written by Charles de la Pommeraye, the founder of the company), which says, "Je sais combien elle peut aider a la propagation de nos idees en Indochine, comme a faire connaitre l'Indochine en France" (I know how I can help spread our ideas in Indochina, as well as how to publicize Indochina in France). "Le cinéma indochinois" [Indochinese cinema], *Revue du Pacifique*, no. 1 (1924): 92–93.

13. Milton Osborne, *The Mekong: Turbulent Past, Uncertain Future* (New York: Grove, 2000), 39–117.

14. Michelle Aubert and Jean-Claude Seguin, eds., *La production cinématographique des frères Lumière* [Films of the Lumière brothers] (Paris: Centre national de la cinematographie, Bibliotheque du Film, 1996), 310.

15. Abe Markus Nornes, *Japanese Documentary Film: The Meiji Era through Hiroshima* (Minneapolis: University of Minneapolis Press, 2003).

16. Aubert and Seguin, *La production cinématographique des frères Lumière*, 408–417.

17. Felix Mesguich, *Tours de manivelle: Souvenirs d'un chasseur d'images* [Turns of the hand crank machine: Memories of a hunter of images] (Paris: Bernard Grassett, 1933).

18. Deac Roussell, *Living Pictures: The Origins of the Movies* (Albany: SUNY Press, 1998), 136–137.

19. See Luke McKernan, "François-Constant Girel," *Who's Who of Victorian Cinema*, http://www.victorian-cinema.net/girel.htm (accessed January 24, 2017). Even though Girel disappeared from the annals of cinema rather abruptly, he was responsible for some of the earliest firsts in film history. Not only was he involved in the first film shooting and first screening in Asia, but probably he was responsible for the first traveling shot, when he filmed from a boat that was approaching the city of Cologne on September 21, 1896. See Martin Loiperdinger, *Film und Schokolade: Stollwercks Geschafte mit lebenden Bildern* [Movie and chocolate: Stollwerck's business with live pictures] (Frankfurt am Main: Stroemfeld, 1999), 193–200; and Uli Jung and Martin Loiperdinger, eds., *Geschichte des dokumentarischen Films in Deutschland* [History of documentary film in Germany], vol. 1, *Kaiserreich (1895–1918)* [Empire (1895–1918)] (Stuttgart: Reclam, 2005), 68.

20. See Wilson, *Colonial Viet Nam on Film*, 175–177.

21. At the Colonial Exhibition in Paris in 1931, the organizers went as far as having coolies from Indochina take the visitors around the exhibition. See Emmanuelle Radar, "'Putain de colonie!': Anticolonialisme et modernisme dans la litterature du voyage en Indochine (1919–1939)" ["Fucking colony!": Anticolonialism and modernism in the travel literature in Indochina] (PhD diss., University of Amsterdam, 2008), 284, http://www.aafv.org/IMG/pdf/EmmanuelleRadar_PutainDeColonie.pdf.

22. Panivong Norindr, "'La trace Lumière': Early Cinema and Colonial Propaganda in French Indochina," in *Le cinématographe, nouvelle technologie du XXe siècle* [Cinema, new technology of the 20th century], ed. André Gaudreault, Catherine Russell, and Pierre Véronneau (Lausanne, Switzerland: Payot, 2004), 331.

23. Martine Astier Loufti, "Imperial Frame: Film Industry and Colonial Representation," in *Cinema, Colonialism, Postcolonialism: Perspectives from the French and Francophone World*, ed. Dina Sherzer (Austin: University of Texas Press, 1996), 21.

24. Philippe Jacquiere and Marion Pranal, *Gabriel Veyre, opérateur Lumière: Autour du monde avec le Cinematographe; Correspondance (1896–1900)* [Gabriel Veyre, Lumière operator: Around the world with the Cinematographe; Correspondence (1896–1900)] (Lyon: Institut Lumière / Actes Sud, 1996).

25. Ibid.

26. Lorin Amaury, *Paul Doumer, gouverneur general de l'Indochine, 1897–1902* [Paul Doumer, governor-general of Indochina, 1897–1902] (Paris: Harmattan, Bagneux, 2004).

27. Jacquiere and Pranal, *Gabriel Veyre, opérateur Lumière*, 195 (italics in original).

28. Wilson, *Colonial Viet Nam on Film*, 239–249, 255–260.

29. Ibid., 257.

30. Ibid., 76.

31. Jacquiere and Pranal, *Gabriel Veyre, opérateur Lumière*, 19.

32. Wilson, *Colonial Viet Nam on Film*, 76.

33. See Andre Touzet, "Une œuvre de guerre et d'apres-guerre: La mission cinematographique du gouvernement general de l'Indochine" [A work of war and postwar: The film mission of the government of Indochina], *La revue indochinoise* [The Indochinese review], March 1919, pp. 575–612.

34. Jacques Marseille, *L'age d'or de la France coloniale* [The golden age of colonial France] (Paris: A. Michel, 1986), 5.

35. Touzet, "Une œuvre de guerre et d'apres-guerre," 575–612.

36. Andre Touzet, "L'Emprunt national de 1917 en Indochine" [The National Loan of 1917 in Indochina], *La revue indochinoise*, 1918, p. 27.

37. Ibid. Note that this provides us with a list of all the cities in Indochina that had cinemas in 1917.

38. *Annuaire administratif de l'Indochine, 1925* (Hanoi: Imprimerie d'Extreme-Orient, 1925), 112. Leon Busy, who worked for Albert Kahn, is listed as an *agent contractual* (contractual agent) to the service.

39. *Annuaire administratif de l'Indochine, 1908* (Hanoi: Imprimerie d'Extreme-Orient, 1908), 61–84.

40. Tully also used this phrase for his book title, *France on the Mekong: A History of the Protectorate in Cambodia, 1863–1953*; the book was published in 2002.

41. *Annuaire administratif de l'Indochine, 1905* (Hanoi: Imprimerie d'Extrême-Orient, 1905), 735.

42. Ibid., 728.

43. Ibid., 701.

44. *Annuaire administratif de l'Indochine, 1908*, 239.

45. *Annuaire administratif de l'Indochine, 1924* (Hanoi: Imprimerie d'Extreme-Orient, 1924), 160, 190.

46. "Cie" is the abbreviation for Compagnie, "Company."

47. *Annuaire administratif de l'Indochine, 1908*, 672, 675, 677, 681.

48. Ibid., 672.

49. Ibid., 338. That a number of different de la Pommerayes are listed in different positions in his various companies throughout the 1910s and 1920s suggests that they were all part of the same family business, probably run by Joseph de la Pommeraye's brothers or sons.

50. *Annuaire administratif de l'Indochine, 1910* (Hanoi: Imprimerie d'Extreme-Orient, 1910), 580.

51. Ibid., 581.

52. Request for permission, file 12861, Correspondence of the *resident superieur* (RSC), National Archives of Cambodia (NAC), Phnom Penh; request for permission, file 12812, RSC, NAC.

53. Muan and Ly, "A Survey of Film in Cambodia," 94.

54. *Annuaire administratif de l'Indochine, 1924*, 157.

55. *Annuaire administratif de l'Indochine, 1910*, 81.

56. *Annuaire administratif de l'Indochine, 1916* (Hanoi: Imprimerie d'Extreme-Orient, 1916), 58.

57. Dinh Quang An, "Film Publishing in Cinema in Pre-liberated Ha Noi," in Lam and Chue, *Vietnamese Cinematography*, 94–99.

58. *Indochine: Adresses, 1ère année 1933–1934; Annuaire complet (europeen et indigene) de toute l'Indochine, commerce, industrie, plantations, mines, adresses particulieres* [Indochina: Addresses, first year 1933–1934; Complete directory (European and native) of the whole of Indochina, industry, trade, plantations, mines, special addresses] (Saigon: Albert Portail, 1922), 177–178.

59. *Tourists' Guide to Saigon, Phnom Penh and Angkor* (Saigon: Albert Portail, 1930), 28.

60. See, for example, requests for business licenses, file 5281, RSC, NAC.

61. For a very detailed overview about early cinema owners and film distribution, see Wilson, *Colonial Viet Nam on Film*, 88–98.

62. Ibid., 92.

63. Flyer, file 35133, RSC, NAC.

64. Letter from Albert Sarraut to *resident superieur* of Cambodia, June 23, 1917, file 5296, RSC, NAC.

65. Reports of the *residents superieur*, file 5299, RSC, NAC. For a discussion of the responses from the governor of Cochinchina and the *resident superieur* of Tonkin, see Wilson, *Colonial Viet Nam on Film*, 140–143.

66. File 5298, RSC, NAC.

67. Film lists, file 30527, RSC, NAC.

68. File 5297, RSC, NAC.

69. Wilson, *Colonial Viet Nam on Film*, 143.

70. File 30527, RSC, NAC.

71. File 24960, RSC, NAC. For a detailed account of the genesis of the arrangement as well as some newspaper reports on the contract, see Wilson, *Colonial Viet Nam on Film*, 150–153.

72. *Annuaire administratif de l'Indochine, 1916*, 50. His involvement in the propaganda films of the colonial government is mentioned in Touzet, "L'Emprunt national de 1917 en Indochine."

73. Quoted from the credits of the movie.

74. "Le cinema indochinois" [Indochinese cinema], *La revue du Pacifique*, no. 1 (1924): 92–93. The fact that the postproduction was done in Indochina contradicts frequent claims in Vietnamese accounts of the colonial period of filmmaking that "the French did not create the material or technical base for filmmaking in Vietnam" and that films were "shot in Vietnam with some Vietnamese actors and actresses and were then taken to France for processing and editing." Ngo Phuong Lan, *Modernity and Nationality in Vietnamese Cinema* (Yogyakarta, Java: Galangpress / Netpac, 2007), 168–169. This might have been true for *Sous l'oeil de Boudha*, but it apparently was not the case for *Kim Van Kieu*.

75. Review, *L'avenir du Tonkin*, March 7, 1924, reprinted in *Communique de la presse indochinoise: Agence economique de l'Indochine* [Bulletin to the Indochinese press: Economic agency of Indochina] 30, no. 4 (1924): 10.

76. Wilson, *Colonial Viet Nam on Film*, 47–49.

77. Maurice Koch, "Le Kim Van Kieu en cinema" [The Kim Van Kieu in cinema], *Les pages indochinoises* [The Indochinese pages], no. 4 (1925): 15.

78. Lam and Chuc, *Vietnamese Cinematography*, 12–23, 17.

79. Wilson, *Colonial Viet Nam on Film*, 587–588.

80. David Henry Slavin, *Colonial Cinema and Imperial France, 1919–1939: White Blind Spots, Male Fantasies, Settler Myths* (Baltimore: John Hopkins University Press, 2001), 60.

81. That they were not made by the Mission cinématographique, however, does not mean that they were completely removed from the colonial effort. Busy was a member of the French army and had even worked for the Mission cinématographique on occasion.

82. For more comprehensive accounts of Kahn's project, including the films that he commissioned, see Paula Amad, "Cinema's 'Sanctuary': From Pre-documentary to Documentary Film in Albert Kahn's *Archives de la planète*," *Film History* 13 (2001): 138–159; Paula Amad, *Counter-archive: Film, the Everyday, and Albert Kahn's "Archives de la Planète"* (New York: Columbia University Press, 2010); Teresa Castro, "*Les archives de la planète*: A Cinematographic Atlas," *Jump Cut* 48 (2006), http://www.ejumpcut.org/archive/jc48.2006/KahnAtlas.

83. For more on Bergson's influence on Kahn and this project, see Amad, *Counter-archive*, 96–132.

84. Autochrome is an early color photography process that was invented by the Lumière brothers in 1903. Lumière camera operator Gabriel Veyre worked extensively with the medium, even though not in the service of Albert Kahn.

85. Parts of the collection can be viewed at the website of the museum, at http://www.albert-kahn.fr.

86. For more production data on the individual films, see Wilson, *Colonial Viet Nam on Film*, 410–416, 507–538.

87. See Sylvie Blum-Reid, *East-West Encounters: Franco-Asian Cinema and Literature* (London: Wallflower, 2003), 13–14; and Fatimah Tobing Rony, *The Third Eye: Race, Cinema, and Ethnographic Spectacle* (Durham, NC: Duke University Press, 2010), which manages to turn even the fact that the young woman in the film puts on her dress again into a proof for the sinister intentions of Leon Busy: "The fact that the female native body is incessantly veiled and unveiled, however, reveals the simultaneous attraction and repulsion felt by the filmmaker for the perceived physicality of the native women" (82).

88. Milton Osbourne, *Sihanouk: Prince of Darkness, Prince of Light* (Chiang Mai: Silkworm, 1994), 177–184; Milton Osbourne, *Before Kampuchea: Preludes to Tragedy* (Bangkok: Orchid, 2004), 47–55; David Chandler, *The Tragedy of Cambodian History: Politics, War and Revolution* (New Haven, CT: Yale University Press, 1991), 152; Elizabeth Romney, "King, Artist, Film-Maker: The Films of Norodom Sihanouk," in Hanan, *Film in South East Asia*, 107–118.

89. See Panivong Norindr, *Phantasmatic Indochina: French Colonial Ideology in Architecture, Film, and Literature* (Durham, NC: Duke University Press, 1996).

90. Lam and Chuc, *Vietnamese Cinematography*, 88.

91. Pham Ngoc Truong, "A Brief History of Vietnamese Films," in Hanan, *Film in South East Asia*, 59–82.

92. Lam and Chuc, *Vietnamese Cinematography*, 19.

93. Ibid.

9 A National Cinema Takes Root in a Colonial Regime

Early Cinema in India

P. K. Nair

Pre-cinema Experience

The pre-cinema experience in India dates back to shadow puppetry, which involves handmade cardboard puppets manually operated from behind a lighted white screen. These silhouetted moving images were accompanied by live singing and sound effects. Scroll paintings (also known as *pat* paintings) depicting successive tableaux images of episodes from Hindu mythology and the *puranas* also foretell the origins of cinema.[1]

These tableaux images, drawn on scrolls of thin cloth or paper, one below the other in a chronological order of action, offered interesting visual narration of the mythical stories from the epics. The images were magnified and projected onto a white screen, using an oil lamp as a light source and a tilted mirror. Coupled with human narration and singing with minimal musical accompaniment, the presentation provided a unique audiovisual experience. The tableaux images were moved manually as the story progressed to synchronize with the live narration and singing.

"Magic lantern shows," which used glass slides with stylishly painted colorful images, then became popular. Some of the original glass slides used by the Patwardhan Bros. of Kalyan (Bombay) for its magic lantern shows are preserved in the National Film Archives India in Pune. Because vegetable dyes were used, the colors have not faded. As the familiar stories of gods and goddesses unfolded before their eyes, through the illusion of choreographed movements and live singing, Indian audiences started experiencing the magic of cinema that emerged later. The oil lamp slowly gave way to a more powerful and steady light source, and the mirrors were replaced with proper optical lenses by the end of the nineteenth century. When Western cinema arrived, it was not much of a wonder for the Indian viewers.

"Lifelike" Yes, but No One Ran Out

When Auguste and Louis Lumière presented their new invention, the Cinématographe, at the Salon Indien in Paris on December 28, 1895, some members of the audience reportedly ran out during *The Arrival of the Train*, shouting, "This is life itself!" But nothing similar happened when the same film was shown by the Lumière representatives at the first public presentation of cinema in India at Bombay's Watson's Hotel on July 7, 1896. As the Indian audience had already experienced the illusion of motion by clever manipulation of static images accompanied by live sounds, the Lumière show was not much of a novelty for most Indians. However, what fascinated one member of the audience was the technical gadget—the Lumière multipurpose camera—which could photograph, process, and project moving images.

Harishchandra Sakharam Bhatvadekar, popularly known as Save Dada, a photographic goods dealer, struck a deal with the Lumières and secured the marketing rights for the equipment in this region. While demonstrating the equipment to his prospective customers in 1899, he showed some scenes shot at Bombay's Gateway of India and the Hanging Gardens at Malabar Hill.[2] Thus, he became the first indigenous filmmaker of the region, by default rather than intention. His amateur recordings include *The Wrestlers* (1899) and *Man and Monkey* (1899).[3] However, two historical events—both of national importance—were covered by Save Dada with the Lumière camera: a public reception held at Bombay's Chowpathy beach on December 7, 1901, to honor the great mathematician Wrangler Paranjpye on his return from England after receiving the "Wrangler" title (an honor given to first-class mathematics undergraduates at Cambridge University),[4] and the Delhi durbar of 1903 (a celebration marking the succession of Edward VII and Alexandra of Denmark as emperor and empress of India).[5] The latter two films are often referred to as the best examples of early Indian motion picture recordings of historical events.

However, the earliest film recordings of Indian life, people, places, and events were done by foreigners who were either professionals or tourists with access to the new technology. It took some time for the natives to obtain the equipment and start recording their own reality on film. One can see a marked difference in perceptions between the selection of images and action in the films shot by foreign cameramen and those shot by the locals. The foreign recordings showed an obsession with the lifestyle of the maharajas, including their palaces, durbars, coronations, wedding ceremonies, hunting expeditions, lions, tigers, elephants, serpents, royal tournaments, and horse races—images associated with the exotic. The Indians opted for the less ostentatious, rather mundane, aspects of daily life, such as a wrestling match or a monkey trainer inducing the animal to perform tricks for the enjoyment of passersby. The seeds of a truly national cinema were sown right from the day the Indians started recording on film their reality as they perceived it.

Pioneers in Indian Cinema

Bhatvadekar recorded interesting snippets of life of ordinary people in the midst of their daily routine activities. In 1903, he shot and showed the Delhi durbar. It was a historical event with Oriental grace and Occidental splendor. The Biograph Company had also recorded the event for world release. Though colonial in content, Bhatvadekar's attempt revealed the open-mindedness of Indians to world events of historical importance.

In Calcutta, Hiralal Sen photographed scenes from some of the popular stage plays at the Classic theater. Brief filmed scenes were shown as added attractions after the stage performances or taken to distant venues that could not be reached by stage performers. The possibility of reaching a large audience through photographic recordings, which could be projected several times, caught the fancy of the people involved in the performing arts, stage, and entertainment business. The first decade of the twentieth century saw live and recorded performances presented together in the same evening's program. Their coexistence did not continue for long, as they were rivals for audience attention. As film gained popularity, all forms of live shows were pushed out of the theatrical space and film virtually dominated the entertainment scene. However, respect for the stage was duly acknowledged by early filmmakers by using its format. Some early films appeared to be photographed plays, with the film camera covering the action on the stage from a fixed viewing position in the auditorium. Dacca-born Hiralal Sen was one of the early pioneers and specialized in this kind of filming.

On Easter Sunday in 1911, at a particularly depressing point in his life, Dhundiraj Govind Phalke (D. G. Phalke), popularly known as Dadasaheb Phalke, happened to see the imported film *The Life of Christ*. Phalke wrote in 1917,

> I must have seen films on many occasions before this—but that day marked the beginning of a revolutionary change in my life. I experienced a strange unassailable feeling. While I was unconsciously clapping my hands at the sight of the noble incidents in Jesus Christ's life, I was mentally visualizing our own gods—Shri Krishna, Shri Ramchandra, their Gokul and Ayodhya. A strange spell gripped me. Could we, the sons of India ever be able to see the images of our own gods and goddesses on the screen?[6]

Phalke was born on April 30, 1870, at Trimbakeshwar near Nasik in western India. He was brought up in a highly orthodox family of Brahmin priests, for whom even watching films was taboo. From a very young age, he was drawn to the medium of cinema because of his interest in photography, magic, and the arts. While struggling to familiarize himself with the intricacies of his imported camera, Phalke exposed single frames over a week to film a seed sprouting and growing into a plant. What he was trying to do then would be known later as time-lapse photography. He titled this early film experiment *Birth of a Pea Plant* (1912), describing it as a capsule history of the growth of a seed into a pea plant. This indigenous "instructional" film helped him obtain financial backing for his first feature film.

The Origin of *Swadeshi* Film

Swadeshi means "native, belonging to one's own land." It was used in contrast to *videshi*, which stood for all that was foreign. The word attained national importance when introduced by the great national leader and freedom fighter Bal Gangadhar Tilak. He exhorted Indians to throw away foreign goods as a first step toward freeing themselves from colonial rule and introduced the concept of *swadeshi* in relation to homemade goods. Phalke, a nationalist at heart, was inspired by this patriotic slogan and worked to implement it in his chosen field—cinema—and thus the *swadeshi* film was born. Except for the raw stock and film equipment, all other items, including finance, came from indigenous sources. In this respect the foreign element was reduced to a minimum.

Setting aside his favorite legend of Krishna project, Phalke chose a comparatively easier subject—Raja Harishchandra (King Harishchandra), also from Indian mythology—that he thought had enough potential to strike an emotional chord with any Indian. Phalke considered this story of a just and honest king who sacrificed his kingdom, wealth, and personal happiness for upholding the values of truth and integrity as valid then as it was in mythical times. He built a studio on Dadar Main Road, wrote the scenario, erected the sets, and started shooting in the summer of 1912. In an interview with *Mouj* magazine in 1939, Phalke declared, "If I had not possessed the artistic and technical faculties required for film-making, namely, the art of drawing, painting, architecture, photography, theatre and magic, and had not shown the courage and daring, the film industry would never have been established in India in 1912."[7]

Phalke's first full-length film, *Raja Harishchandra* (35mm, thirty-seven hundred feet in four reels), was completed in 1912 and released at the Coronation Cinema Bombay on April 21, 1913, for special guests and members of the press. The film was widely acclaimed and proved to be a great success. The film's treatment of the narrative is episodic, following the style of Indian folk theater and the primitive novel. The film has title cards in Hindi (the language of the common people) and English (the language of the elite). Most of the camera set-ups are static, at eye level with a lot of movement within the frame. However, one notices a pan movement to synchronize with the movement of the characters picturesquely reflected in the still river water below as the king goes hunting with his men in the forest scene. The palace sets are so well designed and mounted that the visual impact is as striking and pleasing as the plaster of paris sets seen in later films.

An interesting scene in the film shows the pioneer filmmaker's precocious talent: the indoor bathtub sequence with the spouting fountain at the center and the queen's female attendants playing with it, trying to stop the water spray with the palms of their hands. The king enters the frame and beckons the queen to come near him. The queen comes out of the pond in her wet clothes, and her attendants leave the fountain and walk toward the camera, adjusting their drenched saris and blouses clinging to their wet bodies—this is one of the most sensuous scenes in the film. Only the fertile mind of a creative artist like Phalke could have conceived such an erotic scene in what seemed basically a religious subject. And when we realize all those seductive women in the bathtub are in fact males in female garb, the admiration of the achievement of his art is heightened. Phalke once wrote, "Women refused to act in front of the camera because of the terrible taboo, and so I was forced to cast male actors in female roles."[8] Indian women did not face the camera until the late 1920s. Phalke had to overcome several obstacles before he could make *Raja Harishchandra*, but he was determined to make his dream for a *swadeshi* film a reality.

Why Film Mythological Stories?

That the first Indian film happened to be of a mythological story was not an accident. The first story film of importance in the history of American cinema was *The Great Train Robbery* (1903), a Western that is the mythology of the American West. In India, the subject matter for the first story film could not have come from anywhere else but Indian epics and mythology.

Phalke, we know, came from an orthodox Hindu household—a family of priests with strong religious roots. He was groomed to take over the family profession of the priesthood, but he chose to be a filmmaker instead, against heavy odds. When technology made it possible to tell stories through moving images, it was natural that the Indian film pioneer turned to religious epics and *puranas* for source material. Moreover, the characters, incidents, and plot outline were so much a part of the rich Indian tradition that they were close to the heart of every Indian. Thus, their presentation through the new medium of cinema did not pose any problem of communication and public acceptance. Another significant factor could well be the intense religious ethos inherent in the performing arts and their relationship with spirituality. The traditional performing arts all originate and spring from within the sanctum sanctorum, and performance itself used to take place within the precincts of the religious space, the temple. The performer, whether a musician, dancer, or stage artist, attempts to reach out to the divine being through the performance and in the process attain a state of bliss that is shared with others in attendance.

Since cinema took off as an extension of the performing arts, the same relationship was supposed to exist between the author/creator and the work. However, this did not happen for many early filmmakers, who considered film mainly as business. Phalke was perhaps a major exception, one who maintained a sacred relationship between the author, his creation, and the audience. His intention behind choosing mythological stories was not to transpose his viewers to a fantasy world of gods, goddesses, demons, and dancing damsels but to arrive at some universal truths inherent in Indian epics. He consciously resisted the myth of deification of the gods and treated them as ordinary mortals and next-door neighbors with whom the public could easily identify. There was more neorealism in his mythological than fantasy and miracles. Phalke will be remembered not only as a pioneer and visionary but as someone who could foresee the immense potentials of the film medium.

The Phalke Trail: Film as Business

Phalke Films is the company that Phalke started initially to realize his ambition of becoming a filmmaker, but it was more a cottage enterprise. He borrowed money through personal mortgages and was helped by well-wishers and family friends such as Trymbak B. Telang, whom he trained in the operation of the Williamson camera. The first five films were made under this banner. Later, he found that his personal company was inadequate to handle problems of administration, keep track of returns from distribution, raise capital, and plan more ambitious productions. In keeping with the times, in 1918 he started a purely indigenous company, Hindustan Film Company, as a corporate partnership between Waman Shridhar Apte, Laxman Balwant Phatak, Mayashankar Bhatt, and others. Since he could not handle most of the business dealings, Phalke opted out as partner in 1919, returning in 1923 as chief producer, technical adviser, and artistic creator. Out of the ninety-three films made under the Hindustan banner, Phalke contributed more than forty. The most significant were *Shri Krishna Janma* (Birth of Lord Krishna, 1918), *Kaliya Mardan* (The childhood of Krishna, 1919), *Sant Tukaram* (Saint Tukaram, 1921), *Sant Namdev* (Saint Namdev, 1922), *Sant Eknath* (Saint Eknath, 1926), and *Bhakta Prahlada* (Devotee Prahlada, 1926)—all silent films. S. N. Patankar of Patankar Friends and Company, a contemporary and close associate of Phalke, produced a four-part serial, *Ram Banvas* (Exile of Lord Rama) in 1918.

The Tent Is Pitched, and the Traveling Show Begins

It is a rags-to-riches story, so popular on the Indian screen. Starting as a popcorn boy at Calcutta's Corinthian Hall, Janshedji Framji Madan (1856–1923) rose to become the country's first showman—exhibitor-turned-importer-distributor-turned-producer, studio owner, and theater-chain owner. Launching his first "Bioscope" show (the term used for film exhibition at the time) in a tent at the Calcutta Maidan in 1906,[9] he heralded the first organized public exhibition of films in the country. By 1907, the tent cinema (Elphinstone Bioscope) had developed into a movie palace, and film exhibition became a glamorous business. Cinema theaters sprang up throughout the country. By the end of the 1920s, Madan himself owned a chain of thirty-seven theaters and had built an exhibition, distribution, and production empire, Madan Theatres, modeled after the best of Hollywood.

Along with foreign films, he imported foreign technicians (director E. D. Lignoro; cameraman T. Marconi) and actresses (Patience Cooper, Albertina, and others) to act in *Nala Damayanti* (1920), the most ambitious production of Madan Theatres. His Italian connection continued, casting foreign actresses in Indian mythological and folk tales, as Indian women were still hesitant to expose themselves to the gaze of the film camera. When he died in 1923, the Madan empire, which owned more than one hundred theaters, had extended to the whole of the subcontinent, including Burma, Ceylon, and Singapore. In 1931, although the company failed to make the country's first talkie film, it managed to get the credit for the first Bengali talkie, *Jamai Sasthi* (Son-in-law day, 1931), and followed it up with *Indrasabha* (1932), the country's top musical that include more than sixty songs.

Close on the heels of Madan came another enterprising showman and film magnate. Surat-born Abdulally Esoofally (1884–1957) also began as a tent showman and helped turn the Bioscope into a popular entertainment among Indians. He pitched his makeshift tent in the *maidan* near his hometown, Surat, in Gujarat and started showing film shorts (mostly imported). Once the novelty of the films dwindled, he closed shop, dismantled the tent, and moved to the next venue. For Esoofally, showing films to different audiences at different places was more of a passion than mere business. He moved from place to place with a set of films sufficient for at least two or three programs, which might run for a week or two, starting in parks and empty backyards of big cities and moving to smaller towns and places of religious festivities. The exhibitor-pioneer introduced the concept of "traveling cinemas" as early as 1904, even before Madan. The traveling cinema, later known as "touring talkies," is a vast network of exhibition outlets, operating within prescribed rules fixed by the authorities and their own business transactions. Such cinemas are still prevalent in rural India. Starting from

Calcutta with his tent Bioscope, Esoofally traveled in 1908–1914 to many parts of the Far East, covering Burma, Malaya, Singapore, and Indonesia. By introducing cinema in these regions, Esoofally gets credit (after the Lumières) for popularizing the cinema experience in the Far East through his tent Bioscope shows. He then settled in Bombay, managing the Alexandra Cinema and joining hands with Ardheshir Irani of Imperial Film Company. Later, he built his own Majestic Cinema, where the first Indian talkie film, *Alam Ara* (The ornament of the world, 1931), was premiered.

Reaching Out to a World Audience

Though Dadasaheb Phalke's primary concern was his local audience, he knew making films was a costly proposition. To continue making ambitious projects like *Kaliya Mardan*, he would need a lot of money, much more than the box-office earnings of his first film. He thought this was possible only if he reached out to a wider audience. He was envious of the European and American films that flooded the Indian screens through the distribution network of expert businessmen like Madan and Esoofally. Phalke took a print of his four-reeler film *Raja Harishchandra* to London in 1914 and arranged a few special screenings with the hope of gaining some overseas business. The British press hailed his efforts in glowing terms: "From the technical point of view the film is surprisingly excellent and we wish Mr. Phalke had been born here in England."[10] He was even approached by a London studio owner with a tempting offer to make films in England for the world market, which he politely declined. Even though an American company (probably Warner Bros.) showed interest in distributing *Raja Harishchandra*, the outbreak of World War I shattered Phalke's dreams. In 1920, Los Angeles–trained Suchet Singh engaged an American actress, Dorothy Kingsley, to play the role of Shakuntala in his ambitious production of the Kalidas epic with an eye on the international market. But the film did not create any ripples and disappeared unnoticed. Madan's Italian connections also did not bring him much success.

Coproductions

Bengal-born lawyer-turned-stage director Himansu Rai made his mark in the early years by training at the UFA studios in Berlin under such German masters as Fritz Lang and G. W. Pabst. He was keen to show the rest of the world through the medium of cinema "the glory that was India." With this in view, he and his playwright colleague, Niranjan Pal, joined hands with the Emelka Film Company of Munich and brought to India a team of skilled German technicians—director Franz Osten, cameraman Joseph Wirsching, and production designer Karl Von Sprettin—to make the first Indo-German coproduction, *Light of*

Asia (1925). Based on Edwin Arnold's poem of the same name on the life of Buddha, the film was shot in Indian locations with Indian artists, without makeup and glamour, and with material support from some of the Indian maharajahs. Even though the film had an indigenous flavor and a royal command performance at the Royal Albert Hall in London in 1925, it did not create any strong impressions in the international arena. This was probably due to the beleaguered attempt on the part of the filmmakers to present a stereotyped and conventional (and perhaps worn-out) image of India as projected in the novels of Rudyard Kipling and other English authors. The Rai-Osten team repeated their coproduction exercise with two more ventures—*Shiraz, the Loves of a Moghul Princess* (1928), based on the story of the Taj Mahal, and *Throw of Dice* (1930), inspired by an episode from the great Indian epic the *Mahabharata.*

All three coproductions had more or less the same approach—the emphasis was on exotica—and so met with the same fate: rejection. No doubt the films were technically superior, but they were soulless and turned out to be failed attempts to capture an international market. Indian filmmakers continued the same mistake with talkies. Some thought making films in the English language would be the correct approach, but that did not succeed either. It took some time for the filmmakers to realize that film language was different from spoken language. Not until Satyajit Ray came on the scene in the mid-1950s with his epochal *Pather Panchali* (Song of the little road, 1955) did they find an idiom that could appeal to a world audience. Patronage had been confined to the immigrant Indian population and their ethnic groups, which formed the traditional audience. It has since grown to be a sizable proportion of the world audience. But the distribution network had not caught up with the growing audience, and as a result, the material benefits could not be fully realized.

Regional Expansion and Cultural Identities

R. Nataraj Mudaliar, an automobile spare-parts dealer–turned–filmmaker, is credited with making the first feature film in southern India. His Tamil silent film, *Keechaka Vadham* (The extermination of Keechaka, 1916), heralded filmmaking in the south. As the title indicates, the subject is once again mythological, from the *Mahabharata.* Another film made in Madras, *Valli Thirumanam* (1921), by Whittaker (no records available of his first name) drew critical acclaim and box-office success. Having returned from Hollywood, Ananthanarayanan Narayanan founded General Pictures Corporation in 1929 and established filmmaking as an industry in South India. He became the single largest distributor of silent films in the south. Kolhapur in western Maharashtra was another center of active film production in the 1920s. Baburao K. Mistry, popularly known as Baburao Painter, spearheaded the film scene in the city. He came from the disciplines of stage design, set decoration, backdrop painting, and art direction. His long apprenticeship in cinema gave him valuable experience and firsthand knowledge of the medium. In 1919, he formed the Maharashtra Film Company with the blessings of the maharaja of Kolhapur and released the first significant historical film in 1923, *Sinhagadh*. Because of his special interest in sets, costumes, design, and painting, Painter chose to interpret episodes from Maratha history into the new medium. The historical genre thus became his forte. The exploits of Shivaji and his generals in their patriotic fights against their opponents formed his recurring theme, striking an emotional chord with the people, who were waging noncooperative and nonviolent resistance against a ruthless colonial regime at the time. Historical episodes wherein Indian rulers and the *praja* (the ruled) bravely withstood foreign invasion were cleverly interpreted to enthuse the patriotic sentiments of the people and give a fresh impetus to the country's freedom struggle.

Exposing the false values associated with the Western way of life and their blind imitation by some gullible Indians was humorously brought out by filmmaker Dhiren Ganguly (popularly known as D.G.) in his brilliant satire *England Returned* (1921), the first "social satire," which prompted middle-class Indians and those obsessed with Western values to introspect. It was the beginning of another genre, "the contemporary social." Baburao Painter followed it up with another significant film in 1925, *Saukari Pash* (The Indian Shylock), an attempt at realistic treatment of a village peasant's struggle against a greedy moneylender. From the mythological to the devotional saint film, costume fantasy, action thriller, social satire, and neorealism—all these genres were tried in the silent era of Indian cinema. Though English was the common language used in intertitle cards, the other local languages used gave a clue to the language roots of the film and its regional origin.

The Malay-Singapore Connection

My Japanese friend Tamaki Matsuoka Kanda, a great admirer of Indian cinema, writes:

> The first Malay film, *Laila Majnun*, made in 1933, was the first production of producer [K. R. S.] Chisty and director B. S. Rajhans, two Indian nationals from Bombay.
>
> It was the days of big studios when a number of Indian directors were invited to make Malay films in Singapore. In 1947 the Shaw Brothers film Mogul Sir Run Run Shaw and his elder brother, the late Dato (Sir) Runme Shaw set up Malay Film Production Ltd. (MFP) in Singapore and started to make Malay films.[11]

These two brothers and great showmen invited a number of Indian directors to make Malay films for their company. These Indian directors were crucial to the establishment of the golden days of the Malay film industry through the creation of their own films and their training of a number of Malay filmmakers, actors, and actresses.[12]

Tamaki points out four main reasons for the invitation of so many Indian directors by the Shaw Brothers and Cathay-Keris Film Productions in Malaya:

- India had already developed into a prolific filmmaking country with enough expertise and technical know-how.
- Indian directors were much less expensive than their European and Hollywood counterparts. (It is unfortunate that this holds true even to this day despite the fact the talent available in India is no less competent.)
- Fluency in the English language meant no communication problems with the studio staff.
- Many Indian directors were familiar with the region because the Malay Peninsula had a large number of Indian immigrants already settled there.[13]

The Colonial Regime Intervenes

Cinema in India has always been a private enterprise. The government's involvement from its inception had been confined to documentaries and educational films from the war period. Initially, the colonial regime closely watched what was going on. As film exhibition and filmmaking progressed and slowly expanded into big business, the government stepped in. Appalled by the deplorable conditions in which the public was watching films and the growth of crime, violence, and promiscuity in films, especially in imported films, the authorities realized that they could not be reduced to silent spectators but must take corrective measures immediately. The government intervened and passed the Indian Cinematograph Act of 1918, which made licensing of cinemas and censorship of films shown to the public compulsory.

Management of cinema exhibition halls had to provide adequate safety measures relating to fire hazards and ensure proper hygienic conditions. More important, the films had to have a censor's certificate. Government censorship of films started in 1919 and continued under the national government even after independence in 1947. Soon a bureaucrat from the undivided Bengal decided to impose an "educational cess," or tax, on tickets sold at the box office. Beginning as a negligible one paisa per ticket in 1922, "the entertainment tax" (as it is known now) has since grown into such monstrous proportions that it is sometimes 100 percent or more of the ticket value. This coupled with rampant video piracy has been the biggest bane of the Indian film industry.[14]

Rangacharya Shows the Way

In 1928, the British government set up the Indian Cinematograph Committee under the chairmanship of Dewan Bahadur T. Rangacharya, with the primary task of improving the status of Dominion Empire films, which according to the regime included both British and Indian. Rangacharya understood what prompted the British government to set up the committee. According to Rangacharya, there was no case of discriminating against American films or for offering special privileges to British productions. Being a true nationalist, Rangacharya used the opportunity to study the condition of the Indian film industry and suggested ways to improve it. The committee launched a major investigation, traveling throughout the country, interviewing more than three hundred witnesses, including all involved in Indian film. The resulting material—a report plus five volumes of evidence—provides valuable documentation of the first two decades of cinema in the country.[15]

For the development of the film industry in India, Rangacharya made several recommendations that were far ahead of their times and challenging to implement. Some of his suggestions were to build more permanent cinemas, encourage the growth of traveling cinemas, grant institutional loans for setting up a National Film Library, institute awards and prizes for meritorious films and technicians, produce government documentaries and educational films, and most important, allow the raw material of the industry to be duty-free. Rangacharya submitted the report to the government in 1928 with a note of dissent from two British members of the committee. Since the British government found nothing that was appealing to them, the report was shelved and disappeared into the dusty corridors of bureaucracy. The industry that Rangacharya had so meticulously studied and analyzed was itself poised for a revolutionary change with the technological innovation of sound.

Accent on Nationalism

During the silent era, imported films mostly from America and Europe dominated the Indian screen. The indigenous cinema had to compete with the dominant cinema of the West to obtain films for screening. Only a few nationalist exhibitors showed locally made films. The screening ratio at the end of the silent era was 20 percent national and 80 percent imported. The situation changed dramatically once sound arrived and technology became accessible to make talkies using the various Indian languages, in addition to the national language, Hindustani (which is now Hindi).

Sound gave rise to not one but several cinemas in India. The possibility of seeing films in one's own mother tongue drew a stream of audiences to movie houses. Apart from the major metropolitan cities—Bombay, Calcutta, Madras, and Lahore—filmmaking sprang up in every corner of the country in the respective regional languages, giving a big boost to the overall national film output. The national cinema started asserting itself so strongly that imported films were quickly replaced with Indian-language films. Imported films (by then mostly American) were confined to the urban metropolis, and they were slowly reduced to a meager 10 percent of the overall exhibition time—a complete reverse of the earlier ratio. How this could happen at a time when the country was under British colonial rule is indeed baffling. Very few countries in the region, especially the colonized ones, could claim this distinction of building up a truly indigenous national cinema in the midst of a dominant colonial regime.

Since then, Indian cinema has never looked back. Perhaps India is the only nation that has not allowed imported films to dominate its screens, despite aggressive attempts by American and British distributors to dub their films in Hindi and some South Indian languages and release simultaneously multiple prints to capture the Indian market. Barring a few exceptions such as *Jurassic Park* and *Titanic*, such attempts could not make any headway. The film scene in India continues to be dominated by the national cinema even today. This should be an eye opener to all those who take pride in their respective national cinemas, especially in these days of globalization when American cinema is attempting to dominate the world screen.

Cultural Identity in the Age of Globalization

Indian and other Asian cinemas have shown they have their own cultural identities, distinct from those of Western films. The form and treatment of Asian cinema spring out of strong cultural roots from the countries of the region, whether colonized or not. Their films are basically designed for local consumption and not necessarily targeted for a worldwide audience. For example, the song-and-dance emotion-charged Indian melodrama has its roots in the age-old Indian folk tradition and the performing arts, where serious statements about life and the human condition are made in highly stylized form, something with which local audiences could easily identify. It may seem naïve and frivolous to outsiders, who are not familiar with the local genre or do not bother to search out its nuances or contemporary relevance. The performing arts that preceded cinema in this country evolved on the same principle. Cinema only extended the process through technological means. The ultimate aim for both had been the same, to be entertained and, in the process, be simultaneously enlightened in the spiritual sense.

The bulk of Asian cinema, I believe, has also evolved out of such concerns. Since filmmaking has become such a costly affair, national cinemas have to look beyond their traditional borders both for funding and box-office returns to survive. Whether one likes it or not, globalization is something we have to live with. Under present circumstances, the biggest challenge before the Indian and fellow Asian filmmakers is to reach out to a global audience without endangering the sanctity of their cultural identity.

P. K. NAIR was founder-director of the National Film Archive of India (NFAI), Puna and a film archivist, film teacher, and film festival consultant. He pioneered the film preservation, documentation, and dissemination activities of NFAI and developed it to an institution of international reckoning. He served as chairman and member of several national and international film festival juries and was actively involved in the spread of the archive movement and film literacy in the subcontinent, as well as in the promotion of Indian film studies within and outside the country.

Notes

1. *Puranas* generally refer to the epics *Ramayana* and *Mahabharata* and stories pertaining to gods and goddesses.

2. Sanjit Narvekar, *Marathi Cinema in Retrospect* (Bombay: Maharashtra Film, Stage and Cultural Development, 1995), 7.

3. Ibid.

4. Ibid.

5. Ibid., 8.

6. D. G. Phalke, "Navyug," *Marathi Weekly*, November 1917 (trans. Smti Narmada S. Sahne).

7. Dhundiraj Govind Phalke, interview, *Mouj*, 1939.

8. Phalke, "Navyug."

9. *Maidan* is an open ground where public gatherings and performances are held on special occasions.

10. *Biograph*, 1914.

11. Tamaki Matsuoka Kanda, "Indian Film Directors in Malaya," in *Frames of Mind: Reflections on Indian Cinema*, ed. Aruna Vasudev (New Delhi: UBS Publishers' Distributors, 1995), 43.

12. Ibid., 43–50.

13. Ibid., 50.

14. B. V. Dharap, "National Film Policy," in *Indian Films, 1977 and 1978* (Pune, India: Motion Picture Enterprises, 1979), xi–xviii.

15. Indian Cinematograph Committee, *Report of the Film Enquiry Committee, 1927–28* (Calcutta: Government of India Central Publications, 1928). For more details of the report, see Dharap, "National Film Policy."

10 Colonial Beginnings of Cinema in the Philippines

Nick Deocampo

THE FORMATIVE YEARS of cinema coincided with a major historical juncture in the Philippines: the decline of Spanish rule, the birth of the Filipino nation, and the advance of American imperialism. This includes the outbreak of the Philippine Revolution against the Spaniards in 1896, the declaration of the short-lived Philippine Republic in 1898, the American defeat of Spain at the Battle of Manila Bay, the resulting American occupation of the islands, and the Philippine-American War in 1899, which led to American colonization. Cinema was introduced during this whirlpool of change, and its growth paralleled historical events surrounding and shaping the formation of the Philippine Republic with the approach of the twentieth century. Born as twin to the nation, cinema mirrored historical conditions shaping the destiny of the emerging nation-state. This chapter explains the colonial foundations of what would one day become known as "Philippine cinema." While many presently see this cinema as Filipino, little is known about the foundations of this *Filipino* cinema in its colonial past—its *Spanish* and *American* past.

In defining Filipino cinema's beginnings, one must deal with early cinema (cinema before about 1920) as a starting point for discussion. During this historical period, the prevailing conditions surrounding the arrival and early growth of motion pictures were colonial rather than native, even as cinema was internationalist rather than nationalist in its operation and business. Cinema's Spanish/European and American past provided local cinema with its formative years of development and shaped the cinema we know today. Given this complex beginning, our understanding of early cinema in the Philippines needs to be nuanced and sensitive to the different cultural forces at play. These include (1) the retreating Hispanic culture that tenaciously asserted its receding influence on local society through the latest technology of cinema; (2) the incoming Anglo-American culture that aggressively shaped nascent cinema during the height of the US occupation; and (3) the emerging Filipino consciousness that sought ways to shape cinema through its active reception of, or resistance to, motion pictures and their advancing influence to achieve its own homegrown aspirations.

The complex nature of forces that shaped early cinema in the Philippines formed a "trialectic," best understood if we know who wielded power and who consumed the medium.[1] These forces were not equally dynamic; the Spaniards/Europeans and Americans fought for dominance while the emerging Filipinos were barely visible, save for the power they exercised as a collective body of consumers and movie patrons (and only later as producers themselves, although marginally). They all, however, challenged each other's claims for control over the infant cinema. Interactions between them—their tensions and co-optations, their inadequacies and gains—left lasting marks on the cinema that developed. The cinema that evolved from this period was a cinema that, even if called "Filipino," both spoke of the triumph of the natives and contained elements of the influence of the two colonial agents.

One cannot overestimate the impact that the clash among these competing cultures had on the formation of Filipino identity and film culture. After more than a hundred years, we can look back and discern the ways in which these struggles shaped Filipino cinema. The narrative of this history overlays the national history, a reflection of cinema's role as mirror to society—but also as a cultural practice that did much to shape the nation.

Twilight Year of Spanish Rule Sets the Stage for Early Cinema

The initial public appearance of motion pictures in what was then a Spanish colony, Las Islas Filipinas, happened on January 1, 1897.[2] A cursory look at the active players during this very early phase of cinema already shows its colonial leanings. The Spanish exhibitors Francisco Pertierra and Antonio Ramos, respectively, held the first film screenings using the Chronophotograph and Cinematograph devices.[3] Other nationalities went into the racial mix of early film personalities, such as Swiss business partners Leibman and Peritz, theater operators; the Ullman brothers, French trade importers; and Walgrah, British theater owner. They were all Europeans, with financial capital and social distinction to import and embark on the business of motion pictures.

Although cinema was a visual experience, it was through spoken language that it found its initial entry into local society. Spanish was the dominant language of communication at the time—from newspapers to records that settled judicial matters in court. In the early part of the twentieth century, Filipinos clung to their Spanish upbringing despite America's zealous efforts to change their domestic lifestyle after US forces took control of the country's administration. This was shown in their use of the Spanish language, which increased dramatically during the first few decades of US rule.[4] The Spanish film words remaining in the local vocabulary (even if indigenized) allow us to appreciate cinema's phenomenal acceptance by Filipinos. Even though much of the material evidence from the past has been lost, words remain as proof of the first contact and the deep influence the Spanish language had cast on the evolving Filipino film culture.

Film-related words began to appear in 1896 in Spanish-language newspapers.[5] The short-lived *cronofotógrafo* (from the French word *chronophotographe*) refers to the film device imported by Pertierra. His first film show was called *Espectaculo cientifico de Pertierra* (Pertierra's scientific show), featuring French-made films.[6] Although originally in French, the titles were promoted in Spanish, since Manila was a Hispanic society. Ramos similarly followed, promoting Lumière's films with titles such as *Cortejo arabe* (Arab parade) and *La cena en familia* (Family dinner). Using a *cinematógrafo*, the moving picture machine invented by the Lumière brothers and imported to the country by Ramos, these screenings became popular, as they were in Europe. Not long after, the term found another use. It began to refer to a movie house (*teatro-cinematógrafo* or *cinematógrafo-teatro*), as traditional theaters shared space with motion picture shows until new edifices were built to screen only moving pictures. Only then they were called *cinematógrafos*. The term continued to be popular even during the American period. Later shortened to *cine*, the word became *sine* to refer to film, a term still used by Filipinos today.

Spanish words were also used to name objects and describe experiences related to cinema. These are a few local Tagalog movie-related words (also found in the national language, Filipino) that have a Spanish origin: *pelikula* (Spanish word, *pelicula*: film, movie, cinema); *aktor* (*actor*: actor); *aktres* (*actriz*: actress); *sinematograpiya* (*cinematografía*: cinematography); *eksena* (*escena*: scene); *telon* (*telon*: screen); and *takilya* (*taquilla*: box office).[7] During the silent film period, when no national language was yet in place, combined English, Spanish, and Tagalog subtitles were flashed on the screen. Titles of early silent films—even if they were originally in French, English, German, or Italian—were all written in Spanish, no doubt to appeal to the Spanish-speaking population, the base of support for the emerging entertainment. Popular films of the period such as *Uncle Tom's Cabin* or *Jack and the Beanstalk* were respectively called *La cabaña de tio Tomas* and *Jack y las plantas de habichuelas*. Whether it enriched native vocabulary or increased film's popular patronage, the use of the Spanish language made an impact that one can only begin to appreciate today.[8] Many of the terms we presently use have their origin in words that were introduced during the Spanish era and continued to be used during the early cinema period.

Despite the Spanish influence on the newly arrived moving pictures, at its core were French film practices. Hispanic culture merely provided an outer layer of film's reception in the Philippines. The French provided the films that were imported and shown, the technology used both for filming and projection, the film trade relations, and many other tangible products, but the films' titles were translated into a language acceptable to the colony. The early cinema that grew in the country's capital, Manila, as well as in places such as the southern cities of Ilong-Ilong (Iloilo) and Sugbu (Cebu), was primarily French in origin but cloaked by Hispanic language and culture.[9] Neither a manufacturer of film equipment nor a major center of film production, Spain was itself dependent on French film products.[10] Nevertheless, Philippine exhibitors who appealed to Spanish-speaking audiences (and who often had their own cultural ties to Spain) often made a point of showing films bought from Spain, particularly Barcelona.[11] These might include scenics (films showing landscapes), news films, and fiction films.

The European context of cinema's development would be felt in the Philippines through the mediation of Spanish culture. As the history of early cinema shows, French companies, particularly Pathé, dominated much of the global film market from the late 1890s until the outbreak of World War I. Hollywood's influence would be felt strongly only after this war, which devastated much of Europe and its film industries.

Manila became a popular choice for many European film companies to premiere their films in Asia. Pathé proudly promoted spectacular titles such as Sarah Bernhardt's *Queen Elizabeth* and Victor Hugo's *Les misérables*. Other French companies such as Gaumont and Eclair, as well as the Italian Ambrosio, German Messler, and Danish Nordisk, also provided films. The favored position that Manila enjoyed as a leading film center in Asia, together with Shanghai and Kyoto, could come only from its strong European connections. All these, however, would experience a rapid decline after World War I.

Early Cinema in the Philippines under the American Occupation

The sudden, violent arrival of Americans in the Philippine Islands following the naval battle between Spanish and American warships in 1898 provided an opportunity for motion pictures to exponentially flourish.[12] The United States was not only emerging as a world political and economic superpower; its policies and cultural influences would shape its new colony's emerging cinema. Eventually dislodging French film dominance, American films would serve US imperialist and colonialist interests.

An investigation of early cinema in the Philippines at the time of the US occupation clarifies the decisive role of US colonization. Although private businessmen had first introduced film into the Spanish colony, the US military played a crucial role in facilitating film's reintroduction and subsequent diffusion. In the late 1890s motion pictures were heavily shaped by war—when they were either produced or exhibited. The first published accounts of films screened during the immediate arrival of US troops announced that they were made by Biograph (although as Charles Musser mentions in his chapter, this was only to cash in on the popularity of the brand name). Perhaps not surprisingly, these announcements were published in an English-language newspaper, *Freedom*, on May 23 and 25, 1899. While this newspaper had a small circulation, the rival Spanish-language newspapers that had larger readership carried no mention of the films. Subsequent months would see the screening of films celebrating military themes. Early cinema in the Philippines under American control feasted on war films such as those announced in *Freedom* on September 2, 1899. The advertisement promoted "War Scenes," boasting all of two hundred titles in the program.[13]

Pioneering American Filmmakers

The first films to be made about the new US colony of the Philippines were taken by Americans. Films made about the war—shot both on location or reconstructed—spiked film production in the United States and helped boost the role of cinema as "visual newspapers."[14] Three American filmmakers pioneered the depiction of the Philippines in early American cinema: James Henry White, E. Burton Holmes, and C. Fred Ackerman.

Edison producer James Henry White made two types of films related to US military activity in the Philippines. The first was the actuality type, or factual recording of events; the other used actors and was staged. Among this first group, White and his cameraman Frederick Blechynden filmed *Troop Ships for the Philippines* on May 25, 1898: it was one of the earliest motion pictures to carry a reference to the Far Eastern country.[15] Its main rivals in this regard were Stuart Blackton and Albert E. Smith's *Battle of Manila Bay* (figure 10.1) and French film pioneer Georges Méliès's *Combat naval devant Manille* (Naval combat near Manila), both also shot in 1898.[16] Although White's film was not shot in the Philippines and did not contain images of real Filipinos, its title served as the first invocation of the country in motion pictures by Americans. Absent visually and yet invoked in the filmic imaginary, the Philippines began to enter the consciousness of the American public, who knew little about it before the outbreak of war.

The second type was more elaborate than factual recordings of troop ships on their way to a war zone.[17] Films in this category depicted action-packed battle scenes of Americans as they reconquered and recolonized the Philippines. However, they were "fake" representations shot in the New Jersey countryside and employed African Americans as substitutes for Filipino soldiers. Considered reenactments, the war narratives they depicted were based on newspaper reports and articles written for widely read magazines such as *Harper's Weekly* and *Leslie's Weekly*. Inevitably, fiction and fantasy dominated these depictions of war stories. Among White's reenacted newsreels were *Filipinos Retreat from Trenches* (June 5, 1899), *U.S. Troops and Red Cross in the Trenches before Caloocan (P.I.)* (June 5, 1899), *Advance of Kansas Volunteers at Caloocan* (June 5, 1899), *Capture*

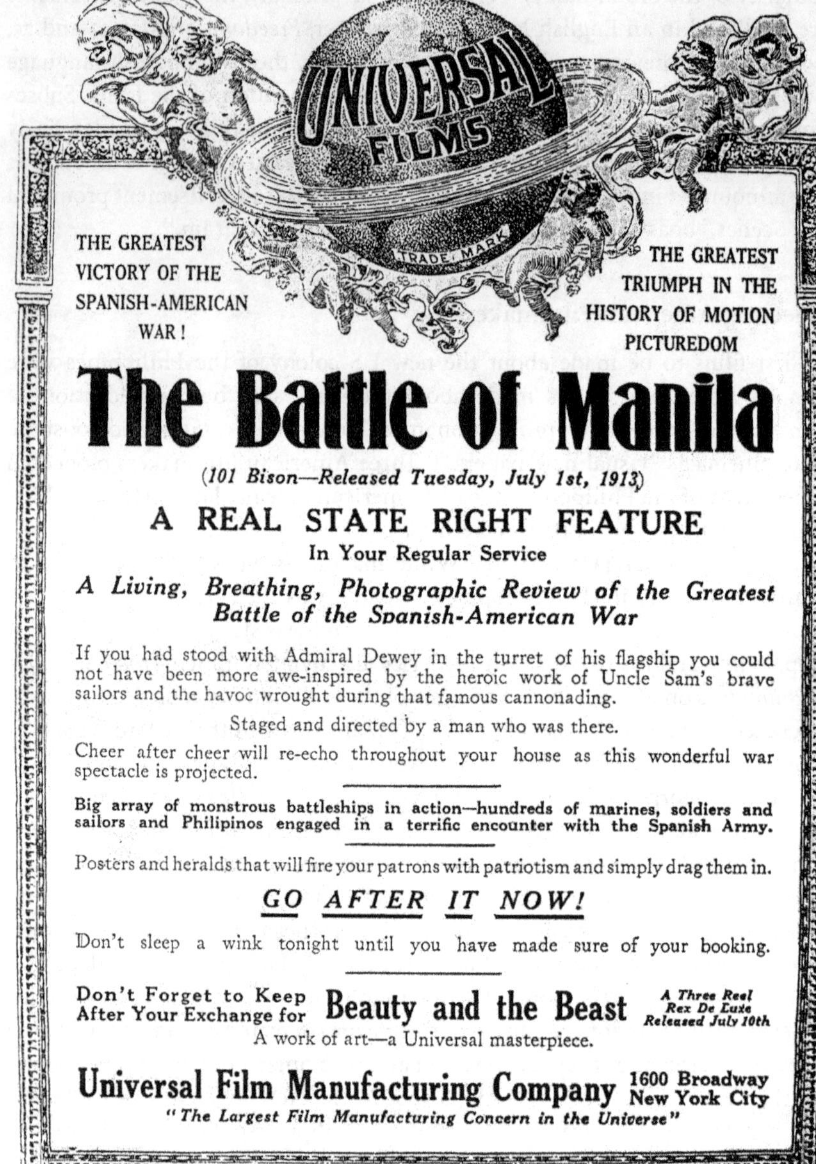

Figure 10.1. "The Battle of Manila" was a celebrated subject during the early motion picture period. The version advertised here was a 1913 movie produced by Francis L. Ford for Bison. Because it was fiction, not a newsreel or documentary, the film was described as "entirely melodramatic." (*Moving Picture World*, June 28, 1913, p. 1317.)

of Trenches at Candaba (June 10, 1899), *Rout of the Filipinos* (June 10, 1899), *The Early Morning Attack* (September 22, 1899), and *Col. Funston Swimming the Baglag River* (September 23, 1899).

The second filmmaker, Elias Burton Holmes, was the first US cameraman to make films in the Philippines. Possibly visiting the colony three times, he made films to accompany his lucrative lecture presentations in the United States and to supply major Hollywood distribution companies such as Paramount with travelogues. Holmes sailed from Hong Kong to the Philippines in June 1899, a year after George Dewey's victory in Manila Bay, and took the first motion pictures of the country and its people.[18] Many of these scenes were staged. Firemen acted out their fire drill before his camera, to Holmes's amusement as well as the entertainment of various bystanders. Although cockfights were a popular Filipino amusement, they were banned by US authorities. Nevertheless, Holmes found "no difficulty in arranging a cockfight for motion picture purposes."[19] He even resorted to filming a sham battle so that he could show audiences back in the United States how American soldiers managed to rout their enemies.

Holmes returned to the Philippines in 1913 with his cameraman and longtime partner, Oscar Depue.[20] Titles from this trip include *The New Manila, Hiking through Luzon,* and *Cruising through the Philippines.* In 1916, Holmes released *A Visit to Bilibid, the Sing-Sing of the Philippines* as part of a series called Paramount–Burton Holmes Travel Pictures. Under this business arrangement, Holmes released films for regular commercial distribution through Paramount. In fact, several of Holmes's films became regular features in movie houses in the Manila capital and other parts of the Philippines.

The third film pioneer, C. Fred Ackerman, worked for Thomas Edison's rival: the American Mutoscope and Biograph Company (AM&B). He was embedded with the US Army to cover the Philippine-American War as correspondent, photographer, and filmmaker. General Elwell S. Otis assigned him to Colonel (later to become General) Franklin Bell's 36th Infantry Regiment.[21] As a special correspondent for *Leslie's Weekly,* he provided the magazine with eyewitness accounts of the raging battle between US and Filipino soldiers. Ackerman's adventurous personality helps explain his presence in the Philippines at the time when America was at war. While other filmmakers contented themselves with reenacting battle scenes in the American countryside, he daringly went to actual battle sites.

Ackerman arrived in the Philippines on September 30, 1899, and stayed until March 1900; he made approximately forty-two films during his almost six-month stay. A closer look at several of his films offers insights into the kind of filmic production taking place during the seminal days of cinema in the US colony. He shot a good number of actualities or travel views: *The Escolta, a Busy Street in Manila* offers a snapshot of Manila's main street where public conveyances passed by. More numerous were films in the military genre. Although none depict actual face-to-face encounters between combatant soldiers, they portray the US military presence as it gradually took control. These include *33rd Infantry Going to Firing Line*, *The Battle of Mt. Ariat* (Arayat), *Repelling the Enemy*, *An Attack on Magalang*, and *A Charge of Insurgents*. Ackerman's attachment to a military unit underscores the complicit relationship early cinema in the Philippines had with the invading US military forces.

None of Ackerman's films were ever shown in the Philippines. The exposed film was shipped back to the New York office and developed there. The films found their way to the US War Department in Washington, D.C., where they were screened for high-ranking officials.[22] Although shown to top-rank military officers, the films were hardly classified information. On the contrary, these screenings were used to promote the films, which were exhibited commercially. Many were later listed in the AM&B's sales catalogues.

All three pioneer filmmakers made films about the Philippines with military themes but with distinctly opposing styles and film formats. Edison films were shot in 35mm, Holmes was using Gaumont cameras with a 60mm film gauge, while Biograph relied on a large-format 68/70mm camera. White's reenactments were shot in the United States, while Holmes and Ackerman engaged in making actualities, films shot in actual places. But while Holmes also shot sham war footage, Ackerman left behind actual footage of American soldiers at the battlefront, in addition to images of civilian life. If cinema in the Philippines grew under a military climate during the 1890s, during the next three decades, film under US colonial administration spread deeper into the fabric of the emerging Philippine society through two other means—economic and cultural.

American Residents Venture into Film Production

As the Philippine-American War subsided, Americans, including soldiers who had fought in that war and chose to stay in the Philippines, began to make films. During this period of pacification, the first American resident to make films may have been Albert W. Yearsley, who shot the Rizal Day celebration at the Luneta in Manila on December 30, 1909. This gregarious American had a prolific career. After 1910 his Oriental Film Manufacturing Company produced news films for the theaters he owned and managed. Yearsley's lead was challenged in 1912 when fellow Americans Harry Brown and Edward Meyer Gross made a film about the country's martyred hero, José Rizal. Their film was destined to become the country's first feature-length film and the first to use well-known actors. Not to be outdone, Yearsley rushed his own shorter version of the Rizal story into production and was able to show the resulting picture a day before his rivals. Yearsley had the advantage of owning Manila's leading movie house, the Majestic, where he could show his film at any time with no booking problem. Brown and Gross might have made use of the Gaiety Theater, which Brown managed, but had already rented the Manila Grand Opera House, an obviously better choice.

For nearly three weeks, Manila became enthralled as these Americans showed the country's first nationalist films, ironically made by foreigners. The heated rivalry finally subsided when Yearsley terminated his screenings on September 1 and the Brown-Gross film announced its last night to be on September 5. So ended a bitterly contested rivalry that did much to lay down the foundations for a domestic film industry.

With films now locally produced, early cinema in the Philippines became assured of continued patronage and loyalty by appealing to homegrown sensibilities. The hallowed space inside the theater, once a preserve only for zarzuelas and operas, was invaded by silent pictures enlivened by musical accompaniment. While the two American films captured local moviegoers' fancy, other films (still made by foreigners) continued to be made. Travelogues, or films depicting local scenes and traditions, appeared to have made up the largest number of local productions from 1905 until 1917. These were closely followed by coverage of public events such as parades, disaster films, and films about government campaigns or local industries such as the hemp industry. Typical of the period, actualities outnumbered fiction films.

Casting the Colonial Gaze: The Film of Dean C. Worcester

In contrast to Yearsley and Gross, who worked full-time in commercial entertainment and made films that appealed to Filipino moviegoers, Dean C. Worcester was an American government functionary and noted anthropologist who saw motion pictures as a device that could advance both the colonialist agenda and his own personal interests. Also a distinguished zoologist from the University of Michigan, Worcester had fortuitously published his book *The Philippine Islands and Their People* in late 1898 to considerable acclaim.[23] President William McKinley then appointed him to successive US commissions on the Philippines, which led to the establishment of a US civil government under William Howard Taft.[24] Worcester subsequently became the first secretary of the interior of the Philippine colonial government (1901–1913),[25] and he soon established a stormy relationship with Filipino politicians and the native press.[26] To deflect these attacks, which included accusations of corruption, Worcester emphasized his achievements in ending the practice of head hunting among the mountain tribes of northern Luzon.[27]

Worcester soon became a strong advocate for the use of film to "civilize" Filipino "natives"; Worcester found in film "the most practical manner to bring about peace among the different tribes in the islands."[28] As correspondent William Altdorfer reported,

Moving Picture shows have penetrated the wildest and most remote parts of the Philippine Islands. After centuries of fruitless effort on the part of the Spaniards to wean the wild men from their unholy pastimes, it has remained for Uncle Sam to adopt the only means to reach their hearts—all with the assistance of the ever-fascinating moving picture show. The wild men have been taught the difference between the clean and unclean ways of living by means of graphic pictures thrown on the canvas.

In the words of an official recently returned from among these people, "Just to watch the many emotions pictured on the faces of the former head hunters when the pictures were first shown was worth the many hardships endured to bring the word of civilization to these children. For they are but children in the simplest sense of the word. They sat on their haunches, or rather squatted in the fashion of the Indian, and there passed across the faces of all present all the emotions of which the human being is capable. Astonishment, amusement and incredulity quickly followed, one upon the other, until it settled to one of extreme pleasure and satisfaction."[29]

In 1911, Worcester submitted a report to Washington, D.C., detailing the results that had been achieved among a number of wild Philippine tribes through the use of motion pictures. Those he called "natives" had abandoned human and animal sacrifices, a change he attributed to the use of film. In *Picture Theater News*, an article on Worcester reported the process of how the moving picture device was enlisted in the sanitary education of tribal natives, as well as in instilling "civilized ways" to run their lives: "Scenes from native and foreign life are shown and the novelty of the picture machine itself enlists the interest of the aborigines. Once the interest has been gained, a basis of helpful work is established and in a comparatively short time remarkable results have been achieved."[30]

During his screenings in the United States, a lecturer explained the pictures. Evident changes happening in non-Christian tribes were proudly recounted in his report:

Head-hunting, slavery and piracy are now very rare. The liquor traffic has been almost completely suppressed. Life and property have been rendered comparatively safe and in much of the territory entirely so. In many instances the wild men are being successfully used to police their own country. Agriculture is being developed. Unspeakably filthy towns have been made clean and sanitary. The people are learning to abandon human sacrifices and animal sacrifices and to come to the doctor when injured or ill. Numerous schools have been established and are in successful operation. The old, sharply drawn tribal lines are disappearing. Bontoc Igorots, Ifugaos, and Kalingas now visit each other's territory. At the same time that all of this has been accomplished the good will of the people has been secured.[31]

Photographs accompanied his report submitted to the Insular Bureau of the US War Department. They showed members of the mountain tribes before and after being introduced to America's civilizing ways. The most graphic among these photographs is that of a "headhunter turned policeman." First, he is shown as a headhunter, "a savage in every respect." In the second, he is shown, after one year of contact with Americans, wearing Western clothes. In a third photograph, he is shown, after two years' contact, as a local policeman wearing a uniform.[32]

Worcester was a die-hard Republican who strongly objected to the presidential candidacy of Woodrow Wilson and the Democratic Party, which expressed a somewhat qualified anti-imperialist, anticolonial ideology. After Wilson took office, Worcester sought to disrupt legislation that would move the Philippines toward independence and claimed that slavery was widespread in the Philippines, even in Manila.[33] Soon after Wilson became president, Worcester stepped down from his post but not to retire. He planned to go on the lecture circuit with as many as nine different illustrated lectures using lantern slides and motion pictures.[34] In the end, his lectures were fewer in number; these were delivered at Carnegie Hall (New York City), the National Geographic Society (Washington, D.C.), and numerous other venues in late 1913 and early 1914.[35] A *New York Times* journalist noted the ways he effectively moved back and forth between photography and film:

> The savage, naked, dirty, and unkempt, was shown in still photographs, while that same one-time savage, clothed, intelligent in appearance, and clean, later was shown in moving pictures. Still photography showed the huts of the savages of the early days of the American occupation, while the moving pictures depicted clean villages, with beautiful public buildings and neat little homes, after a few years of American rule.[36]

Like Ackerman, who was attached to a military regiment, Worcester found himself embedded inside the very government machinery that ruled and shaped the destiny of the Philippines and its people. Ultimately, he filmed *Native Life in the Philippines*, shot by Charles Martin under Worcester's direction (figure 10.2). The film was edited into two evening-length programs: The *Headhunters* and *From Savages to Civilization* (a.k.a. *From Savages to Citizens*). These were released in March 1914 through the Pan-American Film Manufacturing Company.[37]

In his two-part documentary film Worcester sought to achieve a "colonial narrative," which Benito M. Vergara Jr. characterizes as "the inevitable unfolding of events corresponding to an already written 'plot.'"[38] Worcester's two-part film follows in determined fashion a master narrative that came with colonization. This provided the contextual discourse not only for his films but also for other popular media like photographs, stereopticons, and cartoons. They were all part of the flotsam of events and ideas that followed some hidden or implicit text arising from the policies and ideologies arising from US expansionism. Worcester's film is no different in terms of its representation of Filipinos as backward and

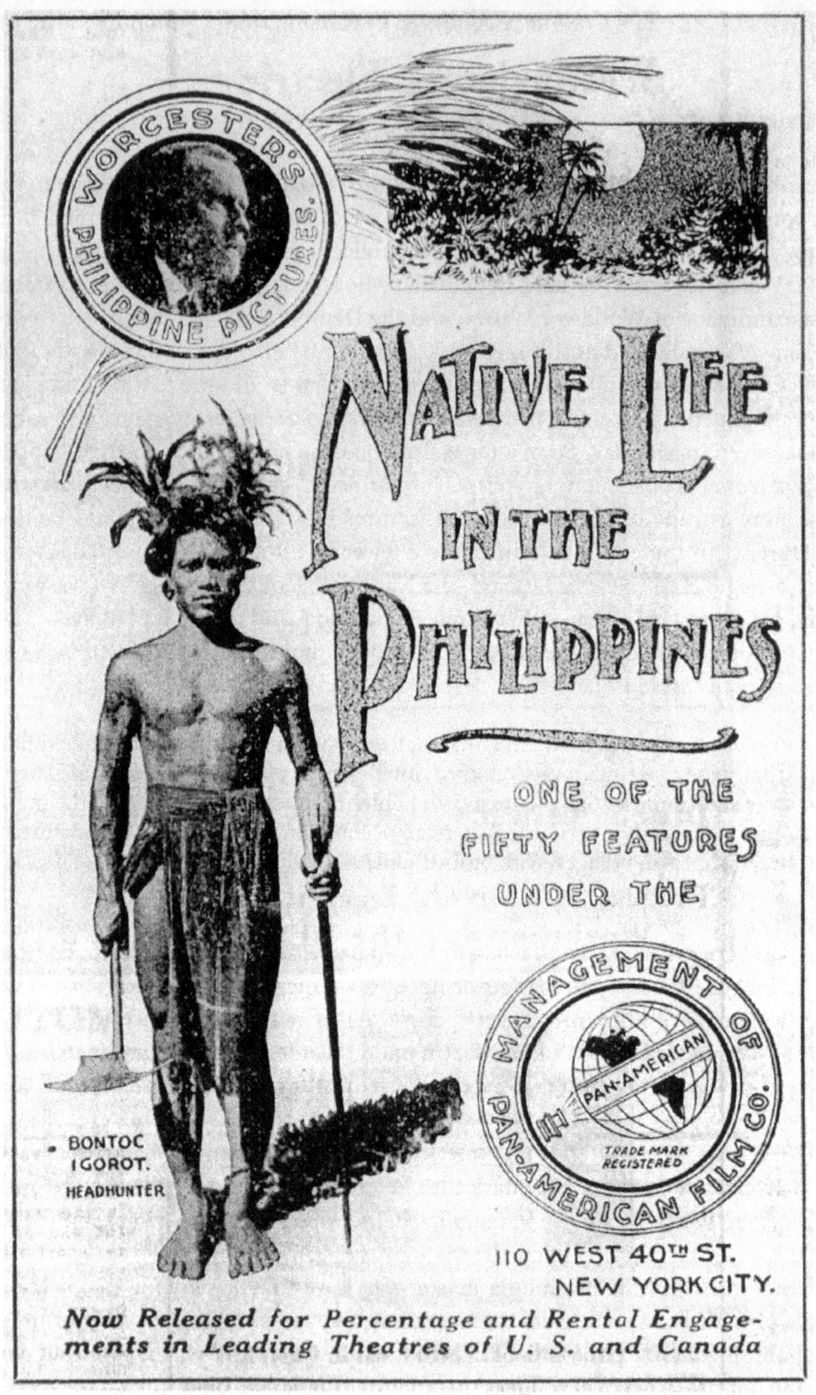

Figure 10.2. Poster promoting Dean C. Worcester's film, *Native Life in the Philippines*, featuring the two episodes *The Headhunters* and *From Savages to Civilization*. (*Moving Picture World*, April 4, 1914, p. 113.)

uncivilized. This representational ploy unequivocally followed the colonialist plot of finding the colonized to be inferior. As in photographs or political cartoons, Worcester's film portrayed Filipinos as "head-hunters," "wild tribes," and America's "little brown brothers." In the course of his filmmaking, the American filmmaker committed another colonializing act—that of showing how these "savages" were transformed into civilized members of society through America's benevolence.[39]

Moving Picture World critic W. Stephen Bush lauded the filmmaker's novel way of civilizing Filipinos through film: "How manfully (the United States) has shouldered the white man's burden and how, with infinite patience and toleration, it has conquered the superstitions, the evils and the crimes of savagery." Bush further wrote, "Among other things, we see how the presence of American civilization in the Philippine Islands replaced savage warfare by rational love of sports and athletics. . . . One cannot help feeling that the Americans, in sharp contrast to the Spaniards, have accepted their responsibilities towards their brown brothers and are discharging their self-imposed duties with great benefit to the objects of their race." In regard to Filipinos, Bush wrote in a patronizing manner: "The Philippino [*sic*] is, in point of intelligence, not much below the white race, and that he is like the Japanese, amiable to kind treatment and very docile."[40] In *The Headhunters*, Worcester depicted only the northern mountain tribes and called them "Filipinos." They were shown half naked and engaged in their "barbaric" rituals of headhunting and dog eating. Christianized lowlanders such as Tagalogs were not considered "pure" Filipinos and received little attention from the surveilling gaze of Worcester's moving picture camera. Not coincidently the release of these two documentary-like programs coincided with the publication of Worcester's two-volume tome *The Philippines: Past and Present*.[41]

For many American newspapers and political figures, Worcester's pronouncements on the Philippines were the final authority. Filipinos had virtually the polar opposite sentiments. Their revulsion to his overzealous acts of educating and civilizing them can be seen in a series of articles printed in a Cebuano newspaper, *Nueva fuerza* (New force). Protesting Worcester's appointment to an executive position in the Visayan Refining Company located on Mactan island, the local paper lambasted the American for holding lectures in the United States and campaigning against granting Philippine independence through the use of his film.[42] In those high-profile illustrated lectures, Worcester continued to insist that Filipinos were primitive in their ways and therefore unworthy of being granted full independence. He tirelessly campaigned in different public forums, insisting that the United States hold on to the Philippines, as it was unfit for self-rule. As Worcester's biographer Rodney J. Sullivan remarked, he insisted that America's duty in the Philippines was "to promote the evolution of savage and barbarous Filipinos to the civilized state." Sullivan further mentions that in the years ahead, Worcester made maximum use of motion pictures to show how American intervention accelerated the Filipinos' ascent toward the American ideal of a "civilized" life, where "under American tutelage dirt gave way to cleanliness, stupidity to intelligence."[43]

When it became apparent that Worcester was to live in Cebu while administering the operations of the Visayan Refining Company, a company in the business of extracting coconut oil, which was in major demand in the United States and Europe, Cebuanos registered their strong revulsion against this "ugly American." With his much-hated reputation preceding him, a large crowd gathered inside Cebu's largest movie house, the Cine Oriente, on June 24, 1915, to protest Worcester's impending arrival on the island.[44] His appointment galvanized the collective concern regarding his acts, which were deemed damaging to the people's desire for self-rule. The city's leading newspaper, *Nueva fuerza*, criticized Worcester, labeling him "an American who is the worst enemy of Filipinos." "During his long stay in power, Worcester's talks about the Philippines were full of damaging defamation of the Filipino integrity," it declared.[45] The article was stinging in its criticism of Worcester's use of motion pictures to delay the granting of Philippine independence:

> In the big cities in the United States he gave "conferences" where he made sure that we Filipinos were not to be granted independence because we are all stupid. Showing proof in meetings, he showed through films several naked *igorrote* [*sic*, Igorots] (with others alleged to be dog eaters), and he claimed that these were the inhabitants of the Philippines. It's true: thousands upon thousands of Americans who listened to him believed that Filipinos were savages and therefore were not fit to be given their independence.[46]

Nueva fuerza then admonished its readers to "avoid Worcester, to ignore him, and not make even a single request of him, so he may see that we Filipinos do not agree with him and are not amused at what he did to us."[47]

In contrast to Worcester, Edward Meyer Gross continued producing story films that appealed to Filipinos. Together with Harry Brown (as producer) and Charles Martin (as cinematographer), Gross formed the Philippines' first major team collaboration in local filmmaking. The same group made other historical films. Aside from his initial productions, *La vida de Rizal* (The life of Rizal, 1912) and *La conquista de Filipinas* (The conquest of the Philippines, 1912), Gross's Rizalina Film Manufacturing Company also produced another dramatic film, *Los tres martires* (The three martyrs, a.k.a. *Gomez, Burgos, Zamora*, 1912), about the killing of three native priests whose deaths inspired intellectuals like Rizal to defy Spanish friar rule. Gross proved to be a prolific filmmaker, making three films in 1912. By producing only story films, he pioneered what would one day become the Tagalog film industry, one that would thrive in the making of narrative films.

Toward a National Cinema

Following the colonial pioneers' local productions, homegrown filmmakers began to make their own films, setting the trialectical process in motion—a process that produced what are generally considered the country's first local cinema productions. This means that while foreign colonial influences remained a continuous source of material and artistic influences, the native influence started manifesting itself and acting on the emergent cinema in ways beyond mere spectatorship. This is best illustrated in the area of production when local talents began to make films.

It has become common knowledge how José Nepomuceno became recognized as the "father" of local filmmaking. Almost every account of Philippine cinema's origin points to him as the maker of the first Filipino film. But while his *Dalagang Bukid* (Country maiden) became the first Filipino-produced feature-length film, this production only happened in 1919. Nevertheless, Nepomuceno and his brother, Jesus, had set up his first film company, Malayan Movies, two years earlier on May 15, 1917. They equipped their company by purchasing film equipment from American pioneers Yearsley and Gross, showing the close ties between the Philippine-born filmmakers and their American benefactors. The equipment Nepomuceno bought from them became his first investments, although according to his biographer, he also bought "equipment from every foreigner who came [to Manila] with movie gadgets."[48] Equipped with a mix of new and hand-me-down devices, Nepomuceno spent the next two years studying and experimenting with the film medium.

In forming Malayan Movies, the Nepomuceno brothers formally started the country's film industry.[49] Initially, Nepomuceno "experimented with documentaries and newsreels before making his first full-length feature film," claims José Quirino.[50] Those short films may be regarded as the first to be locally produced by native-born talent, challenging the long-held belief that *Dalagang Bukid* was the seminal work that started local filmmaking.[51] Long before Nepomuceno made the first all-Filipino feature film, he was a newsreel cameraman who worked with US film interests, supplying films for Paramount (and for Pathé in Europe). However, while engaged in nonfiction film production, Nepomuceno's early feature films strongly illustrate the contending forces that shaped early Filipino productions. His films' narratives and overall production reflected the strong colonial influences on his works. After he made the seminal *Dalagang Bukid*, his next films had Spanish titles, such as *La venganza de Don Silvestre* (The vengeance of Don Silvestre, 1919), *Hoy o nunca besame* (Kiss me now or never, 1920), *La mariposa negra* (The black butterfly, 1920), and *Estrellita del cine* (Movie starlet, 1920). As his career progressed, the titles shifted to the more popular Tagalog, but there were a few in English as well. Nepomuceno's work best exemplifies the three-cornered cultural influences impinging on the early pioneers of local films.

While Nepomuceno clearly favored the Filipino movies' more Hispanic side, another pioneer, Vicente Salumbides, preferred the American and had closer ties to the American filmmaking tradition. While studying law in the United States, Salumbides also studied scriptwriting, acting, and directing in Hollywood, while simultaneously working as a film extra at the Famous Players Company. When World War I broke out, he saw active duty in France under General John J. Pershing.[52] Returning to the Philippines, he finished his law studies and produced his first film, *Miracles of Love* (1925), seeking technical help from the more established Nepomuceno. The film starred American mestiza Elizabeth "Dimples" Cooper and himself as lovers who got married after a long and often humorous set of incidents brought the couple together. With his exposure to Hollywood filming practices, Salumbides claimed he was the first to apply makeup to highlight actors' faces instead of making them appear dark on screen. He also pioneered the close-up to reveal his actors' inner emotions and the use of vision, or superimposed images on the screen meant to visualize what was only in the thoughts of an actor. In terms of editing, he introduced cutaways that highlighted visual rhythm and suspense. Because Salumbides was more Americanized than Nepomuceno, his films were strong in romance and humor—two qualities of Hollywood films that local audiences favored. But his films also addressed the struggle Filipinos had to face in a society that was swiftly changing from its traditional, Hispanic way of life to the more exciting and modern one offered by the Americans. Salumbides's films were early stirrings of local identity finding expression in moving pictures. The new Filipino in the films of both Nepomuceno and Salumbides found new and novel ways to express the contending colonial forces acting and defining the emergent Filipino identity.

In whatever form Philippine cinema may see itself now, understanding its past enriches our understanding of the forms it takes in the present and will take into the future. Early cinema marks a period of ruptures and beginnings that coincides with wars and revolutions. Many of the period's legacies—perhaps hidden from plain view—continue to leave their marks in Philippine cinema.

NICK DEOCAMPO is Associate Professor at the UP Film Institute of the College of Mass Communication, University of the Philippines. He is a filmmaker, author, and scholar who has pioneered several film activities in the Philippines, including the resurgence of interest and study of independent cinema and early cinema. His three books that discuss the colonial cycle of Philippine cinema cover the periods of Spanish, American, and Japanese influences. He has served as member of various international film juries and has organized several conferences on film. He is a member of the International Advisory Board of the

Network for the Promotion of Asia Pacific Cinema (NETPAC) and the UNESCO Memory of the World Philippine Committee.

Notes

1. Inspired by the German philosopher Georg Wilhelm Friedrich Hegel's concept of the "dialectic," the "trialectic" is a way of understanding the interplay of a triad of cultural forces and ideologies shaping early cinema in the Philippines. Composing this triad are two hegemonic cultural forces contained in *Hispanismo* (referring to Spanish cultural influences) and *Anglo-sajonismo* (referring to the aggressive entry of American influences to native society)—both battling each other for dominance over the emerging local cinema. A third force is *Filipinismo*, which resulted from the Filipino people's struggle for independence and self-determination, including what it tried to achieve in cinema. Looking at three cultural influences at play gives a more realistic analysis of the complex colonial and native forces influencing cinema's early years. For more on this discussion, see Nick Deocampo, *Film: American Influences on Philippine Cinema* (Mandaluyong: Anvil, 2011), 6–11.

2. "El Kronofotografo" [The Chronophotographe], *El comercio* [The trade], January 2, 1897.

3. The Chronophotographe was a moving picture machine invented by the Frenchman Georges Demeny. A model manufactured in 1896 is believed to be the one purchased by Pertierra and used to inaugurate the colony's first film show on January 1, 1897. The Cinématographe, invented by Louis and Auguste Lumière, was used by Antonio Ramos for his screenings held on August 29, 1897.

4. Report of the director of education for 1908, cited in "Henry Jones Ford Report," *Philippine Historical Review*, 1913, p. 29.

5. The film-related words appeared, for example, in Spanish-language newspapers such as *El comercio* and other publications such as *La voz española* (The Spanish voice) and *El renacimiento* (The rebirth).

6. Four films were shown with these Spanish titles: *El hombre del sombrero* (Man with a hat), *Los boxeadores* (The boxers), *Baile de negritos* (Negro dance), and *Una calle de Paris* (A street in Paris).

7. See, for example, Teresita Alcantara y Antonio, *Mga Hispanismo sa Filipino* [Hispanisms in Filipino] (Quezon City: Sentro ng Wikang Pilipino / Unibersidad ng Pilipinas, 1999). Alcantara presents findings of a study made by Llamzon and Thorpe, indicating that 33 percent of the Filipino language is derived from Hispanic words; 58 percent are from Tagalog, 4 percent from Chinese and Malay, and 1 percent from English. Alcantara's own study of the widespread use of the Spanish language concludes that among the mass media she surveyed, 22.36 percent of the words used were based on Spanish.

8. In the following years, it became a practice for movie stars to adopt Hispanic screen names, as was the case of Rosa del Rosario (originally Rose Stagner, daughter of an American army official), Nida Blanca (Dorothy Jones), Anita Linda (Alice Lake), and Eduardo de Castro (Marvin Gardner).

9. The pervasive influence cast by language on the local society may be seen as an effect of *Hispanismo*, which is "the existence of a unique Spanish culture, lifestyle, characteristics, tradition, and values, *all of them embodied in its language.*" See Jose del Valle and Luis Gabriel-Stheeman, eds., *The Battle over Spanish between 1800 and 2000: Language Ideologies and Hispanic Intellectuals* (London: Routledge, 2002), 7 (italics in original).

10. See also Alberto Elena and Javier Ordoñez, "Science, Technology, and the Spanish Colonial Experience in the Nineteenth Century," *Osiris* 15 (2000): 70–82.

11. Rafael Roces, owner and manager of the Cine Ideal and other movie houses in Manila, obtained some of his films from Barcelona and even went to Spain to find new films during World War I. See "Philippine Film Man Here," *Moving Picture World*, October 24, 1914, p. 468. Also see Deocampo, *Film*, 169–170, 321–322.

12. The arrival of the United States in the Philippines through the war flotilla commanded by Commodore George Dewey came as a result of the Spanish-American War, which was declared by the United States against Spain in support of Cuban independence after the US battleship *Maine* was allegedly bombed off the shore of Havana. Assistant Secretary of the Navy Theodore Roosevelt commanded Dewey to attack the Philippines, leading to the defeat of the once-invincible Spanish armada in the Battle of Manila Bay on May 1, 1898.

13. An advertisement in *Freedom* on September 2, 1899, claimed that two hundred war scenes would be shown at no. 12 in Escolta. These may have been lantern slides depicting war scenes taken in the Philippines.

14. Robert C. Allen, "Contra the Chaser Theory," *Wide Angle* 3, no. 1 (1979): 7.

15. White and Blechynden's trip in East Asia and their return to the West Coast is traced in Charles Musser, *Edison Motion Pictures, 1890–1900: An Annotated Filmography* (Washington, DC: Smithsonian Institution Press, 1997). James White eventually claimed to have been present at the Battle of Manila Bay and shot footage of this naval battle. There is no contemporaneous evidence to support this claim. See Charles Edward Hastings, "A Cameraman Runs into a War," *Moving Picture World*, January 29, 1927, pp. 327, 362.

16. Blackton and Smith shot *The Battle of Manila Bay* on the rooftop of their American Vitagraph headquarters in New York circa May 19, 1898. As reenactment, the film showed paper ships engaged in mock battle, shot in an upturned tabletop filled with water. Albert E. Smith with Phil A. Koury, *Two Reels and a Crank* (Garden City, NY: Doubleday, 1952), 66–67; Charles Musser, "American Vitagraph: 1897–1901," *Cinema Journal* 22, no. 3 (1983): 13; Roger Boussinot, ed., *L'encyclopedie du cinema* [The encyclopedia of cinema] (Paris: Bordas, 1967), 1045.

17. For details of films made by White in the 1890s, see Musser, *Edison Motion*.

18. Burton Holmes, *The Burton Holmes Lectures*, 10 vols. (Battle Creek, MI: Little Preston, 1901).

19. Ibid., 5:284, 286.

20. "Movies Scare Timid Negritos (Holmes and Camera Men Visit Hill Tribe)," *Manila Times*, June 26, 1913, p. 11. The article reported that "Burton Holmes was accompanied by 'two assistants,' DePue [*sic*] and Cochrane."

21. "Pictures That Will Be Historic," *Leslie's Weekly*, January 6, 1900, p. 18.

22. "The Mutoscope in War," *Kansas City Star*, June 24, 1900, p. 4.

23. "Worcester's Book on the Philippines," *New York Times*, December 31, 1898.

24. "An Important Commission," *New York Tribune*, February 12, 1899, p. B1; "Civil Government for the Filipinos," *New York Times*, February 7, 1900, p. 1.

25. There are several sources of information about Dean C. Worcester: James H. Blount, *American Occupation of the Philippines, 1898–1912* (New York: Knickerbocker, 1913), 571–586; "Dean Worcester," *Bulletin of the American Historical Collection* 25, no. 1 (1997).

26. "Plot to Oust Michigan Men," *Detroit Free Press*, January 18, 1907, p. 2; "Worcester Sues For Libel," *New York Times*, January 24, 1909, p. C4.

27. "Now Educating Head Hunters: Uncle Sam's Latest Job in the Philippines," *Los Angeles Times*, July 5, 1909, p. 14.

28. "Dean Worcester Praises Pictures," *Film Index*, April 8, 1911, p. 4.

29. William L. Altdorfer, "Work of Reclaiming Former Head-Hunters: Moving-Picture Shows Used as Civilizers," *San Francisco Chronicle*, May 7, 1911, p. 5.

30. Untitled article, *Picture Theater News* (London), May 31, 1911, p. 6.

31. Ibid.

32. Benito M. Vergara Jr., *Displaying Filipinos: Photography and Colonialism in Early 20th Century Philippines* (Quezon City: University of the Philippines Press, 1995), 105. This source also reprints a photograph of a Bontoc Igorot who has been transformed in three phases: as a tribal figure, after a year of service after entering the Philippine Constabulary, and then two years later. The photograph's original source is Frederick C. Chamberlain, *The Philippine Problem, 1898–1913* (Boston: Little, Brown, 1913), facing 160. Such images were already being used as illustrations in Altdorfer, "Work of Reclaiming Former Head-Hunters," in 1911.

33. "Filipinos Enslaved, Asserts Worcester," *New York Tribune*, August 25, 1913, p. 4.

34. "Worcester Gives Up Philippines Post," *New York Times*, September 7, 1913, p. 12.

35. Advertisements, *Moving Picture World*, February 28, 1914, p. 1128.

36. "Calls Wild Men Our Wards," *New York Times*, December 31, 1913, p. 7.

37. Advertisements, *Moving Picture World*, February 28, 1914, p. 1128; March 14, 1914, p. 1418; and April 4, 1914, p. 113. See also W. Stephen Bush, "Native Life in the Philippines," *Moving Picture World*, April 18, 1914, p. 365.

38. Vergara, *Displaying Filipinos*, 18. See also Sharon Delmendo, *The Star-Entangled Banner: One Hundred Years of America in the Philippines* (Quezon City: University of the Philippines Press, 2005); and Vicente L. Rafael, *White Love and Other Events in Filipino History* (Quezon City: Ateneo de Manila University Press, 2000).

39. Advertisement, *Moving Picture World*, February 28, 1914, p. 1128.

40. Bush, "Native Life in the Philippines," 365.

41. "Literary Criticism and Book News," *New York Tribune*, February 14, 1914, p. 8.

42. "Worcester," *Nueva fuerza* [New force], August 8, 1915.

43. Rodney J. Sullivan, *Exemplar of Americanism: The Philippine Career of Dean C. Worcester* (Quezon City: New Day, 1992), 183.

44. "Worcester to the Special Mission to the Philippine Islands," August 4, 1921, p. 16, cited in Sullivan, *Exemplar of Americanism*, 195.

45. "Worcester," *Nueva fuerza*, August 8, 1915 (my translation).

46. Ibid.

47. Ibid.

48. Joe Quirino, *Don Jose and the Early Philippine Cinema* (Quezon City: Phoenix, 1983), 14. For a more comprehensive profile of the life and career of José Nepomuceno, see Nadi Tofighian, "The Role of Jose Nepomuceno in the Philippine Society: What Language Did His Films Speak?" (master's thesis, Stockholm University, 2005).

49. Among the documents supporting 1917 as the birth of the Philippines' movie industry are "Treatise on the 50 Years of RP Movies," *Literary Song-Movie Magazine*, August 1, 1966, and Jose's son Luis Nepomuceno's pronouncements in several press write-ups in Hollywood, particularly in "The New Cinema Surge in the Philippines," *American Cinematographer*, October 1966, pp. 698–715, and Luis Nepomuceno, "First Major Color Feature Produced in the Philippines," *American Cinematographer*, July 1967, pp. 474–477.

50. Quirino, *Don Jose and the Early Philippine Cinema*, 16.

51. The claim of the local cinema's birth is based on the establishment of a film company, José Nepomuceno's Malayan Movies, rather than on the first screening of the director's film, *Dalagang Bukid*, a claim that has been made by several historians in the past.

52. Vicente Salumbides, *Motion Pictures of the Philippines* (Manila, 1952), 10.

11 From Shadow Play to the Silver Screen

Early Malay(sian) Cinema

Hassan Abdul Muthalib

Cinema in malaysia can be traced back to a few hundred years before the formal beginning of cinema in 1895. The seeds of cinema were already present in the traditional performing arts of Malaysia in the form of the *wayang kulit* (Malay shadow play), *bangsawan* (Malay opera), and the *sandiwara* (modern Malay theater). Much of the equipment used in these art forms was remarkably similar to the film apparatus. These art forms and cinema served the same social function. The Malaysian performing arts were not only a form of entertainment; they served as a social mirror, and continue to do so, by providing friendly advice, criticism, and comments on the foibles of humans and society. So cinema's arrival at the end of the nineteenth century was not something altogether alien to the peoples of the Malay Archipelago.

The Earliest Film Screenings

Less than two years after the first moving pictures were shown in Paris, signaling the birth of cinema, the first Cinématographe screening was made at the Alhambra in Singapore on August 2, 1897, by a Mr. Paul.[1] It appears to be made up of scenes of the royal procession of the Golden Jubilee of Queen Victoria. At the Alhambra, momentarily forgetting to marvel at the new invention, the audience instead "rose simultaneously and sang a verse of 'God Save the Queen.' This was followed by ringing cheers, the Borneo (Native Police) . . . meanwhile standing at the salute."[2]

In 1897, a screening was held at the Selangor Club in Kuala Lumpur, the capital city of present-day Malaysia. The advertisement in the papers read, "Edison Projectoscope. To-night, Saturday, November 27 at 6.30 p.m. Lifelike representation of scenes from actual life."[3] The audience at the Selangor Club consisted exclusively of members of the club, who were obviously all British. The commoners, however, were given the opportunity three days later to witness a similar screening in a Chinese theater at Petaling Street, a Chinese-dominated area not far from the club.

By the turn of the century, motion picture screenings from Europe and Asia visually introduced the world to Malays. In February 1905, the Grand American Bioscope and Phonograph Company screened newsreels showing scenes of the Transvaal Wars and the Brooklyn Bridge in New York at the High Street Theatre Hall. Also included were short narrative films. Among them were *Cinderella and Her Glass Slipper* (1899) and *The Life and Passion of Christ* (1903).[4] Edwin S. Porter's *The Great Train Robbery* (1903) was another addition to the many screenings of the year.[5] The novelty became profitable, and it was not long before films from Hollywood were brought in by foreign distributors that began to make Singapore their regional headquarters. Serial films then made their appearance, with two reels showing each week. The most popular were Westerns and comedies. The silent movies showing the exploits of Tom Mix, Charlie Chaplin, Buster Keaton, and other popular stars of the day were a hit with the locals, who were made up of Malays and immigrant Indians and Chinese.

The local populace took to the new medium of entertainment easily as films appeared to be simply an extension of the *wayang kulit* performances, which also utilized a white screen and moving images manipulated manually. Ironically, *wayang kulit* was one up on film in terms of sound. Films were silent, and music would be provided by a piano or a band in full view of the audience. Sound for *wayang kulit* came from the voice of the *dalang* (the manipulator of the puppets) and a troupe of musicians who sat behind the screen, and thus the sound appeared to be emanating from the images on the screen.

The Earliest Storytellers

The early Malays inhabited the peninsula, including the surrounding islands of Borneo, Celebes, Sulu, Java, and Sumatra. The fight for survival, coupled with a spirit of adventure, would have given rise to all manner of stories featuring the daring exploits of the menfolk. Many a tale would have been recounted to their children and grandchildren at gatherings around a fire. Like any other traditional peoples, the Malays were used to inventing all manner of tools and artifacts for their daily use constructed from readily available materials. It is possible that this spirit of discovery and innovation, coupled with their traditional performing arts, led the Malays to embrace the medium of film easily when they became involved as actors, singers, and directors in the 1950s.

Entertainment played a very important part in the lives of the people, whether commoners, aristocrats, or royals. The earliest entertainers were the storytellers who moved from village to village, regaling young and old with tales of valor, adventure, and romance, always interspersing them with humor and wit and delivering them, at times, in a singsong manner. W. E. Maxwell of British Malaya, who witnessed Malay storytellers in the late nineteenth century, noted, "A small reward, a hearty welcome, and a good meal await the Malay rhapsodist wherever he goes, and he wanders among the Malay villages as Homer did among the Greek cities."[6] The storyteller was the Malay *penglipur lara* (the soother of woes). He unwittingly played a social and cultural role by keeping alive the numerous stories of the nation handed down through word of mouth. The tales taught stories, carrying with them nuggets of truth and gentle admonition, becoming "vehicles for the transmission of norms and values and as an intermediary between the real and the nether worlds."[7] These storytellers had never heard of Aristotle, but they gave truth to his words that stories are all about how humans should live their lives. When moving from village to village and from town to town, the storytellers adapted the stories and tales of the various districts that they passed through. Over time, their stash of stories increased, and they became adept at their profession until inevitably, they would be invited to perform at the palace. In effect, royalty played an important role in the preservation of the performing arts by becoming its patrons. Important functions such as weddings, circumcision ceremonies, or investitures always culminated in entertainment, both within the palace or in the towns for the benefit of the populace. This partly helped keep alive the traditional arts, but most important, it helped refine and uplift the standards of narrative and aesthetics. As mediums of entertainment evolved, the storytellers kept pace and moved with the times. Where open spaces and street corners used to be venues, the fixed stage slowly became the norm. And so emerged two forms of drama, the puppet show and the *wayang kulit*, which were to be followed some centuries later by the *bangsawan* and *sandiwara*. These were, in effect, the earliest cinema of the Malays.

The Traditional Performing Arts: The Puppet Show

The puppets used in traditional performing arts were little movable dolls, usually carved from wood and colorfully painted and costumed. Their heads, bodies, arms, and legs had strings attached that were manipulated by the puppeteer. A stage and a painted backdrop were all that were necessary for a show. Unlike the *wayang kulit*, more than one voice was used in the acting of the puppets. Mubin Sheppard, a colonial civil servant who has researched and written about the Malay performing arts, is of the opinion that the puppet show is much older than the *wayang kulit* and may have been in existence in parts of Asia more than fifteen hundred years ago.[8] According to Wan Khazim Wan Din, a 1950s actor and violinist who had seen these shows, they were not very popular because the puppet masters and their hands were noticeable to the audience.[9]

Wayang Kulit

The first exhibit at the now-defunct British Museum of the Moving Image in London includes two characters of the *wayang kulit* (see figure 11.1). The museum rightly recognized the *wayang kulit* as the precursor of film. The word *wayang* is a variant of *bayang*, the Malay word for "shadow." *Wayang kulit* (*wayang* meaning "theater"; *kulit* meaning "skin," the hardened cow or buffalo skin used in the making of the puppets) utilizes a white screen propped up on a stage about three feet above the ground, in appearance similar to an outdoor film screening. The *dalang* sits behind the screen holding his puppets, which have articulated arms. An oil lamp (later replaced with a light bulb) is suspended behind him. As he moves the puppets, the shadows cast on the screen by the lamp appear to come to life. Through the lilt and lift of his voice, and accompanied by eight musicians, the *dalang* enthralls his audience with his stories. The accompanying musicians play an oboe (*serunai*), two war drums (*geduk*), two barrel drums (*gendang*), two vase-shaped drums (*gedombak*), a pair of large hanging gongs (*tawak-tawak*), a pair of small gongs placed flat on a low wooden stand (*canang*), and a pair of small brass cymbals (*kesi*).[10] The larger-than-life stories and characters of the *Ramayana* and *Mahabharata* derived from the ancient texts of the Hindu world would later reappear in the stagings of *bangsawan*.

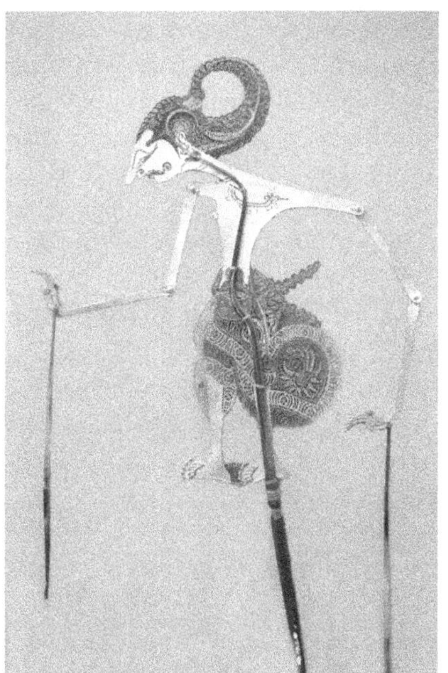
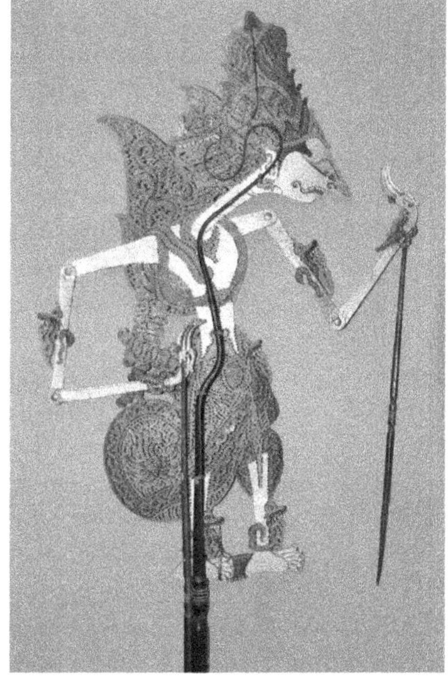

Figure 11.1. These *wayang kulit* puppets made from cow hide once served as the main attractions in Asia's proto-cinema. The puppets acted out scenes in shadow plays similar to the images now seen on the movie screen. The moving images cast on the makeshift screen were accompanied by music and narration by the *dalang*, or narrator. (From the collection of Nick Deocampo.)

According to Ghulam-Sarwar Yousof, an academic who has researched Malay performing arts, the *wayang kulit* is believed to have come to the Malay Archipelago from Hinduized Java during or soon after the Majapahit period (1293–1520) rather than directly from India or Thailand, as popularly believed.[11] However, Usha Malik traces it back even further to its mention in the *Mahabharata* around the ninth century.[12] Berthold Laufer considers *wayang kulit* to have originated even earlier, referring to a legend in China in 121 BC. The legend states that the court shaman "cast shadows on a screen in an effort to recall the spirits" of Emperor Han Wu Ti's dead wife.[13] In fact, performances of *wayang kulit*, with the puppets' articulated arms, could be seen as the first animated cartoons because there is an illusion of movement through manipulation of articulating parts as occurs in the techniques of cutout animation. As if to stress this point, the shadow play literally moved to the cinema screen in 1926. Lotte Reiniger, a German animator, was inspired by Chinese shadow play and created her animated feature *The Adventures of Prince Achmed* in 1926, based on the form. She used the technique of silhouette animation where cutout figures were laboriously made to move frame by frame on a backlit glass table set up under an animation camera.

The word *wayang* was adapted to describe the moving picture medium, as it had all the elements of the *wayang kulit* performance. There was no equivalent word for "film" in the Malay language. Initially, it was designated *wayang gambar hidup*, literally, "live shadow pictures."[14] By the 1920s, the term *wayang gelap* (literally, ark theater) came into fashion, as noted by Philip C. Coote.[15] Eventually the name used was *wayang gambar*, or "shadow pictures." The majority of those involved in films in the 1950s began calling it "filim," perhaps because they could not pronounce the word correctly. Today, it has been simplified to "filem." Another word that has come into common use is the term for the movie theater: *panggung wayang gambar* (literally, theater for shadow pictures). It was shortened to *pawagam* by P. Ramlee, the legendary director and actor, who coined the term from the first few letters of the three words. The first theater built in Kuala Lumpur in the late 1960s and owned by the locals was named Pawagam P. Ramlee. The word is frequently still used by the local Malay press.

Bangsawan and *Sandiwara*

Wayang kulit performances were more dependent on dialogue and were supported by music, but *bangsawan* would not be complete without the actors suddenly breaking into song, sometimes accompanied by dancing. Initially, the song-and-dance combination in *bangsawan* had a practical function. Called "the extra turn," it was performed in front of the curtains and served as a transition that allowed for set and prop changes. The same elements, however, were adapted for films as they had become an integral part of Malay culture. An entry in *Twentieth Century Impressions of British Malaya*, first published in 1908, describes the Malays as "a songful race. . . . Every year sees a new crop of topical songs. Every native operatic troupe has its own versifier to write words to well-known tunes."[16] This love for song was extended into the earliest films in which the hero and heroine suddenly burst into song without any proper motivation.[17]

Bangsawan was not indigenous to Malay culture. It is said to have originated from the *wayang Parsi* or *mendu* (a form of theater from India), which made its way to Penang Island in the north of Malaysia sometime in the 1870s.[18] Its popularity brought the troupe to tour throughout Malaya and down to Singapore. In 1885, the first professional *bangsawan* troupe, the Pushi Indera Bangsawan of Penang, was formed. It had commercial showings in Malaya as well as in Java. In the early 1900s, *bangsawan* had become a popular form of entertainment, and soon a number of *bangsawan* troupes sprang up all over Malaya. But by the late 1940s after the resurgence of cinema, its popularity began to fade, but its styles would live on the silver screen. Wimal Dissanayake and Ashley Ratnavibhushana note, too, that Parsi theater from India arrived in Sri Lanka in the early nineteenth century and became one of the most important forms of urban entertainment there. As in Malaya, it had a formative influence on both Indian and Sri Lankan cinema. The Parsi plays displayed "a curious amalgam of realism and fantasy, music and dialogue, narrative and spectacle, and stage ingenuity, all combined within the framework of melodrama."[19] (Indeed, the story for Malaya's first film, *Leila Majnun* [1933], was one that had regularly been performed in Parsi plays.)

Sandiwara was performed on a fixed stage, and its practitioners held unrelated salaried jobs. *Sandiwara* was, therefore, just a pastime and leisure activity. But for the *bangsawan* players it was a livelihood. Just like a circus, the *bangsawan* troupe toured, and their arrival caused excitement. A stage was built with the name of the troupe prominently displayed, such as the Sri Argandan Opera and Indera Seri Permata Opera. Every troupe had a *Sri Panggung* (prima donna) and an *Orang Muda* (young hero). Both always behaved with decorum, even offstage, in accordance with their stage roles. The prima donna attained a kind of mystique and was eagerly awaited by the audience, especially by the males, while the young hero was breathlessly awaited by the females. Scripts in the accepted sense of the term were nonexistent, as many of the performers were illiterate. They therefore developed prodigious memories. This talent for memorizing could also be seen in the *dalang* in his *wayang kulit* performances. An actor could perform for hours on end, narrating and acting the roles of numerous characters. But they did not rely on memory alone. The *dalang* and the *bangsawan* actors understood their roles instinctively as archetypes and lived their characters with emotion and feeling to such an extent that some *bangsawan* artists became identified with certain roles. With no proper script, they had to rely on the performances and interaction with the other actors. As a result, each night's performance was a slightly different version of the story.

The beginnings of Malay cinema in the 1930s saw actors from *bangsawan* being cast in films. Though introduced to a bewildering new medium, audiences saw familiar faces and the familiar Hindu-influenced stories with their recurring themes of family, romance, and royalty, replete with song-and-dance presentations. The link with the historical and cultural past was thus maintained, so the arrival of cinema was not a culture shock for the locals. Due to its populist nature, film, however, became much more widespread and accessible to the people. No one could have predicted that this new medium would sound the death knell for the various traditional performing arts of the country and bring about their demise in less than three decades.

The first actors in Malaysian cinema were mainly from the *bangsawan* stage. Obviously, they were the only choice because only they could memorize lines of dialogue. There was no set framework of acting at the time; nor did anyone write down the rules of acting. Wan Khazim Wan Din notes that acting methods in *bangsawan* were simple and based on the characters that were played. For example, if the character was an ogre, the actor would utter lines in a booming voice.[20] The players' ability to memorize and improvise gave them an advantage when they entered the film industry. Initially, they brought with them the same stilted and stodgy performances of *bangsawan*. The Indian directors also encouraged this type of acting, which was the style used in the films produced in India. Anuar Nor Arai, writer, lecturer, and film critic, notes that the early Malay films had "gestures that were overdone. The films were mostly melodrama. It was a cinema of sorrow and tears. The actors simply overflowed the audience with their tears."[21]

These early actors adapted easily to the new medium of film and were totally enamored by it, so they were not loath to be involved in all stages of production. This experience led many of them to later become respected film directors. The first Malay director, Armaya (pseudonym of A. R. Tompel), was a *bangsawan* veteran who traveled with a troupe throughout the peninsula and the Borneo territories. He wrote the scripts and dialogues for some of the most memorable films of his generation. Like the immigrant races at the time, the Malays in Singapore also adapted easily to changes.

The acting styles of *bangsawan* and *sandiwara* were carried on in films for many years before new styles of acting began to emerge after Hollywood and other films were screened in Singapore in the 1950s. As Malay cinema gained popularity, audiences for *bangsawan* and *sandiwara* diminished until the curtain finally fell on the two forms in the 1960s. Today, *wayang kulit* and *bangsawan* performances can be seen only at the National Arts Academy, where it is taught under the theater program. *Sandiwara* has moved to a professional stage at the prestigious National Theatre, where its old Malacca sultanate architecture is an homage to the role of royalty in preserving the performing arts.

Early Movie Houses

Until the 1860s, the Malays were the predominant ethnic group inhabiting the Malay Peninsula. Slowly the British brought in Chinese and Indian laborers to work the tin mines and rubber estates. Singapore, Penang, Ipoh, Taiping, and other towns began to expand. For the capitalists, this diverse population and the developments in the region were a ready market and a potential moneymaker for the novelty of the Cinematograph. As films gained more popularity, movie houses were built in many parts of the Malay Peninsula, but almost all were owned and controlled by the Chinese.

Commercial film screening began in Singapore in 1907 at the Alhambra, the premier theater at the time, with music supplied by a band composed of Indians from Bengal. Upton Close, an American adventurer, notes that by the end of the 1920s, most of the screening venues were owned by Chinese, though some were owned by Malays.[22] One was owned by Oli Mohamad, an Indian Muslim. During the same time in Penang, seven permanent theaters had already been built for the increasing population.

The three movie theaters in Singapore were the Alhambra, Harima Hall, and Marlborough. A newspaper report indicates that the Alhambra was said to have been built as early as 1907 by an Englishman named Willis.[23] An entry in the book *Cathay: 55 Years of Cinema* states that the Alhambra was built during that year by Tan Cheng Kee, one of the pioneers of the film industry in Singapore, and that originally it was called Parsee Hall.[24] However, according to a report in the *Malay Mail* on August 3, 1897, the Alhambra was already in existence in 1897. It is possible that it was rebuilt in 1907 to accommodate screenings of the Cinematograph, a novelty that was fast becoming profitable. Prominent among the Chinese entrepreneurs were the brothers Runme and Run Run Shaw, who came from Shanghai in the 1920s and built an empire of cabarets, amusement parks, and cinemas through their company, Shaw Organization. Another was an engineer-turned-businessman, Ho Ah Loke. Next to enter the scene was Loke Wan Tho, a Cambridge-educated businessman who was later identified with the Cathay Organization.

By 1913, there were five movie houses in Singapore with twelve to fourteen theaters being built throughout the peninsula. By 1929, the number increased to thirty-five, operating in sixteen towns.[25] In addition, there were between ten and twenty theaters in smaller towns that occasionally showed films. The abundance of film supply coming from distributors in Singapore made possible the building of more movie theaters. With the movie business booming, it made sense for the importing firms to build movie houses themselves to cater to the increasing audience. Hatta Azad Khan, a filmmaker and academic, mentions Australasian Films (East) building a chain of movie houses in Singapore and in Malaya. Business became so good that four more distribution offices were set up in 1932, bringing the total number to nine, including the Nanking Film Company, which specialized in producing Chinese films. In the next two years, three more film import offices were added: British Empire (East), Kodak, and United Artists. Though exhibition and distribution were totally in the hands of the migrant Chinese, the locals were not left out of the business boom and were to play the main role in the development of local cinema. From the very beginning, actors were entirely Malay; stories were sourced from Malay, Chinese, and Indian legends, folktales, and modern novels.

Prewar Film Production

Two feature films commenced production in 1933. An American-sponsored film, *Samarang*, was directed by Ward Wing and written by his wife, Lori Bara. *Leila Majnun* was produced by S. M. Chisty of the Motilal Chemical Company of Bombay, which used to supply carbon lamps for cinema projectors in the region. It was directed by B. S. Rajhans from India and starred Tijah, Syed Ali Alattas, and M. Suki. The story was of Persian-Arabic origin, and the film was shot more as a stage play in the manner of the *bangsawan*. It is not known if the producers chose consciously to replicate the existing *bangsawan* approach, but the movie had all the song, dance, and melodrama elements typical of the Indian films of the times. Perhaps that familiarity factor led to its acceptance by the local populace. To date, no one living has seen the film and no copies exist. According to Aimi Jarr, a journalist in the 1950s, even M. Suki, who played a leading role, did not have the opportunity to see it because he was touring with a *bangsawan* troupe at the time.[26] *Samarang* flopped at the box office, but *Leila Majnun* was reportedly a hit, perhaps because of the familiar Indian style and its song-and-dance elements. According to Mohamed Zamberi A. Malek and Aimi Jarr, the film was screened in 1934 at the Alhambra in Singapore. The cinema was packed at every screening. Two weeks later, the film was shown in Penang. It seems that it was not widely shown because of distribution and exhibition problems.[27]

A film called *Booloo* (The white tiger, 1938), directed by Clyde E. Elliott and produced by Paramount Pictures, was shot in Singapore and starred Colin Tapley, Jayne Regan, Michio Ito, and Mamo Clark. The Shaws' early films featured *bangsawan* and *sandiwara* actors and were all directed by Chinese, including a Miss Yen and Wan Hai Ling from Shanghai. The films, however, failed to appeal to the local audience since they were all based on Chinese stories. Among the films produced between 1938 and 1941 were *Mutiara* (Pearl), *Bermadu* (Polygamy), *Topeng*

Shaitan (Mask of the devil), *Hanchur Hati* (Heart broken), *Ibu Tiri* (Stepmother), and *Tiga Kekasih* (Three lovers). Press reviews were generally favorable, although there were many technical problems with the films.

There was hardly a local film industry before the Second World War, so foreign films, mostly from Hollywood, ruled. At the time, 70 percent of films shown in Singapore were from the United States, 16 percent were from the United Kingdom, and 13 percent were Chinese. After the war, cinemas were required by law to show British films for at least one week or they would be fined.[28] Criticism of the British, its policies, or the immigrant races was not allowed in Malay films. The hegemony of the British colonialist was evident in more ways than one; thus, a true national cinema was prevented from emerging. Syed Hussein Alatas quotes the scholar J. S. Furnivall, who was not keen on nationalism in British-colonized countries, believing that "nationalism . . . was a disruptive force which tended to shatter rather than consolidate the social order."[29] British policy "was extended to the screen in the representation of the Malays and his or her 'destined' vocation."[30] An analysis of the Singapore-produced films by Timothy Barnard mentions that "representation of the village lifestyle, as if it were authentic, was an imitation of the colonial construction."[31] There were, however, other reasons for the nonemergence of a truly national (Malay) cinema, one that should have spoken eloquently of the nation and its struggles against its colonial masters.

Wayang Kulit and *Bangsawan* in Contemporary Cinema

In the 1950s, elements of *bangsawan* appeared in films, notably in the films of P. Ramlee. In *bangsawan* (as in vaudeville and burlesque), actors would sometimes address the audience when the situation warranted, which delighted audiences. In P. Ramlee's *Pendekar Bujang Lapok* (Raggedy bachelor warriors, 1959), two of the actors turn and talk to the audience. In contemporary times, *wayang kulit* and *bangsawan* have made it to the silver screen in Malaysia, used variously as homage, index, or parody. Anuar Nor Arai's *Johnny Bikin Filem* (Johnny directs a movie, 2007) depicts the struggle and trauma of *bangsawan* actors with their foray into film acting. He uses white screens with shadows cast on them as negative indexes of the hidden hands at work that attempt to disrupt the protagonist's efforts to uplift standards of film storytelling.

Kala Malam Bulan Mengambang (When the moon waxes full, directed by Mamat Khalid, 2008), was shot in black and white with the same kind of stylized acting in the early 1950s reminiscent of the *bangsawan* actors who had moved to the silver screen. The film is ostensibly an homage to the Malay films of the 1950s, which were almost entirely in black and white. It is, in fact, a parody of the present film industry, in which the director laments the low depths that Malay cinema has sunk by churning out films completely lacking substance. One of the characters in the film (played by a veteran actor of the 1950s) even appears in a *bangsawan*-style costume, blissfully unaware (in the film) that he is totally out of touch with the reality of the situation. Parody has always been the forte of Mamat Khalid, and in *Kala Malam Bulan Mengambang*, he satirizes all those involved in the film industry today who are making films that are not much different from the melodramatic films of the 1950s.

Wayang kulit began to resurface in television and films in the late 1990s. In a television episode of the animation series *Kampong Boy* (Village boy, directed by Frank Saperstein, 1997), a puppet master arrives in the village and helps the children solve a problem involving two adults. In the cinema feature, *Perempuan Melayu Terakhir* (The last Malay woman, directed by Erma Fatima, 1999), *wayang kulit* is part of the opening title sequence, symbolizing the confusion and search for identity of the film's protagonist. *Silat Legenda* (Legendary Silat warriors, directed by Hassan Muthalib, 1998), Malaysia's first animated feature, pays homage to *wayang kulit* as the precursor of animation. Javanese shadow puppets appear in a scene as props in an old antique shop in modern Malacca and are then foregrounded in another scene.

Bunohan (Return to murder, directed by Dain Iskandar Said, 2011) was shot in Kelantan, an east coast state in Malaysia famous for its traditional performing arts. *Bunohan* is about a shadow play master puppeteer whose life comes to a tragic end when he is killed by his own son. Subsequently, a young boy who has been enamored by the master's shadow play is left adrift, unable to further his interest to become a puppeteer. Like *Kala Malam*, the film is a subtle criticism of the development of contemporary Malaysian cinema. A torn shadow-play screen and the young boy seen running away (through the tear) become signifiers of the damage wrought on local cinema by mainstream films of amateurish content that disillusion young and talented filmmakers. The film includes numerous scenes of shadowy figures seen against a lit window or on screens, signifiers of the negative nature of the characters and the hidden hands that pit brother against brother and, in the end, results in the death of an entire family.

But it is only in *Wayang* (Shadows, directed by Hatta Azad Khan, 2008) that *wayang kulit* comes back to its original, pristine form. For the first time in Malaysian cinema, a Malay traditional art form becomes the subject for a narrative film. Set in the east coast state of Kelantan (which had banned *wayang kulit* performances as being un-Islamic), *Wayang* is about a puppet master who takes on a blind boy as an apprentice. The boy begins to bring innovations to the *wayang kulit* performance, incurring the wrath of the traditional-minded puppet master. This leads to a conflict between them. Included are scenes of the puppet master being invited by a university to teach young performing arts students. The film poses a profound question about how a traditional art form like the *wayang kulit* can continue to survive amid popular culture. Does it need to make changes to its mode of presentation, and can academia be the answer for its continued existence? This, however, raises the question of whether the art forms of *wayang kulit* and *bangsawan*, once removed from their organic roots, will also lose their original essence.

Conclusion

The traditional *dalang* would be unable to explain the meanings behind the shadows that he projects on the screen. All he can say is that the puppet characters represent the self. In reality, *wayang kulit*, like many of the other traditional art forms, is steeped in Malay cosmology and has very deep religious and spiritual significance that goes beyond normal perception. Every performance has to begin with an ancient ritual that is passed down from master to student and must be diligently adhered to. Hamzah Awang Hamat, a master *dalang*, once told me that a *dalang* who has not attained self-realization is not qualified to be a *dalang*. Many *dalang* are familiar with Sufi teachings, and some are in fact practitioners. Sufi teachings are the perfect vehicle for their purpose as it blends easily with the symbolic elements attached to the epic stories. One of the Wali Songo (nine saints of Java) was reputed to have used *wayang kulit* in the early days of Islam in Java to promote the religion. A manuscript from Cirebon, Java, written about 1820 by Abdulqahar, describes how one of the saints, Sunan Kali Jaga, explained to the king of Demak the mystic dimensions of *wayang kulit*. The *wayang* was "indeed a (reflected) image of the Law. The *wayang* represents all humanity; the *dalang* corresponds to Allah, Creator of the universe. . . . The *wayang* figures cannot move of their own accord, but depend on the will of the *dalang*. Thus, also the Creatures can only act by the Will of the Lord, the Highest, He who manipulates the world."[32] As the populace consisted of Hindus and Buddhists who were already familiar with the spirit world of the *wayang kulit*, it would not have been difficult to win them over. The deeper significance of *wayang kulit* is, however, never revealed to the layman and is privy only to the *dalang*, which would then be passed down to his chosen student.

The shadow has also been significant in Western literature, as seen in its various manifestations, such as Edgar Allan Poe's *Shadows*, Hans Christian Andersen's *The Shadow*, Oscar Wilde's *The Fisherman and His Soul*, and Johann Wolfgang Goethe's *Theory of Color*, with the image of the shadow also frequenting many of Goethe's literary works.[33] Carl Jung, the Swiss psychoanalyst, introduced the shadow as a psychological term—an archetype—one that exists in all of us that must be confronted for us to attain self-awareness.[34] The shadow is the dark side that, if not controlled, would lead one to physical, emotional, or spiritual destruction, as demonstrated in Hollywood gangster movies and film noir of the 1940s and 1950s. In these films, either the characters' faces are seen in shadow or we see their body shadows on walls or on the ground, and the shadows become grim signifiers of the characters' negative and malevolent nature.

Shadow-play elements began to be used in the 1970s in *Star Wars* (directed by George Lucas, 1977): in its characters and the use of silhouettes. *The Year of Living Dangerously* (directed by Peter Weir, 1982), used shadow play to signify the hidden hands at play in the power struggle in Indonesia in 1995 that led to the killing of many innocent people. In Zhang Yimou's *To Live* (1994), Chinese traditional shadow play, which entertains an entire village, is decried as being counterrevolutionary during the Cultural Revolution. In Nina Paley's *Sita Sings the Blues* (2008), which is based on the Indian epic the *Ramayana*, shadow play gets a postmodernist treatment with unscripted, contemporary dialogue by characters who give a personal commentary on the epic. A completely virtual world was created for the "Tale of the Three Brothers" segment in *Harry Potter and the Deathly Hallows, Part 1* (2010), which merged Asian shadow-play puppetry with Lotte Reiniger's silhouette animation style. The four-minute 3D animation segment becomes a metaphor for the protagonists' eventual battle with the antagonist, Lord Voldemort.

Beginning with *Star Wars*, the first film in the series, the portrayal of Darth Vader personifies this character as one who had completely crossed over to "the dark side." The Star Wars series is probably the best example of how the archetypal characters and story of the *Ramayana* prevalent in *wayang kulit* have crossed over into film: Sri Rama (the Hero) becomes Luke Skywalker; Sita Dewi (the Heroine) becomes Princess Leia; Rawana (the Villain) becomes Darth Vader, and Pak Dogol (the Jester) becomes C-3PO. Such characters and stories are found in almost all of the world's myths and legends. Hollywood and Bollywood have successfully appropriated them and made them relevant to the modern age.

The final scene in Hatta Azad Khan's film *Wayang* shows a *wayang kulit* screen with the face of Sri Rama seen in an affectionate image. Sri Rama stands frozen in space-time. Once again *wayang kulit* is one up on film. A similar freeze would be impossible within the film projector, as the celluloid frame would burn up immediately. Sri Rama represents the characters of *wayang kulit* who have not been obliterated by the passage of time. In this scene Sri Rama stands proud, silent, fixed in time and space on a screen within a screen. Like the shadow of Sri Rama, the images of *wayang kulit* will continue to live every time a projector light is switched on. And in every period drama, *bangsawan,* too, will continue to be present. Both these art forms will continue to live on in the cinemas of the world for as long as there is cinema—and for as long as there is a story to tell about the world and the human condition.

HASSAN ABDUL MUTHALIB is a self-taught artist, animator, film director, and writer who has been involved in the Malaysian film industry for more than fifty years. He was Senior Artist-in-Residence at Universiti Teknologi MARA Malaysia and Visiting Scholar at Nanyang Technological University, Singapore. He has written two books, *Malaysian Cinema in a Bottle* and *From Mouse Deer to Mouse: 70 Years of Malaysian Animation*.

Notes

I acknowledge Dr. Hatta Azad Khan for his comments on a draft of this chapter and Dr. Khoo Gaik Cheng for her critical comments on the final version.

1. Untitled article, *Malay Mail*, August 3, 1897. It is possible that "Mr. Paul" is Robert William Paul, a British inventor and producer, as described in John Barnes, "Robert William Paul," *Who's Who of Victorian Cinema*, http://www.victorian-cinema.net/paul.htm (accessed January 24, 2017). This article states that Paul was "one of the first English producers to realize the possibilities of cinema as a means of presenting short comic and dramatic stories." Paul invented a projector called the Theatrograph. By early 1897, the projectors were exported to Europe and British dependencies, which would have included British Malaya and Singapore. Paul advertised it as the Cinématographe.

2. Untitled article, *Malay Mail*, August 3, 1897.

3. Untitled article, *Malay Mail*, November 27, 1897.

4. Untitled article, *Malay Mail*, February 6, 1905.

5. Jamil Sulong, *Kaca Permata, Memoir Seorang Pengarah* [Glass gems: Memoir of a director] (Johor Bahru: Dewan Bahasa dan Pustaka, 1990), 5.

6. Mohamed Taib Osman, *Aspects of Malay Culture* (Johor Bahru: Dewan Bahasa dan Pustaka, 1988), 21.

7. Mohamed Ghouse Nasuruddin, *Traditional Malay Theatre* (Johor Bahru: Dewan Bahasa dan Pustaka, 2009), ix.

8. Mubin Sheppard, *Taman Saujana: Dance, Drama, Music, and Magic in Malaya, Long and Not-So-Long Ago* (Petaling Jaya: International Book Service, 1983), 56.

9. Wan Khazim Wan Din, interview by the author, 2006.

10. Sheppard, *Taman Saujana*, 57.

11. Ghulam-Sarwar Yousof, *The Malay Shadow Play: An Introduction* (Penang: Asian Center, 1997), 10.

12. Usha Malik, "Traditional Puppetry in India," *Indian Horizons* 55, no. 2–3 (2008): 9.

13. Linda Suny Myrsiades, "The Karaghiozis Tradition and the Greek Puppet: History and Analysis" (PhD diss., Indiana University, 1973), 27.

14. Untitled article, *Utusan Malayu* [Malay mercury], August 5, 1908.

15. Philip C. Coote, *Peeps at Many Lands: The Malay States* (London: A. and C. Black, 1923), 24.

16. Arnold Wright, ed., *Twentieth Century Impressions of British Malaya* (Singapore: Graham Brash, 1989), 139.

17. This peculiar use of song in Malay films is mentioned in Hassan Muthalib, "'Winning Hearts and Minds': Representations of Malays and Their Milieu in the Films of British Malaya," in "Britain and the Malay World: Through the Looking Glass of Film, Theatre and

Literature," special issue, *South East Asia Research* 17, no. 1 (2009): 56. The same method was replicated in the production of the first feature film made in Kuala Lumpur by the Malayan Film Unit in 1954.

18. Nasuruddin, *Traditional Malay Theatre*, 2.

19. Wimal Dissanayake and Ashley Ratnavibhushana, *Profiling Sri Lankan Cinema* (Sri Lanka: Asia Film Center, 2000), 4.

20. Wan Khazim Wan Din, interview by the author, 2008.

21. Anuar Nor Arai, interview by the author, 2008.

22. Upton Close, *The Revolt of Asia: The End of the White Man's Dominance* (New York: G. P. Putnam and Sons, 1927), 46.

23. *Utusan Malayu*, 1908, cited in Hatta Azad Khan, *The Malay Cinema* (Bangi: Universiti Kebangsaan Press, 1977).

24. Kay Tong Lim and Tiong Chai Yiu, *Cathay: 55 Years of Cinema* (Singapore: Landmark, 1991), 21.

25. Khan, *The Malay Cinema*, 59.

26. Aimi Jarr, interview by the author, 2005.

27. Mohamed Zamberi A. Malek and Aimi Jarr, *Malaysian Films: The Beginning* (Kuala Lumpur: Perbadanan Kemajuan Filem Nasional, 2005), 77.

28. Ibid., 80.

29. J. S. Furnivall, quoted in Syed Hussein Alatas, *The Myth of the Lazy Native* (New York: Routledge, 2010), 13.

30. Muthalib, "Representations of Malays," 57.

31. Timothy Barnard, "P. Ramlee, Malay Cinema and History," in *Southeast Asian Studies: Debates and New Directions*, ed. Cynthia Chou and Vincent Houben (Singapore: Institute of Southeast Asian Studies / International Institute for Asian Studies, 2006), 162–179.

32. D. A. Rinkes, *Nine Saints of Java* (Kuala Lumpur: Malaysian Sociological Research Institute, 1996), 130. The state of the *dalang* being one with his art is further enunciated as being "*one* in acting, *one* in will, as long as one lives, *one* in involuntary action, *one* in hearing, *one* in seeing, *one* in speaking; that is indeed, 'united.'" Ibid. I am of the opinion that the actors of *bangsawan* who stepped into films were instinctively in this state. Untrained and unlettered, many of them excelled in their newfound art.

33. David Currell, *Shadow Puppets and Shadow Play* (Ramsbury, UK: Crowood, 2008), 7.

34. Carl G. Jung, *Man and His Symbols* (London: Aldus, 1964), 69. *The Penguin Dictionary of Symbols* interestingly describes shadows in terms that are consonant with those of the *dalang*'s beliefs: "When the soul casts no shadow, when the Devil Iblis casts no shadow—the moment of inward peace . . . the very image of fleeting, unreal and mutable things, . . . a symbol of all unpremeditated actions." Jean Chevalier and Alain Gheerbrant, *The Penguin Dictionary of Symbols* (London: Penguin Books, 1997), 868.

12 Iranian Cinema

Before the Revolution

Shahin Parhami

SINCE THE LATE 1980s, postrevolutionary Iranian cinema has been praised in many international forums. What have attracted audiences worldwide to this national cinema are its distinct style, themes, authors, idea of nationhood, and manifestation of culture. In this chapter, I contextualize the emergence of this cinema by situating its relationship to a history of prerevolutionary visual, literary, and performance cultures in Iran up until the late 1970s, with an emphasis on the foundations of filmic art in that region.

If one were to trace the first visual representations in Iranian history, the bas-reliefs in Persepolis (ca. 500 BC) would be among the earliest examples. Persepolis was the ritual center of the ancient kingdom of Achaemenids. As Hugh Honour and John Fleming state, "The figures at Persepolis remain bound by the rules of grammar and syntax of visual language."[1] This style of visual representation reached its peak about a thousand years later during the Sassanian reign. A bas-relief in Taq-e-Bostan (western Iran) depicts a complex hunting scene. Movements and actions are articulated in a sophisticated manner. We can even see the progenitor of the cinema close-up: a wounded wild pig escaping from the hunting ground.[2] After the Arab invasion and conversion from Zoroastrianism to Islam—a religion in which visual symbols were avoided—Persian art continued its visual practices. Persian miniatures are good examples of such attempts. The deliberate lack of perspective enabled the artist to depict different plots and subplots within the same space of the picture.

A very popular form of such art was *Pardeh-Khani* (pictorial storytelling). Similar to the *benshi* of silent Japanese cinema, a *pardeh-khan* (narrator) would uncover the painting as the story progressed. Another type of art in the same category was *Nagali* (minstrelsy). A *nagal* (storyteller) carried out an entertaining performance usually in *ghahve-khanes* (coffeehouses), which were the main forums for cultural interactions between people. As a performing artist, a *nagal* had to possess a good oratorical and singing voice as well as theatrical talent. Above all, the *nagal* relied on his imagination a great deal to improvise according to the audience's feedback and add to the original tales that he was reciting. He also acquired inspiration from the images and pictures on the walls—pictures of religious leaders, sport heroes, epic characters—and appropriated them into his narrative. The dominant themes in *Nagali* were epics depicted from *Shahnameh* (The book of the king) or the story of Alexander's quest for the elixir of life.[3]

There were many other dramatic performance arts popular before the advent of cinema in Iran. *Khaymeshab-bazi* (puppet show), *Saye-bazi* (shadow play), *Rouhozi* (comical act), and *Ta'zieh* (a form of Persian passion play, tragic drama based on the martyrdom of Hossein, an extremely important figure in Shi'ism) are just a few examples.[4]

With respect to Iranian perception of imagery, one should be aware of the long tradition in poetry. From *Yashts* (the ancient Persian hymns) to post-Islamic Sufi poetry, to contemporary Iranian poetry, we can find numerous examples of this fine art of image making. The extravagant use of symbolism and juxtaposition of codes and symbols gives Persian poetry a unique visual sense.

Cinema Reaches Iranian Soil

On August 18, 1900, the first Iranian photographer recorded images of life on celluloid. Mirza Ebrahim Khan Akkas Bashi was the official photographer of Mozaffar al-Din Shah's court, who accompanied the monarch on his first visit to Europe. Akkas Bashi was introduced to the Cinématographe in France while they stayed in Paris in July 1900 to see the Paris Exposition. On the day of the exposition, the shah ordered Akkas Bashi to purchase all equipment necessary for recording and displaying the motion picture in his court. Akkas Bashi took his first images in Belgium while they attended the Festival of Flowers. These images are perhaps the first documentary footage shot by an Iranian in the history of Iranian cinema, even though its main purpose was documenting the shah's visit to Europe.

On his return home, film was brought to Iran by the king as a form of entertainment for members of the monarchy and royal court. After seeing the first film of his life, Mozaffar al-Din Shah writes in his travelogue diary:

> At 9:00 P.M. we went to the Exposition and the Festival Hall where they were showing cinematographe, which consists of still and motion pictures. Then we went to Illusion building. . . . In this Hall they were showing cinematographe. They erected a very large screen in the center of the Hall, turned off all electric lights shand projected the picture of cinematography on that large screen. It was very interesting to watch. Among the pictures were Africans and Arabians traveling with camels in the African desert which were very interesting. Other pictures were of the Exposition, the moving street, the Seine River and ships crossing the river, people swimming and playing in the water and many others

which were all very interesting. We instructed Akkas Bashi to purchase all kinds of it [cinematographic equipment] and bring to Tehran so God willing he can make some there and show them to our servants.[5]

Unlike many other places in the world, where cinema as marketable commodity was used as a mass-entertainment medium, in Iran cinema circulated among courtly nobles and the royal family.[6] Cinematography had to be presented on occasions such as weddings and circumcisions or other festivities in aristocratic settings, usually projected along with French comedy shorts that were imported through Russia.

The first public screening took place in Tehran in 1904, by a private entrepreneur, Mirza Ebrahim Khan Sahaf Bashi. He arranged the screening in the back of his antique shop. In 1905, Sahaf Bashi opened the first movie theater on Cheragh Gaz Avenue in the national capital. There were no chairs in the saloon, and audiences had to sit on the carpeted floor, as they would sit in mosques or at *Ta'zieh* shows. Sahaf Bashi's cinema did not last for more than a month because of his political activities as a nationalist and an individual who was lobbying for a constitutional monarchy. Also, religious opposition provided the shah's police with a sufficient excuse to arrest Sahaf Bashi, close down the cinema, and confiscate his projector and related equipment. He was soon sent into exile. Perhaps this was the first instance of censorship in the history of Iranian cinema.[7]

Two years later, a few Russian and Armenian immigrants individually tried to establish new movie theaters in Tehran. Russi Khan, a Russian immigrant, was the most successful figure among these new cinema owners. With his connections to the royal court, he could expand his business despite religious contentions. The presence of the Russian army in the north as well as in Tehran formed another support for Russi Khan, since they shared the same nationality and provided an additional market for his enterprise. In 1909, after the fall of Mohammad Ali Shah (heir of Mozaffar al-Din Shah) and the success of the constitutionalists, Russi Khan lost his support. Consequently, his film theater and photography studios were destroyed by the public. Soon after, other cinema theaters in Tehran closed down.

Movie theaters sprang up again in 1912 with the help of Ardeshir Khan (an Armenian-Iranian). Farrokh Ghafary, a film historian in Iran, believes it was Ardeshir Khan who fashioned movie theater operation as an organized business. The existence of such an infrastructure encouraged other Iranians to open new movie theaters.[8] Another important person in this era was Ali Vakili, who established a few movie houses and a publication on show business in the late 1920s. Until the early 1930s there were about fifteen theaters in Tehran and eleven in other provinces. By 1978 these numbers grew to 109 in the national capital and 318 in various Iranian cities.[9]

Pioneers of Iranian Cinema

After Akkas Bashi and Russi Khan, who was also hired by the royal family to film court activities, Khan-baba Khan Mo'tazedi was the third Iranian involved with cinematography. As an engineering student living in Paris, Mo'tazedi found work in a film company, where he learned how to operate a movie camera and process film. With his return to Iran in 1916 Mo'tazedi brought film equipment (films, camera, projector, and processing material). What began as a hobby eventually became his profession.

Mo'tazedi also became a court photographer. He shot a considerable amount of newsreel footage during the reign of Qajar and the Pahlavi dynasty.[10] Mo'tazedi is also credited for being the first person to have arranged a public screening exclusively for women before 1920. Beginning in the late 1920s, Mo'tazedi worked in the Iranian film industry and became one of the major cinema owners of the time. He was also the first to add Persian intertitles to foreign films.

In 1925, a young Armenian-Iranian, Ovanes Ohanian (Oganianse), a Russian national who studied film in Cinema Akademi of Moscow, returned to Iran. His goal was to establish a film industry in the country. Since he found it impossible to initiate any production without professionals in the field, Ohanian decided to begin a film school in Tehran. Within five years, he managed to run the first session of the school under the name Parvareshgahe Artistiye cinema (Cinema Artist Educational Center).[11] Acting and performance, rather than film production, were the cornerstones of the institution.

After five months, with a few of his graduates and the financial help of a theater owner, Ohanian directed his first Iranian film, *Abi va Rabi* (1929). The silent film, shot by Mo'tazedi on 35mm black-and-white stock, was fourteen hundred meters long.[12] As Ghafary states, "This film was patterned directly after the comic acts of the Danish cinema couple Pat and Paterson. Iranians had seen [films of] this couple many times in the cinemas and liked them."[13] *Abi va Rabi* was received well by critics and the public. Unfortunately, the only copy of the film burned to ashes two years after its release in a fire in Cinema Mayak, one of the first theaters in Tehran.

By the end of the school's second session, Ohanian had started his next project, another comedy, *Haji Agha Aktor-e-Cinema* (Haji Agha, the cinema actor, 1933). The film was a reflexive construction (as appears in its title) about a traditionalist who is suspicious of cinema, but by the end of the story he recognizes the significance of film art. *Haji Agha Aktor-e-Cinema* did not do well at the box office. Not only were there technical shortcomings, but the release of the first Persian talkie, *Dokhtar-e-Lor* (The Lor girl; produced in India) diminished its prospects for profit. After the failure of his second film, Ohanian could not find any support for further activities. He left Iran for India and continued his academic career in Calcutta. Subsequently, he returned to Iran in 1947, where he died seven years later.

The second Iranian director of that same era was Ebrahim Moradi. As a member of a guerrilla movement in the north of Iran during the late 1920s, the young Moradi sought asylum in the Soviet Union with his father. Moradi lived in Russia for a few years, where he was introduced to the technical aspects of film. In 1929, he established his own film studio, Jahan Nama, in Bandar Anzali, a port city by the Caspian Sea. Moradi started shooting his first film, *Entegham-e-Baradar* (A brother's revenge), about a year later. By 1931, seventeen hundred meters of film were edited, but he had no money left for completing his project.

Privy to some information of cinematic activities in Tehran, Moradi moved there in search of financial help. Yet the young director never completed his first film. In a few months, however, he started a new project, *Bolhavas* (The lustful man), a melodrama released in 1934. This silent film, which received good reviews, was the last Iranian feature production done within its borders until the end of World War II.

Abdul-Hossein Sepenta

Abdul-Hossein Sepenta, the father of Persian talkies, was born in Tehran in 1907. As a young writer and poet, Sepenta went to India in the mid-1920s to study the ancient Persian language and history. In Bombay, his friendship with Professor Bahram Gour Aneklesaria (an expert in old Iranian languages) encouraged him to consider the new and developing medium of film. Through his adviser, Dinshah Irani, Sepenta met Ardeshir Irani, another elite of the Bombay Parsi community. Irani was the executive director of Imperial Film and agreed to invest in Sepenta's first Persian talkie. Sepenta began educating himself about the film medium.

He met with Debaki Bose, a pioneer of Bengali cinema who was also interested in representing his culture in a new, epic form. After an introduction to the theory of film, Sepenta started writing his script, with Ardeshir Irani as technical supervisor and codirector. *Dokhtar-e-Lor*, the first Persian talkie to be released in 1933, is the product of this interaction.[14] The film was a complete success and stayed on Iranian screens for more than two years. Imperial Film was so impressed by the success of the talkie that they offered Sepenta production control over another film. Sepenta made four more films for Imperial Film: *Ferdousi* (1934), *Shireen va Farhad* (1934), *Cheshmhaye Siah* (Dark eyes) (1935), and *Leyla va Majnun* (1936). Interestingly, he also made one film for the East India Film Company in Calcutta. All of his films dealt with the glorification of the old Iranian culture or the optimistic future of a modern Iran.

Sepenta returned to Iran in 1936 with the hope of establishing a film company with the help of government and private-sector funding. Unfortunately, he failed to mobilize any support from either party. Due to his mother's sickness and his financial situation, Sepenta was forced to stay in Iran. To support his family, he started working in a wool factory in Isfahan. Sepenta remained productive, publishing eighteen books and five films, and, as chief editor of two magazines, writing many articles on art and culture. At the age of sixty-two, three years before his death in 1968, Sepenta tried his hand at film once again, but this time in a manner far from the epic form of his earlier work. With a simple 8mm camera, Sepenta recorded everyday reality, but no footage has ever been released for public screening.

Years of Absence

The period between 1937 and 1948 marked a decade of nonproductivity in the history of Iranian national cinema. One can find many reasons for these years of cinema hibernation. The most obvious causes are Iran's general political crisis generated by the Second World War, the country's occupation by the Allies during the war, the undermining of the cinema industry by the establishment, and the domination of foreign films (especially Hollywood).

Reza Shah, the first monarch of the Pahlavi dynasty, came to power in the early 1920s. Despite his fascination with modernization and technology, the shah could not understand the importance of a film industry. The only contributions to cinema he made were the five hundred *toman* awarded to Mo'tazedi for his newsreel based on the Shah's coronation.

After being impressed by Mo'tazedi's newsreel documenting the installation of an Anglo-Persian oil company in Khuzestan, the shah ordered the construction of a new movie theater in Tehran. The industrial sights of his country as seen on celluloid overwhelmed the shah. As Mo'tazedi remembers, the shah remarked, "Marvelous! How well done! What modern installations! But alas they [British oil company] give Iran little money." Right after the screening, the shah ordered the police chief to start building a movie theater in the poor part of town, the Tammadon (civilization).[15] This was the most generous contribution made to Iran's film industry by Reza Shah's regime.

Reza Shah's superficial depiction of civilization and modernity brought many Western values to Iranian society. For instance, he banned the chador for women, dictated a Westernized dress code for men, and forbade Iranian passion plays. Because of their long history of British and Russian colonial interest in Iran, the shah thought them untrustworthy, so he turned to Germany for professional and technological knowledge. By the end of the 1930s, there were about four hundred German skilled laborers working in seven German-based companies in Iran.

Beyond Early Cinema: Birth of a National Cinema

The outbreak of World War II clearly set apart the period of early cinema (until its lackluster aftermath during Rezah Shah's reign) from what consequently happened after the war. The rich pre-cinematic culture gave way to new political and technological developments. The rupture caused by war would later usher in a rebirth of Iranian cinema. During World War II, the Allies found Iran to be a critical strategic zone for supplying Russians with military hardware. In spite of Iran's proclamation of neutrality, the Allies demanded the deportation of German citizens from Iran. Due to negative responses from Reza Shah, Iran was invaded by the British (from the southwest) and the Russians (from the north) on August 25, 1941. With American troops entering in October of the same year, Iran, as "The Bridge of Victory," suffered the woes of occupation by three Western powers. Reza Shah was sent into exile by the British and was replaced by his son in September 1941.[16]

Both the physical presence of Western powers and the cultural domination by the Allies made imperialism ever present in the media. For propaganda purposes more cinema theaters were opened to show dubbed newsreels and expository documentaries. Hollywood productions dominated the screens and left no space for any local cultural activities.[17] Dubbing was one of the few means of participation for Iranians in the film industry during this era.

Since a large percentage of Iran's population was illiterate, they were incapable of reading the explanatory intertitles, and many were unfamiliar with European languages. Dubbing was the ideal solution for distributors and cinema owners to gain further profit. For this purpose, many dubbing studios were established between 1943 and 1965. The demand for the development of dubbing systems in Iran resulted in many local exports in the field of sound reproduction. But it also had side effects, most notably the slowing down of the development of sync sound recording on the set. Because film studios were confident in their highly skilled Foley and dubbing artists, they did not invest in on-the-set sound recording equipment and technicians. This practice of sound reproduction for the entire film at the postproduction stage was predominant until the late 1970s.[18]

In 1947, Esmail Kooshan, an economist with a secondary degree in communications from the Univerum Film Aktiengesellschaft (UFA), returned to Iran.[19] On his way from Berlin he bought two European films, which he dubbed in Persian in a studio in Istanbul. The commercial success of these two films increased his concern about the local film industry. Soon Kooshan established Mitra Film with the association of a few relatives and friends. The first feature production of the studio was *Toofan-e-Zendegi* (Storm of life, 1948), a critical social drama directed by Ali Daryabegi, a theater director/actor who had no experience in filming. The film was a total failure at the box office and received no praise from critics.

Despite withdrawal of a few partners from the company, Kooshan did not give up and made his second film in the same year. This time Kooshan photographed and directed the film himself. *Zendani-e-Amir* (Amir's prisoner, 1948) had relatively better success, which encouraged Kooshan to proceed with his career as filmmaker. Finally, after another disappointing postproduction response for *Varieteh Bahar* (The spring festival, 1949), Kooshan made his groundbreaking film *Sharmsar* (Ashamed, 1950). *Sharmsar* was produced under the name of Kooshan's new company, Pars Film. This romantic musical with a woman as the main character depicts the story of a village girl who ends up in the city after being seduced by an urban man. But soon she recovers from her shock, employs her talents to achieve fame and fortune, and then returns to her village. The lead character was Delkesh, a popular singer at the time. Indeed, it was her presence that guaranteed the financial success of the film.

Meanwhile, other Iranians in the private sector, tempted to test their luck in the film business, stepped into the picture. Mohsen Badie produced the next blockbuster in the history of Iranian cinema: *Velgard* (Vagabond, 1952) by Mehdi Rai's-firooz. This film is a melodrama with moralistic overtones, accompanied by songs and suspenseful action. M. Ali Issari suggests, "It was the combined box office success of *Sharmsar* and *Velgard* . . . that gave the Persian [Iranian] film industry a shot in [the] arm and saved it from extinction."[20]

The movie that really boosted the economy of Iranian cinema and initiated a new genre was *Ganj-e-Qarun* (Croesus treasure, 1951), made by Siamak Yasami. Yasami had worked with Kooshan prior to establishing his own company, Porya Film, in 1960. A huge financial success, *Ganj-e-Qarun* grossed more than seventy million rials (one million dollars). The theme of the film concerns the worthless and desperate life of the upper middle class in contrast with the poor and happy working class, which is "rich" in morals.

Four years later, Masud Kimiaie made *Qeysar*, an award-winning film at the 1969 Tehran Film Festival. With *Qeysar*, Kimiaie depicted the ethics and morals of the romanticized poor working class of the *Ganj-e-Qarun* genre through his main protagonist, the titular Qeysar. But Kimiaie's film generated another genre in Iranian popular cinema: the tragic action drama.

From 1950 to the mid-1960s, the Iranian film industry grew rapidly. Many studios and independent film companies were established. There were 324 films produced during this period (1950–1965). By 1965, there were 72 movie theaters in Tehran and 192 in other provinces.

The foundation of that newborn cinema was commercialism. It was saturated with dominant themes of dance, music, simplistic dramas, and Persianized versions of Western popular movies. But it also brought about the possibility of an independent national cinema. One of the first efforts for such cinema was

Farokh Ghafari's *Shab-e-Ghouzi* (The night of the hunchback, 1964). Filmed in a magic-realist form and based on a story from *One Thousand and One Nights*, *Shab-e-Ghouzi* was the first feature film from Iran selected for international festivals. The other notable film in this category is *Khesht va Aiene* (Mudbrick and mirror, 1965), produced and directed by Ebrahim Goulestan, the owner of Goulestan Studio. Goulestan created an alternative environment out of which sprang several outstanding documentaries throughout its operation until 1978. One of the best-known productions of Goulestan Studio is *Khaneh Siah Ast* (The house is black, 1963), a documentary written and directed by Forough Farrokhzad, a leading poetess in contemporary Persian literature. This film was selected as the best documentary at the 1963 Oberhausen Film Festival.

By 1970, Iranian cinema had entered into its mature stage. The College of Dramatic Arts, instituted in 1963, produced its first graduates at the decade's beginning. Many progressive film co-ops and associations came into existence; and there were a few regular film festivals taking place in the country.

Young Iranians showed great interest in avant-garde forms of cinema, which reflected their activities. One of the best known of such efforts was Cinemay-e-Azad (Free Cinema). The collective was formed by a group of cinema students and interested individuals in the mid-1970s. They started to screen experimental and short Super 8mm films by their members and soon supported and participated in one another's projects. This movement spread around the country, and, in a short time, they had organized their own national festival. The Ministry of Culture and Art also organized similar associations under the name of Anjoman-e-Cinemay-e-Javan (Young Cinema Association) with collaboration of the National TV.

One of the most important organizations that was (and still is) a great help to the development of national cinema is the Institute for Intellectual Development of Children and Young Adults. The institute was founded by Lili Jahan Ara, a close friend of Farah Diba, the Iranian queen. With the support of Farah Diba, a library became the institute's first project. In 1969, it started its cinema department. Soon, many young talented filmmakers and animators joined the organization. The main attraction was its title, which could provide the artists relatively greater freedom of expression than elsewhere. Many prominent directors of Iranian national cinema started their careers there or made films for the institute, such as Bahram Baizai, Amir Naderi, Abbas Kiarostami, Reza Alamzadeh, and Sohrab Shahid-Sales.

The 1970s was a special decade for Iranian cinema. As critic Houshang Goulmakani states, "The Seventies saw the height of the Shah's confidence in his social and political successes. Deluding itself into believing that it had grown unassailably stable, the regime now allowed the making of a few films with critical social themes."[21]

Many important filmmakers emerged from the prerevolutionary era, including Parvis Kimiavi, who made the reflexive masterpiece *Mogholha* (Mongols, 1973), a film that allegorizes the cultural imperialism of TV by comparing that situation to the invasion of Mongols. Bahram Baizai is the director of one of the groundbreaking films of the Iranian New Wave, *Ragbar* (Downpour, 1972). Sohrab Shahid-Sales is an author-director who embodied his original style in his 1975 film *Tabiat-e-Bijan* (Spiritless nature). Abbas Kiarostami is now a well-known director of the 1990s, who directed one of the last films that screened before the revolution in 1978, *Gozaresh* (The report). Dariush Mehrjui, a UCLA cinema and philosophy graduate, directed *Gav* (Cow) in 1969 and the controversial *Dayerehy-e-Mina* (Mina cycle, 1975), which was banned for three years. The latter's subject matter dealt with people involved in the blood business. Interestingly, the film was banned only until the government opened its first blood bank.

The new cultural, political, and economic environment from the mid-1960s to the late 1970s created a unique national cinema that had its roots in Iranian perspectives of art, literature, and culture. The mainstream commercial cinema in the 1970s encountered an innovative form of cinema. The counter-cinema was a political cinema that developed its symbolic language as the result of a long history of censorship. This third cinema was very different from that existing in Latin America, Africa, Asia, or any developing countries, because of different social-historical contexts. Some of the Iranian filmmakers of that period were forced to leave the country because of political circumstances. Many of the artists who stayed on in postrevolutionary Iran challenged the new fashion of religious and moral censorship in the domains of art and culture. The attractive Iranian cinema of today is the outcome of a tradition developed in the prerevolutionary era.

This historical account of the early period of motion pictures in Iran is an effort to locate the formation of a cinematic culture within its sociopolitical and geographic borders while reflecting on its relation to the concept of modernity and a global field of film. I argue that the kinetic qualities of Iranian pictorial, sculptural, narrative, and dramatic forms are linked to contemporary modes of cinematic representation. This is not to posit an essential continuity between forms or across time but rather to gesture toward a genealogy of shared cultural logics and codes embedded in allied artistic genres. That is, the current cinematic language is not an autonomous paradigm but linked to a series of aesthetic precedents and principles that have organized visual production and perception in Iran. While seemingly distant from its early origins, this cinema began in the hands of the Persian royalty as a tool for the sheer entertainment purposes of the courtly nobles and found its way to become one of the world's prominent national cinemas of the last three decades.

SHAHIN PARHAMI has directed several award-winning experimental short and feature films, which have been screened in many international film festivals, art galleries, and universities. His work includes the trilogy *Nasoot, Lahoot,* and *Jabaroot* and the film *Faces.* His latest creative documentary, *Amin,* which was funded by Asian Network of Documentary (AND), has won awards at Yamagata International Documentary Film Festival (Japan), Taiwan International Documentary Festival, and Dubai International Film Festival and was nominated for the best feature documentary at Asian Pacific Screen Awards in 2011.

Notes

1. Hugh Honour and John Fleming, *The Visual Arts: A History* (Upper Saddle River, NJ: Prentice Hall, 1992), 96.

2. Jamal Omid, *The History of Iranian Cinema, 1900–1978* (Tehran: Rozaneh, 1995), 19.

3. *Shahnameh* is a vast epic based on pre-Islamic history and mythology by the poet Ferdausi (tenth century AD) in verse form.

4. A good introduction on art and entertainment in Iran before the advent of cinema is provided in M. Ali Issari, *Cinema in Iran: 1900–1979* (Metuchen, NJ: Scarecrow, 1989), 40–67.

5. Ibid., 58–59.

6. Roy Armes, *Third World Film Making and the West* (Berkeley: University of California Press, 1987), 55.

7. Omid, *History of Iranian Cinema*, 870.

8. Issari, *Cinema in Iran*, 61.

9. Related figures are in Massoud Mehrabi, *The History of Iranian Cinema* [in Persian] (Tehran: Film Publication, 1988), 482, 489.

10. Mo'tazedia also made one of the first fiction films (a short comedy) in three reels. But there is no record or description of this film in available sources on Iranian film history. The only mention of this film is in Issari, *Cinema in Iran*, 96.

11. Government did not permit "school" as part of the title because cinema was not yet considered a serious subject to be studied at school. See Omid, *History of Iranian Cinema*, 42.

12. Ibid., 44.

13. Ghafary, quoted in Issari, *Cinema in Iran*, 97.

14. The title of the film before its first showing in Tehran changed to *Dokhtar-e-Lor ya Irane Diruz va Emruz* (The Lor girl or Iran of yesterday and today).

15. Issari, *Cinema in Iran*, 94–95.

16. Ibid., 118.

17. Omid, *History of Iranian Cinema*, 102–105; Issari, *Cinema in Iran*, 119–120.

18. Omid, *History of Iranian Cinema*, 926–930.

19. Ibid., 926–927.

20. Issari, *Cinema in Iran*, 136.

21. Houshang Goulmakani, "New Times, New Perceptions," *Cinemaya* 4 (Summer 1989): 22.

13 Royalty Shapes Early Thai Film Culture

Anchalee Chaiworaporn

THE ROLE OF royalty in shaping the early years of Thai cinema opens a new page in studying the origins of cinema in Asia. While the growth of most early cinemas in the region happened under the reign of Western colonial powers or through the tutelage of fellow Asians such as the Chinese, Indian, or Japanese film entrepreneurs, film culture in Thailand was formed by both foreigners and locals. This chapter brings out the little-discussed role that the Thai monarchy took in introducing and developing motion pictures in the kingdom once known as Siam.

Film's emergence in Thailand came through an interface between internal and external forces that affected the kingdom toward the end of the nineteenth century. Royal influence on early cinema was strengthened by three factors resulting from the modernization that swept the region with the coming of a new century. First, film was a new and expensive innovation that largely confined its use to the privileged class, mainly the royalty. Second, the country's modernization allowed the royalty to acquire new technology faster and earlier than could neighboring countries. In Iran (then called Persia), for example, the first footage was shot during the Persian king's visit to Europe in 1900; however, the Thai monarch was filmed a few years earlier (in 1897), also while on a tour in Europe during a visit in Switzerland. This led both monarchs to acquire film devices to bring back to their respective kingdoms, but the Thai king gained earlier access to this equipment. The king's travels abroad facilitated the rapid transfer of innovation into the Far Eastern kingdom. Third, because a Thai king possessed absolute rights, coupled with an internal fear of Western imperialism, royal involvement with film activities, when sought in earnest, was fostered with great speed. Technological innovations were immediately shown or reported to the king.

Film as a Path to Modernization

Thailand rapidly opened its land to moving pictures. The first viewing of motion pictures officially recorded was by King Rama V (Chulalongkorn, 1868–1910) in

1896. The first footage showing the Thai people (no less than the king himself) was recorded by a Lumière cameraman one year later, during King Rama V's visit to Bern in Switzerland.

Approaching the end of the nineteenth century, the Thai kingdom was surrounded by political realities it could not ignore as Southeast Asia became engulfed by intense conflicts resulting from the spread of Western imperialism. Along Thailand's southern and western borders, the British established themselves in Singapore, Malacca, and Penang in 1824, increasing their influence in Burma and Malaya from the 1820s; and, at its eastern border, France moved into Indochina in the 1860s. Faced by the aggressive spread of European imperialism around its geographic borders, Thailand had to inevitably open up to allow Europeans to enter the kingdom and deal with their advances politically, but in diplomatic ways.

As a result of these colonial advances, foreigners who settled in surrounding colonies introduced motion pictures.[1] The introduction of cinema in Thailand has some unique characteristics. The first motion pictures were brought in both by foreigners and by local people who directly introduced the film medium after traveling abroad. While film in the West was mostly pioneered by scientists in an intense competition for technological innovation at the turn of the nineteenth century, early film culture in Thailand and Southeast Asia first prospered among the upper class as a form of entertainment. In its very early days, film was an expensive medium that the poor and underprivileged could not yet afford. Later, as lower classes became able to enjoy film entertainment, they did so as mass consumers, although the wealthier class continued to produce films and control their development. This privileged class counted among them foreigners, wealthy families, entrepreneurs, and, of course, the royal family. Foreigners included both permanent residents who lived in the Asian countries for business or diplomatic purposes and temporary showmen who traveled from place to place to profit from the technological innovation.

There were only a few countries in Asia whose early film cultures sprang from the direct intercession of native people, mostly in independent states like Japan, Iran, and Thailand, which were also ruled by monarchies.[2] In Japan, though the first motion picture experience might have been introduced by Thomas Edison's Kinetoscope in 1896, the first Cinématographe was brought in by the Japanese textile merchant Katsutaro Inabata. The Konishi Camera Shop imported the first motion picture device in Japan, used by the photographer Shiro Asano to shoot Japan's (and perhaps among Asia's) earliest films.[3] In Thailand, the monarchy, as the highest class in Thai society, played the major role in pioneering the new technologies in the kingdom, especially during the reigns of Kings Rama V, VI, and VII.

Stephen Bottomore observes that the early monarchs and their extended royal families were attracted to cinema. Monarchies around the world watched moving pictures at specially arranged screenings, appeared in movies themselves, employed royal cinematographers, set up private cinemas, and even had been involved in dramatic film productions.[4] Similarly, all kinds of early film culture in Thailand—including production, exhibition, and related activities like censorship—had been completely in the hands of the monarchy.[5] Although the monarchy did not directly buy the films that were publicly shown, they supported local people rather than Chinese entrepreneurs to do so. Instead of seeing the new technology as threat to their dynasty, as Bottomore puts it, they chose to "attune their image to the new medium, or control over it."[6]

The Thai monarchy opened itself to cinema mainly as a result of external and internal political forces that erupted in the country in the late nineteenth century—the spread of Western imperialism in the region and the local quest for democracy. The kings of Thailand tried very hard to save the kingdom from the onslaught of Western colonization. Several attempts were made by imperialists to take over the country, as they did its neighbors. Instead of fighting against them aggressively, the monarchs decided to modernize the country according to Western standards. King Rama IV employed Westerners to educate his children, including the future king, Rama V. Many new treaties had been made with European nations since the time of King Rama IV, though they had not been fully honored. To adapt themselves to modern times, several kings of Thailand traveled to the Western world. King Rama V made two visits to Europe, after having made several trips in Asia. He also sent his sons to study overseas, including Kings Rama VI and VII. A number of young men in the common class had also been sent to study abroad to help modernize the country after their return. There were eventual political consequences that changed the absolute monarchy into a constitutional mandate.

As travel to the West became easy and entry into the kingdom was made accessible, Western culture, ideology, and innovation flowed into the country, conveyed both by Westerners and returning royalty and Thai students. During the time of King Rama V Thailand made many reforms in almost every aspect of social life: politics, state administration, economics, science, and technology. First, the reforms to society and culture had been streamlined in two directions.[7] A new nation-state ideology was formed, and all administrations were centralized under state control, but Thai society was still ruled by the monarchy. Nationalism was cultivated to replace older beliefs and affiliations based on regional ethnicities. Second, Thailand needed to modernize into a new society. New technologies were adopted. The first railways were constructed throughout the country. In keeping with technological advancements, many old social beliefs and practices were abolished, especially the slave system. During the reign of the king's sons (notably that of King Rama VI), modernization continued, and some signs of attaining democracy began to be seen. For example, a new model town was established by King Rama VI under the name Dusit Thani to allow Thai people to experience freedom and democracy. During the reign of King Rama VII (Prajadhipok, 1925–1935), Thailand physically looked modern, except that it was still controlled by an absolute monarchy. In 1932, the People's Party (Khana Ratsadon) staged a coup d'état, forcing the country to change to a constitutional monarchy. Three years later, on March 2, 1935, King Rama VII abdicated his throne and remained in England with his wife until his death in 1941.

Early Cinema

The study of early Thai cinema begins when King Rama V first saw Thomas Edison's Kinetoscope in 1896 and ends in 1932 when feature films began to be made as the country changed to a democracy. This early phase differs from what occurred in most of the West, when early film or primitive cinema generally denotes an era of filmmaking and film viewing that ends about the 1910s.[8] But as a novelty innovation in Asia, cinema progressed slowly after its sudden spread in the region. For Thais, 1932 not only signaled the end of absolute monarchy but also halted its exploitation of cinema as an object of entertainment. That is, the role of the royalty in the establishment of early Thai cinema culture can be seen in the pioneering but mainly amateurish use of film.[9] The cinema culture later moved toward civil political empowerment when film finally came into the hands of private, professional filmmakers.

Pioneering Film Activities

As a part of their modernization schemes, Kings Rama V, VI, and VII visited several countries both in Asia and in the West, from where they were able to import the new film technology. They were thus among the first in Asia to undertake the region's first activities performed by native Asians.

The first officially recorded viewing of movie-related pictures was by King Rama V. On August 3, 1896, during a trip to Java and Singapore, he was introduced to a machine by an English showman at the Hurricane House Palace in Singapore. He explained, "Something I could not remember how it was called. It looked like a long roll of connecting pictures, and then was inserted into a machine. When the power was on, the machine was rolling and those pictures seemed to be moving. With speed, the pictures looked like cockfighting. First—hitting against each other, and then the cocks were jumping off and on, bowing their heads around. Feathers were falling. The cocks were struggling. Gamblers were yelling, placing their bets. It looked like those pictures were moving. One roll contained the pictures of 1,400 actions."[10]

Thai film archivist Dome Sukvong believes that the machine could be a Kinetoscope, which was created in 1891 by William Kennedy Laurie Dickson, a British employee of Edison. Another account relates that this moving-picture show was introduced to the king by an English showman, forming the first official record about the royal experience with film-related activities. But there is no evidence whether the king tried to bring the new technology home to Thailand. At the same time, no film activities were found to be recorded right after the visit.

One year later, on May 25, 1897, King Rama V visited Bern, Switzerland. The visit was recorded by a Lumière cameraman on celluloid and immediately shown to him. Sukvong claimed it was the first film showing a Thai subject, although the footage was not shot by a Thai, and no copy of the film exists today.[11] The event, however, elicited much interest from the king, who told his brother Prince Sanbhassatra to import the filming equipment after their return to Thailand, the first of its kind to be brought to the kingdom. From this early experience with motion pictures, cinema's development in the country began to move forward. After three years, Prince Sanbhassatra succeeded in shooting short film reels, most of which were about royal ceremonies. He was later honored as the pioneer of filmmaking in Thailand, perhaps among the early film pioneer cinematographers in Asia.

In the beginning, Prince Sanbhassatra's cinematic interest was as an amateur filmmaker. Most of his works were shown in royal screening rooms, but after three years he added an annual show at Benjamabopitr Temple Fair. At that time, the Thai people had already acquired experience in watching films, first through the first exhibitions of S. G. Marchovsky,[12] followed by several traveling showmen. Usually these showmen rented temporary tents or theaters to show films,[13] which contained several shorts, and then moved to another place. But they did not frequently come to the kingdom for long-term screenings because Thailand was only a transit point to other countries. The public had very few chances to see movies. Prince Sanbhassatra's annual show, which charged viewers an entrance fee, played a great part in introducing and instilling film culture in Thailand.[14] He was not only the first Thai cinematographer but also the first Thai showman. Even though an amateur filmmaker, he provided an indigenous perspective to the film culture. No one seems to have challenged his presence as the only Thai filmmaker; Thai students of the common class, who must have been exposed to films in their studies in the West, did not become involved in the motion picture business.

King Rama VI had more personal interest in theater than in film. But at the time, arts and media were being considered influential tools for modernizing the country. Even though the king did not know much about the importance of cinema, he assigned his brother Prince Kambeangbejr, who was the commander of the Thai State Railways, to set up the first professional film organization in 1922 to promote tourism. At that time, railroads had just been constructed throughout the country, and the king wanted to boost traveling by train. The new film unit,

Topical Film Service, undertook making and showing a variety of films—features, documentaries, and newsreels— across the country. Films were dispatched by its mobile unit to be screened in open-air theaters without charge. Topical Film Service was the key player in boosting the cinemagoing culture throughout Thailand, especially in remote areas.

However, since it was the first and only film organization, Topical Film Service had to address every request for its services, not only the demands of its parent organization, Thai State Railways. It operated as a center of all film activities, providing filmmaking services that conducted training. When the first indigenous Thai feature, *Choke Song Chun* (Double luck) was made by Bangkok Film Company (owned by Wasuwat Brothers) in 1926, the crews and filming equipment were hired from Topical Film Service. Similarly, when American director Henry MacRae came to Thailand to make the country's first full-length film, *Suvarna of Siam*, in 1923, the company was also assigned by King Rama VI to assist MacRae. Topical Film Service was the link between amateur filmmaking of the upper class and professional filmmaking of the commoners. With the establishment of Topical Film Service, filmmaking became a full-time and dignified job, where one could be employed as a civil servant and promoted to a higher position by the kings. Making films was no longer confined to the royalty. In fact, the majority of film crew, including stars, in early Thai cinema were noblemen who were permitted by the royalty to act in movies.[15]

Professionalizing Filmmaking

During the time of King Rama VII, filmmaking, both amateur and professional, reached its height. The new king expressed strong interest in cinema and had his own theaters built at several palaces. He made two visits to Hollywood in 1920 and 1931 and met important figures of the filmmaking world, including Thomas Alva Edison, Douglas Fairbanks, and Mary Pickford. The king was an amateur filmmaker and made a number of movies, including features and nonfiction films on festivals, sports, and his own travels abroad. His films were all credited under Pappayong Thai (Royal Shooting Film) before being changed to the company's new name, Amphorn Film. In 1930, he was invited to be an honorable member of the New York–based Amateur Cine League, an international center for amateur filmmakers. He also provided many activities to support the rise of amateur filmmaking in Thailand, and a large number of royal members, noblemen, and rich citizens joined the group. They gathered and set up the Amateur Cinema Association of Siam in 1930 (ACAS), under the official patronage of King Rama VII. According to the *Bangkok Times* on May 29, 1932, ACAS consisted of 122 members, varying from royalty and noblemen to rich commoners and foreigners. The association was divided into three small subcommittees that supported all amateur filmmaking and enriched the film culture in Thailand: the Selling Unit, which handled all selling activities from drinks to film equipment; the Technique Unit, which provided film and print development, film credits, and title making; and the Film Library. Every month, meetings and screenings were arranged at the king's palace. The group supported film criticism and published a monthly newsletter in both Thai and English to promote film culture in the kingdom.[16]

It may be hard to explain why King Rama VII had special interest in cinema. He might have been influenced by his father and his uncles Prince Sanbhassatra and Prince Kambeangbejr to also embark on film activities. However, King Rama VII was the first royal member who understood the power of movies in influencing public opinion. To foster film interest, he enacted several policies to promote film culture in the kingdom, and he used film as a political tool in the counterbalance of power between old and new ideologies.

In the beginning, the royalty used film technology as entertainment and a hobby for themselves. But by the time of King Rama VII, cinema culture was growing beyond its royal affiliation, at which time Thailand was also faced by several political upheavals. The country was swept by nationalism that used film to counter foreign invasion; at the same time, because of flourishing new ideologies and increasing political activities, there was a call for democracy. Cinema was gradually affected by all of those influences. Wittingly or not, film was utilized for political purposes in two ways: in royal attempts at monopolizing the cinema business and the first endorsement of censorship laws.

Rise of Nationalism and the Struggle for Film Monopoly

With the exception of filmmaking in royal hands, early film activities in Thailand developed in a free-trade mode. Anyone could run a business without any control, but mostly in informal ways. Traveling showmen came into the country only temporarily and left after showing their films. It was a traveling film culture until the time of King Rama VI, when he sought to instill nationalism throughout the country. Film could not escape this nationalist impulse, and therefore cinema-related activities became infused by nationalism.

Although most Thai kings agreed to open the country to Western powers in principle, they were often forced to accept unfair bilateral treaties. To protect the country, Thai leaders planted nationalist ideology in the minds of the people so that solidarity would be developed and everyone could play a part in protecting the nation. During the reign of King Rama V, nationalism was not applied in clear-cut fashion. It was not used to develop antiforeigner sentiments and adhere to strict patriotism. It was more a unifying bond to keep Thailand as one nation where all races and ethnicities could live together and share similar beliefs and pride. Education was used to spread the nationalist ideology by creating a

one-single-nation policy. One national language and culture were officially declared as the educational system became centralized. The Ministry of Education
was created, and a single syllabus scheme was used nationwide. But during the
reign of King Rama VII, nationalism took an antagonistic turn. It was aimed
against foreigners, which became widespread in the country, particularly discriminating against the Chinese.[17] One of the key policies came in the guise of the
Boy Scout Unit, a pseudo-military organization that was an extension of the Boy
Scout movement in the country.

At first, film was not affected by the spread of an ultranationalist ideology.
No particular policies were set up to use it to discriminate until the Chinese-
owned Siam Phapphayont, a merger of Roopphayont Krungthep and Phappayon
Phattanakarn, monopolized the film business during the time of King Rama V.
After the merger, the company was vertically integrated in all areas—buying, distributing, and operating the majority of movie theaters. King Rama VI then appointed Chao Phya Ramarakop to set up a new company in 1919, Siam Neeramai.
It used the same model of vertical integration in all aspects of film business—
importing, distributing, and owning several theaters in Bangkok. The Chinese-
owned company went bankrupt one year later.

Siam Neeramai reached its peak during 1922–1925 but started to decline during the Great Depression. By that time, King Rama VII had ascended the throne
(1925) and laid out another monopoly policy affecting the film business. As movies became part of everyday life, each province saw one or two movie theaters
built to accommodate the ever-growing number of viewers. Open-air theaters
were also popular everywhere. The royal attempts at monopoly were now aimed
at running the film business rather than targeting foreign (i.e., mainly Chinese)
competition. But the effort was not successful, as the old royalty-supported Siam
Neeramai went into decline. A new company was immediately set up by the royalty that used the same model of vertical integration. It was registered in 1932
as the United Cinematograph (Saha Cinema). United Cinematograph bought
the Queens theater and soon became the largest cinema operator in Thailand. It
bought several movie theaters and built the most modern and largest, Sala Chal-
ermkrung, directly initiated by the king. According to Sukvong, King Rama VII
possibly started United Cinematograph to celebrate the 150th anniversary of the
Rattanakosin dynasty and to control the film business because it was an influential and highly profitable economic enterprise.[18] However, the company's long-
range plan was interrupted when a coup d'état was staged on June 27, 1932, and
King Rama VII abdicated his throne three years later in 1935. United Cinematograph continued operation until the end of the Second World War.[19]

Although royal members still entered the film industry and continue to
be important figures,[20] there was no other period when royalty was as strongly
involved in the film industry as during the reign of King Rama VII. It can be

argued that if Thailand had not encountered the political change brought about by the coup, the Thai film industry might have developed in another direction than the domination by Chinese Thais that prevails today.[21]

Royalty and Censorship

Censorship law was first endorsed in Thailand in 1931 during the reign of King Rama VII. Between the first film screening by S. G. Marchovsky in 1897 and the endorsement of this law, Thailand had a free-trade system that allowed anyone to show whatever they wanted. This practice was in place for only two decades. By the time the film culture was flourishing, the kings had become the unofficial censorship body. As the highest leaders in the country, who had absolute rights, their consent was solicited for all kinds of activities. For example, Henry MacRae met King Rama VI to introduce himself and ask for the king's permission to shoot, and the king assigned Topical Film Service to assist MacRae. During the reign of King Rama VII, a number of films were often cut, modified, or, in some cases, banned, after viewing by the king. In 1927, the king officially banned the Indian film *Light of Asia* after several media controversies arose regarding the depiction of unfavorable images of Lord Buddha. Even local films had also been affected by this unofficial censorship. The police did not allow *Amnat Mued* (Dark power, directed by Thai Pappayon Taay, 1927) to be shown when they heard of the king's comment on the issue of gambling and prostitution in the film.[22] However, after the film was readapted, reshot, and retitled *Chanapan* (The victory over the hoodlums), it passed the police board, but most theater operators refused to show the film, which was once unsatisfactory to the king.

The censorship law was first drafted during the reign of King Rama VI. On July 18, 1919, the newspaper *Siam Ras* published a commentary against censorship that was placed in the hands of the Interior Ministry: "All of the movies that were brought into Siam had already passed the censor (outside Siam). But it was heard that the Interior Ministry planned to have another law that would be used in the kingdom."[23] In 1928, a sign of censorship was seen when the king assigned Interior Minister Prince Vorapinit to look over the draft. Two years later, on September 20, 1930, the bill was officially promulgated by the king, and an official censorship board was set up. In a controversial move, what was once supervised by the Royal Thai Police Department came under the supervision of the Culture Ministry in 2009.

The role of royalty in early Thai cinema not only helped shape the film culture in Thailand but also promoted it as a kind of popular art. Several times, especially during the absence of royal involvement, the Thai film industry had often been considered an unfavorable culture that was shunned by educated Thais. But after Kings Rama V, VI, and VII shaped early cinema, several royal family members have entered the business and become respected as key figures in the Thai film industry. When Prince Chatreechalerm Yukol began to make films, it was called the first "new wave" in Thai cinema, when new aesthetic innovations were seen on-screen. When Thai cinema was in decline in 1997, Queen Sirikit supported the making of several epics, known locally as the queen's movies, including *The Legend of Suriyothai* and *The Legend of Naresuan* sagas. It can be argued that, without the involvement of the royalty, Thai cinema might not have grown to what it is today.

ANCHALEE CHAIWORAPORN researches Asian cinemas, including those of South Korea, Japan, Philippines, Indonesia, and Thailand, and has been awarded fellowships by the Nippon Foundation, Japan Foundation, and the Asian Scholarship Foundation. She has contributed to a number of publications, including *Cahier du cinema* and *Variety*. She also won awards for Thailand's best film critic in 2000 and best feature writer in 2002.

Notes

1. In Indonesia, for example, the first moving pictures were shown in a house in the Dutch East Indies situated in central Jakarta, and the first production occurred in 1911 by European filmmakers living in Indonesia. Nan Achnas and Marseth Sumarno, "Indonesia: In Two Worlds," in *Being and Becoming: The Cinemas of Asia*, ed. Aruna Vasudev, Latika Padgaonkar, and Rashmi Doraiswamy (New Delhi: Macmillan India, 2002), 153. In the Malay Straits, the first film screenings happened almost in the same year that motion pictures were shown in Bangkok in 1897, while the first Malaysian feature film, *Laila Majnun*, was produced in 1933 by Singapore-based Motilal Chemical; this film was later remade by the Chinese Wong brothers from Shanghai. Hassan Muthalib and Wong Tuck Cheong, "Gentle Winds of Change," in Vasudev, Padgaonkar, and Doraiswamy, *Being and Becoming*, 301.

2. Iran and Thailand share the experience of having their cinemas started through royal intervention, from the first viewing, exhibition, production, and even distribution. Before the first Iranian fiction feature was made in 1930, Iranian cinema was entirely dominated by the production of nonfiction films. Similar to what occurred in Thailand's early cinema, the first nonfiction footage was shot in Ostend, Belgium, on August 18, 1900, when a flower parade of some fifty floats showered the visiting shah with bouquets of flowers. The event was filmed by Mirza Ebrahim Khan Akkas Bashi, the official court photographer, with a Gaumont camera he had bought by order of the shah a few weeks earlier in Paris. Before the First World War, most documentaries were sponsored and viewed only by the Qajar royal family and the upper classes. Hamid Naficy, "Iranian Cinema," in *Life and Art: The New Iranian Cinema*, ed. Rose Issa and Sheila Whitaker (London: National Film Theatre, 1999), 9.

3. Donald Richie, *A Hundred Years of Japanese Cinema* (Tokyo: Kodansha International, 2001), 17.

4. Stephen Bottomore, "'She's Just like My Granny! Where's Her Crown?' Monarchs and Movies, 1896–1916," in *Celebrating 1895: The Centenary of Cinema*, ed. John Fullerton (Sydney: John Libbey, 1998), 173.

5. Thailand has a lot of problems in keeping historical documents on cinema. Thus, only royal activities have been officially recorded, especially in relation to cinema.

6. Bottomore, "She's Just like My Granny!," 173.

7. Likhit Dhiravegin, *The Evolution of Thai Politics and Government*, 2nd ed. (Bangkok: Thammasat University Press, 1990), 101.

8. Robert Sklar, *Film: An International History of the Medium* (London: Thames and Hudson, 1993), 16.

9. In Thailand, there are many levels of titles in defining the status of royal members. Here is a list showing the highest order to the lowest:

> Somdej (His Majesty the King or Queen)
> Phra Barom (crown prince or crown princess)
> Chao Fah (son or daughter of the king and queen)
> Phra Ong Chao (a child of the above royal members with one partner who is a commoner)
> Mom Chao (MC, a child of Phra Ong Chao and a commoner)
> Mom Rajawong (MR, a child of Mom Chao and a commoner)
> Mom Luang (ML, a child of Mom Rajawong and a commoner)

The titles from MC up to Somdej are considered royal members and normally are equal to prince or princess in English. MR and ML are not royal members but considered as commoners.

10. Dome Sukvong, "85 Years of Thai Cinema," *Arts and Culture* [in Thai] 3, no. 8 (1982): 132.

11. Ibid.

12. As reported in the June 9, 1897, issue of the *Bangkok Times*, S. G. Marchovsky was the first man who showed early films in Thailand. See Anchalee Chaiworaporn, "Who Is S. G. Marchovsky?," *The Nation*, January 24, 1997, p. C1.

13. Thailand's first permanent cinema theater, the Japanese Cinematograph, was built in 1905 by a group of Japanese entrepreneurs. In 1911, a new cinema, Phathanakorn Cinematograph, was set up by the locals. In 1916, the Japanese withdrew from the business. Cinema theaters were expanded to the provinces in the 1920s. See Anchalee Chaiworaporn, "Endearing Afterglow," in Vasudev, Padgaonkar, and Doraiswamy, *Being and Becoming*, 441–461.

14. Originally, most of the Thai public entertainment shows were free of charge, similar to some ceremonies such as weddings, ordinations, and funerals. The host paid all expenses. The practice of charging admission began during the reign of King Rama IV and applied only to foreign shows that were brought into the country. The screenings were mostly held in hotels and similar private venues. The first local ticket collection took place after the first permanent theater, Siamese Theatre, was established by a nobleman during the reign of King Rama IV. In the beginning, he held screenings free of charge, and only the upper class, royalty, noblemen, and foreigners were invited. But after a while, because of financial problems, the owner opened the theaters to the public and charged admission. See Sukvong, "85 Years of Thai Cinema," 128–129.

15. Dome Sukvong, *King Prachadhipok and Cinema* [in Thai] (Bangkok: Ton-or Grammy, 1996), 138.

16. Ibid., 64.

17. Originally, Thailand did not discriminate against Chinese people. They were even employed as tax collectors and were noblemen during the reigns of earlier kings.

18. Sukvong, *King Prachadhipok and Cinema*, 121.

19. Ibid., 120.

20. After King Rama VII, other noted royals in the Thai film industry included Prince Phanuphan Yukol, Prince Anusorn Mongkolkarn, and Prince Chatreechalerm Yukol.

21. Most of the production companies in Thailand are owned by Chinese Thais, reflected in the nicknames used by journalists and the public to refer to these owners. These names always mix a Chinese title and a short name. For example, the head of Sahamongkol Film, Somsak Techarattanaprasert, is called Sia Jiang. *Sia* in Chinese means "rich." The head of Grammy's, Paiboon Damrongchaitham, is Ar-koo. *Ar-koo* is the Chinese word meaning "uncle." Hia Hor heads RS Films; *Hia* means "elder brother."

22. In fact, the king gave permission for a temporary screening for the filmmaker to recoup the cost, and then he had the film pulled out immediately. Sukvong, *King Prachadhipok and Cinema*, 145.

23. Ibid., 163.

14 *I Was Born, but . . .*
Some Thoughts on the Origins of Cinema in Asia

Stephen Bottomore

The Arrival

The cinema was introduced to Asia mainly by foreigners. The same is true for countries in other parts of the world (such as Latin America), where the first film shows and film production arrived courtesy of outsiders. The reason is not hard to locate. Inventors in the European and American industrial heartlands had established the photographic and optical basics of the moving picture and then developed the various cinematographs and other devices that made the new medium a practical possibility. The cinematic apparatuses then spread out, usually in the hands of emissaries from these originating countries, to the far corners of the world. In wider historical terms this may be seen as a fairly standard technological diffusion, not unlike the process whereby many generations earlier the Chinese had invented myriad useful devices and techniques that then spread out to the world. In general, a device or technique is developed in one or more places; then others quickly see that this or that new thing is interesting and useful; and they buy, rent, steal, copy, or adapt it.

The cinema was no different, but it seems that this evident truth is a too-bitter pill for some to swallow. As Nick Deocampo points out in the introduction, a number of chroniclers of national cinema in Asia have tried to disown or gloss over the first foreign-dominated years of their film industries. "Our" film industries really began, they suggest, only when "we" took control, and what came before that is of little interest. Even if they do not have this attitude, writers of national film histories often do little to seek out information on the first, foreign-dominated years of their movie businesses.

In some cases such attitudes are understandable and perhaps justifiable, say, where the first foreign-given film shows were so vaguely documented or so ephemeral as to leave little mark or to have no noticeable consequences. For example, little is known (it seems) of the first showing of films in Korea apart from that it took place in 1898 and was arranged so as to advertise the products of an American company.[1] However, in several other Asian countries with more complete documentation—at least in the form of newspapers—little attempt has been made by historians until recent times to research such sources. Yet it appears—based on my own piecemeal research and on more systematic efforts in the last few years by other scholars (Dafna Ruppin, Nadi Tofighian, Tilman Baumgartel, and others)—that quite an extensive cinema exhibition sector, and even some production, was emerging in the early twentieth century in these "forgotten" Asian nations; and this was happening well before national film production began.

The Foreigners

A few examples should illustrate the point. If one looks only at the standard histories of film in Indonesia, one finds virtually nothing about the pre-1920 era in the Nederlands-Indië (as the region was then termed).[2] Yet the newspapers before that date contained considerable information about film exhibition, including titles of films shown and even reviews. For more details one can now see the research by Ruppin and Tofighian,[3] but one wonders why previous scholars had not felt motivated to do such research. One can also find solid information about early film in Vietnam (the French colonialists called the region "Indochine") in the local newspapers and even in the French film trade press of the time. Using the latter source, I have found interesting references to two cameramen working in Indochine in the early film era—Rene Batissou and Andre Wentzel—men whose names are unrecorded in the film history books but who seem to have filmed quite a number of actuality scenes in the region.[4] More significantly, a solid body of work has been undertaken on this subject of colonial-era Vietnamese film not by a native of the country but in New York for a PhD dissertation.[5] For Sri Lanka (then called Ceylon) a little study of the local press reveals several references to a certain Warwick Major, who was a leading film exhibitor on the island around 1912 and an important itinerant presence in the region's entertainment circuits but today is virtually forgotten.[6]

Probably the most significant Asian country at the end of the nineteenth century was India: for its size, its population, and its wealth (as well as its ancient and well-established culture in literature, painting, theatre, etc.). Certainly India was of keystone value to the colonial power. This was, as if we had not heard it enough, the "Jewel in the Crown" of the British Empire.[7] Arguably, cinema developed here more quickly and took root more deeply than anywhere else in Asia.

Film historians in India and elsewhere have made great strides in analyzing the early years of cinema on the subcontinent, but most studies downplay the role of foreign pioneers. I first realized this some years ago as I scrutinized the early film trade press published in Europe, for these journals carried reports about Europeans, including British people, involved with film in India (and indeed in other Asian countries) who are not mentioned in modern film history books and articles. It seems that another scholar had noticed this absence. Stephen Hughes has undertaken scrupulous research in Indian newspapers and archives to reveal the presence of British (and other foreign) film pioneers in South India. He has published one of the most significant contributions to Asian cinema studies in recent years.[8] In his article, Hughes examines some of the theatrical venues in South India from the end of the nineteenth century, as well as the traveling entertainment companies and shows that played in them. He suggests that early cinema was a conveniently "portable technology" that fitted into such transnational entertainment networks, spanning India as well as Singapore, Australasia, and points between and beyond.[9] As instances he offers details on Ada Delroy and her variety entertainment troupe and "Professor" T. Stevenson. The latter has hitherto appeared only in film histories of India as a vague, often misspelled, name, but now we see a fuller picture of this photographic dealer–turned–film showman.[10]

Hughes tells us that "the early period of cinema in India . . . was overwhelmingly European in orientation," meaning that many of the traveling film showmen were Europeans, as were the bulk of spectators for their shows.[11] His detailed investigation substantiates other evidence I have seen over the years about these traveling showmen, and I hope that future accounts of early cinema in the region by Hughes and colleagues will encompass additional forgotten names of this ilk, including Maurice Bandmann; the Corrick family of New Zealand, who gave shows from Australasia through India and beyond; and David Jamilly, who toured his film show from Bombay to Singapore and ended up as a leading member of the British film industry.

A New First in Asia

I have my own small but significant discovery to report in this field, for I have found what I believe is the first known appearance of moving pictures in India. Indeed, it is probably the first instance of this photographic technology in all of Asia (excluding Australia).[12] My new date is December 27, 1895. On that day a certain entertainer named "Dr. Harley," probably British, opened for a few days at Bevan's music warehouse in Calcutta, showing films in a Kinetophone machine (Edison's peepshow Kinetoscope plus phonograph). The details, as stated in the *Englishman* newspaper, are sketchy, but the import is clear: Harley's peepshow moving pictures preceded the hitherto earliest appearance of moving pictures in Asia—the Lumière screening in Bombay in July 1896—by over six months.[13] (The Bombay show remains the first known instance in Asia of *projected* movies.)

The same issue of the newspaper that published the ad for Harley's exhibition included an article describing and commenting on the films he was showing, so perhaps it would not be too far-fetched to say that this date of December 27 marks not only the first films ever shown in Asia but also the first film review in the continent![14] Harley showed his Kinetophone in Singapore the following year, where it was seen by the king of Thailand,[15] and Harley was back in India with films early in the new century.

I originally published this claim in an Indian film festival publication in 2007.[16] I had somehow expected my article to be met with at least a murmur, if not a shout, of excitement—the excitement that often greets the claim of any "first." But there was no excitement, no murmur, not even a response. The rediscovery of Harley's first film activity in Asia went unnoticed and has not been—as far as I know—referred to since. At the time I wondered why, but I think I now know the reason: The news of Harley's pioneering activity was not greeted with interest by Asian film historians because of the reasons I have just discussed. Harley could not be a full-fledged pioneer of Asian cinema simply because he was not "one of us." Indeed, I suspect that his pioneering status will be even less celebrated than the pioneers he has displaced, for the following reason. The screening of films in Bombay in July 1896 was undertaken with the Lumière Cinématographe, a French device, and the show was presented by French technicians. However, Harley was probably British, as was his Calcutta venue, Bevan's, and—worst of all—the announcement of his exhibition was printed in the publication the *Englishman*! So here we have the relatively neutral French being displaced as film pioneers by a representative of the colonial power. This will not be historiographically popular. But popular or not, it is a fact.

Asian Proto-cinema

However, there is a caveat to my discussion of Harley and all the previous discussion, a caveat so large and looming that it cannot and should not be ignored: The pen is not the play; the mason's trowel is not the Taj Mahal; the brush and canvas are not the paintings by Brueghel and Caravaggio. An apparatus is obviously essential to create an art but not sufficient, and cinema was no exception. André Gaudreault suggests in a recent book that the pioneers of the moving image, notably the Lumières, did not invent cinema; they just invented a device. To explain how this device, the Cinématographe, evolved to engender a full-fledged medium and industry, "the cinema," one needs, Gaudreault tells us, to invoke a variety of complex social and cultural forces. One needs to see film emerging in the context of other visual entertainments, spectacles, and media, including theater, photography, and the magic lantern.[17] It was only after several years of contact (and often subordination) to other media that cinema had, as some scholars now say, a "second birth" and was transformed from a novel technology into the medium, the industry, and the building that we know as "the cinema."[18]

In Asia, too, there was this two-stage process. Moving pictures arrived as a novelty, and the technology was exploited for a few years by showmen—foreigners and locals—often in existing entertainment venues and circuits and in traveling tent shows, and the films shown were mainly imported from the West. Gradually the medium became more indigenized and institutionalized (the second birth). At that point the styles and practices of Asian cinema had diverged considerably from Western practices. Many of these distinctive attributes came from long traditions in existing art forms on the Asian continent. As P. K. Nair and Hassan Abdul Muthalib show in their chapters in this book, cinema in India and Malaysia was much influenced by antecedent forms of public entertainment: The stories and myths (such as the *Ramayana*) that had been known and loved by millions of people for generations entered into the movies all across Asia. The diverse social patterns of Asian countries, too, were reflected in their films.

So when some Asian film historians tend to gloss over the foreigners who brought the original cinematic apparatus to their countries, one can see their point. It was not the apparatus alone that created the cinema in Asia and launched it on its long, diverse journey through countries in the region. Much more significant were the conditions into which the apparatus emerged, most notably the preexisting social traditions and artistic and performance practices, all expressed through the talents of the many people who became involved in the cinema(s) of Asia.

The Family Tree

Does that mean that those foreign bringers of the cinematic apparatus—and purveyors of the first foreign films—were insignificant and should be utterly forgotten? I don't believe so. In this context, as so often in life, one can find a lesson in a great film. Yasujiro Ozu's silent film *I Was Born, but . . .* (1932), is about two young brothers whose father is an office clerk. The boys see that their dad constantly tries to ingratiate himself with his boss, to the point that he makes a fool of himself. The boys are mortified and refuse to cooperate with family life; ashamed of their father, they wish to disown him. Only at the end of the film do they come to some kind of reconciliation.

Ozu's charming film reminds us that many of us may not have the parents (or the siblings or grandparents) that we would like—life is not perfect—but it is not a tragedy either. It is just how it is. "Get over it," as the American self-help movement might say; "move on." Asian cinema might not have the parents it would like (or let us say "grandparents," to keep this metaphor on track), but that is not a tragedy either. Those foreigners who brought their cameras and projectors to Asia in the early days are surely worth acknowledging, as well as studying and investigating, because they constitute an undeniable part of the history of cinema on the continent, even if their pioneering work in most cases probably had little influence on the future development of that cinema.

So let us raise our glasses to Dr. Harley and his fellow foreign emissaries of the moving picture to Asia. Their pioneering efforts constitute a brief, little-noticed prequel to Asian film, and like most prequels their story is not essential viewing to understand the main narrative, but surely worth a glance at least. These outsiders were first on the scene and for that reason alone deserve, I submit, to have their names placed somewhere on the family tree of Asian cinema.

STEPHEN BOTTOMORE has worked as Associate Editor of *Film History* and a documentary producer for the BBC. He has directed numerous TV and corporate documentaries worldwide. He is author of many journal articles and two books: *The "Titanic" and Silent Cinema* and *I Want to See This Annie Mattygraph*, a history of early film as seen by magazine cartoonists.

Notes

1. John A. Lent, *The Asian Film Industry* (Bromley, UK: Christopher Helm, 1990), 123.

2. See K. G. Heider, *Indonesian Cinema: National Culture on Screen* (Honolulu: University of Hawaii Press, 1991); and Salim Said, *Shadows on the Silver Screen: A Social History of Indonesian Film* (Jakarta: Lontar Foundation, 1991).

3. See Nadi Tofighian, *Blurring the Colonial Binary: Turn-of-the-Century Transnational Entertainment in Southeast Asia* (Stockholm: Acta Universitatis Stockholmiensis, 2013); Dafna Ruppin, *The Komedi Bioscoop: The Emergence of Movie-Going in Colonial Indonesia, 1896–1914* (Barnet, UK: John Libbey, 2016); Dafna Ruppin and Nadi Tofighian, "Moving Pictures across Colonial Boundaries: The Multiple Nationalities of the American Biograph in Southeast Asia," *Early Popular Visual Culture* 14, no. 2 (2016): 188–207; and Nadi Tofighian, "Watching the Astonishment of the Native: Early Audio-Visual Technology and Colonial Discourse," *Early Popular Visual Culture* 15, no. 1 (2017): 26–43.

4. See, for example, Paul Hugault, "Les explorateurs ignorés" [The ignored explorers], *Ciné Journal*, August 16, 1913, pp. 42–43.

5. Donald Dean Wilson, "Colonial Viet Nam on Film: 1896 to 1926" (PhD diss., City University of New York, 2007).

6. See, for example, "The Moving Picture in Ceylon," *Kinematograph and Lantern Weekly*, May 11, 1911, p. 47.

7. I am here ignoring the "white empire" countries of settlement, such as Canada, Australia, and New Zealand, which shared, almost concurrently, most technological developments with the mother country.

8. Stephen Hughes, "When Film Came to Madras," *BioScope* 1, no. 2 (2010): 147–168.

9. Ibid., 148.

10. I have traced Stevenson beyond his Indian period in the 1890s (as described by Hughes) to the early years of the new century when he was a film showman in China. See, for example, T. J. Stevenson, "Britishers Not Asleep," *British Journal of Photography*, April 5, 1907, p. 262.

11. Hughes, "When Film Came to Madras," 148.

12. I say "known" appearance because it is possible that Harley or someone else brought a Kinetoscope/Kinetophone to India earlier than this December date, for the device was certainly being sent all over the world from 1894. The Kinetoscope was publicly shown in the United States from March 1894 and then in France from July; the United Kingdom and northern Europe from October; then Sydney, Australia, in November 1894 and other locations in Australia from mid-1895 (and in New Zealand from November 1895). The main shipping routes to Australasia went via India, so it would have been perfectly possible for a showman to have stopped over in India and shown his Australia-bound Kinetoscope in India earlier in 1895. For a useful chronology, see the *Who's Who of Victorian Cinema* website, at http://www.victorian -cinema.net.

13. "The Wonder of the Age!," *The Englishman*, December 27, 1895, p. 2. I have recently discovered that Harley was preceded with a Kinetoscope in India by one Henry Grahame. Elsewhere in Asia, the earliest known date for the Kinetoscope is July 1896, in Singapore and Kuala Lumpur. See Tofighian, "Watching the Astonishment."

14. "The Kineto-phonographic Exhibition," *The Englishman*, December 27, 1895, p. 6. The reviewer noted that the show was to take place that evening and described the films he or she had already previewed, including a version of the death of Trilby, a carnival dance, and a bar-room scene.

15. Tofighian, "Watching the Astonishment," 33–34.

16. Stephen Bottomore, "A 'Kinetescope' in the Last Cold Weather," *Osian's Cinefan Festival Daily*, July 24, 2007, n.p. See also "A New Claim," *The Bioscope*, August 15, 2007, https:// thebioscope.net/2007/08/15/a-new-claim/.

17. André Gaudreault and Tim Barnard, *Film and Attraction: From Kinematography to Cinema* (Urbana: University of Illinois Press, 2011).

18. For these insights I thank the organizers of the Second Birth of Cinema conference, Newcastle University, July 1–2, 2011.

15 Before *Moana*

Early Cinema of the Pacific

Stephen Bottomore

SHOULD ONE INCLUDE the Pacific South Sea Islands or Oceania in Asia? Certainly it is within the Asia/Pacific region, though that is not quite the same thing. But if we include the island groups of Japan and the Philippines in our "Asian definition," perhaps the more disparate island places should also not be left out. Probably one could argue about these geographic issues until the dugongs come home, but I have decided to short-circuit the arguments through compromise and brevity, here offering merely a capsule discussion of early cinematic developments in the Pacific.

I begin with Hawaii, because my research suggests that this was the first island group in Oceania to experience cinema, which coincidentally was in 1898, the same year as Hawaii's annexation by the United States. For the Edison company, James White and Fred Blechynden filmed in the island group in May of that year, taking some four scenic views. Travelogue presenter Burton Holmes and his cameraman Oscar Depue came to Hawaii only a few weeks later and showed existing films and shot new ones with their Gaumont film camera, including some coverage of US troops.[1] These pioneers were followed by Robert K. Bonine for the Biograph company, who later established himself permanently in Hawaii as a cameraman. Of these five, all but Blechynden were Americans.

Then came the turn of other Pacific islands. The travelogue lecturer Edward B. McDowell, also American, filmed in Samoa in 1903 and the following year in Fiji, later shooting scenic material in other South Sea locations (and also in the Philippines).[2] In 1907 cameraman Leopold Sutto was at work in the Solomons and other Pacific islands for the French Pathé company.[3] A hint of homegrown cinema arrived in Tahiti when local photographer Maxime Bopp du Pont started making films there in 1912,[4] and early the following year an expedition under Gaston Méliès (brother of Georges Méliès), with a company of actors and two cameramen, spent a month filming on the island.[5]

The Méliès company found film exhibition flourishing in Tahiti: Two large cinemas had been established in the capital, Papeete, and another seven were up and running elsewhere on the island.[6] In the previous couple of years moving pictures had really caught the public's fancy in this part of French Polynesia, and by 1914 there were four cinemas in Papeete (largely financed by the Vicomte de Giron).[7] Cinema exhibition also prospered on other islands in the Pacific, and Hawaii was again in the vanguard: As early as 1908 there were five nickelodeon-type shows in Honolulu, and by the following year five or six more on other islands of the group.[8] But that was just the start of the growth, and in 1915 *Photoplay* reported that there were no fewer than thirty-five film shows in Honolulu alone.[9]

While some audience segmentation was occurring by this time, generally the audiences who attended these Hawaiian shows were racially mixed: Americans, Hawaiian, Chinese, and Japanese.[10] A comparable audience diversity seems to have been the case on some other Pacific islands. The British possession Fiji first enjoyed film shows in 1909, and by 1910 an Australian showman, Arthur Guest, was touring films to mixed Fijian and Indian (Hindu) audiences.[11] By 1913 there were three modern cinemas on the island, running programs by the West, Spencer, and Gaumont companies, the films distributed from Sydney.[12] In Samoa in 1912 a local company was giving three shows a week, also with film prints from Australia.[13]

While distribution of these film prints was controlled from faraway in the industrialized world, audiences in the Pacific had their own special filmic interests that exhibitors tried to satisfy. As well as dramas and comedies, nonfiction "industrials" and news films were screened in the Pacific islands, and local people evinced profound interest in seeing these novel scenes, including views of impressive technology from foreign lands, such as huge locomotives and other machines. People flocked to the cinemas—shows in Tahiti were so popular by 1913 that the authorities kept them closed three nights of the week to avoid cinephilia taking over island life completely.[14] Some accounts—from Guam, for example—report that this love of films even acted as a work incentive, as local people would work longer hours to earn extra money to pay the cinema entrance charges.[15] But on certain islands the colonial authorities considered films that showed fighting and shooting (notably Westerns, one assumes) to be demoralizing for the populations, and by 1914 there was talk of censorship.[16]

Most accounts of South Sea cinema locate the origins of production with Western-made feature-era films such as *Moana* (directed by Robert Flaherty, 1926 [filmed 1923–1924]) and *White Shadows in the South Seas* (directed by W. S. Van Dyke, 1928). Clearly, a great deal of backstory may be added to this conventional historic narrative, and what I have mentioned is a mere lightning sketch of cinematic pioneering in the vast Pacific between the 1890s and early 1920s. Much more remains to be researched, told, and written, using more local material than I personally can ever access.[17] And surely, if we wish to give some kind of complete account of how early cinema in Oceania came about and developed, it would not be out of place to go back even further to the pre-cinema era, for the magic lantern came to the islands decades earlier. For example, there is evidence that the Reverend John Williams of the London Missionary Society projected slides on Samoa in about 1838.[18] That is not film history, but it is surely screen history. Even more relevant to such a complete history of the Pacific screen would be to take into account the rich traditions of storytelling and visual representation within South Sea cultures themselves, which must have influenced indigenous production when it began but also probably influenced how films were received when they were first shown in the 1900s.

STEPHEN BOTTOMORE has worked as Associate Editor of *Film History* and a documentary producer for the BBC. He has directed numerous TV and corporate documentaries worldwide. He is author of many journal articles and two books: *The "Titanic" and Silent Cinema* and *I Want to See This Annie Mattygraph*, a history of early film as seen by magazine cartoonists.

Notes

1. See *Hawaiian Gazette*, July 5, 1898, http://chroniclingamerica.loc.gov/lccn/sn83025121 /1898-07-05/ed-1/seq-7. See also other newspaper articles about Holmes's work in Hawaii in 1898 on the website Chronicling America, at http://chroniclingamerica.loc.gov.

2. Rick Altman, "From Lecturer's Prop to Industrial Product: The Early History of Travel Films," in *Virtual Voyages: Cinema and Travel*, ed. Jeffrey Ruoff (Durham, NC: Duke University Press, 2006), 67; J. S. McQuade, "Chicago Letter," *Moving Picture World*, November 29, 1913, p. 1011.

3. "Bioscope Enterprise," *The Bioscope*, April 29, 1909, p. 21.

4. Patrick O'Reilly, *Les photographes a Tahiti et leurs oeuvres, 1842–1962* [Photographers in Tahiti and their work, 1842–1962] (Paris: Société des océanistes, 1969), 51.

5. "Motion Picture Expedition to Tahiti," *Film Censor*, August 28, 1912, p. 2.

6. Edmund Mitchell, "Filming the South Seas: Adventures of a Motion Camera among Pacific Islands," *Sunset*, November 1913, p. 958.

7. "High Prices to Reduce the Crowds," *Cinema*, June 18, 1914, p. 25.

8. "Moving Pictures in Honolulu," *Dramatic Mirror*, September 5, 1908, p. 8; "Hawaiian Shows," *Film Index*, January 23, 1909, p. 12.

9. Nathaniel Pfeffer, "Honolulu's Garish Night," *Photoplay*, November 1915, p. 147.

10. Ibid.

11. "Oceana [*sic*]," *The Bioscope*, August 19, 1909, p. 35; Stroller [pseud.], "Weekly Notes," *Kinematograph and Lantern Weekly*, September 1, 1910, p. 1065.

12. T. J. West, "Films in Two Hemispheres," *The Bioscope*, November 20, 1913, p. 705.

13. Mason Mitchell, "Samoa," *Daily Consular and Trade Reports*, June 17, 1912, p. 1160.

14. Mitchell, "Filming the South Seas," 958.

15. "The Picture in Guam," *Exhibitors' Times*, July 19, 1913, p. 16.

16. *Exhibitors Overseas Mail*, April 1914, p. 10.

17. A good start is Tony Martin-Jones, "The First Projected Motion Pictures in New Caledonia," 2013, http://www.apex.net.au/~tmj/mp/new-caledonia.htm.

18. Ebenezer Prout, *Memoirs of the Life of the Rev. John Williams, Missionary to Polynesia* (New York: M. W. Dodd, 1843), 362.

16 Early Cinema in Central Asia

The Start of an Ascent

Stephen Bottomore

In writing about the origins of cinema in Central Asia, one is immediately confronted by a question of definition: What is the geographic region "Central Asia"? Which areas are encompassed within it, and which are excluded? A strict definition of Central Asia would include only the "Stans": Kazakhstan, Kirghizstan, Tajikistan, Turkmenistan, and Uzbekistan. But more broadly and historically speaking one could say that Central Asia covers roughly what was formerly known as Turkestan: the territory to the east of the Caspian Sea, west of China, north of India/Pakistan, and south of Russia. In the west that would extend to Afghanistan and parts of Iran, and in the east it would extend to parts of Tibet. Some definitions extend the limits of Central Asia even farther outward.[1]

Given the difficulty in pinning down the geographics of our subject, it seems appropriate that the first documented and verified example of filming that I can find in Central Asia was itself in a borderline part of the region. The photographer and cameraman Vittorio Sella set out in 1909 on an expedition to the Karakoram range on the border of modern Pakistan and Chinese Turkestan. Members of the expedition, led by the Duke of the Abruzzi (1873–1933), a famed mountaineer, managed to climb partway up two mountains, K2 and Chogolisa, in the process ascending to the highest point ever reached on a climb until then. Sella shot various episodes of the expedition, and his film was later released as *Sul tetto del mondo* (On the roof of the world).[2]

If this in 1909 was indeed the first instance of filming in Central Asia, it is not all that early, compared with filming in other parts of the world. After all, the Lumière cameramen (for instance) had been recording views in other parts of the world since the 1890s. Quite possibly earlier examples than this will be found of filming in Central Asia, as other film historians do more research, but it does seem that developments came relatively late to this region, in film exhibition as well as in production, and one is bound to ask why. I might speculate here and suggest that one reason was sheer remoteness.

As Nick Deocampo has mentioned in his introduction, generally the cinema (and other modern devices and developments) came first to Asia at port cities.

Such developments were then slow to reach inland locations—in an age before air travel—and Central Asia was about as inland as one could get. Most existing writings on the cinema of Central Asia mention little happening on the cinema front until the 1920s and even 1930s, when a few films were made, such as *Grass* (directed by Cooper/Schoedsack, 1924) and *Zemlya Zhazhdyot* (Earth thirsts, directed by Yuli Raizman, 1930), and a few were shown. However, while such very late development was the general rule in Central Asia, there were a few earlier stirrings, on both the production and exhibition sides, and I have managed to find some instances of this "precocious" experience of cinema for three countries in the region: Afghanistan, Tibet, and Uzbekistan.

Afghanistan

It is now a well-known fact that cinema came to a number of countries in the world through the influence of their absolute rulers. As Anchalee Chaiworaporn mentions in chapter 13, that was true of Siam, and as I have myself described, it was true of several other states in Asia, Europe, and elsewhere.[3] Something of this sort happened in the mountainous state of Afghanistan, as the ameer (or amir) of Afghanistan developed a considerable interest in cinema.

The Afghan amirs of the late nineteenth and early twentieth centuries are better known for their involvement in stills photography than in film. This interest began in the reign of Abdur Rahman (amir from 1880 to 1901),[4] though photography really blossomed during the reigns of Abdur Rahman's son Habibullah (amir from 1901 to 1919) and grandson Enayatullah (amir briefly in 1929), both of whom were unrelenting modernizers. These two rulers were true enthusiasts for the camera and took many photographs, especially of court life, which remain to posterity as a vivid record of their country in the period up to the 1920s.[5]

Cinema was a development of photography, and this medium, too, was introduced to Afghanistan by the ruling family at the start of the twentieth century. The first report about the new moving pictures in the country came in an article about Kabul by a European woman resident of the city. She described the Afghans' skill in handiwork and their interest in foreign (especially British) fashion and novelties, noting, "The Afghans would take a fancy to the most extraordinary things. One of the late Amir's agents took a cinematograph to Kabul, which greatly amused the people."[6] Note that her exact words are "the late Amir," so this must refer to Amir Rahman, who died in 1901; therefore, either she means a cinema show was given in Afghanistan before 1901, or she is mistaking it for a magic lantern show (for we know that missionaries were projecting lantern slides in Afghanistan by the mid-1890s).[7] Thus, there is a possibility that films were actually shown in the country by around the turn of the century.

However, it was under the following amir that cinema projection became solidly established in Afghanistan. Amir Habibullah was a man with many interests, enthusiasms, and hobbies, from gardening to collecting cars, as well as the aforementioned photography; he employed several foreign experts in his court to help develop such activities, including a British engineer, Frank Martin.[8] A film trade journal reported at the start of 1905 that

> Mr. Martin, the Ameer's engineer-in-chief, had a cinematograph sent up from India, and after getting it into working order, presented it to the Ameer, who duly commanded Mr. Martin and Mrs. Daly to appear before him and to give him an exhibition. The Ameer, who was delighted with his new possession, said: "the magic lantern cannot be compared with it, as the cinematograph shows things alive."[9]

This film projector, which had been ordered from Gaumont in London,[10] became a favorite device of Amir Habibullah, and he started to operate it himself quite regularly. In early 1907 the *Illustrated London News* published a double-page illustrated spread on the amir, lauding his efforts to educate and uplift his country and including an evocative image of him projecting a film to an audience of his courtiers. The caption stated that he showed and commented on selected films "to instruct the Court regarding the world beyond his own borders."[11]

Later that year the amir was himself filmed during a visit to India, and on April 12 the resulting views were shown at the Corinthian Theatre in Calcutta. These were described as the "Visit to Calcutta by the Amir of Kabul" and consisted of two scenes: "Procession from Howrah to Alipore" and "At Chowringhee—Passing in a Motor Car."[12] Curiously, apart from very vague indications,[13] I have found little else about early cinema in Afghanistan. Perhaps there were examples of cameramen coming to the country to film local scenery and life; perhaps isolated screenings were arranged for the local population. Only further research will tell.

Uzbekistan

My information regarding cinema in Uzbekistan and its architecturally famous city of Bukhara, is somewhat broader than for Afghanistan, though sometimes frustratingly vague and unsubstantiated. According to one writer, films began being produced in the country "almost as soon as cinematography was invented." This author states that a pioneer of Uzbek cinema, Hudaibergen Divanov (1879–?) made the first documentary film in Khorezm, Uzbekistan, as early as the spring of 1900.[14] But according to a history of photography in Uzbekistan, Hudaibergen did not begin his film activities that early, and this source tells us more about him.

Hudaibergen was the clever son of an employee of the ruler of the country, Khan Muhammad Rakhim II. Hudaibergen's interest in imaging began with stills (in about 1903), and he was helped in his burgeoning interest by a local German photographer. He soon ran into opposition from Muslim clerics who believed that to make images of human beings was a sin, but relief came when he was offered support by Khan Muhammad. When in 1907 the khan made an official visit to Saint Petersburg in Russia, Hudaibergen was taken along to record this event. He was allowed to stay in the Russian city for two months to study photographic art, and while there, he bought a gramophone and new stills cameras, as well as—and here Uzbek cinema begins—a Pathé ("Pate") Cinematograph.[15] However, it is not clear from the minimal information given whether this was a projector or a camera. Quite possibly it was a camera, because Hudaibergen later became the first Uzbek cameraman at the first Uzbek film studio. If so, he might have been the first person to film in Central Asia, beating Sella.

The example of Hudaibergen offers another instance of cinema arriving in a country through the patronage of a powerful ruler, in this case Khan Muhammad. But subsequent cinematic developments in Uzbekistan seem to have been through more regular commercial channels, and some details of these developments were reported in the press of Western countries. There is, for example, the case of a German named von Papen who demonstrated a phonograph in Bukhara in 1910 and found that it was a considerable attraction. Perhaps buoyed by this experience, he then moved on to moving images, and during a spring festival at the end of March presented an hour-long program of films in a big tent or awning. The films in question—as he reported to a German film trade journal— were mainly French and German reels: magic or trick films, French riding scenes, even daily life in Arabia. He noted that local people watched these films open-mouthed and with "close attention."[16]

Just four years later it seems that cinema had become established in Bukhara, at least according to a brief mention by a writer in the London *Times*. The *Times* man was not happy at this development, however, and decried the arrival in the ancient Muslim city of this newfangled device, as well as other modern technological developments: "Singer's sewing machines are, of course, installed—they are in every town in the wide world. The cinema also has come, and a green poster announces that the Tango will be shown after the presentation of a striking comedy called *The Suffragette*."[17] The latter title was probably the 1913 film starring Asta Nielsen. This would have been an extraordinary choice of film to be screened in such a part of the world, where women's voting rights were not even on the agenda, and the tango film almost equally provocative, this being a dance associated with free-and-easy Western countries. Whether or not these films really were shown (and one should not necessarily believe a technophobe newspaper reporter), cinema did not disappear from Bukhara. Proof of that came in an article published in *National Geographic* magazine in 1918. Noting that Bukhara was still very devout (there were some 364 mosques in the city), the magazine reproduced a photograph showing a group of religious fakirs, and this image also shows—plastered on the wall to the side of the fakirs—a number of posters announcing the latest "movie," as the magazine caption states. The article implies that the Russian influence was strong in the region, and that would seem to be confirmed by the fact that lettering on the posters is in Russian.[18] Uzbekistan came further under the Russian/Soviet influence during this period, and the first feature films were made with the help of Russian technicians during the second half of the 1920s, soon after the formation of the Uzbek SSR (Soviet republic).[19]

Tibet

While cinema was slow to come to Uzbekistan and Afghanistan, it was even slower to penetrate the Tibetan plateau, hidden behind the world's highest mountain ranges. It is perhaps not surprising then that my first example of Tibet "encountering" the cinema comes from just outside the country.

At the end of February 1910 the Grand Lama of Tibet (Dalai Lama) was deposed after the Chinese invaded his country. Forced to flee, he headed across the border to northeastern India and made for the town of Darjeeling.[20] He arrived there on the afternoon of March 1, and the British newspaper *Daily Chronicle* reported that he and his group arrived in a "gorgeous procession, in which the Tibetan community and local Buddhists took part," adding that "the route was lined with photographers and cinematograph operators."[21] A further report confirms that there really were several film cameramen there: "A large number of Bioscope operators were present at the state entry of the Grand Lama into Darjeeling and secured pictures of a quaint and interesting ceremony."[22]

One of the cameramen who aimed his Bioscope at the Dalai Lama that day in Darjeeling was working for the Charles Urban company, and the following month Urban released the result: a film in eight scenes or shots titled *Arrival of the Dalai Lama at Darjeeling.* One trade writer noted that this was a "unique" film of the supreme head of the Buddhist religion and added that it "forms a very impressive spectacle."[23] Unfortunately the film does not seem to survive, though if ever found, it would be an important historical document, marking a significant moment in the increasing domination of Tibet by China throughout the twentieth century. After his escape from his own country to India, the Dalai Lama went to Calcutta on a sightseeing trip and, while in the city, "thoroughly enjoyed a visit to a bioscope exhibition."[24]

Just a year after these events, it seems that some film was actually shot within Tibet itself "to show the work done by missionaries in Thibet [*sic*]"; the footage was screened by a church in Illinois.[25] Then in 1913 the people of Tibet had a chance to see moving pictures for themselves. A German correspondent reported that a film distribution company run by Tibetans had been set up in northern

India, at Kalimpong, a short distance from Darjeeling and the Tibet border. The company had obtained film prints of the Delhi durbar (celebrating the coronation of George V), British military maneuvers, and London street scenes: their first screenings were planned to take place in Gyantse, a town in Tibet with some European inhabitants.[26] The details are vague, but there is an indication that the company then set up a permanent theater in Lhasa. A later report noted that possibly this same company, run by native Tibetans, had purchased a large quantity of European and American films, mostly spectacular subjects and crude comedies.[27] It stated that pictures showing scenes of drinking and fighting were the most popular but added that subjects of a more useful nature had also been purchased: a hope was expressed that moving pictures ought to be a civilizing influence in this "benighted" region.

Because It's There

I began my account of early cinema and Central Asia by discussing Sella's mountaineering film of 1909, and I conclude by mentioning two films of the same kind made in Tibet in the early 1920s. I refer of course to the celebrated features of the 1922 and 1924 Mount Everest expeditions shot by Captain John Noel (1890–1989).[28] *Climbing Mount Everest* and *Epic of Everest* were not the first films made in Tibet, but they were the first feature-length movies made in the country, and in that sense they are significant—significant also in another, very different sense.

Both Sella's and Noel's films were certainly hard-won and admirable records of their respective enterprises and of great interest visually. However, some observers might offer a more cynical judgment on the actual meaning of such motion pictures. Seen from a certain nativist point of view, such films depict the abstruse (and some would even say pointless) activities of rich Westerners in countries they neither know nor understand. Possibly that is an extreme point of view. Nevertheless, even a more temperate observer might admit that such films are examples, and extreme examples indeed, of a certain tendency in the relations between early film and remoter parts of the world.

What is this tendency? In brief one might say that much early filmic activity in the non-Western world was concerned with the interests of the visitors rather than the visited. Films were shot—whether about mountaineering or about other incidents/sights in these countries—by and for the visiting filmmakers. Then in terms of exhibition, it is evident that many films that were chosen to be screened in these countries generally depicted activities—tango dances, London streets— that were irrelevant to the peoples of Central Asia except as curiosities.

But if that is so, does this mean that the Western-oriented history of cinema in this pioneering period (I mean broadly the silent period, up to about 1930) is or should be irrelevant to the film history of these countries themselves? I think otherwise. Whether we or they like it or not, this foreign-induced history did take place in these Asian lands. In some cases there are stirrings of a genuine national consciousness in aspects of this cinematic activity. Details of life in Central Asia and the cultural habits of its peoples were to an extent recorded on celluloid, and there were even instances of Asians deciding to use cinema to advance and promote their own societies: here I refer back to the unlikely case of Amir Habibullah, who projected films to educate and enlighten his countrymen.

A more detailed examination of these issues requires further and deeper research. My account is made up of mere snippets of information that I have been able to gather from mainly Western sources. I suspect that there may be further information on early Asian—notably *Central* Asian—cinema buried in archives and newspapers in these regions. I hope that Asian film historians will in the future (or perhaps it is happening already?) turn their attention to this field and unearth further details. It is, after all, their own history.[29]

STEPHEN BOTTOMORE has worked as Associate Editor of *Film History* and a documentary producer for the BBC. He has directed numerous TV and corporate documentaries worldwide. He is author of many journal articles and two books: *The "Titanic" and Silent Cinema* and *I Want to See This Annie Mattygraph*, a history of early film as seen by magazine cartoonists.

Notes

1. For the various definitions of Central Asia, see "Central Asia," *Wikipedia*, January 23, 2017, http://en.wikipedia.org/wiki/Central_Asia. On the specific case of Tibet, this nation is today (reluctantly) within China and so is thought to be part of East Asia, though historically part or all of Tibet was considered to lie in Central Asia.

2. Piero Zanotto, *Le montagne del cinema* [The mountains of cinema] (Torino: Museo Nazionale della Montagna "Duca degli Abruzzi," 1990).

3. Stephen Bottomore, "'She's Just like My Granny! Where's Her Crown?' Monarchs and Movies, 1896–1916," in *Celebrating 1895: The Centenary of Cinema*, ed. J. Fullerton (Sydney: John Libbey, 1998), 172–181. In some countries such as Morocco and Iran the coming of cinema via a modernizing ruler generated criticism and conflict. See Stephen Bottomore, "The Sultan and the Cinematograph," and Negar Mottahedeh, "Collection and Recollection: On Studying the Early History of Motion Pictures in Iran," in "The Middle East and North Africa," special issue, *Early Popular Visual Culture* 6, no. 2 (2008): 121–144 and 103–120, respectively.

4. However, when this amir came to power, photography was scarcely known in his state, and the population was ignorant and suspicious of this new medium. See Mahomed Khan, *The Life of Abdur Rahman, Amir of Afghanistan* (London: John Murray, 1900), 27.

5. Some of these photographs are held in the Khalilullah Enayat Seraj Collection, Williams Afghan Media Project, Williams College, Massachusetts, and elsewhere.

6. Mrs. Frank Martin, "A Lady at the Court of the Amir," *Wide World Magazine* 8 (February 1902): 575–576.

7. Alice M. Pennell, *Pennell of the Afghan Frontier: The Life of Theodore Leighton Pennell* (London: Seeley Service, 1914), chap. 8.

8. Martin served for eight years under Amir Abdur Rahman and then Amir Habibullah.

9. "The Ameer of Afghanistan and the Cinematograph," *Optical Lantern and Cinematograph Journal*, January 1905, p. 70. I strongly suspect that Habibullah's eldest son, Sardar Enayatullah, who became an enthusiast for photography, was involved in this import of a film projector, for he was in India at about the same time as Martin (he visited India "last cold season," stated a caption in *The Sketch*, October 25, 1905, p. 40). Martin states that Habibullah made his courtiers pay to see one film show. See Frank A. Martin, *Under the Absolute Amir* (London: Harper, 1907), 141.

10. A. C. Bromhead of Gaumont in London stated that he sold the projector to the amir. See "Chats with Trade Leaders," *Optical Lantern and Cinematograph Journal*, February 1905, p. 88.

11. "The Progressive Amir," *Illustrated London News*, January 26, 1907, p. 140.

12. Probhat Mukherjee, *Hiralal Sen: India's First Film-Maker* (Calcutta: Cine Central, 1966), 43.

13. For example, a brief note about "operators for cinema shows" in Afghanistan appears in "Du côté des Afghans" [On the Afghans], *Cine Journal*, June 8, 1912, pp. 49–51.

14. Vladimir Mesamed, "Uzbek Cinema: A Slow Revival," *Central Asia and the Caucasus* 5 (2004), http://www.ca-c.org/journal/2004/journal_eng/cac-05/22.meseng.shtml. Mesamed transliterates Hudaibergen's name as "Khudoibergan" (and later Hudaibergen had "Devanov" or "Divanov" added to his name as an honorific).

15. Tashkent House of Photography, *125 Years of Uzbek Photography*, vol. 1, *The World Sees Us—We See the World, 1879–1940* (Tashkent, Uzbekistan: Tashkent House of Photography, 2002).

16. F. von Papen, "Phonograph und Kinematograph in Buchara [*sic*]," *Der Kinematograph* [The Cinematograph], June 8, 1910. This was probably Ferdinand Graudenz von Papen (1876–?), known as Dr. F. von Papen, author of a 1905 dissertation and a 1921 work on the foreign legion (both published in Berlin). It is presumably not Franz von Papen (1879–1969), vice chancellor (1933–1934) under Adolf Hitler.

17. Stephen Graham, "Wonderful Bokhara [*sic*]," *The Times*, June 8, 1914, p. 51.

18. Maynard Owen Williams, "Russia's Orphan Races: Picturesque Peoples Who Cluster on the Southeastern Borderland of the Vast Slav Dominions," *National Geographic*, October 1918, pp. 245–278. One of the titles of the films listed on the posters in the photograph may be *Peter Petrovka*.

19. Mesamed, "Uzbek Cinema."

20. "Tibet, or Thibet," *Encyclopedia Britannica*, http://encyclopedia.jrank.org/THE_TOO /TIBET_or_THIBET.html.

21. "Darjiling, March 1," *Daily Chronicle*, March 3, 1910, p. 1.

22. "Summarising the Story of the World," *The Bioscope*, March 24, 1910, p. 37, quoting the *Daily Chronicle*. All these modern cameras did not please the *Daily Chronicle* writer, and he chose to take a swipe at this newfangled camera technology: "The thought of a bioscope aimed at the Dalai Lama . . . is the last word in the sacrilege which we in these days commit." He goes on in this way (a "violent clashing of the old and the new," etc.) for several sentences. Ibid. A strange reaction, one might think, when here one simply had cameramen recording a world leader arriving in exile after being forced out of his own country (a situation that continues in Tibet to the present day). There were alternative opinions: a trade journal objected to the

Daily Chronicle's aggrieved remarks, arguing that the film cameramen were simply recording a great historic event for the world to see. See *Rinking World and Picture Theatre News*, April 2, 1910, p. 24.

23. An article in 1910 stated that the cameraman was on an extended filming tour of Asia for the Charles Urban company. See *Rinking World and Picture Theatre News*, April 23, 1910, p. 20. I wonder if this is the same cameraman mentioned in a French journal who was touring China, Japan, and Tibet and who made a film about religion in Tibet? See *Cine Journal*, July 30, 1910, p. 27. Other companies were shooting actuality films of Darjeeling around this time: Pathé Frères in 1910 and Edison (probably shot by James Ricalton) in 1912.

24. "Dalai Lama Sees the Bioscope," *The Bioscope*, March 24, 1910, p. 11.

25. "Missionary Work Shown by Films," *Moving Picture World*, February 25, 1911, p. 418.

26. "Kinos in Tibet," *Der Kinematograph*, August 13, 1913. Gyantse is southwest of Lhasa, halfway to Mount Everest and the Nepal/India border.

27. *Pathe Cinema Journal*, October 11, 1913, p. 68; "Facts and Comments," *Moving Picture World*, September 20, 1913, p. 1259.

28. Kevin Brownlow, *The War, the West and the Wilderness* (London: Secker and Warburg, 1978), 452–464. See also David L. Clark, "Capt. Noel's 1922 Conquest of Everest," *American Cinematographer* 71 (August 1990): 36–40. For information about the 1924 expedition film, see Peter H. Hansen, "The Dancing Lamas of Everest: Cinema, Orientalism, and Anglo-Tibetan Relations in the 1920s," *American Historical Review* 101, no. 3 (1996): 712–747.

29. Since I wrote this article, a book has been published with some brief references (previously unknown to me) about early screening and production of films in Central Asia. See Michael Rouland, Gulnara Abikeyeva, and Birgit Beumers, eds., *Cinema in Central Asia: Rewriting Cultural Histories* (London: I. B. Tauris, 2013), 3.

Appendix: Chronology of Film Beginnings in Asia

Nick Deocampo

December 27, 1895, Calcutta, India	The *Englishman* newspaper reports that an entertainer named "Dr. Harley" shows films in a Kinetophone machine (Edison's Peepshow Kinetoscope plus phonograph) at Bevan's music warehouse. This is an individual viewing made through a peepshow machine, not projected.[1]
July 7, 1896, Bombay, India	Maurice Sestier (cameraman and operator for Lumière brothers) holds a pioneering exhibition using a Cinématographe at Watson's Hotel, including titles like *Arrive d'un train a la Gare de la Ciotat* (The arrival of a train at the Ciotat Station) and *La sortie de l'usine* (Workers leaving the factory). This is the first projected motion picture show here and possibly in all of Asia.[2]
December 30, 1896, Indochina	Lumière camera operator François-Constant Girel shoots *Coolies in Saigon* during a brief stopover on the way from France to Japan; this is possibly the first known film footage ever taken in Asia.[3] No account of Girel showing motion pictures exists.
Late 1896, Kobe, Japan	Motion pictures are publicly shown using Edison's peepshow machine, the Kinetoscope, but there are still no projected moving pictures.[4]
January 1, 1897, Manila, Philippines	Spanish photographer and businessman Francisco Pertierra inaugurates first film show, *Espectaculo cientifico de Pertierra* (Pertierra's scientific spectacle), using a chronophotography device projecting moving pictures on a screen at no. 12, Escolta, Manila.[5]
January 1897, India	James B. Stewart's Vitagraph program shows at Gaiety Theater.[6]

February 15–28, 1897, Osaka, Japan	Katsutaro Inabata arrives in Kobe (February 9) with a Cinématographe device. On hand is Lumière operator François-Constant Girel, who helps him mount the first projected film exhibitions at Osaka's Nanchi Theater (Nanchi-enbujo).[7]
February 21, 1897, Osaka, Japan	Kazuichi Araki uses imported Vitascope to show films at Shinmachi-enbujo.[8]
February 27, 1897, Tokyo, Japan	Arai Shokai uses imported Vitascope to show films at Kabuki-za in Tokyo; another screening starts at Kinkikan Theater on March 6.[9]
March 1897, Batavia (now Jakarta) and Dutch East Indies (now Indonesia)	The Dutch introduce the first film screenings, followed by shows in various parts of the archipelago.[10]
May 22, 1897, Shanghai, China	Film is exhibited to foreign viewers.[11]
May 1897, Singapore	First screenings are presented using the Ripograph projector.[12]
June 4, 1897, Shanghai, China	Films are shown to Chinese audience with a mix of foreigners, followed in July by a film show by American showman James Ricalton.[13]
June 10, 1897, Bangkok, Siam (now Thailand)	S. G. Marchovsky, itinerant showman of unknown nationality, introduces motion pictures at Mon Chaow Alangkan Theater.[14]
August 2, 1897, Singapore	A Mr. Paul holds a Cinématographe screening at the Alhambra.[15]
August 29, 1897, Manila, Philippines	Cinématographe screenings commence with film shows at no. 31, Escolta, managed by Swiss partners Leibman and Peritz, although the actual operator is Spanish soldier-turned-businessman Antonio Ramos. He leaves Manila for China after the outbreak of the Philippine-American War in 1899 and then settles in Shanghai, where his film business prospers.[16]
September–October 1897, Japan	Lumière cameraman François-Constant Girel shoots the first moving pictures in Japan.[17]
November 27, 1897, Kuala Lumpur	The screening at the Selangor Club uses the Edison Projectoscope.[18]

1897, Seoul, Choson (now Korea)	Moving-picture shows are presented at Bongchungjwa, followed by screenings in 1898 at Chunggukin Ch'angko (Chinese Warehouse), located in Namdaemun, Seoul. They may have been private exhibitions because the first public screening does not occur until 1903.[19]
1897, India	Harishchandra Sakharam Bhatvadekar shoots his first footage about a wrestling match at Bombay's Hanging Gardens, followed by footage about a man training circus monkeys; he is possibly the first Asian to shoot films.[20] Unnamed European filmmakers shoot films such as *Our Indian Empire: Delhi, the Rome of Asia* and *Lucknow: Great Inambra Palace.*[21]
Early 1898, Tokyo, Japan	Shiro Asano films geishas in Shinbashi and, together with Bhatvadekar, becomes possibly among the first Asians to shoot film.
February 15, 1898	The Spanish-American War breaks out, and films made about war spike, especially as the war reaches the Philippine Islands.
February 24, 1898, Yokohama, Japan	Edison cameramen James Henry White and Frederick Blechynden arrive and take a shot of coal being loaded onto the SS *Coptic.*[22]
March 7–31, 1898, China	White and Blechynden shoot films in Hong Kong, Macao, Canton, and Shanghai.[23]
April 10–12, 1898, Japan	White and Blechynden shoot films in Nagasaki and Yokohama.[24]
April 1898, Tokyo, Japan	Tsunekichi Shibata shoots actualities in Tokyo streets; he is possibly among the first Asians to shoot film.[25]
May 1, 1898, Manila, Philippines	The Battle of Manila Bay takes place, and films about the American naval fleet defeating the Spanish fleet are made in the United States and France.[26]
May 10, 1898, Hawaii	White and Blechynden shoot films in Hawaii on their way back to the United States.[27]
May 1898, Vietnam	Lumière operator Gabriel Veyre shows films in Hanoi, Vietnam, at the Cercle de l'Union on May 6, 1899.[28]
1898, India	Bengali Hiralal Sen shoots *Dancing Scenes from the Flowers of Persia.*[29]

October 1898–March 1899, Japan	Lumière cameraman Gabriel Veyre shoots Japanese views.[30]
April 1899, Indochina	Paul Doumer, governor-general of Indochina, commissions Lumière cameraman Gabriel Veyre to make five hundred films for the Paris Exposition Universelle.[31]
June 1899, Philippines	E. Burton Holmes visits the Philippines and becomes the first recorded filmmaker to shoot film there.[32]
September 30, 1899, Philippines	C. Fred Ackerman of American Mutoscope and Biograph Company arrives in Manila, embeds himself with US Army as correspondent for *Leslie's Weekly*, and films local views and US soldiers involved in the Philippine-American War. He leaves in March 1900 and goes to China to shoot newsreels.[33]
September 1899, Formosa (Taiwan)	Claims of film screening in this Japanese-colonized island are said to have been made using Edison's Vitascope. The Cinématographe was introduced in 1900.[34]
November 1899, Japan	Working for Konishi company, Tsunekichi Shibata shoots *Momijigari* (Viewing scarlet maple leaves), a scene from a Noh play, outside a teahouse behind the Kabuki-za theater.[35]
1899, Japan	The Arai Shokai trading company invites American projectionist Daniel Krouse to screen films using Edison's Vitascope following earlier similar screenings.[36]
1899, Japan	Shiro Asano begins making his first films such as *Inazuma goto hobaku no ba* (Scene of the lightning robber being arrested).[37]
August 18, 1900, Belgium	Mirza Ebrahim Khan Akkas Bashi films the Persian monarch Mozaffar al-Din Shah during his first visit in Europe.[38]
1900, Tabriz, Persia (now Iran)	Catholic missionaries open Iran's first public cinema, Soleil.[39]
1900, Bangkok, Thailand	Prince Sanbhassatra shoots films in the royal court of King Chulalongkorn (King Rama V), becoming the first Thai filmmaker.[40]
1900, Khorezm, Uzbekistan	Pioneer Uzbek filmmaker Hudaibergen Divanov reportedly makes the first documentary film as early as the spring of 1900.[41]

1900, India	F. B. Thanawala makes two films: *Splendid New View of Bombay* and *Taboot Procession*.[42]
January 16, 1901, Hong Kong	Xilaiyuan, China's first movie house, is built.[43]
November 1901, Taiwan	Japanese film promoter Toyoziro Takamatsu introduces motion pictures and builds the first movie house in Taiwan.[44]
1901, Ceylon (now Sri Lanka)	Film is said to have been first screened to Boer War prisoners detained at Diyatalawa, a tea plantation.[45]
1902, Manila, Philippines	A British national named Mr. Walgrah is the first to screen motion pictures inside a legitimate theater, starting with *Cinematógrafo electrico luminoso Walgrah* (Walgrah's electric light Cinematograph).[46] Earlier films in Manila were shown inside living rooms or tents.
1902, Sugbu (now Cebu), Philippines	Pedro Alario, perhaps an assistant to Mr. Walgrah, mounts a film show titled *Cinematógrafo electro-optico luminoso Walgrah* (Walgrah's electro-optical Cinematograph), featuring films screened inside a warehouse on Magallanes Street.[47]
1902, Afghanistan	The first reported screening occurs in Kabul.[48]
June 23, 1903, Seoul, Korea	The first public film screening is held at Hansong Chonki Hoesa Kigyechang (Hansong Electric Company Machine Warehouse) in Dongdaemun, Seoul.[49]
1903, Colombo, Sri Lanka	The first movie hall is set up.[50]
1903, Samoa	American travelogue lecturer Edward B. McDowell films in this Pacific island and in Fiji the following year.[51]
1903, Japan	The first permanently constructed movie theater, the Denki-kan (Electric Theater), is established in famous Asakusa Prefecture in Tokyo's entertainment district.[52]
1903, Shanghai, China	Spaniard Antonio Ramos, having left the Philippines, starts exhibiting films at Ching-Lin-Ko teahouse.[53] His business eventually expands into a huge enterprise.
1904, Tehran, Iran	The first public screening takes place in Tehran. Mirza Ebrahim Khan Sahaf Bashi holds screenings at the back of his antiques shop.[54]

1904–1905, Japan	Japanese documentaries are produced that cover the Russo-Japanese War.[55]
1905, Peking (now Beijing), China	Considered China's first silent film, *Conquering Jun Mountain* is made, and photographer Ren Qingtai directs the film.[56] He is also known as the builder of Peking's first film theater, the Daguanlou Motion Picture Theater.
1905, Tehran, Iran	Sahaf Bashi opens the first movie theater in Cheragh Gaz Avenue in Tehran.[57]
1905, India	Theater manager Jamshedji Framji Madan establishes Elphinstone Bioscope Company, which later dominates India's film production.[58]
1905, Bangkok, Thailand	Thailand's first permanent film theater, the Japanese Cinematograph, is built by Japanese Tomoyori Watanabe.[59]
1907, India	India's first permanent movie palace, the Elphinstone Picture Palace owned by J. F. Madan, opens.[60]
1907 Solomons, Pacific islands	Cameraman Leopold Sutto shoots films for Pathé.[61]
December 1908, Shanghai, China	Antonio Ramos builds his first formal movie house, the Hongkuo Motion Picture Theater. Although mistakenly regarded as Shanghai's first movie house, it is preceded by two earlier ones—the Huanxian Theater and possibly the Qingliangse Theater, built perhaps in 1907.[62]
1908, Japan	The first film studio begins operation in Japan.[63]
1909, Japan†	*Katsudo shashin kai* (The cinématographe), the oldest-known film magazine in Japan, is published.[64]
1909, Central Asia	Photographer and cameraman Vittorio Sella shoots scenes of a mountain expedition to Karakoram range on the border of modern Pakistan and Chinese Turkestan. It is later released as *Sul tetto del mondo* (On the roof of the world).[65]
July 29, 1910, Manila, Philippines	Manila's first modern movie house, the Majestic, made of concrete and built by American Albert Yearsley, is opened.[66]
1910, Indochina	*Annuaire administratif de l'Indochine, 1910* (Administrative directory of Indochina, 1910) lists Cinématographe Pathé Frères, making it possibly the first permanent movie house in Indochina.[67]

1911, Indonesia	Local film production begins. Dutch filmmakers G. Kruger and F. Carli produce the first documentaries on Indonesia.[68]
August 23, 1912, Manila, Philippines	The Philippines' first feature film, *The Life of Dr. José Rizal*, made by Americans Edward Meyer Gross and Harry Brown, is shown. Fellow American Albert Yearsley rivals the two with a short newsreel, *La vida y muerte de Dr. José Rizal* (The life and death of Dr. José Rizal; sometimes known as *El fusilamiento de Dr. Jose Rizal* [The execution of Dr. José Rizal]), shown a day earlier than the Gross-Brown film.[69]
1912, Tahiti	Local photographer Maxime Bopp du Pont begins making films.[70]
1912, India	India's first feature film, *Pundalik*, is made by Englishman R. G. Torney.[71]
1912, Philippines	A censorship law is passed, and three American-produced films are censored.[72]
1912, Japan	In a move toward business consolidation, Nikkatsu (Nippon Katsudo Sashin) is established from four film companies: Yoshizawa, Yokota, M. Pathé, and Fukuhodo.[73]
1913, India	The first Indian feature film, *Raja Harishchandra* is made, directed by Dhundiraj Govind Phalke.[74]
1913, Tahiti	Gaston Méliès (brother of French film pioneer Georges Méliès) shoots films in Tahiti.[75]
1914–1918	The First World War breaks out and severely affects European global dominance of the film business. Hollywood leads the world film market after the war.[76]
1916, India	The first Tamil-language film, *Keechaka Vadham* (The extermination of Keechaka), based on the epic the *Mahabharata*, is made directed by R. Nataraj Mudaliar.[77]
1917, Manila, Philippines	José Nepomuceno sets up Malayan Movies, signaling the birth of Filipino cinema.[78]
1917, Japan	The first frame-by-frame animation, *Imokawa Mukuzo, genkanban no maki* (The story of the concierge Mukuzo Imokawa), is made, directed by Oten Shimokawa.[79]
1918, India	The Indian government passes the Indian Cinematograph Act of 1918, which makes licensing of cinema compulsory and establishes film censorship.[80]

1918, Philippines	Hollywood's Universal Studios sets up a distribution office in Manila, and other American studios follow.[81]
1919, Manila, Philippines	The first Filipino feature film, *Dalagang Bukid* (Country maiden) is made, directed by José Nepomuceno.[82]
1919, India	Baburao Painter (Baburao K. Mistry) forms Maharashtra Film Company and releases the first significant historical film, *Sinhagadh*, in 1923.[83]
1919, Japan	Norimasa Kaeriyama begins work at Tenkatsu studio (Nikkatsu's rival) and makes *Sei no kogayaki* (The glow of life) and *Miyama no otome* (Maid of the deep mountains) as examples of "pure film," leading to the modernization of Japanese films.[84]
1921, China	The first docu-drama, *Yan Ruisheng*, is shot in China, produced by China Film Research Society.[85]
1921, India	*England Returned*, a well-known satirical film, is made, directed by Dhiren Ganguly (popularly known as D.G.).[86]
1922, Cebu, Philippines	The first Cebuano feature-length film, *El hijo disobediente* (The disobedient son) is made, directed by Florentino Borromeo.[87]
1922, Bangkok, Thailand	Royal Thai State Railways produces actualities depicting Thai social life after setting up a film production department, Topical Film Service.[88]
1922, Taiwan	The first indigenous production, *The Eyes of Buddha*, is released, directed by Tanaka King.[89]
1923, Bangkok, Thailand	Thailand's first feature film directed by a foreigner, *Nang Sao Suwan* (Sovarna of Siam) is made, directed by American filmmaker Henry MacRae.[90]
1923, Hong Kong	The first feature-length film is produced in Hong Kong.[91]
1923, Korea	The first Korean feature-length film, *The Plighted Love under the Moon*, directed by Yun Paengnam, is produced.[92]
1924, Vietnam	*Mot dong kem tau duoc ngua* (A penny for a horse) marks the beginning of national cinema in Vietnam; Nguyen Lan Huong (or Huong Ky) directs.[93]
1925, Taiwan	The Taiwan Motion Picture Study Society attempts to become the first film organization to produce native films. Liu Xiyang directs the company's first feature-length venture, *Whose Fault Is This?*[94]

1926, Bandung, Indonesia	The first Indonesian feature film, *Loetoeng Kasaroeng* (The enchanted monkey), is produced by Dutch filmmakers G. Kruger and L. Heuveldorp.[95]
1927, Thailand	The first locally produced Thai film, *Chok Song San*, is released.[96]
1929, Indonesia	The first sound films are screened in Indonesia.[97]
1930, Iran	The first Iranian feature-length film, *Abi va Rabi* (Abi and Rabi) is made, directed by Armenian-Iranian Ovanes Ohanian.[98]
1930, China	China's first sound film, *Genu Hangmudan*, is made.[99]
1931, India	The first Indian sound film, *Alam Ara*, is made.[100]
1932, Manila, Philippines	The first Filipino sound film, *Punyal na Guinto* (Golden dagger) is made, directed by José Nepomuceno.[101]
1932, Thailand	The first Thai sound film, *Long Tong*, is made.[102]
1933, Singapore	The first Malay feature film, *Laila Majnun*, directed by B. S. Rajhans, is produced in Singapore by the Montilal Chemical Company of Bombay.[103]
1933, India/Iran	The first Persian-language sound feature, *Dokhtar-e-Lor* (The Lor girl), codirected by Iranian Ardeshir Irani, is shot in India.[104]
1935, Korea	The first Korean sound film, *The Tale of Chunhyang*, is made, directed by Yi Myongyu.[105]
1936, Sri Lanka	The first Sinhalese silent film, *Pagliaganeema* (Revenge), is made, directed by musician-turned-director W. John Edward.[106]
1937, Indonesia	The first Indonesian sound film, *Terang Bulan* (Full moon), is produced by ANIF (Algemeen Nederlandsch-Indisch Film).[107]
1937–1938, Vietnam	*Canh dong ma* (The haunted field), is made; Vietnamese Tran Phi directs Vietnamese actors, although the film is shot entirely in Hong Kong.[108]
1938, Cebu, Philippines	*Bertoldo-Balodoy*, Cebu's first Visayan-language feature film, is made, directed by Piux Kabahar.[109]
1939, Japan	The Film Law is instituted. All matters related to cinema in Japan are subject to government supervision and control.

1941, Cambodia	King Norodom Sihanouk, considered Cambodia's first filmmaker, makes his first films in 16mm.[110]
1941–1945	World War II breaks out. Japanese military forces occupy Hong Kong, Malaysia, Singapore, Dutch-India (Indonesia), Burma (Myanmar), and the Philippines.
1947, Sri Lanka	The first Sinhala-language feature film, *Kadavunu Poronduva* (Broken promises), is made, directed by B. A. Jayamanne.[111]

Notes

1. "The Wonder of the Age!," *The Englishman*, December 27, 1895, p. 2; see also chapter 14.

2. See Eric Barnouw and S. Krishnaswamy, *Indian Film* (New York: Oxford University Press, 1980); Paul Willemen and Behroze Gandhy, eds., *BFI Dossier, No. 5: Indian Cinema* (London: British Film Institute, 1982); Ashish Rayadhyaksha and Paul Willemen, eds., *Encyclopedia of Indian Cinema* (London: British Film Institute, 1994); Suresh Chabria, ed., *Light of Asia: Indian Silent Cinema, 1912–1934* (New Delhi: Phoenix Computer Center, 1994); K. Moti Gokulsing and Wimal Dissanayake, *Indian Popular Cinema: A Narrative of Cultural Change*, 3rd ed. (London: Trentham Books, 2004); and Yves Thoraval, *The Cinemas of India* (New Delhi: MacMillan India, 2000).

3. Dean Wilson, *Colonial Viet Nam on Film: 1896 to 1926* (New York: City University of New York, 2007); see also chapter 8.

4. National Film Center of Japan museum exhibit on the history of Japanese cinema, 2011.

5. "Fonografo Pertierra/Espectaculo cientifico de Pertierra," *El comercio* [The trade], January 2, 1897; see also Nick Deocampo, *Cine: Spanish Influences on Early Cinema in the Philippines* (Manila: National Commission for Culture and the Arts, 2003).

6. Untitled article, *Times of India*, January 4, 1897.

7. Hiroshi Komatsu, "Le Cinematographe Lumiere et la production du cinema au Japon dans ses premiers temps" [The Lumiere Cinematographe and the production of film in Japan during its early years], in *Lumière! Les frères Lumière et le Japon, 1895–1995* [The Lumière brothers and Japan], ed. Futoshi Koga (Tokyo: Asahi Shimbun, 1995).

8. Ibid.

9. National Film Center of Japan museum exhibit on the history of Japanese cinema, 2011.

10. Untitled article, *Bintang-Barat* [Star-West], March 8, 1897; see also chapter 7.

11. See chapter 3.

12. Untitled article, *Straits Times*, May 12, 1897; see also chapter 7.

13. See chapter 3.

14. Untitled article, *Bangkok Times*, June 11, 1897; see also Dome Sukwong and Sawasdi Suwannapak, *A Century of Thai Cinema* (London: Thames and Hudson, 2001); and chapter 13.

15. Untitled article, *Malay Mail*, August 3, 1897. It is possible that "Mr. Paul" is Robert William Paul, a British inventor and producer, as described in John Barnes, "Robert William Paul," *Who's Who of Victorian Cinema*, http://www.victorian-cinema.net/paul.htm (accessed January 27, 2017). See also chapter 11.

16. Deocampo, *Cine*.

17. See Koga, *Les frères Lumière et le Japon*.

18. Untitled article, *Malay Mail*, November 27, 1897; see also chapter 11.

19. Young-Il Lee, "The Establishment of a National Cinema under Colonialism: The History of Early Korean Cinema," paper presented at the Beginnings and Development of Early Asian Films conference, Second Pusan International Film Festival, October 16, 1997, Pusan, South Korea.

20. There appears to be some confusion about the year Bhatvadekar filmed the wrestling match. While Barnouw and Krishnaswamy put the year as 1897, two other sources provide contradictory dates. Barnouw and Krishnaswamy's date is affirmed in Paul Willemen and Behroze Gandhy, "Scanning Indian Cinema," in Willemen and Gandhy, *BFI Dossier, No. 5*. Rayadhyaksha and Willemen's *Encyclopedia of Indian Cinema* gives the date as 1898.

21. Firoze Rangoonwalla, *A Pictorial History of Indian Cinema* (London: Hamlyn, 1979).

22. Charles Musser, *Edison Motion Pictures, 1890–1900: An Annotated Filmography* (Washington, DC: Smithsonian Institution Press, 1997).

23. Ibid.

24. Ibid.

25. See Koga, *Les frères Lumière et le Japon*.

26. Several filmmakers in the United States and France made films immediately after the Battle of Manila Bay. For information on the film made by J. Stuart Blackton and Albert E. Smith in New York, see Albert E. Smith with Phil A. Koury, *Two Reels and a Crank* (Garden City, NY: Doubleday, 1952), 66–67. For information on Georges Méliès's film shot in Paris, see Roger Boussinot, *L'encyclopedie du cinema* [Encyclopedia of cinema] (Paris: Bordas, 1967), 1045.

27. Musser, *Edison Motion Pictures*.

28. Refer to Pham Ngoc Truong, "A Brief History of Vietnamese Film," in *Film in Southeast Asia: Views from the Region: Essays on Film in Ten South East Asia-Pacific Countries*, ed. David Hanan (Hanoi: SEAPAVAA, Vietnam Film Institute and the National Screen and Sound Archive of Australia, 2001).

29. Yves Thoraval, *The Cinemas of India*.

30. See Koga, *Les frères Lumière et le Japon*.

31. See chapter 8.

32. Burton Holmes, *The Burton Holmes Lectures*, vol. 5 (Battle Creek, MI: Little Preston, 1901).

33. See Nick Deocampo, *Film: American Influences on Philippine Cinema* (Mandaluyong: Anvil, 2011), 97–105.

34. See chapter 5.

35. National Film Center of Japan museum exhibit on the history of Japanese cinema, 2011.

36. Ibid.

37. Koga, *Les frères Lumière et le Japon*.

38. Shahin Parhami, "Iranian Cinema: Before the Revolution," *Offscreen* 3, no. 6 (1999), http://offscreen.com/view/iran2.

39. Hamid Naficy, "Iranian Cinema," in *Life and Art: The New Iranian Cinema*, ed. Rose Issa and Sheila Whitaker (London: National Film Theatre, 1999), 12–24.

40. Sukwong and Suwannapak, *A Century of Thai Cinema*.

41. Vladimir Mesamed, "Uzbek Cinema: A Slow Revival," *Central Asia and the Caucasus* 5 (2004), http://www.ca-c.org/journal/2004/journal_eng/cac-05/22.meseng.shtml; see also chapter 16.

42. See chapter 1.

43. Li Suyuan and Hu Jubin, *Chinese Silent Film History* (Beijing: China Film, 1997).

44. Ibid.

45. Wimal Dissanayake, "Cinema, Nationhood, and Cultural Discourse in Sri Lanka," in *Colonialism and Nationalism in Asian Cinema*, ed. Wimal Dissanayake (Bloomington: Indiana University Press, 1994), 190–201.

46. "Teatro Filipino," *El Comercio*, June 14, 1902. See also Deocampo, *Cine*, 99.

47. Nick Deocampo, *Films from a "Lost" Cinema: A Brief History of Cebuano Films* (Quezon City, Philippines: Mowelfund Film Institute, 2007); see also Resil Mojares, "Resurrecting Visayan Movies," *Sun Star Weekend*, May 21, 1995.

48. Mrs. Frank Martin, "A Lady at the Court of the Amir," *Wide World Magazine* 8 (February 1902): 575–576; see also chapter 16.

49. Lee, "Establishment of a National Cinema under Colonialism."

50. Dissayanake, "Cinema, Nationhood, and Cultural Discourse in Sri Lanka."

51. Rick Altman, "From Lecturer's Prop to Industrial Product: The Early History of Travel Films," in *Virtual Voyages: Cinema and Travel*, ed. Jeffrey Ruoff (Durham, NC: Duke University Press, 2006), 67; J. S. McQuade, "Chicago Letter," *Moving Picture World*, November 29, 1913, p. 1011; see also chapter 15.

52. National Film Center of Japan museum on the history of Japanese cinema, 2011. See also Aaron Gerow, "Japan," in *Encyclopedia of Early Cinema*, ed. Richard Abel (London: Routledge, 2005), 433.

53. Jay Leyda, *Dianying: An Account of Films and the Film Audience in China* (Cambridge, MA: MIT Press, 1972).

54. See chapter 12.

55. National Film Center of Japan museum exhibit on the history of Japanese cinema, 2011.

56. Zhiwei Xiao, "Chinese Cinema," in *Encyclopedia of Chinese Film*, ed. Yingjin Zhang and Zhiwei Xiao (London: Routledge, 1998), 3–30.

57. See chapter 12.

58. See chapter 1.

59. Sukwong and Suwannapak, *A Century of Thai Cinema*.

60. Willemen and Gandhy, *BFI Dossier No.5*.

61. Untitled article, *The Bioscope*, April 29, 1909; see also chapter 15.

62. Antonio Arenas, "Una vida de cine" [A life in movies], *Ideal*, July 16, 1996.

63. National Film Center of Japan museum exhibit on the history of Japanese cinema, 2011.

64. Ibid.

65. Piero Zanotto, *Le montagne del cinema* [The mountain of cinema] (Torino: Museo Nationale della Montagna "Duca degli Abruzzi," 1990); see also chapter 16.

66. Untitled article, *Manila Times*, July 28, 1910; see also Deocampo, *Film*, 219.

67. See chapter 8.

68. H. Misbach Yusa Biran, "The History of Indonesian Cinema at a Glance," in Hanan, *Film in Southeast Asia*, 160–191.

69. Deocampo, *Film*.

70. Patrick O'Reilly, *Les photographes a Tahiti et leurs oeuvres, 1842–1962* [Photographers in Tahiti and their work] (Paris: Société des océanistes, 1969); see also chapter 15.

71. See chapter 1.

72. Jose Marino, "La censura cinematográfica" [Film censorship], *Renacimiento Filipino* [Filipino rebirth], November 1911. Although the film censorship board was formally put in place in 1912, the first moves to set it up on a Manila municipal level started in 1911. See untitled article, *Manila Times*, November 6–7, 1911.

73. National Film Center of Japan museum exhibit on the history of Japanese cinema, 2011.

74. Suresh Chabri, "India," in Abel, *Encyclopedia of Early Cinema*, 318–320.

75. Untitled article, *Film Censor*, August 28, 1912.

76. See Kristin Thompson, *Exporting Entertainment: American in the World Film Market, 1907–1934* (London: British Film Institute, 1985).

77. See chapter 9.

78. Deocampo, *Film*.

79. National Film Center of Japan museum exhibit on the history of Japanese cinema, 2011.

80. See chapter 9.

81. Thompson, *Exporting Entertainment*.

82. Deocampo, *Film*.

83. See chapter 9.

84. National Film Center of Japan museum exhibit on the history of Japanese cinema, 2011.

85. Li and Hu, *Chinese Silent Film History*.

86. See chapter 9.

87. Deocampo, *Films from a "Lost" Cinema*; see also D. M. Estabaya, "First Visayan Movies Recalled," *Republic News*, August 28, 1975.

88. Anchalee Chaiworaporn, "Endearing Afterglow," in *Being and Becoming: The Cinemas of Asia*, ed. Aruna Vasudev, Latika Padgaonkar, and Rashmi Doraiswamy (Delhi: Macmillan India, 2002), 441–461.

89. Li and Hu, *Chinese Silent Film History*.

90. Sukvong and Suwannapak, *A Century of Thai Cinema*.

91. Cheuk-to Li, "Zest and Anguish," in Vasudev, Padgaonkar, and Doraiswamy, *Being and Becoming*, 92–123.

92. Hyae-joon Kim, "The Politics of Memory," in Vasudev, Padgaonkar, and Doraiswamy, *Being and Becoming*, 281–300; see also chapter 1.

93. See chapter 8.

94. Li and Hu, *Chinese Silent Film History*; see also Gene-Fon Liao, "In and Out of Shadows," in Vasudev, Padgaonkar, and Doraiswamy, *Being and Becoming*, 418–440.

95. Marseth Sumarno and Nan Triveni Achnas, "In Two Worlds," in Vasudev, Padgaonkar, and Doraiswamy, *Being and Becoming*, 152–170; see also Biran, "The History of Indonesian Cinema at a Glance."

96. See chapter 1.

97. Harun Suwardi, "Indonesia," in *The Films of ASEAN*, ed. Jose F. Lacaba (Pasig City: ASEAN Committee on Culture and Information, 2000), 15–48.

98. Naficy, "Iranian Cinema"; Houshang Golmakani claims it was in 1929. See Houshang Golmakani, "Stars within Reach," in Vasudev, Padgaonkar, and Doraiswamy, *Being and Becoming*, 186–204.

99. See chapter 1.

100. Ibid.

101. Deocampo, *Cine*; Deocampo, *Film*.

102. See chapter 1.

103. Jade Uhde and Yvonne Ng Uhde, *Latent Images: Film in Singapore* (Oxford: Oxford University Press, 2000); see also Hassan Abdul Muthalib and Wong Tuck Cheong, "Gentle Winds of Change," in Vasudev, Padgaonkar, and Doraiswamy, *Being and Becoming*, 301–328.

104. See chapter 12; see also M. Ali Issari, *Cinema in Iran: 1900–1979* (Metuchen, NJ: Scarecrow, 1989).

105. See chapter 1.

106. Ibid.

107. Ibid.

108. See chapter 8.

109. Deocampo, *Films from a "Lost" Cinema*; see also Estabaya, "First Visayan Movies Recalled."

110. Ingrid Muan and Ly Davaruth, "A Survey of Film in Cambodia," in Hanan, *Film in Southeast Asia*, 71–80.

111. See chapter 1; see also Dissanayake, "Cinema, Nationhood, and Cultural Discourse in Sri Lanka."

Selected Bibliography

Archival Magazine and Newspaper Sources

American Cable News, 1912
Bangkok Times, 1897–1917
Bintang-Barat [Star-West], 1897
The Bioscope, 1909–1916
British Journal of Photography, 1907
Cable News American, 1909–1914
Cebu Chronicle, 1912
Chinese Mail, 1864–1946
Cine Journal, 1910–1912
Cinema (London), 1914
The Citizen, 1919
Daily Chronicle (London), 1910
Daily Consular and Trade Reports (Washington, DC), 1912
De Nieuwe Vorstenlanden [The new frost countries], 1913
Der Eisbar [The polar bear], 1917–1919
Der Kinematograph [The kinematograph], 1910–1913
Dramatic Mirror, 1908
El comercio [The trade], 1897–1902
The Englishman (Calcutta), 1895
Exhibitors Overseas Mail, 1914
Exhibitors' Times (New York), 1913
Film Censor (London), 1912
Filmen [Filmmaking], 1915
Freedom, 1899
Film Index, 1909
Hawaiian Gazette, 1898
Illustrated London News, 1907
The Independent, 1922
Katsudo no sekai [Activity world], 1917–1918
Kinema rekodo [Kinema record], 1915–1916
Kinematograph and Lantern Weekly (London), 1910
Kommersiella Meddelanden [Commercial messages], 1921–1924
La revue du Pacifique [The Pacific review], 1924
La revue indochinoise [The Indochinese review], 1918–1919
Les pages indochinoises [The Indochinese pages], 1925
Los Angeles Times, 1909–1925
Malay Mail, 1897–1915
Manila Times, 1899–1912

Motography, 1911
Moving Picture News, 1912–1913
Moving Picture World, 1910–1919
National Geographic, 1918
New York Clipper, 1899–1900
Nickelodeon, 1911
Optical Lantern and Cinematograph Journal (London), 1905
Pathé Cinema Journal, 1913
Pemberita-Makassar [Makassar reporter], 1914
Perak Pioneer, 1911
Photoplay, 1915
Picture Theatre News, 1910–1911
Rosenstock's Manila City Directory, 1914
Siam Observer, 1913–1914
Straits Times, 1897–1917
Sunset, 1913
Taiwan nichi nichi shinpo [Taiwan daily news], 1899–1935
Taiwan shinmin ho [Taiwan new people's news], 1932
The Times (London), 1914
Utusan Malayu [Malay mercury], 1908
Wide World Magazine, 1902
Xinwen Bao, 1897

Other Sources

Abel, Richard, ed. *Encyclopedia of Early Cinema*. London: Routledge, 2005.
Abel, Richard, Giorgio Bertellini, and Rob King, eds. *Early Cinema and the "National."* Eastleigh, UK: John Libbey, 2008.
Alatas, Syed Hussein. *The Myth of the Lazy Native*. New York: Routledge, 2010.
Amad, Paula. "Cinema's 'Sanctuary': From Pre-documentary to Documentary Film in Albert Kahn's 'Archives de la Planète.'" *Film History* 13 (2001): 138–159.
———. *Counter-archive: Film, the Everyday, and Albert Kahn's "Archives de la Planète."* New York: Columbia University Press, 2010.
Amaury, Lorin. *Paul Doumer, gouverneur general de l'Indochine, 1897–1902* [Paul Doumer, governor-general of Indochina, 1897–1902]. Paris: Harmattan, Bagneux, 2004.
An, Dinh Quang. "Film Publishing in Cinema in Pre-liberated Ha Noi." *Vietnamese Cinematography: A Research Journey*, by Xuan Lam and Dao Xuan Chuc (Hanoi: Gioi, 2007), 94–99.
Anderson, Benedict. *Imagined Communities: Reflections on the Origin and Spread of Nationalism*. London: Verso, 1983.
Annuaire administratif de l'Indochine, 1905 [Administrative directory of Indochina, 1905]. Hanoi: Imprimerie d'Extreme-Orient, 1905.
Annuaire administratif de l'Indochine, 1908 [Administrative directory of Indochina, 1908]. Hanoi: Imprimerie d'Extreme-Orient, 1908.

Annuaire administratif de l'Indochine, 1910 [Administrative directory of Indochina, 1910]. Hanoi: Imprimerie d'Extreme-Orient, 1910.

Annuaire administratif de l'Indochine, 1916 [Administrative directory of Indochina, 1916]. Hanoi: Imprimerie d'Extreme-Orient, 1916.

Annuaire administratif de l'Indochine, 1924 [Administrative directory of Indochina, 1924]. Hanoi: Imprimerie d'Extreme-Orient, 1924.

Annuaire administratif de l'Indochine, 1925 [Administrative directory of Indochina, 1925]. Hanoi: Imprimerie d'Extreme-Orient, 1925.

Appadurai, Arjun. *Modernity at Large: Cultural Dimensions of Globalization.* Minneapolis: University of Minnesota Press, 1997.

Aubert, Michelle, and Jean-Claude Seguin, eds. *La production cinématographique des frères Lumière* [The cinematographic production of the Lumière brothers]. Paris: Centre national de la cinématographie, Bibliothèque du Film, 1996.

Barnes, John. *The Beginnings of the Cinema in England.* Vol. 1. London: David and Charles, 1976.

Barnouw, Erik. *Documentary: A History of the Non-fiction Film.* Oxford: Oxford University Press, 1974.

Barnouw, Erik, and S. Krishnaswamy. *Indian Film.* New York: Oxford University Press, 1980.

Bean, Jennifer, and Diane Negra, eds. *Feminist Reader in Early Cinema.* Durham, NC: Duke University Press, 2002.

Beng, Tan Sooi. *Bangsawan: A Social and Stylistic History of Popular Malay Opera.* Singapore: Oxford University Press, 1993.

Bhabha, Homi. *Nation and Narration.* London: Routledge, 1990.

Bloom, Peter J. *French Colonial Documentary: Mythologies of Humanitarianism.* Minneapolis: University of Minnesota Press, 2008.

Blum-Reid, Sylvie. *East-West Encounters: Franco-Asian Cinema and Literature.* London: Wallflower, 2003.

Bordwell, David, Janet Staiger, and Kristin Thompson. *The Classical Hollywood Cinema: Film Style and Mode of Production to 1960.* New York: Columbia University Press, 1988.

Bordwell, David, and Kristin Thompson. *Film History: An Introduction.* New York: McGraw-Hill, 1994.

Borthwick, Mark. *Pacific Century: The Emergence of Modern Pacific Asia.* Boulder, CO: Westview Press, 2007.

Bottomore, Stephen. "A 'Kinetescope' in the Last Cold Weather." *Osian's Cinefan Festival Daily,* July 24, 2007.

———. "The Sultan and the Cinematograph." In "The Middle East and North Africa," special issue, *Early Popular Visual Culture* 6, no. 2 (2008): 121–144.

Bowser, Pearl, Jane Gaines, and Charles Musser, eds. *Oscar Micheaux and His Circle: African American Filmmaking and Race Cinema of the Silent Era.* Bloomington: Indiana University Press, 2001.

Brocheux, Pierre, and Daniel Hemery. *Indochina: An Ambiguous Colonization, 1858–1954.* Berkeley: University of California Press, 2009.

Brownlow, Kevin. *The War, the West and the Wilderness.* London: Secker and Warburg, 1978.

Castro, Teresa. "*Les Archives de la Planète*: A Cinematographic Atlas." *Jump Cut* 48 (2006). http://www.ejumpcut.org/archive/jc48.2006/KahnAtlas.

Chabria, Suresh, ed. *Light of Asia: Indian Silent Cinema, 1912–1934*. New Delhi: Phoenix Computer Center, 1994.

Chaiworaporn, Anchalee. "Who Is S. G. Marchovsky?" *The Nation*, January 24, 1997.

Chandler, David. Review of *Indochina: An Ambiguous Colonization, 1858–1954*, by Pierre Brocheux. *Contemporary Southeast Asia: A Journal of International and Strategic Affairs* 32, no. 2 (2010): 302–304.

———. *The Tragedy of Cambodian History: Politics, War and Revolution*. New Haven, CT: Yale University Press, 1991.

Chatterjee, Partha. *Nationalist Thought and the Colonial World: A Derivative Discourse*. London: Zed Books, 1986.

Chou, Cynthia, and Vincent Houben, eds. *Southeast Asian Studies: Debates and New Directions*. Singapore: Institute of Southeast Asian Studies/International Institute for Asian Studies, 2006.

Ciecko, Annie Tereska, ed. *Contemporary Asian Cinema*. Oxford, UK: Berg, 2006.

Clark, David L. "Capt. Noel's 1922 Conquest of Everest." *American Cinematographer* 71 (August 1990): 36–40.

Close, Upton. *The Revolt of Asia: The End of the White Man's Dominance*. New York: G. P. Putnam's Sons, 1927.

Coote, Philip C. *Peeps at Many Lands: The Malay States*. London: A. and C. Black, 1923.

Craig, Austin. *Lineage, Life and Labors of Jose Rizal, Philippine Patriot*. Manila: Philippine Education, 1913.

Currell, David. *Shadow Puppets and Shadow Play*. Ramsbury, UK: Crowood, 2008.

Del Mundo, Clodualdo A. *Native Resistance: Philippine Cinema and Colonialism, 1898–1941*. Manila: De La Salle University Press, 1998.

Deocampo, Nick. *Cine: Spanish Influences on Early Cinema in the Philippines*. Manila: National Commission for Culture and the Arts, 2003.

———. *Film: American Influences on Philippine Cinema*. Mandaluyong: Anvil, 2011.

———, ed. *Lost Films of Asia*. Manila: Anvil, 2006.

Dhiravegin, Likhit. *The Evolution of Thai Politics and Government*. 2nd ed. Bangkok: Thammasat University Press, 1990.

Dissanayake, Wimal, ed. *Colonialism and Nationalism in Asian Cinema*. Bloomington: Indiana University Press, 1994.

Dissanayake, Wimal, and Ashley Ratnavibhushana. *Profiling Sri Lankan Cinema*. Colombo, Sri Lanka: Asian Film Center, 2000.

Dome Sukvong. *King Prachadhipok and Cinema* [in Thai]. Bangkok: Ton-or Grammy, 1996.

Duras, Marguerite. *L'amant de la Chine du Nord* [The lover of North China]. Paris: Gallimard, 1991.

———. *L'Eden cinema* [Cinema Eden]. Paris: Mercure de France, 1977.

———. *Un barrage contre le Pacifique* [The sea wall]. Paris: Livre de Poche, 1968.

Elsaesser, Thomas, ed. *Early Cinema: Space, Frame, Narrative*. London: British Film Institute, 1990.

Engberg, Marguerite. *Dansk Stumfilm: De Store Ar* [Danish silent film: The great year]. Copenhagen: Rhodos, 1977.

Erichsen, Chr. *Siam som Handelsland og "Det Ostasiatiske Kompagni"* [Siam as a trading country and "The East Asian Kompagni"].Copenhagen: H. Hagerups Forlag, 1900.

Featherstone, Mike, Scott Lash, and Roland Robertson, eds. *Global Modernities.* London: Sage, 1995.

Fell, John, ed. *Film before Griffith.* Berkeley: University of California Press, 1984.

Fell, John, Jay Leyda, Neil Harris, Richard Koszarski, Stephen Gong, and Charles Musser. *Before Hollywood: Turn-of-the-Century American Film.* New York: Hudson Hills, 1987.

Fernandez, Doreen G. *Palabas: Essays on Philippine Theater History.* Quezon City, Philippines: Ateneo de Manila University Press, 1996.

Fullerton, John, ed. *Celebrating 1895: The Centenary of Cinema.* Sydney: John Libbey, 1998.

Gaines, Jane, and Radha Vatsal, eds. *Women Film Pioneers Sourcebook.* Vol. 1. Champaign: University of Illinois Press, forthcoming.

Gaudreault, André, and Tim Barnard. *Film and Attraction: From Kinematography to Cinema.* Urbana: University of Illinois Press, 2011.

Gaudreault, André, Catherine Russell, and Pierre Véronneau, eds. *Le Cinématographe, nouvelle technologie du XXe siècle* [The Cinematographe, new technology of the 20th century]. Lausanne, Switzerland: Payot, 2004.

Gellner, Ernest. *Nations and Nationalism.* Oxford, UK: Basil Blackwell, 1983.

Gerow, Aaron. "Writing a Pure Cinema: Articulations of Early Japanese Film." PhD diss., University of Iowa, 1996.

Giddens, Anthony. *The Nation-State and Violence.* Cambridge: Cambridge University Press, 1985.

Gokulsing, K. Moti, and Wimal Dissanayake. *Indian Popular Cinema: A Narrative of Cultural Change.* 3rd ed. London: Trentham Books, 2004.

Goulmakani, Houshang. "New Times, New Perceptions." *Cinemaya*, no. 4 (1989): 22.

Gunning, Tom. "The Cinema of Attraction(s)." *Wide Angle* 8, no. 3–4 (1986): 63–70.

Habermas, Jurgen. *The Structural Transformation of the Public Sphere.* Cambridge, MA: MIT Press, 1992.

Hammond, Paul. *Marvellous Méliès.* New York: St. Martin's Press, 1975.

Hanan, David, ed. *Film in South East Asia, Views from the Region: Essays on Film in Ten South East Asia-Pacific Countries.* Hanoi: SEAPAVAA, Vietnam Film Institute, and National Film and Sound Archive of Australia, 2001.

Hansen, Miriam. *Babel and Babylon: Spectatorship in American Silent Film.* Cambridge, MA: Harvard University Press, 1991.

———. "Early Cinema, Late Cinema: Permutations of the Public Sphere." *Screen* 34 (Autumn 1993): 197–210.

Hansen, Peter H. "The Dancing Lamas of Everest: Cinema, Orientalism, and Anglo-Tibetan Relations in the 1920s." *American Historical Review* 101, no. 3 (1996): 712–747.

Heider, K. G. *Indonesian Cinema: National Culture on Screen.* Honolulu: University of Hawaii Press, 1991.

Hernandez, Tomas. *The Emergence of Modern Drama in the Philippines, 1898–1912.* Honolulu: University of Hawaii Press, 1976.

Hobsbawm, E. J. *Nations and Nationalism since 1780: Program, Myth, Reality.* Cambridge: Cambridge University Press, 1990.

Hu, Jubin. *Projecting a Nation: Chinese National Cinema before 1949.* Hong Kong: Hong Kong University Press, 2003.

Ichikawa, Sai. *Ajia Eiga No Sozo Oyobi Kensetsu* [Creating and developing an Asian cinema]. Tokyo: International Movie News Service, 1941.

Ileto, Reynaldo Clemeña. *Pasyon and Revolution: Popular Movements in the Philippines, 1840–1910.* Quezon City, Philippines: Ateneo de Manila University Press, 1979.

Imamura, Kanae. *Eiga sangyo* [The film industry]. Tokyo: Yuhikaku, 1960.

Issa, Rose, and Sheila Whitaker, eds. *Life and Art: The New Iranian Cinema.* London: National Film Theatre, 1999.

Issari, M. Ali. *Cinema in Iran, 1900–1979.* Metuchen, NJ: Scarecrow, 1989.

Jacquiere, Philippe, and Marion Pranal. *Gabriel Veyre, opérateur Lumière: Autour du monde avec le Cinématographe-Correspondance (1896–1900)* [Gabriel Veyre, Lumière operator: Around the world with the Cinematographe-correspondence (1896–1900)]. Lyon: Institut Lumiere / Actes Sud, 1996.

Jung, Carl G. *Man and His Symbols.* London: Aldus, 1964.

Jung, Uli, and Martin Loiperdinger, eds. *Geschichte des dokumentarischen Films in Deutschland* [History of the documentary film in Germany]. Vol. 1, *Kaiserreich (1895–1918)* [Empire (1895–1918)]. Stuttgart, Germany: Reclam, 2005.

Kapur, Anuradha. "The Representation of Gods and Heroes: Parsi Mythological Drama of the Early Twentieth Century." *Journal of Arts and Ideas*, no. 23–24 (1993): 85–107.

Kapur, Geeta. *When Was Modernism: Essays on Contemporary Cultural Practice in India.* New Delhi: Tulika Press, 2000.

Kar, Law, and Frank Bren. *Hong Kong Cinema: A Cross-cultural View.* Lanham, MD: Scarecrow, 2004.

Kedourie, Elie. *Nationalism.* London: Hutchinson, 1960.

Khan, Hatta Azad. *The Malay Cinema.* Bangi, Malaysia: Universiti Kebangsaan Press, 1977.

Khan, Mahomed. *The Life of Abdur Rahman, Amir of Afghanistan.* London: John Murray, 1900.

Koga, Futoshi, ed. *Les frères Lumière et le Japon, 1895–1995* [The Lumière brothers and Japan, 1895–1995]. Tokyo: Asahi Shimbun, 1995.

Komatsu, Hiroshi. "From Natural Colour to the Pure Motion Picture Drama: The Meaning of Tenkatsu Company in the 1910s of Japanese Film History." *Film History* 7, no. 1 (1995): 69–86.

———. "Hisutoriogurafi to gainen no fukususei: Taikatsu o rekishikasuru tame ni" [Historiography and conceptual multiplicity: Historicizing Taikatsu]. *Eigagaku* 13 (1999): 2–11.

Komatsu, Hiroshi, and Frances Loden. "Mastering the Mute Image: The Role of the *Benshi* in Japanese Cinema." *Iris*, no. 22 (1996): 33–52.

Kramer, Paul A. *The Blood of Government: Race, Empire, the United States and the Philippines.* Chapel Hill: University of North Carolina Press, 2006.

Lacaba, Jose F., ed. *The Films of ASEAN.* Pasig City, Philippines: ASEAN Committee on Culture and Information, 2000.

Lam, Xuan, and Dao Xuan Chuc. *Vietnamese Cinematography: A Research Journey.* Hanoi: Gioi, 2007.

Lan, Ngo Phuong. *Modernity and Nationality in Vietnamese Cinema.* Yogyakarta, Indonesia: Galang / Netpac, 2007.

Larsen, Lisbeth Richter, and Dan Nissen, eds. *100 Years of Nordisk Film.* Copenhagen: Danish Film Institute, 2006.

Law, Wai-ming. "Hong Kong's Cinematic Beginnings, 1896–1908." Translated by Stephen Teo. In *Early Images of Hong Kong and China*, edited by Law Kar, 20–26. Hong Kong: Urban Council, 1995.

Lecasse, Germain. "Du bonimenteur quebecois comme pratique resistante" [Du bonimenteur quebecois as a resistant practice]. *Iris*, no. 22 (1996): 53–66.

Lee, Daw-Ming. "How Cinema Came to China: Some Theories and Doubts." In *Early Images of Hong Kong and China*, edited by Law Kar, 16–19. Hong Kong: Urban Council, 1995.

———. "Taiwan Dianyingshi Diyi Zhang: 1900–1915" [Chapter one of Taiwan film history: 1900–1915]. *Film Appreciation* 13, no. 1 (1995): 1.

———. "You Dianying Keneng Zi Xianggang Chuanlai Taiwan Kan Shijiu Shijimo Dianyingren Zai Taiwan Xianggang Riben Zhongguo yu Zhongnanbandao jian de Liudong" [Movement of manpower in the film exhibition business between Taiwan, Hong Kong, Japan, China, and Indochina in the late nineteenth century: Speculation that Hong Kong was the origin of cinema in Taiwan]. In *Proceedings of the Conference on History of Early Chinese Cinema(s) Revisited.* Hong Kong: Hong Kong Film Archive, 2009.

Lent, John A. *The Asian Film Industry.* Bromley, UK: Christopher Helm, 1990.

LeRoy, Eric. "Le Fonds cinématographique colonial aux Archives du film et du depot legal du CNC" [The colonial film fonds in the film archives and the legal deposit of the CNC]. *Journal of Film Preservation*, no. 63 (2001): 55–59.

Leyda, Jay. *Dianying: An Account of Films and the Film Audience in China.* Cambridge, MA: MIT Press, 1972.

Lim, Kay Tong, and Tiong Chai Yiu. *Cathay: 55 Years of Cinema.* Singapore: Landmark, 1991.

Liu, Xiaolei. *Zhongguo Zaoqi Huwai Diqu Dianyingye de Xingcheng, 1896–1949* [The beginning of film business in areas outside Shanghai: Early years of China, 1896–1949]. Beijing: Zhongguo Dianying Chubanshe, 2009.

Lo, Ming-cheng M. *Doctors within Borders: Profession, Ethnicity, and Modernity in Colonial Taiwan.* Berkeley: University of California Press, 2002.

Malek, Mohamed Zamberi A., and Aimi Jarr. *Malaysian Films: The Beginning.* Kuala Lumpur: FINAS, 2005.

Malik, Usha. "Traditional Puppetry in India." *Indian Horizons* 55, no. 2–3 (2008): 9.

Martin, Frank A. *Under the Absolute Amir.* London: Harper, 1907.

McMahan, Alison. *Alice Guy Blanche: Lost Visionary of the Cinema.* New York: Continuum, 2002.

Mehrabi, Massoud. *The History of Iranian Cinema.* Tehran: Film Publication, 1988.

Mesguich, Felix. *Tours de manivelle: Souvenirs d'un chasseur d'images* [Turns of the hand crank machine: Memories of a hunter of images]. Paris: Bernard Grassett, 1933.

Muan, Ingrid, and Ly Daravuth. *Cultures of Independence: An Introduction to Cambodian Arts and Culture in the 1950s and 1960s.* Phnom Penh: Reyum Institute, 2001.

Mukherjee, Probhat. *Hiralal Sen: India's First Film-Maker.* Calcutta: Cine Central, 1966.

Musser, Charles. *Before the Nickelodeon: Edwin S. Porter and the Edison Manufacturing Company.* Berkeley: University of California Press, 1991.

———. "The Early Cinema of Edwin S. Porter." *Cinema Journal* 19, no. 1 (1979): 1–38.

———. *The Emergence of Cinema: The American Screen to 1907.* Berkeley: University of California Press, 1990.

———. "Nationalism and the Beginnings of Cinema: The Lumière Cinématographe in the United States, 1896–1897." *Historical Journal of Film, Radio, and Television* 19, no. 2 (1999): 149–176.

Musser, Charles, and Carol Nelson. *High-Class Moving Pictures: Lyman H. Howe and the Forgotten Era of Traveling Exhibition, 1880–1920.* Princeton, NJ: Princeton University Press, 1991.

Musser, Charles, and Hiroshi Komatsu. "*Benshi* Search." *Wide Angle* 9, no. 2 (1987): 72–90.

Muthalib, Hassan. "'Winning Hearts and Minds': Representations of Malays and Their Milieu in the Films of British Malaya." In "Britain and the Malay World: Through the Looking Glass of Film, Theatre and Literature," special issue, *South East Asia Research* 17, no. 1 (2009): 47–63.

Myrsiades, Linda Suny. "The Karaghiozis Tradition and the Greek Puppet Theater: History and Analysis." PhD diss., Indiana University, 1973.

Nasuruddin, Mohamed Ghouse. *Traditional Malay Theatre.* Johor Bahru, Malaysia: Dewan Bahasa dan Pustaka, 2009.

Negt, Oskar, and Alexander Kluge. *The Public Sphere and Experience.* Minneapolis: University of Minnesota Press, 1993.

Noletti, Arthur, Jr., and David Desser, eds. *Re-framing Japanese Cinema.* Bloomington: Indiana University Press, 1992.

Norindr, Panivong. *Phantasmatic Indochina: French Colonial Ideology in Architecture, Film, and Literature.* Durham, NC: Duke University Press, 1996.

Nornes, Abe Markus. *Japanese Documentary Film: The Meiji Era through Hiroshima.* Minneapolis: University of Minneapolis Press, 2003.

Omid, Jamal. *The History of Iranian Cinema, 1900–1978.* Tehran: Rozaneh, 1995.

O'Reilly, Patrick. *Les photographes a Tahiti et leurs oeuvres, 1842–1962* [Photographers in Tahiti and their work, 1842–1962]. Paris: Société des océanistes, 1969.

Osbourne, Milton. *Before Kampuchea: Preludes to Tragedy.* Bangkok: Orchid, 2004.

———. *The Mekong: Turbulent Past, Uncertain Future.* New York: Grove, 2000.

———. *Sihanouk: Prince of Darkness, Prince of Light.* Chiang Mai, Thailand: Silkworm, 1994.

Osman, Mohamed Taib. *Aspects of Malay Culture.* Johor Bahru, Malaysia: Dewan Bahasa dan Pustaka, 1988.

Pennell, Alice M. *Pennell of the Afghan Frontier: The Life of Theodore Leighton Pennell.* London: Seeley Service, 1914.

Pham Vu Dung, Do Lai Thuy, Thieu Thi Bich Huong, Nguyen Hien Luong, Pham Van Lu, Nguyen Dang Nghi, Pham Lan Oanh, Dinh Duc Tien, Dao Mai Trang, and Tran Quang Vinh, eds. *Vietnamese Cinematography: A Research Journey.* Hanoi: Gioi, 2007.

Popple, Simon, and Joe Kember. *Early Cinema: From Factory Gate to Dream Factory.* London: Wallflower, 2004.

Prout, Ebenezer. *Memoirs of the Life of the Rev. John Williams, Missionary to Polynesia.* New York: M. W. Dodd, 1843.

Quirino, Joe. *Don Jose and the Early Philippine Cinema.* Quezon City, Philippines: Phoenix, 1983.

Radar, Emmanuelle. "Putain de colonie: Anticolonialisme et modernisme dans la littérature du voyage en Indochine (1919–1939)" [Fucking colony: Anticolonialism and modernism in Indochina travel literature (1919–1939)]. PhD diss., University of Amsterdam, 2008.

Rafael, Vicente L. *White Love and Other Events in Filipino History.* Quezon City: Ateneo de Manila University Press, 2000.

Rajadhyaksha, Ashish. "The Phalke Era: Traditional Form and Modern Technology." *Journal of Arts and Ideas* 8 (1987): 14–15.

Ramsaye, Terry. *A Million and One Nights.* New York: Simon and Schuster, 1926.

Rayadhyaksha, Ashish, and Paul Willemen, eds. *Encyclopedia of Indian Cinema.* London: British Film Institute, 1994.

Richie, Donald. *A Hundred Years of Japanese Cinema.* Tokyo: Kodansha International, 2001.

Riggs, Arthur Stanley. "The Drama of the Filipinos." *Journal of American Folklore* 17, no. 67 (1904): 279–285.

———. *The Filipino Drama [1905].* Manila: Intramuros Administration, 1981.

Rinkes, D. A. *Nine Saints of Java.* Kuala Lumpur: Malaysian Sociological Research Institute, 1996.

Rittaud-Hutinet, Jacques. *Auguste et Louis Lumière: Les 1000 premiers films* [Auguste and Louis Lumière: The first 1,000 films]. Paris: Philippe Sers Editeur, 1990.

Rony, Fatimah Tobing. *The Third Eye: Race, Cinema, and Ethnographic Spectacle.* Durham, NC: Duke University Press, 2010.

Roussell, Deac. *Living Pictures: The Origins of the Movies.* Albany: SUNY Press, 1998.

Ruoff, Jeffrey, ed. *Virtual Voyages: Cinema and Travel.* Durham, NC: Duke University Press, 2006.

Saaler, Sven, and Christopher W. A. Szpilman, eds. *Pan-Asianism: A Documentary History.* 2 vols. Lanham, MD: Rowman and Littlefield, 2011.

Sadoul, Georges. *Histoire generale du cinema* [History of cinema]. Vol. 2, *Les pionniers du cinema, 1897–1909* [Pioneers of cinema, 1897–1909]. Paris: Éditions Denöel, 1948.

Said, Salim. *Shadows on the Silver Screen: A Social History of Indonesian Film.* Jakarta, Indonesia: Lontar Foundation, 1991.

Sanjugo, Naoki. "Nihon eiga oyobi eigakai" [Japanese film and film world]. In *Naoki Sanjugo zenshu* [Complete works of Sanjugo Naoki], vol. 31, 208–216. Tokyo: Kaizosha, 1935.

Sato, Tadao. *Zohoban Nippon Eiga Shi* [History of the Japanese cinema]. Vol. 1, *1896–1940.* Rev. ed. Tokyo: Iwanamishoten, 2006.

Scheel, Fritz. *A.-B Svenska Ostasiatiska Kompaniet: Dess tillkomst och verksamhet under 20 ar* [A.-B Svenska Ostasiatiska Kompaniet: Its attendance and activities for 20 years]. Gothenburg, Sweden: Wald. Zachrissons Boktryckeri AB, 1928.

Segrave, Kerry. *American Films Abroad: Hollywood's Domination of the World's Movie Screens from the 1890s to the Present.* Jefferson, NC: McFarland, 1997.

Sen, Krishna. *Indonesian Cinema: Facing the New Order.* London: Zed Books, 1994.

Sherzer, Dina, ed. *Cinema, Colonialism, Postcolonialism: Perspectives from the French and Francophone World.* Austin: University of Texas Press, 1996.

Shibata, Yoshio. *Eiga no keizagaku* [The economics of film]. Toyohashi, Japan: Eigakai Kenkyujo, 1954.

Sklar, Robert. *Film: An International History of the Medium.* London: Thames and Hudson, 1993.

Slavin, David Henry. *Colonial Cinema and Imperial France, 1919–1939: White Blind Spots, Male Fantasies, Settler Myths.* Baltimore: John Hopkins University Press, 2001.

Slide, Anthony. *Early American Cinema.* Metuchen, NJ: Scarecrow, 1994.

Stauven, Wanda, ed. *Cinema of Attractions Reloaded.* Amsterdam: Amsterdam University Press, 2006.

Steinberg, David Joel, ed. *In Search of South East Asia: A Modern History.* Honolulu: University of Hawaii Press, 1987.

Sukvong, Dome. "85 Years of Thai Cinema." *Arts and Culture* [in Thai] 3, no. 8 (1982): 128–132.

Sulong, Jamil. *Kaca Permata, Memoir Seorang Pengarah* [Glass gems: Memoirs of a director]. Johor Bahru, Malaysia: Dewan Bahasa dan Pustaka, 1990.

Takahashi, Masao. "Shinema Rigu to Kogyo Mondai" [Cinema League and the issue of exhibition]. *Eiga Seikatsu* [Movie life] 3, no. 4 (1932): 2–48.

Tanaka, Jun'ichiro. *Hiroku: Nihon no Katsudo Shashin* [Secret minutes of Japanese motion pictures]. Tokyo: Wides Shuppan, 2004.

———. *Nihon Eiga Hattatsu-shi* [Developmental history of Japanese film]. Vol. 1. Tokyo: Chuokoronsha, 1975.

Thompson, Kristin. *Exporting Entertainment: America in the World Film Market, 1907–1934.* London: British Film Institute, 1985.

Thorsen, Isak. "Nordisk Films Kompagni Will Now Become the Biggest in the World." *Film History* 22, no. 4 (2010): 463–478.

Tofighian, Nadi. "The Role of Jose Nepomuceno in the Philippine Society: What Language Did His Silent Films Speak?" Master's thesis, Stockholm University, 2005.

Tsukada, Yoshinobu. *Nihon Eigashi no Kenkyu* [Studies of Japanese film history]. Tokyo: Gendaishokan, 1980.

Tsurumi, Yusuke. *Goto Shinpei Den* [The biography of Goto Shinpei]. Vol. 2. Tokyo: Fujiwara Books, 2005.

Tully, John. *France on the Mekong: A History of the Protectorate in Cambodia, 1863–1953.* Lanham, MD: University Press of America, 2002.

Vasudev, Aruna, Latika Padgaonkar, and Rashmi Doraiswamy, eds. *Being and Becoming: The Cinemas of Asia.* New Delhi: Macmillan India, 2002.

Waller, Greg. *Main Street Amusements: Movies and Commercial Entertainment in a Southern City, 1896–1930.* Washington, DC: Smithsonian Institution, 1995.

Wang Hui sled Matthew A. Hale. "The Politics of Imagining Asia: A Genealogical Analysis." *Inter-Asia Cultural Studies* 8, no. 1 (2007): 1–33.

Warner, Michael. *The Letters of the Republic.* Cambridge, MA: Harvard University Press, 1990.

Weghofer, Beate. *Cinema Indochina: Eine (post-)koloniale Filmgeschichte Frankreichs* [Cinema Indochina: A (post-)colonial film history of France]. Bielefeld, Germany: Transcript Verlag, 2010.

Williams, Raymond. *Problems of Materialism and Culture.* London: Verso, 1980.

Wilson, Donald Dean, Jr. "Colonial Viet Nam on Film, 1896 to 1926." PhD diss., City University of New York, 2007.

Wright, Arnold, ed. *Twentieth Century Impressions of British Malaya.* Singapore: Graham Brash, 1989.

Yau, Shuk Ting. *Honkon Nihon Eiga Koryu Shi* [Interrelations between the Japanese and Hong Kong film industries]. Tokyo: University of Tokyo Press, 2007.

Yousof, Ghulam-Sarwar. *The Malay Shadow Play: An Introduction.* Penang, Malaysia: Asian Center, 1997.

Zanotto, Piero. *Le montagne del cinema* [The mountain of cinema]. Turin, Italy: Museo Nationale della Montagna "Duca degli Abruzzi," 1990.

Index